THE
END OF THE
WORLD AND THE
ENDS OF GOD

THEOLOGY FOR THE TWENTY-FIRST CENTURY

CENTER OF THEOLOGICAL INQUIRY

Theology for the Twenty-first Century is a series sponsored by the Center of Theological Inquiry (CTI) located in Princeton, New Jersey, an institute dedicated to the advanced study of theology. This series is one of its many initiatives and projects.

The goal of the series is to publish inquiries of contemporary scholars into the nature of the Christian faith and its witness and practice in church, society, and culture. The series will bring investigations into the uniqueness of the Christian faith. But it will also offer studies that relate the Christian faith to the major cultural, social, and practical issues of our time.

Monographs and symposia will result from research by scholars in residence at the Center of Theological Inquiry or otherwise associated with it. In some cases, publications will come from group research projects sponsored by CTI. It is our intention that the books selected for this series will constitute a major contribution to renewing theology in its service to church and society.

WALLACE M. ALSTON, JR., ROBERT JENSON,
AND DON S. BROWNING
SERIES EDITORS

What Dare We Hope?
by Gerhard Sauter

God and Globalization
edited by Max L. Stackhouse with Peter Paris

The End of the World and the Ends of God
edited by John Polkinghorne and Michael Welker

THE
END OF THE
WORLD AND THE
ENDS OF GOD

SCIENCE AND THEOLOGY ON ESCHATOLOGY

edited by
John Polkinghorne and Michael Welker

TRINITY PRESS INTERNATIONAL
Harrisburg, Pennsylvania

Trinity Press International, P.O. Box 1321, Harrisburg, PA 17105
Trinity Press International is a division of the Morehouse Group.

Cover art: William Blake, "The Ancient of Days," Frontispiece of *Europe, A Prophecy,* 1794. The Pierpont Morgan Library, New York/Art Resource, New York.

Cover design: Corey Kent

Library of Congress Cataloging-in-Publication Data
Polkinghorne, J. C., 1930–
    The end of the world and the ends of God : science and theology on eschatology / John Polkinghorne and Michael Welker.
        p.   cm.
    Includes bibliographical references and index.
    ISBN 1-56338-312-8 (pbk. : alk. paper)
    1. End of the world. 2. Eschatology. 3. Religion and science. I. Welker, Michael, 1947–   II. Title.
BT882 .P65 2000
236–dc21
                                                                                    99-058543

Printed in the United States of America

00   01   02   03   04   05   06   10   9   8   7   6   5   4   3   2   1

CONTENTS

ACKNOWLEDGMENTS

The work of our group falls naturally into the four sections that follow, concerned with approaches to eschatological themes deriving respectively from the natural sciences, the social sciences, biblical studies, and systematic theology.

1. Concepts from Science: Catastrophes and Hope

2. Cultural Contexts: The Shaping of Eschatological Thought

3. Biblical Traditions: Themes of the End-time

4. Theological Insights: Hope, Joy, and Eternal Life

Such a division is, of course, a presentational convenience; it should not be mistaken for a compartmentalized treatment. Readers will see that the writers in each section draw also upon the insights and concerns expressed in the other parts of our volume. This genuine interdisciplinarity is something that we all value greatly and wish to offer to a wider public.

The project would have been impossible without the generous and enthusiastic support of the Center of Theological Inquiry, Princeton, and in particular the participation and guidance of its director, Wallace Alston, and its academic directors, successively Don Browning and then Robert Jenson. The staff of the Center, and in particular Mary Beth Lewis and Kathi Morley, dealt with all the administrative demands, including much circulation of drafts of contributions, with admirable courtesy and efficiency. To all of them, our heartfelt thanks are due.

As the project was nearing completion, a significant conference on its theme was held at the Internationales Wissenschaftsforum, Heidelberg. In addition to the regular participants in the consultation and to those contributing to this volume, there were present also Werner Bestgen, Sigrid Brandt, Gregor Etzelmüller, Dirk Evers, Klaus Fricke, Ralf Frisch, Michael Hampe, Hubert Meisinger, Bernd Oberdorfer, Andreas Schüle, and Günter Thomas. We are most grateful to them for their contributions that helped to make the conference so stimulating, and to the Internationales Wissenschaftsforum and the Volkswagen-Stiftung, whose generous financial support made it possible.

Introduction

SCIENCE AND THEOLOGY ON THE END OF THE WORLD AND THE ENDS OF GOD

JOHN POLKINGHORNE AND MICHAEL WELKER

Science and Theology on a Realistic Eschatology: A Challenging Dialogue

Not only our individual life but also the universe is doomed to physical decay! This scientific insight of the twentieth century poses a great threat to theology and the faith of all religions. How can we believe in God and think of God and God's intentions with the world when human remembrance and history will finally come to an end? Should we settle with a "just me and my God" ideology, which does not care much about the creator of heaven and earth and the God of the world? Should we join those who are not very much concerned about a future beyond two generations down the road? Or should we be haunted by the notion of the finitude of the universe and its effects on our understanding of the power of God over reality, history, and the future? Should we be haunted by the threat of apathetic and cynical moods, caused by the impression that, if the universe is finite, then there is only silence in the end. In the long run everything will be in vain! This book deals with these difficult questions.

At the same time this book is a contribution to the currently expanding and intensifying dialogue between science and theology. In the last fifteen years this dialogue has moved from a "methodological phase," through a "physics phase," into a stage in which theological topics and questions have become more and more important.[1] The discourse between science and theology on the subject of "the end of the world and the ends of God" clearly belongs to this last phase. Its topic, called *eschatology*, is a particularly challenging one for the theology and science discourse. It seems to provoke an irreconcilable split between the sciences and theology by implying that there are two distinct realms of reality.

> There is, on the one hand, the realm of cosmic and natural reality that forms the unique subject matter and domain of the sciences.

---

1. Cf. Ted Peters, *Science and Theology: The New Consonance* (Boulder, Colo.: Westview Press, 1998), 5ff.

1

On the other hand, there seems to be an *eschaton* — some type of supernature or hyperreality — as the realm of religious ideas and theological exploration.

The present volume questions this view of theological and scientific inquiry.

The book starts from a simple but startling observation. Most eschatological symbols and texts in the classical and canonical religious traditions do not at all concentrate on any realm of pious wishes and fantasy about the end of the world and the ends of God. Instead, they speak of the *continuity and discontinuity* between this world and the world to come. For instance, they use the terms *new creation*, or *new heaven and new earth*, in order to indicate that there are continuities between the creation and the so-called eschaton, between our heaven and earth and the heaven and earth to come after our earthly life will have ended. The eschatological promises and images tell us that "flesh and blood will not inherit the kingdom of God" while at the same time they insist on the "resurrection of the body." This logic of continuity/discontinuity provides an admittedly difficult ground for a common discourse. The sciences are challenged to face an area or mode of reality beyond their usual realm of competence. The theme of eschatology requires that science expand its scope of concern and avoid reductionistic assumptions about the nature of reality. "The universe," as Henry David Thoreau once put it, "is wider than our views of it." Eschatological symbols, with their strange logic of continuity/discontinuity, challenge the sciences to forgo equating our views of the universe with the universe itself. However, the same logic presents a challenge to theology.

All too often theology has used eschatology to move into speculations about a *virtual reality*, something that science will not readily accept. In this way, theologians have tried to immune their claims from the judgment of the sciences. If the sciences are challenged by eschatological symbols to expand the scope of inquiry, theology, for its part, is made to confront in the most rigorous way possible the demand of publicly warranted truth claims. The interest in a dialogue with the sciences about the strange reality called *eschaton* or *eschata* requires theology to seek a new approach. The contributions to this volume seek this new approach. They agree that their common topic is a *realistic eschatology* and that the discourse between science and theology should help us to explore grounds of hope and joy in the face of physical death and the threat posed by a finite world and universe.

Eschatology is not only a demanding topic in the "third phase" of the science and theology exchange. The multidisciplinary discourse found in the following pages of this book makes it a new and unique enterprise as well. Under the rubric "Science and Theology" most discourses in the past have brought together natural scientists, systematic or philosophical theologians, and scholars in the field of religious studies. The three-year consultation on eschatology from which this book arose, held in Princeton and Heidelberg, made an effort to facilitate interactions by natural scientists and social scientists with systematic theologians and ethicists, but also with biblical scholars. The wager was that the careful study of the biblical texts might aid in the finer decoding of eschatological images, symbols, and modes of thought.

To be sure, the first meeting of this consultation led many of us to feel that we were trying to rebuild the tower of Babel. Some colleagues complained about their difficulty in understanding the discourse, rationalities, and methods of the other fields. Some even spoke about a chaotic situation. But, from meeting to meeting, we gained coherence while still holding to the complexity of the topic. In this respect, we avoided one standard tactic in navigating conceptual differences among disciplines. We did not succumb to the use of reductionistic ideas or formulae that would have allowed us to move on a single but abstract level of thought depleted of content. For example, we avoided the existential eschatology of the *here and now* characteristic of much earlier twentieth-century theology. Such a position reduces the complexity of eschatological symbols to ciphers of inner self-consciousness. Yet we also jettisoned a sociomoralistic eschatology of an endless societal and global future in need of shaping and reshaping. In our determination to cling to the thickness, and even messiness, of creaturely and eschatological reality, we reached a surprising level of coherence. We certainly hope that our readers will get a feeling for this multidisciplinary striving for a realistic eschatology which aims at coherence of insights while keeping the complexity of the topic in mind.

This introduction highlights some basic, yet important, claims, each taken up in one of the following sections. First, it is not theology alone that must make a reality and entities unseen intelligible, but also the sciences. Second, it is not science alone that has to warrant difficult truth claims, but also theology. Third, these analogous challenges, however, do not yet provide a comfortable common ground of exploration. Rather they call into question many all-too-familiar clichés:

Theology deals with realities unseen, science deals with visible reality.

Theology deals with feelings, science deals with facts.

Theology deals — at best — with personal certainty, science deals with objective truths and so on.

Once these clichés are shown to be problematic, an investigation of the current cultural context in which science and theology operate in Western societies can reveal several shared concerns. Fourth, among these is the common concern for a realistic eschatology that seeks to understand the ends of God in and with a world that will come to an end as surely as we all will go through physical death and decay.

Science and Theology in General:
Making Belief in Reality and Entities Unseen Intelligible

Both science and theology have to speak about unseen realities in the course of their rational discourse. The dark companion of Sirius is invisible to us and we have to infer its existence indirectly from its apparent perturbing gravitational effect upon its bright partner. More fundamentally, the contemporary account of the nature of nuclear matter attributes to quarks and gluons the role of basic constituents, while at the same time asserting that they will never be observed individually. This is because they are "confined," that is to say, they are so tightly bound within the protons and neutrons that they compose that no impact will ever be strong enough to expel them. When we ask the elementary particle physicists why they believe so firmly in these elusive entities, they reply that it is because the assumption of their existence makes sense of great swathes of physical experience that otherwise would seem mysterious to us. The observable particles of nuclear matter form a series of families whose patterns and properties exactly correspond to what would result from their being made up of quarks. When high-energy projectiles impinge on protons and neutrons in what is called a deep inelastic scattering process, they "bounce back" in just the way that corresponds to their hitting pointlike quark constituents inside.

The assumption of the existence of these unseen realities is then not a wild "leap of faith" against all we know about the universe. On the contrary, the assumption of their existence is warranted by what we already know about the universe. There is, we might say, continuity and discontinuity in scientific claims about the complexity of reality. Similarly, theologians can claim that belief in the unseen reality of God or more specific beliefs of this kind, such as in the Trinity and the Incarnation, are also well motivated because they make sense of great swathes of spiritual experience. This is, again, not a leap of faith or Pascal's wager. What the theologians seek, no less than the scientists, is a clearer perception of the reality in question. What is sought is a careful and yet realistic picture of reality. Only in this way is theology saved from reducing its claims and insights solely to matters of consolation and search for meaning.

In both disciplines, intelligibility is the key to reality, but reality is what funds intelligibility. The universe is wider than our theories about it, but we also and always grasp that reality in and through distinctly human ways of knowing. We are thus warranted in holding to the reality of what enables us to think in a comprehensive and satisfying way about our encounter with the way things are. This is the modest, but important, realism basic to this book. If our concepts are to carry this ontological conviction, they will have to go beyond the attainment of mere explanation and confer the deep intellectual satisfaction that we call understanding. This distinction is crucial. Explanation is concerned with correlative strategies operating at a single level. Understanding aims at a comprehensive sense of what we see as "the whole" respectively, making sense of complex constellations and interconnections of events. Hence our emphasis in this volume on thick accounts in both the sciences and theology.

Many theories of "understanding" are operative in theology and the sciences. Here, too, just as with eschatological symbols, the authors of this volume have opted for some version of realism. This means that human understanding demands of inquirers a willingness to allow the object of understanding to form the concepts with which we frame our account of it. There is no universal epistemology, no single interpretative key that will unlock every ontological door. No one view captures the universe. Realism demands epistemic humility and also the tenacity to continue inquiry attentive to multiple perspectives or frames of reference. This point is readily illustrated from within physical science.

Scientists know the everyday world of classical physics in one way, the sub-atomic quantum world in quite another. If we were to demand of quantum entities the clear, picturable, and predictable properties of Newtonian particles, they would be totally unintelligible to us. Quarks and electrons can only be known on their own terms, in their Heisenbergian uncertainty. They then become con-vincingly intelligible, but the rationality that exhibits this intelligibility has its own idiosyncratic character (there is even a quantum logic, different from the classical logic of Aristotle).

Similarly, the divine nature is to be known in the way that God has deter-mined to reveal it. It would be the reverse of being rational to demand of theology that it submit its inquiry into the transpersonal nature of God to protocols de-rived from the inquiries of a methodologically atheist science. But in saying this we are not reintroducing the old assumption that science deals with facts and truth while theology handles meaning and value. Our claim is more subtle and demanding: science and theology are both concerned with realities (facts and meanings; truth and value) attentive to the connection between understand-ing and what is presented to be understood. This entanglement of the "what" and "how" of understanding is the famous hermeneutical circle: how entities are known must accord with their nature; that nature is revealed in what we know of them. No discipline of thought and inquiry can escape its own epistemological circle.

These considerations suggest that, despite the differences in their subject mat-ter, the sciences and theology share a cousinly relationship in the common search for truth about reality. The conviction that this is so is what undergirds the inter-action between science and theology generally, and the specific project reported in this volume in particular.

Science and Theology in General:
The Challenge to Evaluate and Warrant Truth Claims
with Respect to Nature, Culture, and Religion

For a long time it has not been widely or adequately recognized that the dialogue between science and theology should have a genuinely *theological* focus. Many previous discourses worked on historical questions, ethical concerns, general methodological reflections, or the endeavor to test a certain style of philosophy as a potential interface for dialogue. This has now changed.

In 1993 the Center of Theological Inquiry at Princeton sponsored a four-year consultation in which a highly interdisciplinary group (including the fields of cos-mology, physics, chemistry, biology, environmental studies, philosophy, religious studies, and theology) moved from an exchange of individual approaches over the discussion of general religious topics to a progressive specification of a common theological ground of discourse. For the second year of that initial project the notion of *God's activity* was selected; the third year focused on the notion of the *temporality of God's action in the world.* Finally, the consultation centered on the two topics: *eternity and temporality* and *eternity and contingency.* Throughout the discourse scientifically and philosophically trained reflection were brought into a fruitful tension with theologically and exegetically trained thinking.[2]

Why is this type of discourse so important? In Western cultures, public expectation relies predominantly on scientific procedures and not much, if indeed at all, on theology or the human sciences in the endeavor to come close to truth and evaluate evidence. Likewise, we seek to gain certainty and reliability in relation to difficult and critical issues through scientific inquiry. Despite the current crisis in scientific epistemology, and a growing suspicion as to the actual benefits of much of technological progress, the common assumption in Western societies is that the measure and model for truth claims is found in the sciences. Indeed, the "modern age" itself is often associated with the rise and dominance of science.

This stance can have many ideological side effects. Instead of complaining about this, theology must rise to the challenge. It cannot give up seeking to make its impact on common sense and on contemporary mentalities. Christian theology has to expose and expound its theological truth claims in public discourse. It has to warrant its claims to truth. All endeavors to score points for theology by simply opposing the sciences should be discouraged. At the same time, theology and science have to clarify the limits of scientific insights.

There are signs of developments in the natural sciences that begin to encourage a richer account of reality and truth — even within their own circumscribed domain — than that of a strictly reductionist physicalism. The old Newtonian picture of a mechanical world of individual atoms, moving in the spatial container of the void, is certainly dead. General relativity describes an interrelational reality in which space, time, and matter are closely tied together. Quantum theory and chaos theory have shown that tame predictability is not a feature of most of nature. The infant science of *complexity theory* begins to suggest that the presence of unexpected powers of self-organization in complex systems means that the *pattern-forming concept of information* has to be added to the long-familiar concepts of matter and energy for an adequate scientific account of their behavior. Perhaps most surprising of all, it has been shown that quantum systems exhibit a counterintuitive "nonlocality" (togetherness in separation). When two entities have interacted with each other they will retain a power of mutual influence however widely they may subsequently separate. This "EPR effect," as it is called, implies that the subatomic world cannot be treated atomistically.

The metaphysical implications of these remarkable scientific developments are still matters for discussion and argument, but it is clear that physical reality is certainly more subtle, and probably more supple, than had been supposed in the past by classical physics.

---

2. The discourse resulted in many individual publications (books and articles) of the participants. A collection of some of these contributions appeared in *TToday* 55 (October 1998).

Why Eschatology?
Seeking Orientation in Shifting Eschatological Moods with Their Impact on Worldviews and Ethos: Common Concern of Scientists and Theologians

Eschatology might seem to be a demanding — if not impossible — topic for the interaction of science and theology, but it proves to be a most promising starting point to demonstrate the fruitfulness of the dialogue. The last thirty years have witnessed an astounding shift in eschatological moods. In the sixties, Jürgen Moltmann's *Theology of Hope* with its "messianic" optimism became one of the most influential theological books of the second half of the century. A mere thirty years later, apocalyptic and even exterministic modes of eschatological thinking and feeling dominated the scene. The proclamation by the sciences of the definite finitude of the world has come as a cultural shock. In the face of the environmental crisis, the continuing surge of global poverty, and the threat by an age of increasing conflict, scarcity, and despair, many people around the world look to a future without hope or joy. The hard facts of life have shocked many from a naive anthropocentrism wherein reality and reality's God exist to insure the fulfillment of the human project. A universe moving from big bang to hot death or cosmic crunch hardly seems to lend comfort to the human heart!

Human life is short. Even the span of human memory is short, when compared with the time-scales over which science describes the evolving development of the universe and the changes and chances of terrestrial history placed within that cosmic story. The scientific account of this "story" is not merely retrospective but also prospective, for science can speak of future possibilities as well as past events. When it does so, the outlook is gloomy when considered over very long time-scales. As we explain in the first part of this book, there are contingent hazards to life on earth arising from its potentially dangerous environment. There are also absolutely certain catastrophes, such as the explosion of the sun and the collapse or decay of the universe, which cannot be averted.

While these destructive events lie far into the future, their influence on theological thinking cannot be ignored. One obvious reason is that they call into question any notion of an ultimate fulfillment brought about through the unfolding of present cosmic history alone. At best, we see a transient fruitfulness that leads to final futility, with the certain eventual disappearance of all life from the universe. These images of catastrophe feed cultural moods of nihilism and apocalyptic despair that are powerfully present in contemporary societies.

How should theologians respond to this eschatological mood and the scientific claims that often back it? Is the task of theology to offer consoling fantasies and thus to calm the human heart? Should theologians simply concede the scientific point, join the current mood, and thereby abandon all claims about God's involvement with and care for creation? If theology wants to avoid the judgment that eschatology is nothing but false consolation, a way of talking people into a vague hope for the future, then it has a threefold task:

Theology will take the notions of finitude formulated by the natural and social sciences seriously. These notions are far from simple and they demand careful formulation. Theology must participate in testing their limits.

Theology also will ask whether, and if so how, our cultural symbol systems resonate with the notions of finitude expressed by the sciences (for instance, in the talk about exterministic cultures or cultures of death), and it must examine the boundaries of these approaches.

Above all, Christian theology will reexamine its views of hope, joy, the divine future, the new creation, and eternal life. This will be undertaken not only in the light of the biblical traditions and the traditions of faith, but in a critical and self-critical dialogue with the social and natural sciences in their diagnoses of the finitude of the world.

In such a dialogue between science and theology, both sides should demonstrate their advocacy of truth, showing that this is not a simple task, but one that must contend with many vague and simplistic answers offered from both sides.

The topic of eschatology is of the utmost interest in a situation in which we experience a major shift in our worldview and in the set of values correlated with this worldview. It is important to grasp the novelty of this situation. On the one hand, the eschatological mood of the day is often a response to the seeming insignificance of human purposes within the immense time-span of the universe. In this respect, human perceptions of time and evaluations of human destiny are being elongated. We readily speak of "billions of years"; schoolchildren are confronted with the pace of planetary history and its episodes of crisis and extinction. And yet, on the other hand, our age — the so-called postmodern age — is also marked by a compression of time, a shortening of our perception of the temporal flow of reality. While the physical sciences press us to expand our consciousness of time, recent cultural developments collapse time-consciousness back into the immediate present. Many of the essays in this volume explore these surprising cultural developments and their meaning for eschatological beliefs and convictions.

In past decades a radically changed attitude toward the world has emerged with the spread of the electronic media, and especially in connection with the fast and global expansion of television and now the Internet. The worldwide spread of television and the Internet has been accompanied by a *depreciation of cultural memory*, of the hierarchy of the classics, of the canonic, and of recourse to historical memory in the crises of the present moment. The new media bring with them an enormous inflation of a flow of data, constantly demanding fresh attention. The amount of concentration needed to grasp the world of today, and of the near future, increases enormously. The effective "habitation" and common "animation" of the past decreases drastically. The formula "dechronologization of the world and spatialization of the world"[3] has been used to grasp this process.

---

3. See David Harvey, *The Condition of Postmodernity: An Inquiry into the Origin of Cultural Change* (Oxford: Blackwell, 1990).

Cultivation of *cultural memory* is displaced by the reinforced and demanding collective attention paid to the present and the near future. This necessary attention to the present and the near future is accompanied by a constant excitement. It conceals the fact that the displacement of a common remembrance and cultural memory leads to a "cooling down" of human life together. Jan Assmann, the renowned Heidelberg Egyptologist, has developed insights of Claude Lévi-Strauss's by distinguishing between "hot" and "cold" memory. *Cold memory* deprives events of their singularity and extraordinariness. It deprives events, and the community affected by them or ascribing them to itself, of their power to form history. Thus it also weakens the potential to nourish hope, to build complex common expectations, and to live in the *perseverantia sanctorum*. The current media and market stimulate *cold memory* in abundance. The abundance of memories, the manner of their presentation, and the dominance of attention to today and tomorrow provide for a constant cooling-down of life and remembrance. Long-term expectations and hopes are cut off.

A second devaluation of cultural memory reinforces and accelerates the first and is itself reciprocally reinforced by it. The presentation of the world through the media radically questions the naive "unity of history" and the naive "unity of the life world" (*Lebenswelt*). The otherness, indeed foreignness, of the forms of life, of the ideas of wholeness, and of the recourse to tradition in other areas of the world becomes manifest each and every day. This leads to broken and distanced attitudes toward one's own history and life world. Sensitization through the mass media to foreign life worlds and traditions not only changes relations to the world. It also brings with it a sensitization of people to the differences of the various life worlds and traditions in one's own culture. It intensifies the tendency to pluralism. This more differentiated and more complex view of the world demands a new orientation. It no longer seems advisable to grant one's own tradition and one's own classics a monopoly in that orientation. Insecurity, experiments with one's identity, caution in self-commitment, and weak links with any form of one's cultural heritage appear desirable ways of life. If a memory is cultivated at all, then let it be as cold as possible!

This change in mentality has an effect on many other cultural phenomena. The cultural evaluation of the old and young changes. The complex world with its quickly changing "today and tomorrow" does not demand wisdom, maturity, and self-possession. It demands the power to grasp things quickly and an intelligence that is able to attune and change. The "Old World" is left to specialists and museums. The real world belongs to young people. The concept of education (*Paidaia, Bildung*) is changing. The educational ideal changes from accumulating and cultivating ordered knowledge to selecting knowledge according to situation and function. We have reached a stage where the expectations of kindergarten and elementary school that children learn something by heart seem to amount to molestation, almost like bodily injury! Flexibility of attention must not be disturbed by fixed remembrance and memory. All these factors add greatly to processes of individuization (not to be confused with individualization in the sense of building personality!), under which current Western cultures suffer greatly.

Finally, this cultural stress is strengthened and heightened by an exterministic mentality, which is fueled by the insight of the sciences, that not only humankind and this earth but also the universe itself are doomed to final decay.

Our point is not to celebrate some golden past when cultural memories were strong, education uniformly attained, and wisdom the expected product of age. Such a time has never existed. Past ages, cultural memories, have at best been ambiguous, often marked by tyranny, ignorance, violence, and want. And too often in our own day cultural memories are *hot*, as one ethnic group violently rages against another. The point we are making, then, is that current cultural developments alter experiences of time and thus necessarily bear on theological claims about eschatological realities.

If this cultural analysis is in some measure correct, then theology has to find an eschatological approach that takes the meaning of common and individual history very seriously. Theology must not idolize those histories, foster merely new tribal mentalities, nor revive the grandiose ideology of "universal history." Theology must come to grips with a reality that resists the effects of a media culture and its drive toward a world where experience and imagination become indistinguishable. In this attempt to be truthful to the earth and, at the same time, live up to a reality that is not of the earth, the critical and self-critical dialogue with the sciences becomes crucial. A realistic theology is at stake, a theology that distinguishes its task clearly from entertainment or easy consolation. The dialogue between theology and science is by no means a luxury, but a crucial task in a time in which (and not for the first time in cultural history either) the historical worldview crumbles. A critical and self-critical realistic theology should not shun but rather seek dialogue with the sciences.

For this enterprise the topic of eschatology is a most suitable one. It will help clarify and cultivate the difference between truth claims in both fields. It enables us to formulate our eschatological truth claims in the face of the finitude of the world. It challenges us to work on a clear differentiation between the sustenance of the world and the new creation: to differentiate between infinity and eternity, between the mere totality of times and the eschatological fullness, and between the different types of hope related to one or the other. The capacity of the theme "eschatology" to spark inquiry into the conjunction of natural and cultural realities has shaped the very structure of this volume.

Perspectives beyond Transient Life and Universe: The Ground of Dignity and Realistic Hope

Together, these scientific and cultural developments pose powerful questions to theology. What are the true purposes of the Creator of such a world of change and decay? What ends are being brought about within it by the divine purpose? Should there not be an unflinching recognition that despair is the real foundation for human thought about the future, bringing about the end of belief in the

Christian God of hope, with Shiva the Destroyer the only honest possibility for a replacement?

Certain common stances underlie the variety of the approaches set out in this volume. One is belief in a tempered rationality and in a critical realism, both in science and in theology. Both disciplines are seen as seeking to grasp and understand reality, to speak of what is the case, within the limitations of human ability. (We print as an appendix some further discussion of this point, derived from a paper presented to the group by Hans Weder.) It is precisely this common trust in reality, and belief that its nature is not wholly hidden from us, that give rise to the possibility of a fruitful interaction between science and theology. A number of specific consequences follow from this realist position and are particularly significant for the discussion of eschatological themes.

A second common stance, already noticed, is the commitment to give a *thick*, many-layered account of reality. An oversimplified reductionism, whether of scientific or fideistic kind, is scrupulously to be avoided. Many forms of discourse will be needed to match the richness of reality, with poetry, metaphor, and symbol playing an indispensable role alongside more prosaic forms of expression. It will also be necessary to do full justice to the profoundly relational character of reality, particularly in connection with an understanding of the person as being much more than an isolated individual. A highly significant aspect of an adequately thick account will be the subtlety and power of the interrelationship of past and present, together with a proper recognition of the richly textured character of the nature of human temporal experience. Another important recognition is that of the reality of death. Christian thinking does not seek to diminish the bleakness and stripped-down character of this depth experience. After all, at the heart of Christianity lies the cross of the crucified Christ.

Scientific prognosis puts to theology the question of whether it is not, in fact, ultimate (and perhaps, defiant) despair that is the appropriate human attitude to the world in which we live. Theology's response is to replace despair with hope and joy. Perhaps one of the most innovating developments to arise out of the dialogue, documented in this book, is the possibility of two distinct and yet related theological responses to ultimate despair. Some theologians among us understand the most appropriate response to our age to be rooted in *joy*, a profound acceptance and gratitude for life in all of its limitation and fragility. For these theologians the challenge of our age with its confusing eschatological mood strikes to the very core of Christian conviction. At issue is whether or not and to what extent Christians can and may and must say "yes" to a reality we now know scientifically to be crated for ultimate futility. Does the radical displacement of human purposes from the center of an account of reality count against belief in a loving God? For these theologians, the radicality of this challenge has required a shift in focus from the "theology of hope" to explore the meaning, truth, and practical significance of a realistic joy completely mindful of the finitude of the world and of human life.

Other theologians among us continue the important legacy of the theology of hope. For these thinkers it has been crucial to insist that hope is very different from optimism. Its basis is neither wishful fantasy nor calculated prediction. Instead, its basis is trust in the everlasting faithfulness of the living and eternal God. This is the only reality that can be set against the reality of the scientific predictions of catastrophe. Theology does not deny these predictions, but it transcends them. Christian hope is not a consoling fantasy that somehow death is an illusion. Death is real, but death is not ultimate. Only God is ultimate. The Christian hope is death and resurrection, not merely spiritual survival.

At the heart of that hope is, of course, belief in the resurrection of Jesus Christ. In the experiences of the first witnesses, the resurrection had both an objective dimension (moment of recognition, even touching and offering food) and a subjective dimension (hearts warmed and heavenly light shining forth, the conviction that Jesus lives). It had both an individual dimension (it is the crucified Jesus who is risen, still with the scars of the passion) and a collective dimension (believers are incorporated into the body of Christ and they have the role of the witnessing community).

These responses to the current eschatological mood and its undercurrent of despair are in fruitful conversation throughout this book. Yet each addresses the strange logic of eschatology — the connection of continuity/discontinuity noted above — in its own way. Among theologians of hope, faithful existence always involves a degree of tension between the already and the not yet: present experience of life transformed in quality and depth, and future expectation of life beyond death in which there is neither sighing nor sorrow anymore. For theologians who explore the theme of realistic eschatological joy, the tension of faithful existence is between joy in God's continual presence and governance and the radical discontinuity between being and nothingness science seems to predict as the fate of our universe. Different Christian thinkers have, from the first, struck the balance between continuity and discontinuity in different ways and with different religious foci. This diversity and its complementarity are happily reflected in the essays that follow.

The strongest theme to emerge from all our discussion, and one that is widely reflected upon in our writings, is the need to wrestle with the necessity for both continuity and discontinuity in any adequate account of eschatology. Take the example of personal identity. Too great an element of discontinuity would threaten the trust that it is "Abraham, Isaac, and Jacob" (and not some new persons bearing those names) who live with God. It must be that each generation will attain to fulfillment, never merely serving as a stepping stone to the future of others, and that those whose lives have been cut short by oppression and violence receive what was denied to them on earth. Yet too great an element of continuity would threaten belief in the new creation, redeemed from the old creation's bondage to death and decay. Insights are offered in this book into how we might try to think of this continuous/discontinuous relationship of the new creation to the old creation. Attention may be drawn to some of the ideas discussed.

A revival of the notion (as old as Aristotle and Thomas Aquinas) of the soul as the form (information-bearing pattern) of the body may offer a credible concept serving to carry across identity from the life of this world to the life of the world to come. If it is intrinsic for human beings to be embodied in some form (so that resurrection, rather than spiritual survival, is the Christian hope), then it may be that they are intrinsically temporal beings. If that is so, the life of the new creation will have its own new time and its own new, salvific process. Judgment will then involve a coming to terms with the reality of ourselves, and a purgation of what we are in order to become what God wills us to be. Fulfillment will not happen in a timeless moment of illumination but through an everlasting exploration of the riches of the divine nature, an experience that may be characterized as our entering into "eschatological joy."

Necessarily, accounts of human destiny post-mortem have a degree of speculation about them. Some people might think: the best answer to too much eschatological curiosity about details is to say, "Wait and see!" The writers of this book share a common trust in a faithful Creator, a merciful Redeemer, and a sanctifying Spirit. They believe that it is of the highest importance that the Christians and the Christian church should not lose nerve in witnessing to our generation about the eschatological hope that is set before us. They offer this book as a resource toward that end.

Part 1

ESCHATOLOGY IN THE NATURAL SCIENCES

CATASTROPHES AND HOPE

Introduction to Part 1

ESCHATOLOGY
AND THE SCIENCES

John Polkinghorne

Science is concerned with present experience and its future extrapolation. It may raise questions of total meaningfulness that can be held to demand answers lying beyond any such extrapolation, but it could not usurp theology's role in speaking of what God might do by way of a new creation. However, if that new creation is to be related to the present creation in a way that involves both continuity and discontinuity (as the Christian resurrection hope suggests), then science may have something to say about the conditions of consonance and credibility that the continuity aspect of the relationship might be expected to fulfill.

William Stoeger gives a careful and detailed account of risks of catastrophes that would be destructive of life on Earth. He emphasizes the reliability of these scientific prognoses, which are based on well-founded theory and on observations of similar phenomena occurring elsewhere. Stoeger also makes it clear that the universe itself will eventually decay or collapse, ending in cosmic futility. Yet he concludes by drawing our attention to the amazing life-giving characteristics of present physical reality.

John Polkinghorne begins by asserting that these anticipated futilities raise for theology the question of the nature of its eschatological hope of true fulfillment. He believes that the response will have to be framed in terms of a resurrection concept of continuity and discontinuity, linking the present creation to God's new creation, brought about as the expression of divine faithfulness. Metascientific responses that make no use of theological insight, whether they take the form of the heroic defiance of a meaningless world, or the speculative form of a physical eschatology, are held to be insufficient to restore a sense of total meaningfulness to the cosmos. Concepts from science that may help in framing the continuity side of a resurrection hope include an increasing recognition of the significance of relationality and of the need for holistic accounts of physical reality, and the realization that the conventional matter-energy approach of physics needs supplementation by a holistic concept of pattern-forming information. The latter insight is held to encourage a revival of the Thomistic notion of the soul as the form of the body. At death that human "pattern" is held in the divine memory, to be re-embodied in the "space-time-matter" of the new creation. Such a hope

17

can only spring from a conviction of the faithfulness of God, but it is not contrary
to what a this-worldly science can say about human nature.

In a short contribution written from the point of view of a neurophysiologist,
Detlef Linke draws our attention to the complex temporalities present in the functioning of the brain. He uses these insights to present an interesting speculation
about the experiences of a realized eschatology.

Fraser Watts approaches these issues from the point of view of the human science of psychology. He believes that this provides an important corrective to the
insights and influence of the natural sciences. His contribution is woven around a
series of linked polarities: natural science/human science; propositional aspects of
eschatology/attitudinal aspects of eschatology; optimism/wishful fantasy. In a discussion of Christ's resurrection, Watts poses a further duality: resurrection body
(objective aspect)/grief experiences of the disciples (subjective aspect). He emphasizes that either half of each of these dichotomies is unsatisfactory on its own.
Watts believes that theology must operate in the "inbetween land" that mediates
between these polarities. He gives a careful discussion of the nature of hope,
a concept that also has this mediating character. For Watts, eschatology needs
the balance between already/not yet, and its expectation is concerned with open
promise and not closed prediction.

Chapter 1

SCIENTIFIC ACCOUNTS OF ULTIMATE CATASTROPHES IN OUR LIFE-BEARING UNIVERSE

William R. Stoeger, S.J.

Introduction

Despite the more or less successful efforts of believing scientists, philosophers, and theologians to reconcile Christian faith with the account the natural sciences give of the evolutionary history and structure of the world and the universe, our contemporary scientifically and technologically oriented culture strongly challenges Christian, or other religious, visions of afterlife, resurrection, "the new heavens and the new earth." Any meaning or hope in an ultimate destiny tied to such conceptions is considered by many pure illusion, without any shred of real foundation in reality, and with no support from anything in our experience. They are simply projections of our own yearnings for meaning and significance, or symbols embedded in the universe of cultural meaning we have established to allow us to live happy and productive lives. Thus they have little or no bearing on what our ultimate fate — of ourselves as persons and communities, of our species, of the universe — really will be. From all the indications we have from the neurosciences, biology, physics, astronomy, and cosmology, death and dissolution are the final words. There is no scientifically supportable foundation for the immortality of the soul, the resurrection of the body and the person after death, a transformed new heavens and new earth.

Certainly there are many who vehemently and persistently react against this pervasively negative and hopeless account of our future, relying heavily on belief in the literal meaning of symbols of hope and ultimate destiny available in Christianity and other religious traditions. For Christians these have their basis in the revelatory events of Jesus' life, death, and resurrection, and all that flows from them — or in analogous events and personages for other religious traditions. However, in taking this stance, one must inevitably either deny the scientific accounts of our proximate and distant future, as many have done, or at least discount the capability of the scientific evidence for revealing our ultimate destiny. If we are to take the truth discovered by the sciences seriously, denying the scientific description of death and the more reliable scientifically supported accounts of eventual certain life-ending and earth-ending catastrophes is really

19

not an option. Choosing that course leads us to reject unreasonably a great deal of overwhelming evidence concerning how life and its nurturing environments emerged, developed, and are structured, as well as very well substantiated conclusions concerning past catastrophic events and the potential for such events in the future.

Thus, the other alternative — that although the human species, life, the earth, the sun, and the universe will end, that end is not ultimate but somehow leads to a fuller, transformed reality, to which the natural sciences provide no access, and to which our human experience gives us only obscure, but nevertheless real, intimations and indications — has achieved growing dominance in some communities. For Christians, for instance, this transformed reality in which we shall find our ultimate destiny is revealed to us by God through Jesus, on the evidence and testimony of scripture, tradition, and our individual and communal experiences of the transcendent and the personal. Accepting that evidence and testimony is a matter of faith — faith in God and faith in Jesus. The death and dissolution we experience, which the natural sciences predict, is real and will certainly occur. But, as the Christian message proclaims, eternal life, salvation, and redemption will be realized precisely through those disconcerting events — in a way that we do not yet fully understand and on which we have only a partial analytical purchase. Even if we choose this second, more measured approach, however, consistency requires us to explain why the sciences are incapable of dealing with this transcendent or spiritual reality and to bolster the evidence and support for it by a critical and careful evaluation of those phenomena that seem to demand it, against the reductionistic or projectionistic accounts given by some philosophers and natural scientists.

That will be attempted in some of the other contributions in this volume. In this chapter I shall provide part of the context for those discussions by describing the results from the physical sciences which have direct bearing on this question. I shall briefly outline and substantiate the types of apocalyptic scenarios which they predict as inevitable, given what we know about the physical and material universe and its constitution and dynamics. As a balance to this overview, I shall conclude with a description of the vastness, intricacy, and dynamic, life-generating qualities of physical reality as we know it from scientific research.

Astronomical and Cosmological Catastrophes

Nature and the cosmos are characterized by order and reliability, and most strikingly by their life-generating character. As we contemplate the wonders of this earth of ours, the abundance, variety, and persistence of life are startling and overwhelming. And, as we come to appreciate the origin and evolution of life more deeply through what the sciences reveal about them, we find ourselves even more impressed. The universe is life-bearing, and even seems to be specially ordered to produce life. And yet, paradoxically, at the same time death is also a pervasive experience throughout nature. In fact, it is only through the disappearance, disintegration, and death of structure, systems, and organisms that emergence and birth of others that are new and more advanced occur. From a distance these transitions sometimes seem gentle and automatic, but when we look at the details and the mechanisms, the large-scale and catastrophic nature of many of these events hits home.

Contemporary natural science presents very reliable descriptions of catastrophic events that are capable of wiping out life on earth, the earth itself, and altering the sun very radically in its life-giving properties. These occurrences are far from just speculation. We know that they have happened in the past on our earth, or we have seen them happen to other planets and stars. We witnessed the successive impacts of fragments of comet Shoemaker-Levy on Jupiter in 1994. The craters on the moon and on earth — as well as mass extinctions in the fossil record, the frequent arrival of small meteorites, and the periodic near misses by large ones we have detected — witness to the devastation our planet has undergone in the past and will inevitably undergo again sometime in the future.

Stars much like our sun have eventually become red giants, expanding to enormous radial size and enveloping their inner planets, and much later shedding their outer layers in a planetary nebula to become a highly collapsed white dwarf. Other stars, much more massive than our sun, go through similar phases toward the end of their existence but finally explode in supernovae, scattering their metal-enriched material throughout their cosmic neighborhoods. The universe itself, from what we surmise from the data of cosmology, will eventually either collapse under its own weight in a fiery big crunch or expand forever, dissipating itself in entropy death.

Isaac Asimov, in his well-known book *A Choice of Catastrophes,*[1] has catalogued the various possibilities in detail. They have been discussed, represented, and slightly modified or made more precise in quantitative detail many times since he wrote the book in the late 1970s. Here I shall briefly discuss the most reliably supported world-ending, life-terminating astronomical disasters. Most of the catastrophes I shall describe are extremely remote from our experience and occur on time-scales of the order of more than 50 million years, much longer than the time-scales on which our species may significantly evolve or disappear, or our ecology significantly and possibly disastrously change, through disease, episodes of flooding or volcanism, pollution, and global self-destruction.[2] Why, then, should we concentrate on these scenarios? The primary reason for discussing them in detail here is because, though they are remote and of long time-scale occurrence, they are certain to happen. They also represent the ultimate demise of life on this planet, and, in the case of the universe, of the cosmic life-bearing womb itself. As such they present a very formidable challenge to our religious understanding of what ultimate destiny, eternal life, the resurrection of the body, and the new heavens and the new earth might mean.

---

1. Isaac Asimov, *A Choice of Catastrophes: The Disasters That Threaten Our World* (New York: Simon and Schuster, 1979).

2. I am indebted to Professor Bestgen for emphasizing these points at our discussion in Heidelberg.

Impacts by Asteroids and Comets

On June 30, 1908, a stony asteroid only about 30 to 60 meters (m) in diameter exploded about 5–10 kilometers (km) above the Tunguska region in northern Siberia. Though it left no crater, it destroyed everything within the nearly 2,150–square-km blast area and left evidence in the form of asteroid fragments embedded in tree resin at the site.[3] Had it exploded over a large city, it would have destroyed it in its 1,520–megaton blast.

Near the town of Winslow in northern Arizona people can visit the 1.2-km-diameter meteor crater caused by a metallic asteroid about 30 m in diameter which fell about 50,000 years ago. Though many meteorites and asteroids this size burn up or explode before hitting the ground, this one, being composed of metal, was tough enough to impact.[4] In January 1991 astronomers discovered the asteroid 1991 BA just hours before it passed within 0.0011 AU of us — less than half the distance between the earth and the moon.[5] And in 1994 James V. Scotti of the University of Arizona Spacewatch Program discovered an asteroid that passed within 105,000 km of the earth, about the same distance as the 1991 near miss.[6]

Over a period of six days in July 1994, twenty-one fragments of the comet Shoemaker-Levy 9 crashed into Jupiter and exploded.[7] The impacts were monitored very closely by astronomers around the world. The comet itself had undergone fragmentation during a previous close swing around Jupiter in July of 1992. Scars on the surface of the planet (in its atmosphere) from this succession of collisions remained for more than a year. Shoemaker-Levy 9 was originally only about 1.5–2 km in diameter, and its largest fragments were not more than about 700 m in diameter. Yet the dark blemishes each inflicted upon Jupiter's atmosphere were larger than the size of the earth.[8] If any one of these fragments had impacted the earth, it would have caused a global catastrophe. All of the impacts together could well have wiped out life on earth as we know it. This spectacular event is an example of what is called "coherent catastrophism," in contrast with stochastic catastrophism (catastrophes occurring randomly in time).[9] There was not just one impact, but a whole succession of closely related impacts. Such swarms of catastrophes are not infrequent within the history of the solar system and represent one of the more unsettling prospects in facing the long-term future of life on earth.

---

3. V. V. Adushkin and I. V. Nemchinov, "Consequences of Impacts of Cosmic Bodies on the Surface of the Earth," in *Hazards Due to Comets and Asteroids* (hereafter *HDCA*), ed. Tom Gehrels (Tucson: University of Arizona Press, 1994), 721–78, and references therein; Patricia Barnes-Svarney, *Asteroid: Earth Destroyer or New Frontier?* (New York: Plenum Press, 1996), 169–71; Richard P. Binzel and others, "The Origins of the Asteroids," *Scientific American* 265 (October 1991): 88–94.

4. Tom Gehrels, "Collisions with Comets and Asteroids," *Scientific American* 274 (March 1996): 54–59.

5. Binzel and others, "Origins of the Asteroids," 91.

6. Gehrels, "Collisions with Comets and Asteroids," 58–59.

7. David H. Levy and others, "Comet Shoemaker-Levy 9 Meets Jupiter," *Scientific American* 273, no. 2 (August 1995): 84–91.

8. Barnes-Svarney, *Asteroid*, 125–27.

9. Duncan Steel, *Rogue Asteroids and Doomsday Comets* (New York: Wiley and Sons, 1995), 247–59.

If we look at the history of the earth, it is very clear that asteroid and comet impacts happen from time to time. As of 1994 140 terrestrial impact craters were known, with a discovery rate of new craters at three to five per year. Most of these are greater than several kilometers in diameter, and many are tens of kilometers in size.[10] The most famous and impressive such impact crater is the one detected and confirmed near Chicxulub in Yucatan, Mexico. It is about 180 km in diameter and was formed about 65 million years ago when an asteroid at least 10 km in diameter crashed into the earth, releasing more that 100 million megatons of energy. There is extremely good evidence from a number of independent sources that this event caused or substantially contributed to the Cretaceous-Tertiary (K/T) mass extinction during which the dinosaurs and many other species disappeared.[11] So global terrestrial catastrophes have happened before, and it is clear that they will probably eventually happen again. As if to underline this fact, the fossil record has recorded a large number of extinctions, including five major mass extinctions. In at least three of these cases there is significant evidence that asteroid or cometary impact was a contributing factor.[12] However, the most pervasive of all mass extinctions — that which occurred at the end of the Permian era, 250 million years ago — was probably not caused by the impact of an extraterrestrial visitor, but rather by a combination of receding seas, oxidation of carbon, a prolonged massive episode of volcanism, and the resulting short-term cooling followed by long-term warming.[13]

Now that we have summarized the principal evidence for periodic catastrophes due to asteroid and comet impacts, we need to discuss briefly the cosmic context that leads to these events. Besides the nine planets, our solar system is populated with a large number of smaller bodies. Some of these are comets, and some are asteroids and meteorites. The asteroids and meteorites originate in the belt between Mars and Jupiter. Due to collisions among them and with comets, fragments of many sizes (from about 10 km in diameter to grains of dust) populate the inner solar system in the region of the earth. Many of these asteroids and fragments have earth-crossing orbits — their paths through space regularly cross that of the earth — or orbits that, while not crossing the earth's, come very near and could eventually be perturbed into an impact orbit. Thus, these objects pose a potential hazard to us. As of 1996 there were about 250 such near-earth objects known, ranging in diameter from 32 km to about 100 m, with more being discovered all the time.[14] It is estimated that the total number of medium-size near-earth asteroids (one kilometer in diameter and larger) is about 1,000 to 2,000. Statistically we expect one such object of this size to hit the earth every 300,000 years. Near-earth asteroids an order of magnitude larger — 10 km in

10. Richard A. F. Grieve and Eugene M. Shoemaker, "The Record of Past Impacts on Earth," *HDCA*, 417–62, and references therein.

11. David Morrison and others, "The Impact Hazard," *HDCA*, 59–91, esp. Table II, 72–73.

12. David M. Raup, *Extinction: Bad Genes or Bad Luck?* (New York: Norton, 1992).

13. Douglas H. Erwin, "The Mother of Mass Extinctions," *Scientific American* 275, no. 1 (July 1996): 73–78.

14. Barnes-Svarney, *Asteroid*, 212–13.

diameter and above — are fortunately much less numerous. There are perhaps only about ten of them, and we would expect an object of this size to impact the earth only about every 100 million years.[15] As we have seen above, it is an asteroid of this size which would cause a mass extinction.

Besides asteroids, we also have comets, which originate much farther out in the solar system and are rocky objects covered with ice. They travel on highly eccentric orbits around the sun, sublimating their ice along with dust in spectacular tails as they interact with the solar wind. Some comets originate in the Oort Cloud that envelops the solar system and consists of probably about 10 trillion objects. There is another belt of comets much closer — the Kuiper Belt — just beyond the orbit of Neptune. Every so often an object is knocked out of these regions and sent on a highly elliptical or parabolic orbit toward the sun. These comets can be anywhere from a kilometer to more often 20–30 km across and pass by us with much higher relative velocities than asteroids — of the order of 60–70 km/sec.[16] They obviously pose a significant long-term threat to the earth, as we can see from what comet Shoemaker-Levy 9 did to the surface of Jupiter.

Finally, it is instructive to describe briefly the physical effects of an impact such as that which caused the K/T mass extinction. As Tom Gehrels summarizes it,[17] from the impact of the 20-km-diameter object traveling in excess of 20 km/sec, a tremendous fireball of rocks and steam would be ejected into the atmosphere, triggering earthquakes and 200 m tidal waves around the globe. Some of the ejected rock would return to the earth — over the whole globe — from extremely high altitude in a rain of meteors creating a firestorm, igniting fires throughout undampened regions of the earth, using vast quantities of oxygen, and creating much carbon dioxide and dust. Dust would cover the globe for years, inducing a "nuclear winter" during which much of what had survived the initial explosion, firestorm, and tsunamis would perish. Acid rain would fall for years, and over the next decades and centuries greenhouse warming would ensure further destruction and global climate alteration. There is evidence that all of this actually occurred 65 million years ago. It could occur again.

The Ultimate Fate of the Sun

If civilization and life on earth survive periodic impacts of large asteroids and comets, or other possible global catastrophes,[18] they will certainly not survive the eventual catastrophic changes in the sun. Just as surely as the sun has given us life and continues to do so, it will eventually ensure our demise — unless we succeed in colonizing other planets and sun systems. This will not happen soon, but it will happen. We have a very good knowledge of stellar evolution, and of the physics of our star, the sun.

---

15. Gehrels, "Collisions with Comets and Asteroids," 57.
16. Ibid., 54, 55–56.
17. Ibid., 57.
18. See, for instance, Asimov, *Choice of Catastrophes*.

Our sun has been existence for about 5 billion years (we know that the earth itself is 4.8 billion years old). It will burn hydrogen in its core and stay more or less as it is (remaining on the main sequence) for another 5 billion years. Once core hydrogen burning ceases (all the hydrogen in the sun's core has been burnt to helium), the sun will begin to burn the hydrogen in the shell around the core. The core then will contract and rise in temperature, and the hydrogen burning shell will continue to eat outwards. The increased luminosity and inner temperature will cause the outer atmosphere of the sun to expand and cool so that it becomes a red giant.[19] The red-giant solar atmosphere will have expanded to envelop the inner planets, Mercury and Venus at least, and eventually will either envelop or nearly envelop Earth — either way destroying all life on it, if not the planet itself. The red-giant sun will be 2,000 times more luminous than the present sun, even though its outer temperature will be cooler.

The sun will continue in this red-giant phase for about one billion years. Then as hydrogen shell burning declines, it will again shrink. As it collapses, its core will heat up to tremendous temperatures (100 million degrees), so that helium burning will be initiated. It will now be a pulsating yellow giant (an RR Lyrae variable star). Once the helium is mostly consumed, it will again enter a red-giant phase, becoming even more extensive and luminous than before, extending much farther than the present orbit of the earth. However, the cool outer layers of the star, which now contain carbon and silicon dust, will be pushed away from the star itself and form a planetary nebula. Eventually the core will collapse to become a very dense, degenerate remnant, called a white dwarf. We know other stars like our sun have followed this evolutionary path. Eventually it will do the same, putting an end to our earth as we know it.

It is worth pointing out that our sun is probably not massive enough to end its life in a supernova explosion the way some more massive stars do. Supernovae are the most energetic and spectacular catastrophes stars can undergo. Interesting enough, it is only because of supernova explosions that we exist. Without them some crucial heavier elements like calcium would never be synthesized, and the full range of manufactured elements within the cores of stars would not be dispersed through intergalactic space for providing the building blocks for complex molecules and life. However, like the red-giant phases of the sun, supernova explosions could induce catastrophes here on earth. We examine this possibility and some other possible life-ending cosmic catastrophes in the next subsection.

Other Cosmic Life-Ending Catastrophes

Would the supernova explosion of a nearby star threaten the existence of life on earth? Certainly, if our own sun went supernova, it would be the end. But, as we saw above, that is unlikely to be the case. It is much more likely that our end

19. For a summary of these details, see William J. Kaufmann III, *Universe*, 4th ed. (New York: W. H. Freeman, 1994), 385–88; Thomas T. Arny, *Explorations: An Introduction to Astronomy*, 2d ed. (New York: WCB/McGraw-Hill, 1998), 387–89, 398–402.

will come via a solar red-giant phase. But how about a supernova that occurred, say, 30 light years away from us? Richard P. Kirshner estimates that the closest possible supernova would not be closer than this, and he studied its possible effects.[20] He found that, although it would disrupt some terrestrial systems, such as the weather, and would be an awesome and unforgettable experience, it would not be directly catastrophic. Even a supernova would at that distance still be less than 1 percent of the sun's luminosity. He points out, however, that perhaps its most damaging effects would be the huge increase in the high-energy particle (cosmic ray) background, which would result in thousands of years of markedly increased rates of genetic mutation — probably severely damaging some species but possibly aiding in the improvement of others.

With the frequent detection and knowledge of cosmic gamma-ray bursts, a much more lethal catastrophic possibility has become apparent — the collisional coalescence of two neutron stars to form a black hole. Neutron stars (often referred to as pulsars when they are emitting rapid regular bursts of radiation as they spin on their axes) are extremely collapsed objects — one having the mass of our sun would only be about 20 or 30 miles in radius, and would have a matter density of a thousand trillion grams per cubic centimeter. We know that these objects exist, and we also know there are cases where two neutron stars are orbiting one another. The orbit will gradually decay, and the two neutron stars will eventually spiral into one another at nearly the speed of light, releasing an incredible amount of energy and forming a black hole. For an instant this collision would produce more energy than all the other stars in the galaxy, possibly in the form of gamma rays (very high energy X-rays) and other radiation. Several researchers in recent years have estimated that such a merger would be lethal to all life if it occurred within 1,500 to 3,000 light years of the earth.[21] They have also calculated that we might expect three such mergers in our galaxy, the Milky Way, every 100 million years. There are presently two such systems known roughly within this distance from us, PSR B1913+16, which is estimated to merge in about 410 million years, and PSR B1534+12, which is estimated to collide in about 2.73 billion years.

Finally, it has been pointed out that the "silent," invisible collapse of a massive star within a few tens of light years of the earth would unleash an incredible number of hyperenergetic neutrinos that could wipe out many species on earth through cancer and genetic mutations, in a similar but possibly more extreme way than what a nearby supernova would do.[22]

The Fate of the Universe Itself

Though the earth and the sun are destined for eventual destruction by the very forces that gave them existence, we might be inclined to suppose — or at least

---

20. Richard P. Kirshner, "Supernovae and Stellar Catastrophe," in *Understanding Catastrophe*, ed. Janine Bourriau (New York: Cambridge University Press, 1992), 527.

21. See Robert Zimmerman, "When Neutron Stars Collide," *Astronomy* 25, no. 4 (April 1997): 52–55.

22. Philip Yam, "Attack of the Killer Neutrinos," *Scientific American* 274, no. 4 (April 1996): 20.

hope — that the universe as a life-generating ensemble is eternal. However, from all that we know about the evolution and dynamics of the observable universe, and about the laws of nature that govern it, this is not true. The universe itself will eventually evanesce or possibly collapse in a fiery final conflagration (the big crunch).

It has been recognized for many decades that either one of these two final cosmic scenarios is the fate of the universe. Which one will occur depends upon the amount of mass contained in the universe. If that is above a certain critical threshold, the gravity due to that mass will eventually bring the expansion to a halt and induce contraction and collapse.[23] That will reheat the universe and eventually destroy everything that it has produced. If, on the other hand, the mass within the universe is less than that critical amount, the universe will expand forever, and eventually run down and disperse to the point that no further star formation, galaxy formation, or anything else will occur (this is what is called cosmological heat death). The universe will no longer be life-bearing. In the past few years the weight of evidence has swung in favor of an open (that is, a low-density, forever expanding) universe.[24] The time-scale on which this will occur is of the order of trillions of years. Furthermore, it is also reasonably certain, if protons are not eternally stable (it is likely that they are not), that at a extremely distant era all the baryonic matter in the universe will have decayed, leaving a sterile configuration of weakly interacting particles and a low-level energy background.[25]

The Life-Giving Characteristics of Physical Reality

Given the focus of this chapter, it is all too easy to see the universe and physical reality only as death-dealing and to forget about the essentially life-generating character of nature. And so for a few moments I wish to return to the other side of the coin. The natural sciences have revealed the universe and all of material reality to be vast and incredibly intricate, capable of hierarchical organization on many, many different levels from the atom to the human person, possessing the wonderfully complex human brain. The dynamisms within nature render it autonomous in many ways, capable on its own of generating all that has emerged from it, and relational, tending toward complexity and higher organization. It was endowed with these dynamisms from the beginning. In fact, the intricacy, organization, and potentialities within nature far exceed what we have understood. We understand a great deal, but essential and very puzzling mysteries at the heart of reality remain, especially when we ask about the properties of complex organisms, about mind and consciousness, and about ultimate origins — the origin, for instance, of the laws of nature themselves.

---

23. For a readable review of the basics of physical cosmology as it pertains to these questions, see Stuart Clark, *Towards the Edge of the Universe* (New York: Wiley and Son, 1997), esp. chaps. 4 and 9.

24. See Peter Coles and George F. R. Ellis, *Is the Universe Open or Closed?* (New York: Cambridge University Press, 1997).

25. For a detailed treatment, see Fred C. Adams and Gregory Laughlin, "A Dying Universe: The Long-Term Fate and Evolution of Astrophysical Objects," *Reviews of Modern Physics* 69 (1997): 337–72.

One spinoff of our vastly increased knowledge of the universe is that it is open to life and consciousness. Not only can life and consciousness exist within it, but it seems peculiarly fine-tuned for life. Changing any number of the physical and chemical properties of matter and its interactions by just a little bit would render our universe completely sterile. This fact is what is often referred to as "the anthropic principle."[26] As I have already mentioned, supernova explosions, which destroy stars and anything near them, are essential to the evolution of a galaxy toward a life-bearing phase. So many processes that generate life and new possibilities do so only by taking life and destroying a previous generation of objects and organisms. It is very unlikely that we would be here without the demise of the dinosaurs, or the other episodes of mass extinction that occurred during the four-billion-year history of life on this planet.

What we do have to say is that whatever nature fashions — and nature continues to fashion a marvelous diversity of objects and beings, here and probably elsewhere — is temporary and destined to be replaced by others. The mystery of life and death is written into the very heart and essence of material creation.

---

26. See John D. Barrow and Frank J. Tipler, *The Anthropic Cosmological Principle* (New York: Oxford University Press, 1986), and references therein.

Chapter 2

ESCHATOLOGY

Some Questions and Some Insights from Science

John Polkinghorne

Introduction

If eschatological fulfillment were to be conceived of in terms of an unfolding evolutionary optimism about the end of cosmic history (such as seems to be the case in the thought of Teilhard de Chardin), then science would have a partially determinative role in what could be said. Otherwise, science's contribution to eschatological thinking will necessarily be more modest. By its nature, it is concerned with what can be learned from, and extrapolated from, present physical process and, correspondingly, science's conclusions are limited in scope. As we shall see, when cosmologists peer into the future, their story is one of eventual futility rather than one of fulfillment. From this point of view, therefore, the principal role of science is to pose to theology, with considerable sharpness, the question of what meaning there could be in the hopeful belief that "in the end all will be well."

If the answer to that question were to be framed in the apocalyptic terms of a discontinuous abolition of the old and a sudden revealing of the totally new, then science could not pretend to be able to say what that "new" would be like. It would be utterly beyond its competence to describe or to constrain what an absolute exercise of Creatorly power could bring into being. All that science (or, rather, metascientific reflection on the general nature of the process of the cosmos) could contribute would be to point to the fact that the shuffling and fruitful explorations of potentiality that have taken place within our presently evolving universe are suggestive of the idea that, if the will and purpose of a Creator lie behind this unfolding story, the God thus revealed is One who is patient and subtle, content to work through creaturely process. A sharp change of divine character would then seem to be the implication of any sudden and discontinuous act of apocalyptic transformation.

To the problem thus presented, concerning the nature of divine consistency, could also be added the theological perplexity of what would have been the role of the old creation if the new creation were to be so totally different. Putting it bluntly, why did God not straightaway create a world free from death and suffering, if such a world is an eventual possibility? The Christian answer, it seems to me, is that the new creation is not due to God's wiping the cosmic slate clean and starting again. Instead, what is brought about is the divine redemptive transformation of the old creation. The new is not a second creation *ex nihilo*, but it is a resurrected world created *ex vetere*.[1] Involved in its coming to be must be both continuity and discontinuity, just as the Lord's risen body bears the scars of the passion but is also transmuted and glorified.

If continuity/discontinuity is the case, then science may have something to contribute to the discussion. The nature of the discontinuities will be the province of theology, but the nature and degree of the continuities, required by consistency if the eschatological world is to be truly a resurrected world, are things on which science may hope to comment to some degree, and even contribute some modest insight into the form of coherent possibility. The link will be provided by what may more accurately be called metascience, for it involves the distillation of certain general ideas from the scientific exploration of many particulars. Examples would be the significance of relationality in a modern understanding of physical reality; the recognition, emerging from the study of complex systems, that the concept of information of a pattern-forming kind must be added to the familiar ideas of matter and energy; a dynamic view of physical reality in terms of open becoming rather than static being.

Frustration and Futility

Scientific prognostications of the future divide between identification of contingent possible disasters and the prediction of definitely expected events.[2]

Contingency

There are many possible threats to the earth resulting from the misuse of the power that scientific technology provides. These include the devastating effects of nuclear or biological warfare and the degradation of the environment through various forms of global pollution. Many of these threats of human-induced disasters are linked with the effects of increasing world population.

There are also potential naturally induced disasters due to viral or bacterial mutations, of which the impact of the HIV virus is an anticipatory experience. The incidence of these events is unknowable, for potentially they could occur at any time. They could be very destructive, but it is unlikely that they would wipe out human or animal life altogether.

The normal biological lifetime of a species is a few million years before evolution produces its successor. What this implies for the natural future of humanity is hard to say because of uncertainty about how the Lamarckian process of cultural evolution has modified the effects of the Darwinian process of biological evolution, as far as the genus *homo* is concerned. The human transmission of

---

1. J. C. Polkinghorne, *Reason and Reality* (Valley Forge, Pa.: Trinity Press International, 1991), 102–3; Polkinghorne, *The Faith of a Physicist* (Princeton: Princeton University Press, 1994), chap. 9.
2. See also William R. Stoeger, "Scientific Accounts of Ultimate Catastrophes in Our Life-Bearing Universe," in this volume.

acquired knowledge affords a much more effective way of conveying useful information from one generation to the next than is provided by the slow and uncertain process of the natural selection of genetic mutations. In just a few tens of thousands of years, the effects of human cultural development have produced enormous consequences for the terrestrial environment and for other forms of life on earth. Humanity now stands at the threshold of being able to intervene directly in the process of life itself, through the ambiguous power conferred by genetic engineering.

Finally, there are contingent threats of catastrophe originating from outside the earth. Meteorites large enough for their impact to have global consequences may be expected to hit our planet every hundred million years or so, on average. It is widely believed that such a collision 65 million years ago brought about the demise of the dinosaurs. Very considerable technological effort and accuracy would be needed to provide an artificial protection against the recurrence of such a disaster.

Certainty

The nuclear processes in the interiors of stars like the sun are well understood. In about five billion years it will have exhausted all its hydrogen fuel and it will then enter a new phase of stellar development. The first consequence of this will be the sun swelling to become a red giant, thereby engulfing and destroying the whole of the habitable solar system. Of course, by then life may well have migrated elsewhere in the galaxy or even into the wider universe.

That universe itself, on the largest possible scale on which we observe it, is balanced between the competing effects of the initial big bang (blowing matter apart) and the pull of gravity (drawing matter together). Our knowledge is not sufficiently accurate to enable us to be sure which tendency will ultimately win, but either way the observable universe is condemned to eventual futility. If expansion predominates, the galaxies will continue to move apart forever, at the same time condensing and decaying within themselves into ever-cooling low-grade radiation. If contraction predominates, the universe will eventually collapse upon itself into the fiery melting pot of the big crunch. Neither way is an obvious evolutionary fulfillment to be found.

Metascientific Response

A variety of metascientific responses have been given to the bleak picture of the cosmic future outlined in the last section.

Heroic Defiance

On this view, there is no answer to the actual fact of ultimate futility. Humanity, with all its knowledge and insights, all its art and culture, is but a transient episode in what is fundamentally an inane cosmic history. The same will eventually prove true for all forms of carbon-based life. All that we can do is inhabit our little island of meaning in a world of unmeaning, maintaining a stoic defiance in the

face of the dark and hostile universe that surrounds us. Such views have been
advocated with powerful rhetoric by writers such as the two Nobel Laureates
Jacques Monod[3] and Steven Weinberg.

Weinberg has written, "The more the universe seems comprehensible, the more
it also seems pointless.... The effort to understand the universe is one of the very
few things that lifts human life a little above the level of farce, and gives it some
of the grace of tragedy."[4] This stance is not without its austere nobility, but it is
a deeply pessimistic view. Science is built upon the foundation of the search for
understanding and its reward is the sense of wonder induced by the discovery
of the deep intelligibility of the universe, revealed in the rational beauty and
rational transparency it is found to possess. Yet, at a deeper level still the world
would be meaningless. Although the universe, in its beautiful order and fruitful
history, might seem to be a cosmos, it would have to be asserted that ultimately
this is an illusion. In the end, the waters of chaos will engulf everything. The most
astonishing event in cosmic history known to us — the emergence of persons by
which the universe has become aware of itself — would be no more than a happy
accident in a flux of absurdity.

What this point of view does for us is to make it clear what is at stake in
the questionings of eschatology. Fundamentally, the issues center on the ultimate question, "Does the universe make *complete* sense, not just now but always,
or is it in the end, 'a tale told by an idiot, full of sound and fury, signifying
nothing'?" Weinberg's remarks make it plain that for many scientists moments
of insight, or the recognition of the realized fruitfulness of evolutionary process,
satisfying as these perceptions are, are insufficient for attaining total meaningfulness. That would require that cosmic history had an ultimate fulfillment as well
as transient fertility.

Physical Eschatology

While it is certain that human life, and indeed all carbon-based life, can only
form a limited and finite part of cosmic history, might it not be the case that
"intelligence," having once come into being with *homo sapiens*, will maintain
itself, continually reengineering its own physical embodiment in ways appropriate to current cosmic circumstances, and ever changing as those circumstances
change? According to the advocates of the strong Artificial Intelligence program, we already see this happening with computers, which are primitive forms of
"silicon-based life." Highly speculative "physical eschatologies" of this type have
been discussed, particularly by Freeman Dyson and Frank Tipler.[5] Dyson considers the case of an ever-expanding universe, in which information processing
could continue indefinitely, albeit at ever slower rates and in large and distributed
physical systems that would have to husband their dwindling supplies of energy

3. Jacques Monod, *Chance and Necessity*, trans. Austryn Wainhouse (New York: Knopf, 1971).

4. Steven Weinberg, *The First Three Minutes* (New York: Basic Books, 1977), 149.

5. Freeman J. Dyson, *Infinite in All Directions*, Gifford Lectures given at Aberdeen, Scotland,
April–November 1985 (New York: Harper and Row, 1988), chap. 6; Frank J. Tipler, *The Physics of
Immortality: Modern Cosmology, God, and the Resurrection of the Dead* (New York: Doubleday, 1997).

by enduring long periods of dormancy. Tipler, on the other hand, considers the case of a collapsing universe. He speculates that eventually the whole universe could be engineered to become a cosmic information-processor. Although this universe would have a finite lifetime, in its final instants of collapse the cosmic computer would race ever faster, achieving the processing of an infinite amount of information in its final dying gasp.

These ideas are excessively speculative in the assumptions that they make about physical processes in unexplored circumstances, particularly in Tipler's case. The closing instants of a collapsing universe involve physical processes at energies vastly in excess of those of any regime of which we could claim to have an understanding. In this respect, his speculations are vastly more bold than those of quantum cosmologists (see below) who make guesses about the behavior of the extremely early universe. They talk about times of the order of 10^{43} seconds, while Tipler talks about times less than 10^N seconds, where $N = 10^{10}$!

The speculations of the physical eschatologists are also chillingly reductionist in tone. Life is equated to the mere processing of information. Only if one believes that humans are no more than "computers made of meat" could one regard their replacement by "computers made of bizarre states of matter" as affording a picture of continuing fulfillment. In my opinion, these attempts at a physical eschatology are best understood as illustrating the ultimate bankruptcy of an eschatological optimism exercised simply within current evolving process.

Endless Fertility

Even more speculative are certain ideas that have emerged from the thinking of quantum cosmologists.[6] They are scientists who are seeking to apply quantum theory to the universe itself, an activity requiring much skating on intellectual thin ice, since the cosmic structure of space-time is described by Einstein's general theory of relativity and no one has succeeded — despite much effort having been expended — in reconciling that theory with quantum mechanics in an internally consistent way. In consequence, many different proposals have been made for quantum cosmology, all of equal scientific uncertainty. Basic to the endeavor are two component ideas: quantum fluctuations (the fact that Heisenberg's uncertainty principle permits transient eruptions of energy from the vacuum, which in quantum thinking is an active medium and not a void) and inflation (a speculative, but motivated, conjecture that in certain circumstances small fluctuations can be "blown up" exceedingly rapidly to sizes that will permit the subsequent evolution of universe-sized entities). Various schemes result in which worlds are forever bubbling up out of an urvacuum state (the ideas are reminiscent of those of the pre-Socratic philosopher Anaximander). *Our* world's fate will be futility, but never mind because on the broadest scale everything will go on bubbling away forever. Many will think that the best that this point of view could achieve,

---

6. See C. J. Isham, "Quantum Theories of the Creation of the Universe," in *Quantum Cosmology and the Laws of Nature: Scientific Perspectives on Divine Action*, ed. Robert John Russell and others (Berkeley, Calif.: Center for Theology and the Natural Sciences, 1993), 49–89.

were it to be correct, would be an everlasting randomness, an eternal lottery in which occasional, but transient, prizes might be won. One is back with a picture of possible islands of meaningfulness within an engulfing ocean of absurdity.

Insights from Science

If scientists forswear scientism and are content that science should act in a complementary role toward theology, not pretending that it can give a complete account of what is the case and what we might hope for, then it has some insights to offer which might prove to be of wider metaphysical value. Twentieth-century science has seen the death of a merely mechanical, deterministic, atomized account of the physical world. This loosening-up, and conceptual expansion, of the story that science has to tell needs to be taken into consideration by theology, and it may even afford modest help in the latter's thinking about the coherence and credibility of eschatological hope. A merely clockwork world would simply tick away until its spring ran down. A dynamic universe, whose history repeatedly contains the evolution of genuine novelty (life, consciousness, self-consciousness) going far beyond simply new arrangements of old components, might be going somewhere, even if its eventual destination lay beyond simple extrapolation of present process. Some ideas characterize contemporary scientific thinking that may prove useful insights for the construction of a wider understanding of reality.

Relationality and Holism

Twentieth-century science differs from that of preceding centuries in its recognition of the relational character of physical reality and in a consequent acknowledgment of the need to consider totalities as well as constituent bits and pieces. In different ways, relativity theory, quantum theory, chaos theory, and the thermodynamics of systems far from equilibrium all point in this direction.

Newton had envisaged physical process as taking place within the container of absolute space (which he identified as being the "sensorium of God") and in the course of the even flow of an absolute time. Einstein realized that a more instrumental approach was required, based on (idealized) procedures for the actual measurement of space and time. Synchronizing the clocks of spatially separated observers required that the relevant information of clock settings could be transmitted between them with a known message velocity, thus enabling corrections to be made which were necessary to allow for the time elapsed in transit. Fundamental to the special theory of relativity is the assumption that light provides this universal means of signaling, its velocity being an absolute constant of nature which is found to be the same by all observers, whatever their state of motion relative to the light. This is a highly counterintuitive assumption (naively, one would expect that movement would affect the speed observed, in the same way that the speed of a river current appears different to an observer in a boat than it does to an observer on the bank). It led to other counterintuitive consequences, including the result that the judgment of the simultaneity, or otherwise, of two distant events is dependent on the particular state of motion of the observer who makes the assessment. Absolute notions of space and time were abolished and a relational aspect was introduced into the character of spatial and temporal properties. However, there is also an underlying structure that enables the reconciliation of the differing accounts given by different observers. There is a space-time measure, called "interval," on which all agree, and the ordering of causally related events is not observer-dependent. All observers will agree that the cause precedes the effect.

Later, Einstein made a second discovery that exhibits a further, and even more unexpected, relational character present in the physical world. He did so with two young collaborators, Boris Podolsky and Nathan Rosen, and the phenomenon is usually called the EPR effect.[7] In essence, it asserts that the subatomic world of quantum theory cannot be described atomistically. Once two quantum entities have interacted with each other, they retain a power of mutual and immediate causal influence upon each other, however far they subsequently separate. In a real sense, they continue to constitute a single system. If one stays here and the other goes "beyond the moon" (as we conventionally say), a measurement made upon the one here will have an instantaneous effect upon its distant companion. It is important to emphasize that this is an ontological effect and not merely epistemological. If there is a black ball and there is a white ball in an urn, and you and I both put our hands in and draw a ball out in our closed fists, then if I open my fist later, after you have left, and find that I have the black one, immediately I know you have the white one, however far away you now may be. There is nothing at all surprising in this; you always had the white one and I have simply learned now that this is so. The EPR effect is quite different from this trivial epistemological consequence; the measurement here has brought about something *new* beyond the moon, which was not previously the case. There is a real entanglement of the two quantum entities, which implies that they should be thought of as constituting a single system.

Einstein thought that this "spooky" effect was so crazy that it showed that quantum theory was in some way incomplete. However, some brilliant experiments by Alain Aspect and his collaborators in the 1980s showed that this strange "togetherness inseparation" (nonlocality) is an actual property of nature. The subatomic world is interconnected in a way that means that it can never adequately be thought of as a collection of separate bits and pieces. Quantum field theory reinforces the message. Elementary particles (such as electrons) are not to be pictured as individual and atomistic entities but as energetic excitations in a common electron field.

This holistic, integrated story continues at the Newtonian level of everyday process. The discoveries of what has, somewhat unfortunately, been called chaos theory have revealed the existence of many systems of exquisite sensitivity to circumstances — they are clouds and not clocks. The slightest disturbance will totally change, in an unpredictable way, the pattern of their future behavior. (In a serious joke, this is often called "the butterfly effect" — the earth's weather

---

7. See J. C. Polkinghorne, *The Quantum World* (London: Longman, 1984), chap. 7.

systems can be so sensitive that an African butterfly stirring the jungle air with its wings today could produce effects that would magnify to give a storm over London in about three weeks' time.) Chaotic systems of this kind can never truly be isolated from their environments, since their sensitivity makes them vulnerable to the slightest variation in surrounding circumstance. They must be considered holistically. Their future is not totally haphazard, however, for it is contained within a certain range of possibilities, called a "strange attractor." Order and disorder intertwine in the process of the physical world.

Finally, what are called dissipative systems, drawing energy from their environment and consequently far from thermal equilibrium with it, can spontaneously generate impressive patterns of long-range order. For example, in certain well-defined circumstances, fluid contained between two horizontal plates, with the lower plate hotter than the upper, can develop motions that take place within a highly orderly structure of hexagonal convection cells. This phenomenon involves the correlated movement of literally trillions and trillions of fluid molecules.

Science has been methodologically reductionist, partly because the "divide and rule" strategy has enabled it quite often to reduce consideration of complex situations to discussion in terms of manageable components. Many valuable insights have been gained in this way, but it has become increasingly clear that only part of nature's story can be told in this fashion. The physical world fights back against a merely bits and pieces account. The more we understand the universe and its processes, and the more we understand life and its processes (the claims of a genetic reductionism notwithstanding), the more reality takes on an interrelated character.

We encounter here concepts that are consonant with the ideas of those thinkers in the realm of human experience who emphasize the distinction between a person, irreducibly involved in, and indeed constituted by, a network of human relationships, and the abstracted notion of an isolated individual. These scientific insights of the significance of relationality will also come as no surprise to theologians, who see the nature of creatures as being fully comprehensible only if their relationship to the Creator is taken into account. Finally, such understandings make credible the emphasis found in parts of the New Testament (particularly Romans 8 and Colossians 1), that the destiny of human beings and the destiny of all created things are inextricably intertwined in the eschatological providence of God.

Energy and Pattern

This recognition of the inadequacy of a merely reductionist account of physical reality has encouraged attempts at the study of the behavior of complex systems. Simultaneously, the availability for the first time of extensive computing power has enabled the investigation of the behavior of computer models of such systems. The result is the infant science of complexity theory. Currently it is at the "natural history" stage of deriving partial insights from the exploration of exemplary "for instances," but as yet there is no general theory to hand. However, there are enough insights, and unexpected and unexplained regularities, to suggest that a profound new paradigm is awaiting to be unveiled. Its discovery is probably hindered by the current limitations of our mathematical imaginations.

Reductionist science gained many of its insights from mathematical techniques based on the twin themes of continuity and linearity. Continuity is concerned with smooth variation, the kind of curves we can sketch with pen on paper and the kind of variation that Newton's splendid discovery of calculus is perfectly formulated to discuss. It seems that holistic complex systems have associated with them an altogether more jagged geometry, involving the famous fractals,[8] entities whose proliferating microstructure never settles down to smooth variation. Linearity refers to simple additivity of effect; increasing the number of entities simply adds in their (independent) further contributions. Holistic complexity is nonlinear: adding a new component totally changes the situation in a radical way. It is also reflexive: effects react back upon their causes in a feedback process.

What makes the infant science of complexity theory intriguing is that, though the situations it attempts to discuss are so much more complicated than those of reductionist science, nevertheless there are encouraging indications that there is a subtle patterning in what is going on. One example would be chaos theory's limiting the apparent haphazardness of behavior to the confines of the strange attractor.

Another example of this generation of pattern amid complexity would be provided by the spontaneous order found to arise in some computerized experiments conducted by Stuart Kauffman.[9] He studied the digitalized analogue of an array of lightbulbs, each of which has its state of being on or off influenced in a certain simple way by the state of two other members of the set. Naively, one would expect that if a large array of this kind is started off from some not particularly orderly initial configuration, it will flicker away in a random fashion forever. This is not the case. Quite quickly, the system settles down to a pattern of behavior conforming to cycling through a very limited number of states. (If there are N bulbs, there are approximately the square root of N states involved in the limit cycle.) A deep theory, currently unknown to us, must surely lie beneath these astonishingly orderly phenomena.

What does seem to be becoming increasingly clear is that, in the description of realistically complex physical process, two complementary modes of description will be necessary for an adequate account of what is happening. One deals with energy (equivalently, matter), and its natural discourse is the reductionist mode of scientific thinking in which causality acts from the bottom up among the constituents of the system being considered. The other deals with what one might, in some highly generalized sense, call "pattern": the formation of interrelated structure by which a top-down causality of the whole acts upon the parts. In the duality of energy and pattern we see the glimmerings of a revival in modern dress of the Aristotelian notions of *hyle* and *logos*.

---

8. See James Gleick, *Chaos: Making a New Science* (New York: Viking, 1988), chap. 4.
9. S. Kauffman, *The Origins of Order* (New York: Oxford University Press, 1993), chap. 5.

Mathematics

Science makes extensive use of mathematics, not least as a heuristic tool. It seems that the laws of nature are expressed in terms of "beautiful equations," so that it is a technique of discovery in fundamental physics to seek for such equations. (Mathematical beauty is an austere form of aesthetic experience, but one that mathematicians can readily recognize and agree upon.) That is how Einstein discovered the general theory of relativity, after an eight-year search. But what is mathematics itself?

Most mathematicians find it impossible to think of their subject simply in terms of human construction. They seem to discover mathematical truths through the exploration of a noetic world that contains them, and not just to make them up. It is hard to believe that the Mandelbrot set (a fractal entity of inexhaustible complexity that arises from a deceptively simple definition) only came into existence when Benoit Mandelbrot first began to think about it. Surely it was already there, awaiting its discovery, so to speak. Mathematicians are instinctive platonists.[10] Such thoughts encourage taking seriously the existence of nonmaterial aspects of reality. This statement need not be interpreted in the sense of advocating a Cartesian dualism. It is possible to conceive of (however hard to articulate) a dual-aspect monism that supposes that created reality consists of one kind of stuff (substance), existing and experienced in the complementary polarities of mind/matter.[11] Perhaps the intertwining of energy and pattern in the scientific understanding of physical process provides a glimmer of insight pointing in that direction.

Continuity and Discontinuity

The conclusion must be that an unaided scientific account of the world does not succeed in making complete sense of cosmic history. If that were all that could be said, one sees the point of Weinberg's pessimistic judgment. An apocalyptic theology fares no better, for it introduces a surd-like rift into the story of creation. I do not feel content with either option, for I cannot give up so readily the search for a truly unified "theory of everything."

I believe, in fact, that the latter will be found in a theological understanding of reality. The claim is a big one and its defense can only be sketched here. In my opinion, if the universe is to make complete sense, it will be through something like the continuity/discontinuity of the Christian resurrection hope. The theological motivation for entertaining that hope lies in the resurrection of Jesus and the faithfulness (*chesed*) of God. Yet there is also the metaphysical question of the coherence of such a hope. Could the degree of discontinuity necessary to deliver human and cosmic destiny from being a mere resuscitatory revival, with its dismal implication of slavery to an eternal return, be compatible

---

10. J. C. Polkinghorne, *Belief in God in an Age of Science*, The Terry Lectures (New Haven, Conn.: Yale University Press, 1998), chap. 6.

11. J. C. Polkinghorne, *Science and Creation* (London: SPCK, 1988), chap. 5.

with the degree of continuity necessary to ensure that it is *this* person, or *this* world, whose fulfillment lies beyond the threatening fact of anticipated demise?

The complementary dichotomy of energy and pattern may be of help in considering this eschatological dichotomy of continuity and discontinuity. The "matter-energy" of the world to come will certainly have to be radically different in its physical properties to the matter-energy of this present creation. As Saint Paul said, flesh and blood will not inherit the kingdom of God (1 Cor. 15:50). The matter of this universe is perfectly adapted to its role of sustaining that evolutionary exploration of potentiality which is theologically to be understood as the old creation being allowed to "make itself." In an evolving world of this kind, death is the necessary cost of life; transience is inevitably built into its physical fabric. New possibilities are realized "at the edge of chaos," regimes where there is a balance between order and disorder. The entities arising in this way are sufficiently structured to endure for a while and sufficiently flexible to develop and grow, but they can only sustain their dynamic patterns for limited periods. In our world, the cost of the evolution of novelty is the certainty of its impermanence.

If the world to come is to be free from death and suffering, its "matter-energy" will have to be given a different character. There will have to be a discontinuous change of physical law. It is surely significant that the empty tomb implies that the Lord's risen body is the transmutation and glorification of his dead body. In Christ there is then a hope for matter as well as for humanity. Indeed, if created reality is intrinsically dual-aspect in character, in the way previously suggested, this would have to be so. But the matter of the new creation will be divinely transmuted matter.

Where the continuity between the two worlds can be expected to be expressed is in a carryover of pattern. In other words, we can hope to revive the Thomistic Aristotelian notion of the soul as the form, or pattern, of the body, so that its restoration to psychosomatic existence in a divine act of resurrection constitutes the element that links the one who dies in this world to the one who lives reembodied in the "matter" of the world to come. However, this modern understanding of the soul will take a less individualistic form than that of its predecessors. In acknowledgment of all that has been said about the significance of relationality, it is important to recognize that the pattern that is the soul is not simply carried by an embodiment contained within the confines of our skin. The pattern that is me must include those human relationships that do so much to make me what I am, and also it must express the nature of my unique creaturely relationship with God. (It is surely significant that Christian hope has as one of its articulations the incorporation of all believers into the one Body of Christ.) It would seem a coherent hope that this vastly complex pattern that is a human person could, at death, be held in the divine mind to await its reembodiment within the life of the world to come.

In modern scientific thought, space, time, and matter all belong together in the single package of general relativity theory. We might expect this nexus of relationship to be characteristic of the created order generally. In that case, resurrected beings will not only be embodied in the "matter" of the new creation, they will also be located in its "space" and immersed in its "time." Understood in this way, the continuity of human nature would imply for humanity an everlasting destiny, rather than some timeless experience of eternity.[12] The modern recognition of the role of becoming in the unfolding history of the present creation encourages a dynamic concept of being and of being's perfection. Change does not imply imperfection. To take a musical illustration, each of the thirty Goldberg variations is perfect in itself, and we may hope that redeemed humanity's destiny involves God's ceaseless variation on our individual themes. The beatific vision, then, will not be an atemporal experience of illumination but the unceasing exploration of the riches of the divine nature.

Although the new creation is the transformation of the old creation, it is not necessarily the case that time and "time" should be in a strictly sequential relationship, with the new "time" beginning "after" the ending of the old. The mathematically minded will find it easier than most to envisage a variety of possible relationships. What they would naturally think of as the vector spaces of the old and new creations could be "alongside" each other, with the continuity of resurrection being the result of a structure-preserving mapping from one space into the other. From this point of view, it would be conceivable that all persons arrive at the general resurrection at the same "time," irrespective of the time of their deaths in this world. The "clock" of the world to come need not be synchronized with the clocks of the old creation. (If Christ's resurrection is the seminal event from which the new creation springs, then something like this must be so. The resurrection appearances are then intersections between these two spaces.) If this picture is correct, it would not be necessary for theology to speculate about an intermediate state in which the information patterns (souls) of the dead are held prior to their reembodiment at the resurrection of the dead.

There is another aspect of continuity that one might expect to link the old and the new creations. The history of this universe is that of an unfolding process, and we have already said that the life of the world to come may also be expected to involve a similarly unfolding process.[13] This will surely take the form of an everlasting encounter with God, as the divine nature is made accessible in that world of the new creation which is totally infused with the presence of the Creator. I do not accept panentheism as a present reality, but I believe it will become an eschatological reality.[14] The old creation is a world that contains sacraments, particular covenanted occasions in which God's presence is most transparently perceived. The new creation will be wholly sacramental, for God will be "all in all" (1 Cor. 15:28). Ultimate human fulfillment will be a continuing sharing in the life of God (theosis), not a timeless moment of illumination.

Another aspect of anticipated continuity reinforces this idea. The present universe is a world whose evolving history is to be understood in terms of God's will

---

12. These ideas are consonant with those expressed from a theological perspective by Miroslav Volf, "Enter into Joy! Sin, Death, and the Life of the World to Come," and from a perspective of New Testament study by Hans Weder, "Hope and Creation," both in this volume.

13. Volf, "Enter into Joy!" and Weder, "Hope and Creation."

14. Polkinghorne, Faith, chap. 9.

for an unfolding act of *creatio continua*. It is not to be expected that the patient and subtle Creator, who is acting in this way, will suddenly change and no longer continue to act in an analogous fashion in the world to come. Among other things, this recognition seems to require some recovery of a suitably demythologized concept of purgatory.[15] The hope of purgation must be part of the transforming process that fits human beings for everlasting encounter with the reality of God. It will surely not be brought about by an instantaneous act of divine magic.

Ironically, it is the lack of a positive and dynamic concept of continuing exploration into God that renders pallid and unsatisfactory process theology's reduction of individual eschatological hope to a static remembrance in the divine mind, with the only locus of everlasting development being the consequent nature of God.

An eschatological theme of considerable traditional importance that has not found a place in the discussion so far is that of judgment. Science, with its official position of not dealing in questions of value,[16] has little to say on this matter. It is silent for a reason similar to that which condemns it to having little to say about the complementary theological theme of the Fall.[17] Of course, physical death did not originate with our hominid ancestors, nor did the emergence of humankind bring about change in the physical constitution of the cosmos. Traditional notions need to be reinterpreted in terms of valuational perception (the emergence of the experience of mortality at a time of dawning hominid consciousness of future death, and the consequent sadness at the transience that this implied). Similarly, judgment will involve recognition of, and response to, a clarified perception of reality (cf. John 3:19–21). A self-limited science has closed its eyes to considerations of this kind but, from a wider perspective, human perceptions of value are as much windows onto reality as are scientific accounts of physical process.

In eschatological discourse, science mostly poses some of the questions and looks to theology principally to provide the answers. Yet the form these answers take will have to bear a sufficiently consonant relation to the process of this present universe so as to be persuasive that, amid the redemptive transformation of the old through God's gracious action, there is enough continuity to make sense of the conviction that it is indeed Abraham, Isaac, and Jacob who live everlastingly in the divine presence.

---

15. See Jürgen Moltmann, "Is There Life after Death?," in this volume.

16. But see J. C. Polkinghorne, *Beyond Science* (New York: Cambridge University Press, 1996), chap. 8.

17. Cf. Polkinghorne, *Reason and Reality*, chap. 8.

Chapter 3

THE LORD OF TIME
Brain Theory and Eschatology

DETLEF LINKE

The Coding Problem: Information and Energy

There exists a fundamental difference between the human brain and a computer. In the computer, time is defined by a pacemaker, so that for any given point on the line of time, a well-defined interval of time can be correlated with it. On this ground, it is possible to use a binary code for information processing in the computer. It is quite understandable that brain scientists were searching for well-defined time quanta, but there is no common pacemaker by which intervals of time could be defined in the brain. On the more basic level of sensorimotor reaction times, some tendencies for rhythmic clustering of reactions appear, proving that there are some time characteristics for facilitated action. The data, showing some tendency to develop rhythmicity on a sensorimotor level, complicate the time problem for the nervous system, because these time quanta are not generalizable for all activities of the brain. The data therefore demonstrate that the brain is not a clock in the physiological sense. The question of time determinism nevertheless may come up, if we allow a more far-reaching scope of investigation. That means that the inclusion of theological and cosmological perspectives may give a new and different interpretation of the situation.

Physiological studies show that the electrophysiological correlates of cognitive processes are not phase-bound in relation to the basic rhythms of the electroencephalogram. The relation is rather the other way around: the manifold of cognitive and perceptive processes influences the varying rhythms of the electroencephalogram. In the 40-Hz range, time coherences have been shown in perception experiments involving low-distance activities in the visual cortex. It is assumed that percepts are constituted by coherent firing of neuron-cell populations in this 40-Hz range. However, there is not enough experimental evidence to show that conscious phenomena in general are related to coherent cell firing in the 40-Hz range. The binding problem — the question of coherent cell firing for the constitution of cognitive entities — is still concerned with the problem of higher order relations, for example, between different percepts, and for the realization of decision processes. Certainly different time-scales are used for all these different processes, leaving the idea of a common pacemaker far behind. Information processing in the nervous system is not realized by reference to constant basic rhythms. In fact just the opposite is true, as too much rhythmic synchronization is deleterious for informational content, and generalized rhythmic synchronization of the brain is a well-known pathological condition. The question of information coding therefore has to be seen as a complex system of different time-scales in which a complete presence of all the information would destroy the complex hierarchical and heterarchical interactions.

In investigations in which one hemisphere of the brain is separately brought into anesthesia, it can be shown that subjective time estimation differs, depending on which hemisphere is in anesthesia. For the right hemisphere, the flow of time is experienced as slower than for the left hemisphere. This gives an additional complication to the development of the subjective experience of time. In German idealism, the genesis of time was seen as a product of imaginative capabilities. If one combines this conception with the neuropsychological finding that imaginative power is more distributed to the right hemisphere, then one comes to the conclusion that the generation of time by imaginative power shows a time characteristic of its own. Seen from this perspective, imaginative time would function more slowly than the time used in other areas of the brain. Possibly, this is not only a paradoxical finding, but it shows that the shifting between different scales of time experience can give rise to the well-known experience of variable passing of time. To counteract this experience, one would have to stick to one of two extremes, either reflecting on time constantly, or never thinking of time at all. These two forms of coping with time have their own characteristics of time perception.

True paradoxes of time can be explained by the way the nervous system performs parallel processing of information. The multiplicity of time-scales for different processes in the nervous system is the condition for the possibility of paradoxical perceptions of time, such as dream experiences in which the action of the dream converges on an event that objectively was the cause of the dream. Such an example is a dream in which a man with a gun in his hand is coming toward the dreamer, who awakens at the moment of shooting. When awake, he notices that he was woken by the sound of a misfiring car engine on the street. Interpreted on a linear scheme of time, the sound of the misfiring was the cause of the dream and the cause for the awakening at the same time. This paradox can be solved by knowledge of parallel processing in the brain. At the moment when the left hemisphere became awake because of the noise in the street, the right hemisphere started a dream that later was recollected by the right hemisphere. Such parallel-processing phenomena may occur between different systems of the brain, not only between the two hemispheres.

The fact that no system of defined time quanta within the brain exists allows the interpretation of many peculiarities of brain function. We would like to put forward a formal descriptive system within which those neuronal impulses, which do not find the appropriate time window, are generally bare of informational content and therefore can be handled nearly as free energy, a contribution to the general activity and arousal level of the nervous system. To a certain degree this may even be supportive of cognitive processes. But when the informational coordination of the signals in the nervous system decreases, the overwhelming energetic flow may disturb precise control and processing of information. Certainly, the free energy is not completely free, because a certain relation to defined time-scales still remains; but it is quite possible that such signals are apt for new categorization processes. The language function of the left hemisphere plays an important role in the categorization of inner experiences or, if we take the neuronal level, of neuronal activities that switch between different time-scales and are sometimes partly free from them. The relative independence of neuronal spikes from the neuronal activities correlated to language in the left hemisphere can be taken as scope for the interpretation of emotional states, which are much more related to the processes of the right hemisphere. In such a model, the right hemisphere is related to states of excess, emotion, and trauma, especially because the categorization of these impulses by the left hemisphere is not close. In this perspective, a part of biography arises out of the recategorization of those neuronal activities that were not primarily categorized. In this sense, one way of life belongs to the way from the right to the left hemisphere.

The Fullness of Time

Reflection takes time and therefore makes a difference to the passing of time. Many philosophical considerations have been directed toward this difference. I think that this difference need not be painful but it can, instead, be taken as the possibility of the brain being a host to others. There are good reasons to keep up differences and time-scales when they could be the origins for better contact with alterity. But the question of unity therefore remains, especially the question of the ability of being a host while being preserved in unity.

Certainly the frontal lobes of the brain play a role in the organization of information processing in the brain. According to some models, the frontal lobes possess a gate control for information converging into them. I think that this model can be turned around in the sense that the content of the information being processed in the frontal lobe influences the selection of information in the other parts of the brain. Thus the Lord, being expected in our attentive consciousness, could influence our whole brain. The different times and codes of the brain could be decoded in his name. He, and our attitude toward him, would activate such a state of expectancy and welcome in the frontal lobes, which could allow the activation of suitable neuronal activity in other parts of the brain. In the advent of the Lord, the selection of the neuronal group activities appropriate for him is accompanied by joy, which on the physiological level may be described as the possibility of the frontal lobes activitating serotonergic mechanisms. In the joy of selection, judgment and salvation become the same.

Hope

It is not a global mathematical formula (though even this idea might help us at times) that gives the solution to the different time-scales of the codes in our brain. By our hope and expectation toward his coming, we already influence all our activity. In the transformation of our formerly fractured codes, we also find the reframing for our free energy, which can live in love toward him. In the meeting of hope and grace, the purely linguistic and axiomatic misuse of his name and his suffering is precluded. (The balancing activities of the frontal lobes would fall back into the mathematics of the parietal lobes if grace were taken as an axiom, which would allow us to shift our attention away from him.) If one does not take his sufferings as a grace toward which one has to respond with love, then there is the danger of taking alterity into a formula in which it may be neglected for the axiomatic foundation of the ego. There is no axiomatic system possible for grace. Grace gives the plenitude of our codes of times and even for what we could not code. It is not in opposition to the ego. If one adopts this perspective, religious problems, which arose around the axiomatization around the ego, fall away. Jean-Paul Sartre formulated the paradox that I will achieve immortality only when I'm modest and, because wanting to achieve immortality is immodest, I therefore can achieve immortality only when I don't want to achieve it! But the idea of grace and his loving goes beyond the alternative of affirmation or negation and receptivity or activity of the ego.

Neuronal Thermodynamics and Theology

The further development of a theory of neuronal functions not only in the terms of information theory but also in terms of a theory looking for thermodynamic aspects may be crucial for the further development of theological thinking.

Present information theory concepts of the brain put energetic concepts far aside to the areas of a metaphorical psychoanalysis. Not only the necessity of self-sustainment of information precessing (which may be enforced by interrelations) but also the theoretical proximity of a concept of information, entropy, and energy opens up perspectives for an advanced and sophisticated neuronal thermodynamics which takes account of all the interrelations of information, energy, and entropy in this subject. This offers the possibility to describe circles of self-sustainment in neuronal function in which coherent information may overflow into energetic contexts (e.g., joy) which give the basis for new, thoughtful informational experiences.

On this view eternity would not be a concept of elongated serial time but would be open to a description as a life in which the abundance of energy is in a steady transgression into informational contemplation, which again gives rise to energy. So not the seriality of an ordered time that would decay into mere quantity but the onlasting productive process of overflow from information to energy and finding informational structure would also make the hope for his disclosure more than a mere ordering of time: It would be full of surprise.

References

Gray, C. M., P. König, A. K. Engel, and W. Singer. "Oscillatory Responses in Cat Visual Cortex Exhibit Intercolumnar Synchronization Which Reflects Global Stimulus Properties." *Nature* 338 (1989): 334–37.

Koch, Christof. *Biophysics of Computation*. New York: Oxford University Press, 1999.

Linke, D. B. *Das Gehirn*. Munich: C. H. Beck Verlag, 1999.

———. *Hirnverpflanzung: Die erste Unsterblichkeit auf Erden*. 2d ed. Reinbek: Rowohlt Verlag, 1996.

Reuter, B. M., D. B. Linke, and M. Kurthen. "Stehen kognitive Prozesse in Phasenbeziehung zum 40 Hz-EEG?" *Zeitschr. EEG-EMG* 23 (1992): 62–66.

Singer, W., and C. M. Gray. "Visual Feature Integration and the Temporal Correlation Hypothesis." *Ann. Rev. Neurosci.* 18 (1995): 555–86.

Chapter 4

SUBJECTIVE AND OBJECTIVE HOPE
Propositional and Attitudinal Aspects of Eschatology

Fraser Watts

In this chapter, I will examine Christian eschatology in the context of interdisciplinary dialogue, selecting two other disciplines for consideration, the natural sciences and psychology. I will argue that which discipline is chosen for dialogue affects how eschatology itself is understood. In particular, dialogue with the natural sciences emphasizes its propositional aspects, whereas dialogue with the human sciences, such as psychology, emphasizes its attitudinal aspects. I will argue that these different aspects need to be held together in authentic eschatological thinking, and that it is important to conduct the dialogue with other disciplines in a way that doesn't destabilize this discourse.

This will also allow me to consider another theme, the pathologies of eschatological hope. Here I will argue that authentic hope depends on holding together these objective (propositional) and subjective (attitudinal) strands. Hope can disintegrate into *either* a mere propositional expectation that the future will be good (which is optimism rather than hope) *or* a mere wishfulness or fantasy about the future, which equally fails to inspire hope. Also, as I will argue, various pathologies of hope can be discerned in which, in different ways, there is a breakdown of the proper relationship between the "here and now" and the "hoped for."

Dialogue with Natural Science

First, let us consider how dialogue with the natural sciences affects eschatological thinking. The natural sciences make predictions about the future of the universe. One basis for such predictions is the second law of thermodynamics, which appears to predict that the universe is running down into disorder. Indeed it was the second law that first initiated a dialogue between eschatology and natural science. People became concerned that the disordered future predicted by science was incompatible with the Christian hope. Actually, it is not entirely clear what the second law does predict about the universe, because it is not clear that the universe is the kind of closed system to which it applies at all; also it does not necessarily predict inexorable progress toward disorder. However, leaving aside such complications, the second law focused the question of whether the Christian hope was compatible with bleak cosmological predictions.

These days the second law is less central to such cosmic anxieties than the issue arising from big bang cosmology of where the universe is headed. As earlier chapters in this volume have made clear, there are two possible scenarios, one in which the universe will implode on itself in a "big crunch," and another in which it will expand infinitely, with gradual heat loss. Both scenarios are bleak, and again raise issues about compatibility with the Christian hope.

However, Christian eschatology belongs to a completely different world from the impersonal predictions of cosmology. For one thing, eschatology is essentially moral. It is about a *good* future: the Christian future is one promised by a loving and faithful God. When theologians speak of the hoped-for future they are not generally speaking of a particular point in temporal chronology that will one day be the present, and then the past. Rather, they are speaking of a different kind of future, intended by God and hoped for by humankind. Indeed, eschatology is more a matter of promise than of prediction, and relates to eternity more than to the chronological future.

It is thus clear that Christian eschatology operates in a very different world from scientific predictions about the future of the universe. But yet Christians feel a residual unease about how the cosmology of the future impinges on their eschatological thinking. Granted that Christian eschatology is not *primarily* a set of propositions about the future of the universe, can it be completely independent of the future predicted by cosmology? To press the point, suppose that there was a confident scientific prediction that the whole universe was going to implode next year. Would that really make no difference at all to the proclamation of the Christian hope? Bringing scientific predictions about the future of the universe into dialogue with eschatology can lead to a misrepresentation of eschatology as being more concerned with the scientific future than it really is. However, to say that eschatology has nothing whatsoever to say about the scientific future may misrepresent it in a different direction.

It may be helpful here to refer to George Lindbeck's well-known identification of three ways of understanding Christian doctrine.[1] The first is the propositional. The dialogue between doctrine and science can easily result in taking doctrine more propositionally than many theologians would think appropriate. As Lindbeck points out, there are other ways of taking doctrine: the expressive and the linguistic. Dialogue with the natural sciences can lead to neglect of these latter aspects of the function of doctrine. Many theologians would probably share that concern about the nature of Christian doctrine becoming misrepresented. The uncertainty is about how far to press it. Granted that eschatology is not *primarily* a set of propositions about the future of the universe, is it about that *at all?*

There is a parallel point about the relationship of the doctrine of creation to natural science. Here again it is easy for those operating in the borderland between natural science and theology to misunderstand the doctrine of creation as being about the origin of the universe. Surely it is not primarily about that, but about

---

1. George A. Lindbeck, *The Nature of Doctrine: Religion and Theology in a Postliberal Age* (Philadelphia: Westminster Press, 1984).

a different kind of dependence of everything in creation on God. Does it have any implications at all for what we think about the origin of the universe? And if not, how can it altogether avoid having such implications without becoming empirically vacuous? There are different instincts here. Many would be inclined to say flatly that the doctrine of creation is just not about the origin of the universe at all. Others would say that it must have some implications for the origin of the universe, even if that is not its primary focus.

On the other hand, theologians have often been concerned about doctrine becoming overpsychologized. The widespread reaction against Paul Tillich's theology arose in part from theologians sensing a danger that, along the road on which Tillich was traveling, Christian doctrine would be "psychologized away." Against that danger, if that is what it is, theologians have often wanted to claim some kind of propositional content or objectivity for Christian doctrine. Yet it is not easy to see how any "objective" aspects of Christian eschatology can be explicated without saying something propositional about the future of the universe and the human race.

Although popular scientific writing about the future of the universe — whether it will end in a "big crunch" or in "heat death" — appears to be propositional, it may not in fact be as narrowly propositional as it seems. There is currently what Larry Bouchard calls a "moodiness about cosmology."[2] It is reasonable to ask why so many people are so intrigued by bleak predictions about the future of the universe. In fact, cosmology is not the only source of bleak predictions; concerns about a nuclear holocaust or a major environmental disaster have gripped the imagination in similar or even more vivid ways. It can be argued that what seem to be mere impersonal predictions about the future are in part projections of spiritual realities and concerns onto the scientific or political arenas. Reflecting on this, John Davy has argued that we need to "begin to read what we call the external world as the outer face of our own inner realities."[3] The way in which we are preoccupied with the end of the universe says something about us, not just about the universe.

The nature of Christian eschatology, in the context of natural science, arises in particularly acute form in integrations of science and eschatology developed by scientists. Over the last hundred years or so, many areas of apparently secular thought have taken over religious themes and given them new life. This migration of ideas from the religious to the apparently secular world has been most clearly recognized in the case of ideologically based political movements such as Marxism. There has been less awareness of the extent to which the *scientific* enterprise has also incorporated religious themes. It is important for theologians to realize that eschatology is no longer a theological preserve. Indeed, contemporary practitioners of naturalistic quasi-eschatology are probably more widely read than any recent theological eschatology. Christian eschatology cannot reasonably

---

2. See Larry Bouchard, "Contingent Futures: Imagining the Ethics of Cosmology," chap. 7 in this volume.

3. J. Davy, "Discovering Hope," in Davy, *Hope, Evolution and Change* (Stroud, Gloucestershire: Hawthorn Press, 1985).

continue oblivious of this recent wave of secularized eschatology; it is necessary at least to engage with it.

The most notable outcropping of quasi-eschatological ideas in the scientific domain is to be found in Frank Tipler's book *The Physics of Immortality*.[4] Tipler draws here on a variety of sources to concoct a heady brew of cosmology, artificial intelligence (AI), and eschatology. The implications of cosmology for eschatology are a central theme of this volume, but AI is another area of modern science where ideas of a recognizably eschatological character are strongly entrenched.[5] AI has been marked, since its inception in the 1960s, by a highly optimistic view of the extent to which human intelligence can be simulated in computer form. Tipler argues that if the essence of human beings can be embodied in programmable information processing, that essence can be preserved in a form that is not dependent on the vagaries of the human body. He sees a person's way of processing information as a close equivalent of the classical idea of their soul. Thus, to Tipler, AI offers a way of preserving indefinitely what is effectively the human soul.

Although the religious roots of contemporary scientific eschatology such as Tipler's are not difficult to discern, it is clear that eschatological ideas have taken a very different turn. For one thing, it is not clear that they are a message of hope, in the way that traditional eschatology has always been. Indeed, it is not clear why anyone should care whether these ways of processing information will be preserved indefinitely in computer form. Eschatology seems to have become too exclusively prepositional, and does not speak sufficiently to the attitude of hope.

Also, it is not clear how much sense eschatology makes without God. For example, Christian eschatology maintains a careful balance, avoiding saying either that we are helpless victims of fate, or that we are masters of our future. That sense of balance is missing in scientific eschatology. The assumption is that we will have the power to bring about the future that we wish, an optimistic assumption that on the face of things seems exaggerated, even irrational. However, a key part of the appeal of scientific eschatology seems to lie precisely in this proclaimed ability to control our destiny. To put it crudely, God-like powers are implicitly being claimed for human beings. Because theology ascribes omnipotence to God, an atheist eschatology seems to need to claim it for humanity.

Eschatology and the Human Sciences

Let us now turn to the very different dialogue between eschatology and psychology, which brings out different facets of eschatological thinking.

In eschatological hope, there is a distinctive relationship between the here-and-now and the hoped-for. There has probably never been a settled tradition of

---

4. Frank J. Tipler, *The Physics of Immortality: Modern Cosmology, God, and the Resurrection of the Dead* (New York: Doubleday, 1997).

5. Fraser Watts, "Artificial Intelligence," in *Ten Scientists Consider Humility Theology*, ed. R. L. Hermann (Philadelphia: Templeton Foundation Press, forthcoming).

Christian eschatology that is wholly consistent internally. From the earliest years, there have been contrasting strands of thought, albeit sometimes held concurrently. Some have adopted a wholly "realized" eschatology, that the kingdom is now; eternal life is nothing more than a quality of life in the present. Others have located eschatology wholly in the future, though there have been further divisions about where this future was to be located. Some have seen it as "beyond the grave," some have allowed it to recede into a wholly indeterminate future. Yet others, though mostly on the unorthodox fringes of Christianity, have adopted a specific and detailed futurist eschatology, in the sense of believing that there is a specific date in the future when Christ will come again and establish his kingdom and the dead will be raised. During Christian history there have been repeated outbreaks of eschatological extremism along these lines. The sensible and predominant view is that eschatological extremes will not do, that the kingdom is "inaugurated"; it is both "now already" *and* "not yet."

I want to emphasize why this matters psychologically. Hope requires a sense of continuing inauguration. In a completely realized eschatology, there is nothing left to hope for. In a wholly futurist eschatology of a confident and specific kind, the future seems too inevitable; it is too determined and predictable for *us* to be part of the hope. Hope thrives on a sense of what is inaugurated and possible, but always still coming into being.

It is important to make clear what kind of future we are concerned with in the context of eschatology. We can think about the future in various ways. There is, for example, an ideal future to which we might aspire. In contrast, there is the foreseeable future that we expect or predict will actually come to pass. For example, Moltmann has made a distinction between the "*futurum*," the anticipated future, and the "*adventus*," the radically new future.[6] One danger is simply to confuse these two very different concepts. The other danger is that the link between the foreseeable future and the ideal future can become too tenuous. The transforming power of the hoped-for future depends on its being adequately linked to the present and the expected future. Calling what is hoped for the "future" may imply a stronger link with the present than is actually the case. In eschatology, the hoped-for future needs to remain inseparably linked to the predicted future without being confused with it.

The requirement of eschatological hope has formal parallels with the requirement in Chalcedonian theology neither to "confound the persons" nor "divide the substance," as the Athanasian Creed puts it. In a similar way, proper eschatological thinking does not confuse the present and the future, nor even confuse the predicted future with the hoped-for future in the way that millenarianism does. This is the equivalent of not "confounding the persons." Equally, proper eschatology does not so rupture the link between the present and the hoped-for future that there is no transaction between the two. That would be the equivalent of "dividing the substance."

---

6. See Jürgen Moltmann's essay in *The Future of Hope*, ed. Frederick Herzog (New York: Herder and Herder, 1970).

In a similar vein, W. W. Meissner has recently offered a Freudian analysis of the pathology of eschatological thinking found in Utopian millenarianism. He sees millenarian eschatology as involving an undifferentiated fusion of the ego and ego-ideal; the two are simply not distinguished in the way that they need to be. He suggests that this failure to differentiate the ego and ego-ideal has its roots in infantile narcissism. Often the millenarian vision is wedded to violent and destructive fantasies about the events by which the final union of the "hoped for" with the "here and now" will be realized, indicating an abdication of the superego. However, not all eschatological hope has the features that Meissner diagnoses in extreme millenarianism. We need, as he says,

> to draw a distinction between the hopeful illusions that sustain life and increase the measure of tolerance for human existence and those fanatical visions that exceed the bounds of meaningful hope and sow the seeds of ultimate despair and discord, between an authentic faith that confirms life and identity and the fanaticism that leads away from reality and dooms its adherents to autistic solutions that solve nothing but substitute pure fantasy for the harshness of reality.[7]

Hope needs to maintain a clear link between the foreseeable future and the ideal future. It is only if this connection is maintained in human consciousness that the actual future is likely to take on some of the characteristics of the hoped-for future. Otherwise, the hoped-for degenerates into something that is merely wished for, or fantasized about, with no actual hope for it, and consequently no commitment to bring it to pass.

Meissner's Freudian analysis of millenarian eschatology could be given a parallel in Jungian thought in terms of the axis between the ego and the "Self" (i.e., the complete and true self). In a healthy personality, the axis between the ego and Self remains open. The ego does not become so diminished or alienated that it has no contact with the Self. Equally, the ego does not become so inflated that it masquerades as the Self, failing to recognize its "otherness."

Dysfunctions of eschatological hope can, in this sense, be seen as parallel to a dysfunctioning of the ego-Self axis. The "hoped for" in eschatological thought can function, for a whole religious movement, in a way that parallels how the symbol of the Self functions for the individual. Equally, the relationship of the present to the eschatological future can become dysfunctional, rather as the relationship of the ego to the Self can become dysfunctional within the individual.

In millenarian eschatology, there seems to be an "inflation" of the imminent chronological future that fails to distinguish it adequately from the hoped-for future. In completely realized eschatology, there is a different kind of inflation in which the present is wholly identified with the hoped-for future. However, there are other pathologies of eschatological thinking in which the eschatological future has no discernible link with the present, and so is not able to inspire hope. That represents a rupturing of the axis between the present and the hoped-for that is equivalent to a rupturing of the ego-Self axis.

---

7. W. W. Meissner, *Thy Kingdom Come: Psychoanalytic Perspectives on the Messiah and the Millennium* (Kansas City: Sheed and Ward, 1995).

Resurrection

It may be helpful in focusing these issues about Christian hope to look briefly at a related area of eschatology, the nature of the resurrection. The resurrection of Christ can be discussed in dialogue with either the natural or the human sciences, and which dialogue partner is chosen nudges the understanding of the doctrine in one direction or the other.

It is, of course, the idea of the resurrection of a *body* in which the natural sciences would take most interest. One question would be about the possibility of physical resurrection, and many would be inclined to say that it was a scientific impossibility. Certainly, in ordinary experience, bodies simply do not resurrect. However, it seems to me that science always has to be careful about saying that events *could* not happen. What we call the "laws of nature" operate under a certain range of conditions. Outside their boundary conditions, it is unpredictable what might happen. Jesus may have been such an unusual person that the normal boundary conditions, under which resurrection is impossible, were transgressed in a way that made it possible.

Another question the natural sciences would want to raise about the resurrection is the nature of the resurrection body of Christ. The indication from the New Testament is that it is not an ordinary mortal body. That is clear both from the gospel resurrection narratives, and also from the interesting discussion in 1 Corinthians 15 about different kinds of flesh. If there was indeed a physical resurrection of some kind, it seems clear that the resurrection body was not an ordinary mortal one, the resurrection was not simply a resuscitation, as Michael Welker emphasizes later in this volume.[8] That leads to the interesting question about what kind of body the resurrection body was, something that could be discussed in dialogue with the natural sciences.

Yet another area of dialogue with natural sciences about the resurrection is its relation to time and space, something that has already been fully discussed by Thomas Torrance.[9] One could suggest that the resurrection body has the same kind of relationship to ordinary space as the eternity of the risen Christ bears to time. The latter has been much discussed, the former much less. However, the understanding of the relationship between space and time in our post-Einsteinian world might nudge us toward developing parallel accounts of the relationship of the resurrection to space and time. There is also the question Torrance addresses of the "Lordship of Christ" over space and time, and the way in which space and time in general may have begun to be transformed by the resurrection.

These matters could be pursued at length, but my concern here is more with whether these are appropriate questions to be pursued at all. It is clear that they are questions that most contemporary theologians do *not* choose to pursue. That might be either because they do not feel competent to do so, or because they feel such questions involve a misunderstanding of the nature of the resurrection.

---

8. See Michael Welker, "Resurrection and Eternal Life: The Canonic Memory of the Resurrected Christ, His Reality, and His Glory," chap. 18 in this volume.

9. Thomas F. Torrance, *Resurrection, Time, and Space* (Edinburgh: Handsel Press, 1976).

This kind of approach seems to imply an understanding of the resurrection that is too literal and propositional.

It can certainly be conceded that the resurrection is not just about what happened to a body; the New Testament sees the resurrection as having much broader significance. Some would say that it is not primarily a physical but a spiritual event. Yes, but is it exclusively a spiritual event? We are back to an issue rather like the relationship of the doctrine of creation to the origin of the universe. The doctrine is primarily about origins, but does it have any implications for origins at all?

Also, the worldview of the New Testament, and indeed most premodern theology, does not make the sharp distinction we all too easily make between physical and spiritual. Many contemporary theologians want to handle these questions in a way that is more faithful to the premodern worldview. Great subtlety is often brought to bear in that task — in reflecting, for example, on the complicated nuances of meaning associated with the term *body* in the New Testament.

However, it sometimes seems that wariness of getting into dialogue with the natural sciences about resurrection comes from the fear that if the concept of resurrection is brought into dialogue with natural science it will appear indefensible, and that the only way of safeguarding the doctrine of the resurrection is to keep it well away from the context of the natural sciences. The approach of most contemporary theologians seems to be influenced by an implicit assumption that many key tenets of Christian doctrine would be indefensible in the contemporary world if they were interpreted in a way that left them open to scientific challenge. It is a matter for concern that contemporary science seems to exercise such a tyranny over theological discussion, but this is not often admitted openly.

Shall we then choose a different dialogue partner and consider resurrection in connection with the human sciences? Here again, there is much of interest to be discussed. One obvious line of interest is the way in which belief in the resurrection arose out of the grief processes of the disciples. In fact, it is in fact very common for bereaved people to see and hear their loved ones after they have died. That is surely part of the background for the disciples seeing and hearing the risen Jesus. For example, the way in which the Johannine farewell discourses deal with the departure of Jesus maps very closely onto our modern psychological understanding of grief processes.[10]

There is much to be explored here, for example, about the transformation of memory in the grief process and about the sociology of collective grief. Welker explores some of these issues in this volume when he considers of the role of cultural memory in resurrection belief. However, the key question is again about the relationship of such interdisciplinary dialogue to how the doctrine of resurrection is understood. One possibility is to take the resurrection in a sharply reductionist way, that the belief in the risen Jesus was "nothing but" the manifestation of standard grief processes. However, an emphasis on the role of grief processes in the resurrection experience would also be compatible with a more "realist"

---

10. See Yorick Spiegel, *The Grief Process: Analysis and Counseling*, trans. Elsbeth Duke (Nashville: Abingdon, 1978). Also P. Harvey, *Death's Gift* (London: Epworth Press, 1985).

understanding of the role of God in the resurrection, along the lines that God fostered a belief in the risen Jesus through the kind of processes by which people normally respond to a bereavement.

Looking at resurrection in dialogue with the human sciences thus presses the interpretation of resurrection in a different and opposite direction from looking at it in dialogue with the natural sciences. It takes us toward seeing resurrection as essentially a matter of faith, in which the disciples came to believe in the risen Jesus, experienced his spiritual presence with them beyond the cross, were transformed by it, and embarked on the dissemination of what has become a major world faith tradition two thousand years later.

But, if taken too far, this also seems not quite right. Just as looking at resurrection in dialogue with the natural sciences seems to overemphasize the objectivity of the event, so looking at it in connection with the human sciences seems to overemphasize its subjectivity in a way that very easily leads to the conclusion that the resurrection was a merely subjective or cultural event. My conclusion is that the natural and human sciences can illuminate different aspects of the nature of resurrection, but that it is elucidated most adequately and in the most balanced fashion when they are both taken into account.

Beyond Objectivism and Subjectivism

Perhaps part of the problem here is the way in which our thought world fragments into the objective (propositional) and the subjective (attitudinal). When it becomes clear that neither choice is a happy one, it is right to question the choice. Do we have to choose between overobjective and oversubjective modes of interpretation of Christian doctrine? An increasing number of voices suggest that we do not.[11]

To gain some historical perspective, let us note that the present connotations of the terms *objective* and *subjective* are a development of the scientific era. A *volte-face* took place in the meaning of the word *subjective* in the seventeenth and eighteenth centuries, from the Aristotelian sense of "existing in itself" to the modern one of "existing in human consciousness."[12] ("Objective" also changed meaning, albeit less decisively, and in a roughly opposite direction.) These changes in meaning are an indication of the radical rethinking of the nature of objectivity and subjectivity which came in the early modern period with the dawn of what has been called the "onlooker" or "spectorial" consciousness.[13] It culminated in the sharp division in the latter part of the nineteenth century between science on the one hand and art, poetry, and religion on the other.

---

11. Richard J. Bernstein, *Beyond Objectivism and Subjectivism: Science, Hermeneutics, and Praxis* (Philadelphia: University of Pennsylvania Press, 1983).

12. Owen Barfield, *History in English Words* (London: Faber and Faber, 1953).

13. Nicholas Lash, "Observation, Revelation and the Posterity of Noah," in Lash, *The Beginning and the End of "Religion"* (Cambridge: Cambridge University Press, 1996). Also C. Davy, *Towards a Third Culture* (London: Faber and Faber, 1961).

Currently, we have two broad views about epistemology, one that believes in a rather naive way in the possibility of complete objectivity ("subjectless objectivity"), and another that assumes that no objectivity is possible ("nonobjectifying subjectivity"). Sadly, all too many people seem totally entrenched on one side or other of this divide. Scientific discovery is often accompanied by a failure to recognize that all discoveries are, in an important sense, discoveries about language and point of view. Equally, those who have grasped the importance of language and point of view often have no interest in any kind of objective discoveries; too often postmodernism seems to want to win the battle against any kind of objectivity. However, there is nothing to be gained from trying to win this battle for one side or the other; what is needed is cooperation. As Owen Barfield puts it:

> Perhaps each needs the clasp and support of the other in his half-blinded staggering towards the light. Perhaps there is not one prison cell but two: the non-objectifying subjectivity in which the humanities are immured, and the adjoining cell of subjectless objectivity, where science is locked and bolted; and maybe the first escape for the two prisoners . . . is to establish communication with one another.[14]

These considerations are part of the background to the problems that arise over *either* the overpropositional understanding of eschatology that tends to result when it comes into dialogue with the natural sciences *or* the overattitudinal understanding of it that results when it comes into dialogue with psychology. Theology is best located in the in-between land that is neither wholly objective nor wholly subjective. This place where the objective and the subjective meet is of enormous importance. Donald Winnicott, the child psychoanalyst, talked about it as a "transitional" world, a space that is "outside, inside, at the border."[15] This is the place where, I suggest, good theology is done.

For those of us committed to the interdisciplinary study of Christian doctrine, the question is how to benefit from interdisciplinary partners without allowing them to dislodge us from this important transitional space. It may be that, to hold the "transitional" ground, we need two interdisciplinary partners, not one. We need the balance between the objectifying tendencies that come from dialogue with the natural sciences *and* the subjectifying tendencies that come from dialogue with human sciences such as psychology.

The Grammar of Hope

The need to avoid the extremes of overpropositional and overattitudinal interpretation of Christian doctrine applies in a particularly powerful way to the concept of hope. Authentic hope is not just a matter of holding optimistic propositional beliefs about the future. Neither is it simply a matter of a wish or desire about the future that fails to engage with what is actually likely to happen. Grasping

---

14. Owen Barfield, "The Language of Discovery," in *The Rediscovery of Meaning and Other Essays* (Middletown, Conn.: Wesleyan University Press, 1977).

15. D. W. Winnicott, *Playing and Reality* (New York: Basic Books, 1971). See also Fraser Watts and Mark Williams, *The Psychology of Religious Knowing* (New York: Cambridge University Press, 1988).

the nature of hope makes it clear that it necessarily stands in a transitional world between the objective and the subjective. A good starting point for a conceptual analysis of hope is the excellent monograph *Rules of Hope*, by James Averill, G. Catlin, and K. K. Chon.[16] The view of hope taken there is broadly consistent with that taken, within a different intellectual tradition, by Gabriel Marcel in *Homo Viator*,[17] but Averill's formulation is more systematic. In elucidating the nature of hope, there are two related concepts from which it needs to be distinguished. Hope is different from optimism; it is also different from wishing, wanting, or desiring.

Though there is a clear *conceptual* distinction between optimism and hope in the sense that will emerge in the present analysis, the situation is muddied by the fact that the word *hope* can be used in a way that is virtually synonymous with optimism. The clearest difference between hope and optimism lies in the confidence with which a future event is predicted. The more likely something is to happen, by definition, the more optimistic you are that it will happen. This is not true of hope. Indeed, hope characteristically occurs in situations of darkness or uncertainty in which optimism would be impossible or out of place. For example, when you are seriously ill, you may hope to recover, even though the medical prognosis does not allow you to be optimistic. Or if you are being held in a concentration camp, you may hope to live and eventually to be released, even in circumstances that hardly justify optimism.

Hope thus differs from optimism in its relation to the rational probability of an occurrence. Because of this, it commands less confidence about the future to talk about hope than about optimism. Politicians who said only that they "hoped" the economy would improve would inspire no confidence that it would actually happen. On the other hand, if they said that they were "optimistic" that the economy would improve they at least intended to convey a measure of confident expectation.

Extreme pessimism makes hope as inappropriate as does extreme optimism. There is a prudence about hope. People feel it is imprudent to hope for what is extremely unlikely to happen. Many maxims about hope warn against imprudent hope, for example, "the houses hope builds are castles in the air." Indeed, as Nicholas Lash has pointed out, hope eschews the certainties of both optimism and pessimism.[18] It is altogether more reticent; it adopts an "interrogative" mood in relation to the future.

The difference between hope and optimism is one of four "rules of hope" that Averill has formulated in his grammar of hope. The second he calls a moralistic rule. Hope is circumscribed by moral values in a way that optimism is not. You can be optimistic about any desired event, but you can only allow yourself to hope for what is good. Again, it is instructive to listen to how politicians talk. They

---

16. James R. Averill, G. Catlin, and K. K. Chon, *Rules of Hope* (New York: Springer-Verlag, 1990).

17. Gabriel Marcel, *Homo Viator: Introduction to a Metaphysics of Hope* (1951; New York: Harper and Row, 1965).

18. Nicholas Lash, "All Shall Be Well: Christian and Marxist Hope," in *Theology on the Way to Emmaus* (London: SCM Press, 1986); also Lash, "Hoping against Hope, or Abraham's Dilemma," in *The Beginning and End of "Religion."*

use the language of hope, not for more technical matters of public policy, but for when they are trying to reach for the moral high ground. They talk, for example, of their hopes for a society that is kinder, more tolerant, more just. Hoping is constrained by morality in a way that optimism is not.

Third, you normally only hope for what is important to you. Hoping is such a serious matter that people rarely hope for trivial things. Optimism is again unconstrained in this way. The fourth rule of hope is an action rule. People are normally prepared to take action to bring about what they hope for. Optimism does not carry any specific commitment to action. If you confidently expect something to happen, you can simply wait for it to arrive. Hope, in contrast, demands action. This constrains what you can hope for. Unless you are prepared to work for something, you are in effect constrained from hoping for it.

These rules of hope are also relevant to distinguishing wishing, wanting, and desiring from hope. Wishing is unconstrained by probabilities. In particular, it is unconstrained by considerations of prudence. Though people generally do not allow themselves to hope for what is very unlikely, there are no constraints on *wishing* for something that is pure fantasy. Again, wishing is not constrained by morality. You can wish for purely selfish gratifications. What you wish for may be not only *a*moral, it may actually be *im*moral. What you wish for may be quite trivial. You can wish for a delicious dessert, but it might be stretching the grammar of hope to say that you hoped for one. Finally, wishing carries no commitment to action. It can be simply a matter of "wouldn't it be nice if . . . " with no obligation to try to ensure that it comes to pass.

The commitment to action is a key factor in translating wishes into hopes, as Meissner has also pointed out.[19] You may have wishes that have the potential to become hopes in that they are important and moral, but it is the engagement with reality involved in accepting a commitment to bring them about that marks the dividing line between wishing and hoping. Wishing may sometimes be the source from which hoping arises. However, even if wishing is a necessary precondition for hoping, it is certainly not a sufficient one.

Optimism and wishing are equally unconstrained by the rules of hope, but in other aspects they are very different, even opposite. Optimism is objective, in the sense that it reflects probabilities that can be determined in a purely rational, even mathematical way. Wishing, in contrast, can be highly subjective, and represents a retreat into a personal, primitive, even autistic world. It *can* be, though it perhaps need not always be, a retreat into the infantile world in which wanting something is all important; whether it is actually available in the real world is an irrelevant distraction from the subjective power of the wish.

The nature of hope can be elucidated further by looking at its antithesis, that is, hopelessness, or despair. Is hopelessness a lack of optimism or a lack of hope (as defined above, with the benefit of Averill's rules of hope)? The current psychological research literature on hopelessness defines it in terms of expectations, either the expectation that highly desired outcomes will not occur (which would

---

19. W. W. Meissner, *Life and Faith* (Washington, D.C.: Georgetown University Press, 1987).

be a lack of optimism) or the expectation that highly aversive outcomes will occur (which would be pessimism).[20] Such definitions of hopelessness thus link it conceptually to optimism, pessimism, and expectations for the future, rather than to a lack of hope in the strict sense.

However, I suspect that a lack of optimism is, psychologically, a less significant phenomenon than a lack of hope. The hypothesis under consideration in current psychological research is that hopelessness is a sufficient cause of depression. However, I doubt whether lack of optimism about the future always leads to depression. We live in a bleak world, in which negative expectations about the future are probably justified by the reality of our situation. It is implausible that such negative expectations should always lead to personal depression. Also, negative expectations about the future are by no means incompatible with hope. Indeed, if we follow Gabriel Marcel, it is precisely in situations in which the future looks bleak that hope comes into its own. My suggestion is that negative expectations about the future only lead to depression when *hope* fails.

James Hillman, a Jungian psychologist, has some reflections that are relevant here. He writes movingly about the value and importance of the abandonment of hope, though I believe he is thinking more of the abandonment of optimism. When he says, for example, that the religious meaning of hope implies the sacrifice of all hoping, I think it is optimism that he thinks has to be sacrificed. Hillman sees optimism as not just different from hope, but actually antagonistic to it. However, when optimism is abandoned, it may initially be unavoidable that hope should be sacrificed too. Hillman sees, in the loss of hope that accompanies the suicidal moment, a time of opportunity. He also suggests that the abandonment of what he calls hope is a valuable precondition for psychoanalysis:

> To be weak and without hope . . . is often a highly positive condition at the beginning of analysis. It does not feel positive. . . . But death is going on and a transformation is probable. An analyst may encourage his patient to experience these events, to welcome them, even to treasure them — for some get better by getting worse. If he starts to hope with the patient to "get rid of" them he has begun to repress in a medical way.[21]

The task of the therapist, as Hillman sees it, is to be "with" patients in their moments of hopelessness, and that is surely also sometimes the task of the Christian pastor. Hopelessness cannot always be cured, and perhaps should not be. Out of the collapse of optimism, a new hope can be rebuilt that does not depend on optimism.

So, is hope objective or subjective? I suggest that it stands at the intersection of the two. It arises at a point of intersection at which creativity, imagination, emotion, and religion also stand. In this sense, there is probably no more religious emotion than hope. In the terms I have used in this chapter, hope integrates the propositional and the attitudinal.

---

20. James Hillman, *Suicide and the Soul* (New York: Harper and Row, 1964).
21. Lauren B. Alloy, ed., *Cognitive Processes in Depression* (New York: Guilford Press, 1988).

The concept of hope, as I have defined it, and distinguished it from optimism and wishing, was relatively rare in Greek literature before the New Testament. Certainly the word *elpis* and related forms occurred, and these are often translated as hope. However, as J. L. Myers[22] has pointed out, it is clear that the concept involved was really "rationally based optimism." Hoping for something that might not be rationally expected, that is, hope as I have defined it here, was a usage first found in Thucydides, but one that comes into its own in the New Testament.

The Old Testament had a rather different concept of hope, focusing mainly on trust, especially in the context of hoping in God. This often lacks any specific concern with future events. There are passages in the New Testament, especially those quoting the Hebrew Bible directly, that use hope in exactly this sense. In Paul, both concepts of hope are found, sometimes one sense being predominant, sometimes the other. However, the significant thing is that Paul brings together strands of the Greek concept of hope as optimism and the Jewish concept of hope as trust.

It would be going too far to say that this broader concept of hope was coined within Christianity. However, I think it would be reasonable to say that the blending of elements of trust and optimism in the concept of hope was one that Christianity found very congenial and which was given impetus by Christianity.

---

22. See J. L. Myers in *The Classical Review* 63 (May 1949): 46.

Part 2

ESCHATOLOGY IN THE CULTURAL SCIENCES AND ETHICS

THE SHAPING OF ESCHATOLOGICAL THOUGHT

Introduction to Part 2

CULTURAL PERSPECTIVES ON ESCHATOLOGY

LARRY BOUCHARD AND WILLIAM SCHWEIKER

The following essays explore eschatology from the perspective of cultural analysis. The authors reflect a shared, but too little emphasized, consensus among a wide range of contemporary scholars. Human beings are participants in the processes and patterns of reality. Insofar as that is the case, then human developments — cultural forms and dynamics — are not only enabled and limited by the physical universe, but cultural practices also contribute to the shaping of the universe itself, for better and worse.

The ecological crisis, for instance, is largely a matter of the impact of human action on the environment, action that is guided and informed by deep cultural beliefs and practices. On the human level, no doubt, cultural evolution has decisively shaped the natural development of the species, all the more so in an age in which genetic manipulation and disease control have become possible. There is, then, a reflexive relation between nature and culture. The authors represented below examine this reflexivity in the realm of eschatology. More specifically, the essays explore eschatology in various cultural contexts in terms of different disciplines: physics, literature and the arts, theology, and ethics. Yet, ultimately, the authors assess the cultural horizons of scientific cosmology against the scriptural promise of a "new creation," a new reality that will be both in continuity and in discontinuity with the ways we have construed or imagined nature and culture.

William Stoeger, from the perspective of physics, describes the way science interacts with culture in terms of the disappearance of transcendence. To the extent that modern Western cultures valorize human achievement and material well-being as ultimately significant, then the eventual demise of humanity in the natural future might well correlate with a sense of the disappearance of transcendence now. Stoeger also indicates ways in which, in relation to science and culture, this disappearance of "visible transcendence" might be reconsidered.

Theologian Janet Martin Soskice reminds us that looking to scientific cosmology with a sense of despair is not merely a late-twentieth-century phenomenon. It is also rooted in what some call the "Victorian crisis of faith," which involved an apparent failure of some poetic imaginations to envision how a nominally Christian moral framework might yet remain deeply connected with a scientific worldview, that is, with a cosmos that seemed bereft of transcendence, a universe in which humanity was homeless.

Working with art and literature, Larry Bouchard considers how this sense of cosmic pointlessness was further enforced by the catastrophes of the twentieth century, including its wars and threat of nuclear war, its episodes of ethnic oppression and genocide, its structures of injustice and ecological crises. Bouchard also suggests that cultural pluralism and fragmentation mean that stories of implicit despair are not the only cultural dramas being enacted. There are aspects of contemporary art and literature that correlate with more hopeful visions of scientific cosmology. These correlations need to be assessed theologically and ethically. Are they really visions of a "new creation"?

William Schweiker, a theological ethicist, notices how, partly as a result of modern science and cosmology, we live in a time-obsessed world. We are anxious about how little time we have to satiate our desires and about the cosmic ocean of endless time in which we are lost. As interpreting and valuing creatures, human beings are driven to make sense of time, to give it some cast of meaning. Beliefs about time are at the core of any culture; they constitute nothing less than a moral space of life. Schweiker suggests we look at the ways scientific and speculative cosmologies (e.g., mythological and theological) intersect with "moral cosmologies," that is, with pictures of how human beings can and ought to live in a universe that can be interpreted in an astonishing variety of ways. In such a universe, is it not possible to discern new creation as a divine gift, one in which we respond to God's transformation of values and meanings?

From a variety of perspectives the essays below engage the "reflexive" relation between nature and culture in terms of eschatology. They seek to shed new light on the religious and moral significance of Christian conceptions of time. Yet the labor of analysis and interpretation is not the only point of each individual author's work. Given that cultural forms and dynamics now decisively shape the physical world, it is also necessary to suggest ways we might direct lives and societies better to reflect upon convictions about new creation. In this way, our lives as participants in reality become a means for joyful and hopeful devotion to the God of all creation.

Chapter 5

CULTURAL COSMOLOGY AND THE IMPACT OF THE NATURAL SCIENCES ON PHILOSOPHY AND CULTURE

William R. Stoeger, S.J.

Introduction

Contemporary Western, and the emerging global, culture betrays pervasive pluralism and even fragmentation in its values and orientations. In fact, disorientation, hopelessness, and a profound sense of the ultimate meaninglessness of life and reality prevail among a large proportion of the population in developed countries. Short-term goals and satisfactions generally provide some meaning and motivation, but these often serve as well to divide and separate groups from one another, and individuals from groups. For many — perhaps even for most — the ultimate outlook is grim. All seems to be destined for death and disappearance. There is little sense or conviction of any ultimate meaning or destiny beyond what is immediately available and attainable — beyond the individual's and the group's immediate life and fulfillment. Images, expressions, and stories of hope, final destiny, eternal life are dismissed as unfounded and illusory. Some religiously and culturally influential groups continue to live by beliefs and convictions in the ultimate significance and transformation of human life and of the world around us. But the dominant cultural critique discredits their vision and renders their influence ineffective. On the American scene, there are influential religious constituencies, but they rarely present an adequate or compelling testimony of ultimate meaning and hope to our scientifically and technologically sophisticated culture — particularly when they, as they sometimes do, call for the outright repudiation of scientific results and conclusions. What has happened? And what can be done to retrieve a sense of ultimate meaning and orientation in our society?

In an earlier paper[1] in this volume I discussed the essentially life-generating character of our universe — of physical reality as we know it — and the principal scenarios contemporary astronomy, geology, cosmology, and physics give us for

---

1. William R. Stoeger, S.J., "Scientific Accounts of Ultimate Catastrophes in Our Life-Bearing Universe," chap. 1 in this volume.

the demise of life on this planet or of the universe itself. "The mystery of life and death is written into the very heart of creation itself." That constitutes reliable scientific knowledge and is helpful for realistically confronting the cultural and religious issues of orientation and of ultimate meaning and destiny. We might at first think that the life-ending catastrophes and detailed analysis of finitude and death which the sciences provide would be dominant influences in discrediting or undermining any images, stories, beliefs, and convictions of hope, eternal life, or a realized destiny in death. However, I believe there is good evidence that it is the materialistic and reductionistic gloss on our contemporary scientific and technological culture, rather than the biological reality of death or ultimately inevitable catastrophic events, which leaches the essential value and meaning from our cultural perceptions — or, as I shall characterize it later, our cultural cosmology.

The exterministic scenarios we have examined earlier,[2] and those that have been acted out in the social and political arena in the last century, do disconcert us and strongly reinforce our sense of the temporary and transient character of our lives, and of material reality as we know it. But they do not directly undermine the personal and the spiritual, and call into question intimations of transcendence and immortality, as a reductionistic materialism does. Christianity and other mature religions have always insisted on the reality and inevitability of personal death and moral failure, as well as on the inevitability of crime, violence, and war, which trade in them. Furthermore, they have continually and insistently stressed that physical reality as we know it must pass away, and that that passing will occur through global and cosmic cataclysms that will seem to be the absolute end of everything. The natural sciences do not present us with anything essentially new along this line — just with the details and a reinforcement of their inevitability.

But Christianity and the other major religious systems of thought and prac-tice — as well as the worldviews of many traditional cultures — have at the same time always proclaimed and emphasized the dominance of an ultimate or final reality beyond, or hidden at the core of, the material, the transient, and the dying. The temporary and the mortal are the gateway to the eternal and the permanent. The spiritual and the "immaterial" are revealed through accepting the death of the "material" and the physical, and are at the basis of the des-tiny toward which we all tend and for which we all hope. It is this basis — this ultimate reality — which absolutized, uncritically expansionist philosophical ver-sions of the conclusions of the natural sciences have systematically challenged and removed. And it is this removal that drains the meaning and significance from our culture and our contemporary lives — and undermines the truths about our ultimate destiny and that of the universe we struggle to find, articulate, and maintain in revelation and religious belief. Philosophies and general perspectives based on these scientistic accounts do this by purporting to demonstrate that there is nothing in reality beyond what is physical and material, in the scientific meaning of those terms, and by thus reducing all human experience, including

---

2. Ibid.

the mental, the aesthetic, the personal, and the spiritual to what dies and decays. Our experiences of what seem to transcend the material and the purely physical are considered to be completely explainable in terms of physics, chemistry, and biology. What seems to endow our personal and cultural lives with ultimate meaning and value, and what seems to indicate an eternal individual and communal destiny beyond death, is proclaimed to be the result of wishful thinking and projection. There are no truths or realities — no foundation — capable of giving ultimate meaning and hope to us.

This reductive materialism is strongly imaged and expressed in many obvious and subtle ways in our culture — in art, literature, education, advertising, and the mass media, in our economic and political policies. I shall not develop this part of my case here. The strong and almost universal tendency to privilege science and technology as the preeminent forms of knowledge and practice, along with the failure to recognize the limits and boundaries of science and the complementary strengths of other forms of knowledge, explanation, and expression, significantly reinforce the influence these views have within our culture. In many quarters they are simply taken for granted.

Certainly, despite this there are, as I have said, large numbers of people who strongly resist these conclusions and adhere faithfully to religious and cultural traditions in the face of this challenge. But very influential social, political, and educational forces insist either that such belief is completely unjustified and contrary to all the evidence that can be brought to bear upon it or, at the other extreme, that the natural sciences themselves are bankrupt and by and large instruments of distortion and falsehood. One can choose one or the other, but some middle ground is frequently argued or perceived to be intellectually impossible and dishonest. Furthermore, the results and the products of science and technology are so overwhelming impressive — so well substantiated and proven — and so essential to our way of life and our thinking that it is very difficult for most individuals, and even for dominant but critical cultural groups, to counteract philosophical conclusions and perspectives apparently based on them. So, many who have attempted to reconcile their religious convictions and their intellectual and scientific integrity end up without cultural impact or voice, or even yield to the prevailing enthusiasm.

In this chapter I shall draw on three sources to shed some light on what has occurred in our contemporary scientific culture. These are the insights of cultural anthropology — particularly in regard to the prevailing myths and cosmologies that carry the values, meanings, and orientations of a culture; the ideas of the American philosopher Albert Borgmann with regard to "the deictic" and its importance in societies and cultures;[3] and the framework the Belgian philosopher Jean Ladrière has provided for the analysis of the impact of science and technology on cultures.[4] Using these I shall show that our cultural cosmology has been

---

3. Albert Borgmann, *Technology and the Character of Contemporary Life* (Chicago: University of Chicago Press, 1984).

4. Jean Ladrière, *The Challenge Presented to Cultures by Science and Technology* (Paris: UNESCO, 1977).

depleted of some of its essential characteristics and, furthermore, that the ultimate orientations, meanings, and values that are expressed in certain resources available to us are effectively discredited or contradicted by the prevailing assumed scientistic philosophy and myth. However, those resources are still present, and with their renewed appreciation we can recover our metaphysical and moral orientation. Those events, persons, and situations that are special and that give us hope *do* provide clues to rediscovering ultimate meaning and purpose.

Cultural Myths and Cosmologies

Over the past fifty years cultural anthropologists have shown that every society develops a set of myths — stories, images, rituals, and places that are, in a definite sense, sacred. These express or present "realities and events from the origin of the world that remain valid for the basis and purpose of all there is."[5] These usually speak of the birth or creation of the universe, the world, humankind, and so on, thus describing in an imaginative way space and time prior to the world we now inhabit and endowing our present era with meaning and significance.[6] Thus, the core of this body of myths is often referred to as "cosmogonic" or "cosmological" myths. As such they authoritatively present and celebrate what the world and reality are about — they do not argue, discuss, or analyze the world and the universe.[7] Also unlike contemporary scientific cosmological stories, traditional cosmological myths or cosmologies have humanity, human persons, and human society as their central focus. "[T]he cosmos is always the world of man, and not an external object of inquiry."[8]

The nature of the world and of the universe as imaged in these deeply embedded cultural myths provides the basis for ethical and social behavior. What is required of the people of a given society is contained in germ in accounts of the world's origin and structure.[9] Not only that, but the portrayal of the origin of reality is often the way in which the resources, possibilities, limitations, and validations of the meaning of human existence are expressed and communicated to the community.[10] In this connection, it needs to be stressed that these cosmogonic myths — what I shall refer to from now on as "cultural cosmology" — refer not only to the origin of the universe or of the world, but also to the origins and disposition of all important aspects of human living and organization, including the origin and legitimation of particular institutions and authority structures, the meaning of suffering and death, the role of work and family structures, and so on. The cultural cosmology invites and effects the relating of our time and

---

5. Kees W. Bolle, "Myth: An Overview," in Mircea Eliade, editor-in-chief, *The Encyclopedia of Religion* (New York: Macmillan, 1987), 10:261.

6. Charles H. Long, "Cosmogony," *Encyclopedia of Religion*, 4:94–100.

7. Bolle, "Myth," 262.

8. Kees W. Bolle, "Cosmology: An Overview," *Encyclopedia of Religion*, 4:100–107.

9. Ibid., 104.

10. Long, "Cosmogony," 99.

circumstances to the time and circumstances of the myths, thus linking us to the fundamental and primordial dynamisms and principles of creation.[11]

Finally, in this brief and focused summary of myths — cultural cosmologies — and their crucial function in cultures and societies, it is significant that eschatological myths, which describe the end of the world and of humankind — their ultimate destiny — are not disconnected from cosmological myths. All genuine eschatological myths function as assurances of and invitations to renewal or completion of the real origin of things — putting us in contact with the originating principle or divine being (e.g., Jesus Christ as the new Adam, or in Marxism a classless society as the restoration of humanity, as it was originally).[12]

From this brief excursus into the findings of cultural anthropology, we see that a cultural cosmology is much more than an imaginative and fanciful unscientific description of the origin and makeup of the world, the universe, and physical reality. It expresses in primitive and uncritical but very powerful form the beliefs, perspectives, orientations, and values — the transcendent principles or truths — which embody a society's ultimate origin and its destiny. These realities are tacitly or explicitly assumed and presupposed by that culture.[13] It thus provides the individual and the community with both a cultural and a social identity, and with ultimate meaning and orientation, thus unifying and animating it. Furthermore, it is reflected in innumerable obvious and subtle ways in its art, literature, religion, social, political, and economic structures. For example, the "moral space" or the "moral cosmologies" William Schweiker discusses in his chapter and the "canonical memories" Michael Welker refers to in his contribution on resurrection appearances of Jesus constitute important elements in the cultural cosmologies of large groups within Western society.[14] If the society or culture is well integrated, stable, harmonious, and basically life-giving, there will be a well-defined cultural cosmology that finds more or less universal support and expression in its dominant institutions. There will be agreed-upon goals, values, truths, and a viable, believable, and influential story of its origin, along with an engaging vision of its destiny. If there is conflict, disharmony, fragmentation, and stagnation within the culture or society, this will not be the case. However, it is important to note that a unified and homogeneous cultural cosmology does not prevent a society from prejudice or from repression against some of its constituents, or against other societies. Cultural cosmologies often contain discriminatory elements, distortion, and blind spots.

At this point we need to ask what components constitute our cultural cosmology. More important, is there a cultural cosmology that embodies agreed-upon and accepted expressions of essential values, orientations, ultimate meanings, and destinies? If so, what are these elements? And, if not, what elements are available for constituting an adequate cultural cosmology, and what conflicts, fragmenta-

---

11. Paul Ricoeur, "Myth: Myth and History," *Encyclopedia of Religion*, 10:273.

12. Bolle, "Myth," 264.

13. Ibid., 262ff.

14. William Schweiker, "Time as a Moral Space: Moral Cosmologies, Creation, and Last Judgment," chap. 9, and Michael Welker, "Resurrection and Eternal Life: The Canonic Memory of the Resurrected Christ, His Reality, and His Glory," chap. 18 in this volume.

tions, and distortions prevent them from functioning as such? I shall come back to these questions later.

Before going on to consider the two other resources we wish to use in analyzing our basic problem, however, it should already be obvious that the stories and descriptions of the origin and structure of the world and the universe we have from contemporary astronomy, cosmology, and physics, and of the origin of life, and humankind as individuals and societies, from biology, anthropology, and the other human sciences — well substantiated, influential, and wonderful as they are — are not enough to constitute our cultural cosmology. These accounts usually lack an anthropological focus, in the sense Kees Bolle emphasized above, and abstract from those aspects of reality that deal with ultimate origins and destinies, and from other features of the natural and human world which are capable of bestowing meaning, orientation, and value on our culture and society. Our cultural cosmology is strongly affected by the strictly scientific accounts but cannot be constituted by them alone.

Borgmann's Concept of "the Deictic"

In his book *Technology and the Character of Contemporary Life* Albert Borgmann develops the concept of "the deictic." "The deictic," a word that comes from the Greek, meaning "that which can be pointed out or indicated," signifies the special, the particular — that which cannot be subsumed under general laws of operation and behavior. Deictic explanations articulate things and events in their uniqueness and in their concrete significance, through such media as art, poetry, religious or political celebrations. They express and communicate ultimate concern in what Borgmann refers to as "focal things, persons and practices" — those that "center and illuminate" our lives — and move us to action. As such, they complement scientific (apodeictic) and paradigmatic explanations. More specifically, deictic elements in our experience engage us with these issues of ultimate concern, thus providing values and norms, and thus concrete orientations in personal and social life.[15]

This category of reality — which may include events, persons, institutions, places, experiences, or situations (for example, the Exodus event for the Jewish people, which they celebrate at Passover) — is of basic importance to societies and cultures, as will become apparent, and, though Borgmann does not put it this way, is essential to an adequate cultural cosmology, or body of foundational myths. The natural sciences and philosophy deal with particulars only by subsuming them under more general laws and categories. Neither really deals with them in their very specialness and uniqueness, in the local, historical, and personal connections that characterize them. And yet it is most often these special and particular features that give meaning, significance, focus, orientation, and value to human life and society. Thus, "the deictic" is that which cannot be adequately described or accounted for — it can only be pointed out or indicated — but it is precisely that which endows our life and that of our community or society with

15. Borgmann, *Technology and the Character of Contemporary Life*, 4–5, 25–26, 71, 72, 179–81.

meaning and orientation. Examples would be the person who is central to our life, the event that gives meaning to our situation — such as the event that gives independence or freedom to a nation or a people — or gives us hope by revealing our ultimate destiny, such as the death and resurrection of Jesus.

Although deictic experiences and deictic elements are special and unique and endow our personal, social, and cultural life with meaning and orientation, they are not absolute. They are subject — and must be subject — to ongoing discernment and critique. The key question always is: Do these events, places, persons, experiences that are important or sacred to us — and the values, orientations, and actions they embody and elicit — lead to fulfillment, sensitivity, and compassion toward others, openness and social harmony? Or rather do they instead promote disintegration, violence, distrust, alienation? By their fruits, you shall know them.

An important insight deriving from Borgmann's analysis is that "the devaluation of the deictic" in a culture or a society leads to disorientation, loss of meaning, and fragmentation.[16] Furthermore, he suggests that one of the most important negative influences of science and technology on culture and society is precisely such undermining of the deictic elements that are basic to its identity and equilibrium. This happens for a variety of reasons, including the privileging of scientific knowledge and technological practice, the consequent demeaning or discounting of other forms of knowledge — precisely those such as art, religion, and politics, which transmit deictic elements except insofar as they can be justified in terms of science — and the neglect of those aspects of culture and community that are not directly connected with the economic, technological, and scientific sectors of society. Another way of expressing this is that technology can lead us to treat things and persons as either devices or commodities, desensitizing us to the local, historical, aesthetic, and religious relationships and meanings they may have for us. Thus, we have a strong tendency to view them only for how they can be used for us and for our projects, and not for what they are in themselves, or for what they reveal to us about what is beyond our projects and our immediate concerns.

Jean Ladrière's Analysis of Cultural Dynamics

In his monograph *The Challenge Presented to Cultures by Science and Technology*,[17] Jean Ladrière analyzes the impact science and technology have on cultures and societies, and the dynamics involved. His treatment abstracts from cultural anthropological perspectives. However, as I summarize his framework, it will be apparent that it complements them and can shed some light on the evolution of cultural cosmologies.

First, Ladrière distinguishes between a broader and a more narrow sense of "culture." More broadly "culture" consists of

---

16. Ibid., 78–113.
17. Ladrière, *Challenge Presented to Cultures by Science and Technology*; see also William R. Stoeger, "Astronomy's Integrating Impact on Culture: A Ladrièrean Hypothesis," *Leonardo* 29 (1996): 151–54, for a summary.

all the institutions — considered in terms of their functional and normative aspects — in which a certain social totality is expressed and which represent for individuals belonging to it the inescapable framework which moulds their personalities, defines their possibilities and traces in advance the pattern of their lives, that which will give them actual shape.[18]

In a more restricted sense, "culture" refers to certain components of "culture" in the broad sense. In this narrow sense it "embraces all those areas of life which enable an individual, in a given society, to develop his or her sensibilities, his or her critical sense, his or her capacity for knowledge, and his or her creative abilities."[19] In other words, "culture" in this narrow sense denotes all those aspects of a society that are oriented toward personal and communal fulfillment.

Next, Ladrière points out that the components of culture, broadly speaking, can be separated into various fields — the field of institutions, the field of values, and the field of meanings.[20] It is helpful at this point to distinguish between "meanings" and "values." Perhaps the clearest simple relative description of these two concepts has been given by the American philosopher Robert Nozick:

> Value involves something's being integrated within its own boundaries, while meaning involves its having some connection beyond these boundaries. The problem of meaning itself is raised by the presence of limits. . . . To seek to give life meaning is to seek to transcend the limits of one's individual life.[21]

Having defined "culture" and distinguished its constituent fields, Ladrière goes on to describe the types of systems found in culture (broad sense) and society. There are political, economic, and cultural (narrow sense) systems.[22] Cultural systems, our principal focus here, ensure the informational and axiological (value-bearing) aspects of social and cultural (broad sense) life: values, standards, systems of representation, expressive and symbolic systems, including education, religion, and science.

In order to induce modifications in a system, science and technology must be concretely represented within that system (59ff.). So how are they typically represented? Within society they are embodied in a number of different ways — first by those who are professionally engaged in those pursuits and by the institutions and networks they form in order to collaborate and communicate with one another, with other elements of the scientific and academic communities, and with society at large. Second, there are those who follow science and technology and use it, appropriating the new knowledge to varying degrees, using it and the products it has generated. Thus, science and technology become represented in education, in mass media, in economic and production-oriented institutions, in the evolving

---

18. Ladrière, *Challenge Presented to Cultures by Science and Technology*, 57.
19. Ibid.
20. Ibid., 57–58.
21. Robert Nozick, *The Examined Life* (New York: Simon and Schuster, 1989), 166.
22. Ladrière, *Challenge Presented to Cultures by Science and Technology*, 58 (subsequent page references appear in the text).

language and images we use, in art and literature, and even in religion — in the symbols we employ there.

As we have indicated above, a large part of the impact of science and technology will be on cultural subsystems — that is, at the level at which society forms an image of reality and of itself, at the level of mental and symbolic representations. Among these subsystems that are either directly or indirectly affected are (1) the mythical (ritual and symbolic) elements of society and culture; (2) the systems of beliefs, which are religious or traditional and communicate meaning and value through, for example, an expression of what our individual and corporate destiny is believed to be; (3) the systems of theological representations, which are more speculative than beliefs; (4) the systems of a metaphysical character, which embody our empirical, prescientific knowledge; and (5) the systems of ideological elements, which are representations relating to society and to the individual's place in it, which serve to justify existing social and political structures (66).

Using the concepts he has so far established, Ladrière models in some detail the generic history of the process of influence, impact, and eventual assimilation of scientific and technological novelty in a culture. His description of the dynamics within cultures appears to be approximately correct and helps us understand the tensions and conflicts, and the subsequent accommodations, that mark the history of culture and ideas.

At first, according to Ladrière, a development in science is a *foreign body* in the cultural subsystems of representation we described above (66). It may at first be very isolated relative to them, without implications beyond the narrow scientific context within which it originated. But eventually the new scientific knowledge begins to be propagated outside the scientific community, through education and the mass media, as well as through the contacts the scientists themselves have with the larger community (66–67). The knowledge itself is accessed, at least in its basics, by society at large and begins to affect its language, and eventually its symbolic structures (e.g., art). It is thus assimilated and integrated into the representational systems of the culture, inducing changes in them — changes in perspectives, values, horizons, and meanings. What is important to notice is not so much the small changes induced by individual bits of new scientific knowledge, but rather those effected by the cumulative impact of continuing new developments and directions — for instance, of astronomy and cosmology during the last seventy-five years, or that of biology during the last forty years.

Ladrière goes on to divide the impact process into two phases: *destructuration* and *restructuration* (69ff.). Each of these phases will have political, economic, and cultural components. What is the destructuration phase? It obviously refers to the preintegration, or preassimilation, part of the impact process. For a culture to be effective in coordinating and regulating society by means of norms and meanings, it must act in a coherent, coordinated manner, rendering the whole self-stabilizing. Values are again crucial here. Destructuration, in the context of cultural subsystems, is the disturbance or disruption of systems of representation, and therefore of systems of values and meanings.

There are three aspects of such cultural destructuration. First, there is the direct effect of the scientific and technological activities on the cultural systems of representation we have just described — challenging them or confirming them. Second, there is the growing acceptance of the scientific or technological perspective or project, and the image of and design for the future it implies. This has further influence on values and meanings. Finally, as a result of this, there is the establishment of a new corresponding *form of temporality*. Many areas of sciences and technology envision the future as planned, controlled, and transformable by human activity. This induces a sense of time as rich in possibility and more and more fulfilling our expectations, our needs, and our plans. The threatening, the uncertain and unexpected, and the uncontrollable in temporality are mitigated. Other areas of science, especially those connected with contemporary scientific cosmology and astronomy, act against this overall trend by inducing a sense of a vastly expanding future that we cannot totally control or plan, and which in the long term presents us with our ultimate demise, and that of the universe, in an insistent and disconcerting way. If taken as the final word and unmitigated by other complementary personal or religious considerations, the impact of this mode of temporality will induce a sense of ultimate meaninglessness and point-lessness. Scientific eschatological scenarios fail to put us in touch with the sources of life and wholeness; instead, they definitively undo what nature has fashioned.

The second phase of the process of cultural impact, according to Ladrière, is restructuration (86ff.). This is the phase of reintegration and reunification of culture and its subsystems on a new level, based on new or modified representations, meanings, and values, or on new interpretations of old ones. It, too, generally, has three aspects or subphases. First, there is the rejection of new elements of representation by some aspects of the culture and acceptance of them by others. This is not necessarily by different groups of people, but more often by different subsystems, and leads directly to a dualism, or a pluralism. Second, there is a phase of careful criticism and delimitation of spheres of competence, which resolves or moves toward resolving the conflict expressed by the dualism. Finally, there is the restoration of a unity of vision. This can be negative, if the reunification spurns real integration and embraces instead a radical scientistic rationalization — for instance, a reinterpretation or explanation of theology in purely scientific terms and models. Or restructuration can be a very positive achievement, in which culture subsumes the essential kernel of scientific knowledge under new and more expansive theological, psychological, and philosophical interpretations. What appears to be decisive in the conflict stages of restructuration are the maintenance of a critical and self-critical spirit, and systematic and cumulative growth in both knowledge and in the critically integrative, open, and fruitful character of our perspectives.

The Impact of Science and Technology on Our Cultural Cosmologies

Bringing these descriptive and analytic resources to bear on our present situation, several conclusions can be drawn. First of all, from what we have seen from cultural anthropology, the scientific accounts of origins we have from cosmology, astronomy, geology, and biology, while providing images and narratives we use in constructing our cultural cosmology, cannot provide key elements, those that provide meaning, orientation, and value and insert us as individuals and as communities in an understandable and significant way within the physical context they portray. Religious, traditional, personal, and communal accounts of foundational experiences can do that. However, prevailing philosophies espousing metaphysical reductionism and scientism call those accounts into question in the name of science.

Thus, there is a perceived mismatch between our physical cosmology and the other essential elements available for our cultural cosmologies. I contend that the mismatch is only apparent relative to certain inadequate interpretations of the range and significance of scientific knowledge and of the validity of other forms of knowledge and understanding. But it is, in many quarters, a strongly perceived and influential incompatibility nevertheless. In Ladrièrean terms, we are still in an intermediate phase of restructuration, in which we are dealing with conflicts caused by a pluralism of interpretations and are being tempted to fabricate a scientistic reunification.

In earlier centuries, the prevailing physical cosmology reinforced the cultural cosmology, including its perceived transcendent and anthropological elements, providing a more or less hospitable framework for them. For instance, under the Ptolemaic system, there was always a place for transcendent elements — the unchangeable heavenly bodies, circular motions, and a place for the prime mover.[23] Even after Copernicus, Galileo, Kepler, and Newton, there was a definite place for the divine in the understanding of the physical constitution and ordering of the universe, unsatisfactory as that really was. The visible structure of the world provided a coherent and powerful, if inadequate, witness to what is eternal and ultimately meaningful. We are not idealizing these past cultural integrations. The price they exacted in terms of their narrowness, superficiality, and oppressiveness was enormous. We are merely pointing out the coherence between the physical cosmological components and the religious, philosophical, and anthropological perceptions they manifest.

That is no longer considered the case today — in fact, it is presumed *not* to be the case. There are the clues provided by the anthropic principle,[24] which seem to indicate that the universe is fine-tuned for life. But these have not provided compelling symbols or images of purpose, ultimate meaning, or orientation in the face of reductionistic accounts, evolutionary accident, and ultimate cosmic demise. Physical cosmology provides "laws" and regularities that are relatively stable and eternal but does not present an ultimate origin or purpose for those regularities and processes that would bestow meaning and significance on cultural cosmology.

---

23. For a brief description of ancient and medieval cosmologies, particularly the Ptolemaic paradigm, see A. G. Pacholczyk, *The Catastrophic Universe: An Essay in the Philosophy of Cosmology* (Tucson: Pachart Publishing, 1984), 11–27.

24. John D. Barrow and Frank J. Tipler, *The Anthropic Cosmological Principle* (New York: Oxford University Press, 1986), and references therein.

Nor should it. From a broad point of view, however, physical cosmology should be kept open to deeper harmonization with other cultural and religious elements that do so. Even though increasing numbers of scientists and philosophers admit that the regularities and processes of nature may very well have their origin in a divine being or principle, and that they are indeed fundamentally compatible with some religious perspectives, influential materialistic interpretations of the results and significance of the natural sciences (and of physical cosmology itself) continue to call any eternal or transcendent reality into question.

Thus, we have the situation where dominant institutions within our society — science and technology, and the other institutions that heavily rely upon and communicate them — often manifest deep and radical disagreement and conflict with essential beliefs, values, and perceptions we have inherited and upon which we rely for meaning and orientation. Our physical cosmology has been used to undermine the cultural cosmologies upon which we have depended, and threatens to replace them, anthropologically and philosophically inadequate as it is. Something else must provide these essential components to our operative cultural cosmology. And the only area from which that can come is from a renewed analysis and appreciation of the limitations of the natural sciences and of expressions of our human experience which cannot be adequately accounted for, evaluated, and interpreted by the natural and human sciences.

Along with this deep separation of our physical cosmology from cultural cosmologies is the scattering, fragmentation, and relativization of the elements that are or could be important meaning- and value-bearing components of our cultural cosmology. These are religious, traditional, human-oriented, and nature-oriented stories, symbols, and celebrations that are part of everyone's heritage, as well as the eloquent witness of outstanding people and communities of integrity and holiness in our recent past. These elements still exert powerful attraction for many people, but their significance and meaning have been diluted, dulled, marginalized, and disengaged from the images and priorities that really dominate. Although they continue to communicate effectively and express transcendent and even ultimate meanings to some groups, they no longer do so to the majority of people. In light of a strictly reductionistic and scientistic philosophy, the meaning and orientation they convey have been effectively rendered illusory. The challenge is not to return to the past, but to forge new and more profound integrations that rely on the richness, rigor, and the critical spirit of the natural sciences but which also express and celebrate the values, meanings, and insights of other more nourishing areas of human experience.

Much of the problem, as we have already seen, is "the devaluation of the deictic."[25] A significant part of this is due to the unwarranted exclusive privileging of scientific knowledge and explanation, and the consequent dismissal of other forms of knowledge and understanding. If only those phenomena that can be scientifically described and validated, and only those pursuits that lead to technological application and control, count for anything, then all those particular

---

25. Borgmann, *Technology and the Character of Contemporary Life.*

and special events, persons, pursuits, and objects that endow our lives with meaning, focus, and orientation are merely pragmatic necessities. They are effective in entertaining us, soothing us, and relaxing us — creating a sense of harmony and peace with ourselves, our surroundings, family, friends, and colleagues, and with reality at large. But they really do not convey or express any true ultimate meaning or value. We construct such useful fictions in order to be able to live and function more happily, efficiently, and easily.

Finally, in our cultural and moral disorientation, we are hounded by two conflicting senses of time. On one side, as Ladrière has said, time and the future are apparently under our control. Anything that happens or does not happen is the result of our action or our negligence — our foresight or our lack of awareness. We are under the compulsion to use time well and to bring all future events in line with our projects. But on the other side, in the long range, it does not make any difference. It is all for naught. Ultimately, death will have the last word, and humanity, our world, our universe will yield to entropy and dissolution. Thus, we are faced with the intense demands of living and working and struggling for a purely temporary achievement — that is what gives meaning and orientation to our lives. But that achievement will not last. Our lives and our accomplishments are victims of a temporally hostile and meaningless world. In terms of cosmogonic and eschatological myths, the prevailing impression is that our universe happened and gave birth to us in a series of blind and purposeless accidents. It will sooner or later destroy us in a similar series of accidents and then gradually disperse, losing all its potential for further regeneration, and leaving no perceptible or significant trace. Such a cultural cosmology provides no meaning, orientation, or moral compass.

These are some of the central dynamisms which I believe are at work in our contemporary Western culture at present, and which strongly contribute to the hopelessness, alienation, and sense of disorientation so many people experience. Fortunately, as is obvious from our discussion, the resources for remedying this malaise are already in our possession — the deictic elements in our personal and cultural experience, and the roots of a more profound appreciation of the range and the limits of human knowledge, including particularly those of the natural sciences.

Note: I am particularly thankful for the help and suggestions I have had from other members of the Center of Theological Inquiry Consultation on Science and Theology in preparing and revising this contribution, particularly John Polkinghorne and Michael Welker, and for the valuable suggestions and criticisms of Professor Günter Thomas.

Chapter 6

THE ENDS OF MAN AND THE FUTURE OF GOD

JANET MARTIN SOSKICE

Theology and Science: On Eschatology

Internationales Wissenschaftsforum, Heidelberg, March 24–28, 1999

Hope is one of the three theological virtues, but hope seems to us different from faith and charity. You can dispose yourself to faith and charity — try to be more kind or more devout. With hope, however, you either have it or you do not. In contemporary culture hope is represented, even by the churches, as a psychological mood. Lack of faith and charity can be treated by prayer but lack of hope is treated with antidepressants. Surely this points to what is flawed in this commonplace, modern understanding of hope, at least for theological purposes. Christian hope is neither a psychological mood nor an emotional commodity but a gift and a grace. The same is true of faith and love. We do not "possess" these — or a certain quantity of them — as commodities, any more than we will possess God as a commodity when we see God face to face. Rather, we are constituted in these theological virtues by God. This is perhaps what is meant, in part, by saying that hope, like faith and love, *abides.* Karl Rahner even suggests that hope is not to be dispensed with in the hereafter. Hope abides, he says, as distinctly and irreducibly itself even in heaven. Christian hope will not dissolve once it possesses its "object" as do profane hopes, because Christian hope is not directed toward some *object* or finite goal but toward God. Hope, Rahner says, is an attitude that bears upon God as God is in and for Godself. It is an attitude toward God who, even in total givenness, remains mystery.

Many theologians have pointed to the difference between this hope *in God* and profane hopes. J.-B. Metz has said that the difference between Christian hope for the coming of God's kingdom and a secular utopian vision is this: the secular utopias envision a time that would be marvelous for those lucky enough to be alive at the time but offer little solace to those whose lives have been a means to this glorious end. But Christian hope looks forward to God's time, the kingdom, when all will be well and when every tear will be dried, when all the suffering of the world through its ragged and jagged history will be made whole. Such hope could only be hope in God.

However, religious hope is not simply directed toward the future state of well-being but is an abiding knowledge that all is God's and God is all, no matter how grim things may be. Christian hope is not only hope for the future but hope for the present and past. This hope is quite different from the Hollywood optimism that "blue skies are just around the corner." Christians have learned from Jews out of the horror of the Shoah that hope in God can abide even in the midst of profound evil, and without ignoring that profound evil.

Just as hope in God is not simple optimism, the opposite of hope in God is not pessimism or even despair but nihilism.[1] Whereas despair is a transient mood, nihilism, like hope, is a fundamental orientation to the world. You can have happy, even jolly nihilists. There are many of these people around — garrulous dinner-party nihilists who are optimistic about pay raises or their summer holiday but skeptical as to questions of meaning, truth, values, goodness, or integrity.

Depending on whom one listens to in the intellectual cacophony, nihilism is in the ascendant in the postmodern West and hope on the way out. From the religious point of view the period of European modernity has been one of sustained and continuing loss of beliefs, loss of belief in the authority of scripture, church, tradition, and even common sense. God, in dying — so this story goes — has dragged other cherished fancies to the grave. Most recently we have seen loss in belief in those "idols" that tried to take the place of the absent God — loss in belief in progress, in beauty, in Marxism, in the Enlightenment, in psychoanalysis, all the secular narratives of salvation — a true twilight of the idols.

There is a consensus that science has played a large part in stripping away traditional certainties, in "disenchanting" the universe. On this view the growth of scientific knowledge, with its convincing accounts of order in the world, is directly responsible for the decline in religious belief and the values of traditional culture. The phrase "disenchanted universe" is Max Weber's, but has a recent update in François Lyotard's book *The Postmodern Condition,* where the writer argues that this postmodern condition is undoubtedly the product of the progress of science.

What interests me about this putatively "empirical" account of modernity and the decline of faith is that it has so little empirical warrant. There is no direct correlation between advance in scientific knowledge and decline of religious allegiance. Where we see dramatic declines in church attendance, say, in modern Greece between the 1950s and the 1990s, it is not new scientific knowledge paving the way, although secularism may have something to do with advancing technology and technocratic culture. The causes of religious decline are undoubtedly complex, and Western Europe should not be our template. It is not the case that everywhere modernity has meant the loss of religion. It may even be quite distinctive to the modern West. Three billion of the world's people are still religious and these are not all "unmodern" people. Indeed, secularization has proceeded at

---

1. This is a somewhat overworked term and I do not, for the purposes of this essay, intend to give an extensive account of the varieties of European nihilism, whether philosophical or other. Let it rest, for our purposes here, in the contrast with despair. Nihilism in this sense is not an emotional state.

quite different rates in Western countries where acquaintance with the scientific culture was roughly the same.

What, in any case, are we meant to have learned from science that was so shocking to the religious mind? Is science meant to have shown that there is a totalizing and atheistic explanation of the universe? No scientific explanation has achieved as much.[2] Are Christians meant to be shocked by the revelation that the Bible is not useful when read as a book of astrophysics? Are they meant to be shocked by the possibility that the universe was not really made in six days? Sometimes we are given the impression that all Christians were biblical literalists until Darwin.

We do a disservice to our great-grandparents to imagine their faith uniformly so simple that the trauma of the nineteenth century in matters of science and re-ligion was simply one of fundamentalists encountering Darwinists. Paradoxically, it is not because a great gulf had emerged during the Enlightenment between sci-ence and religion that the nineteenth century saw a crisis. In Britain we might say that the reverse was true — *because* the theological apologetics of the eighteenth century had been so closely wedded to the science of their time, with its support for the arguments from design, the controversies over evolutionary theory came in the nineteenth century as a powerful blow. Religion's dearest ally had turned on it. Science, which had been proving the truths of religion only a hundred years before, now proposed naturalistic explanations for the perfections and order of the natural world. The divine clockmaker was redundant.

But what is the nature of this fall? What was destroyed? What was it about scientific advance that so devastated the Victorians? I have already indicated that we do them a disservice to imagine that they all were biblical literalists, stunned into sudden atheism by the suggestion that the world was not made in six days.

Consider the case of two of the most distinguished minds of Victorian England, the art critic John Ruskin and the poet Alfred, Lord Tennyson.

Ruskin's aesthetic theory in the early parts of *Modern Painters* brimmed with praise for the ingenuity of creation. The fluting and veining of a leaf, the way in which the clouds were formed, the way in which water divides over a cascade all received his devout attentions. And all of this was connected with his belief in a divine providence ordering all that is and all that we see. When scientists produced explanations to rival — indeed, to better — that of the grand designer, it was not simply that Ruskin feared he would lose his faith in God. He feared to lose his *faith in beauty*. How can we say the leaf is really beautiful if it just happens to be that way for adaptive reasons — for reasons that can be determined completely scientifically? A gap seems to yawn between the world as described by science (the "real world" of quantification and measurement) and the world as seen by "merely" human beings. If the leaf and the clouds are not designed, why do we call them beautiful? Are they not just there? Are they not just themselves biological or physical phenomena that we happen to call beautiful? Does our judgment of

---

2. And were someone to produce so totalizing an account it is interesting to ask whether we would call it science rather than ideology.

beauty, then, have nothing to do with the world as it really is in itself, the world as described by science, but is merely subjective? Even more worrying than this loss of foundation for aesthetics, must we not say that all human values, whether aesthetic or moral, are merely subjective?

The same fears haunt one of the finest nineteenth-century works on the tensions of science and religion — or at least one of the most anguished, Tennyson's "In Memoriam." Ostensibly, this poem mourns the loss of Arthur Hallam, a young college friend, but at another level what is lost and mourned in the poem is a world where God's providence and man's pre-eminence are unquestioned assumptions. Tennyson was a keen reader of scientific writings and his poem is punctuated throughout with references to then-contemporary scientific ideas. Particularly influential, in these pre-Darwinian days, were the finds of the geologists. Tennyson was deeply affected by the demonstration, from fossil records, that whole species such as the "giant reptiles" (dinosaurs) should have flourished and now are no more. On such a cosmic scale, where whole species have gone into extinction, what matters the life and work of a single man like Hallam or, for that matter, Tennyson?

> Are God and Nature then at strife,
> That Nature lends such evil dreams?
> So careful of the type she seems,
> So careless of the single life;
>
> (LV)

> "So careful of the type?" but no.
> From scarpèd cliffs and quarried stone
> She cries, "A thousand types are gone:
> I care for nothing, all shall go."
>
> (LVI)

All forms of life, man amongst them, are destined for extinction.

In another place Tennyson describes a visit to the street where Hallam had lived.

> Dark house, by which once more I stand
> Here in this long unlovely street.

The word "unlovely" is carefully chosen. The street, once lovely, is now unlovely. It is not a merely neutral street, it is positively ugly. His friend has gone; it is empty. The natural world, too, once lovely because suffused by God's purpose and providence, is now empty. Tennyson, writing again of Hallam, but also of God, says

> He is not here; but far away
> The noise of life begins again,
> And ghastly through the drizzling rain
> On the bald street breaks the blank day.
>
> (VII)

Tennyson's choice of phrase suggests a parody of the angel's words to the women disciples at the empty tomb: "He is not here, but is risen" (Luke 24:6). But in Tennyson's vision there is no resurrection and no life. What we have is bald streets and a blank day. A clearer statement of the anxiety of modernity you will find nowhere. It is a world empty of God and empty of hope — a vision of cosmic futility.

If I may draw together the themes that I have been tracing under three points, they are these: (1) In the modern period "man"[3] seems to have been swiftly demoted from being the crown of God's good creation to being just one more creature in a line of creatures destined for extinction, just another episode in the history of nature. (2) A gap seems to have emerged between the world as it is in itself and the world as we just happen to see it. (Sometimes this is described as the world of facts and the world of values.) (3) The single individual — the individual man or woman, or the individual ivy leaf or drop of water — seems of no importance compared to the law-like generalizations that govern the whole.

These philosophical anxieties, or ones close to them, predate the nineteenth century. Already in the eighteenth century some feared the hegemony of science. Yet Romantic soul-searching was not simply nostalgia, or hostility to progress, but was motivated by fear that, despite the benefits that science brought, science was suggesting that its description of the world was the only one and that the real world was a world of brute facts to which values, whether aesthetic or ethical or religious, were merely inessential decoration. It was, they feared, being suggested by the ideology of science, if not by science itself, that the real accounts of the world were those subsumable under laws and generalities and the real truths about the world were quantifiable and susceptible to formal analysis. In this the particular, the singular, and the individual were lost. As I have said, not just religion but ethics and aesthetics — all merely human values — on this account look fake.

The Nobel prize–winning scientist Ilya Prigogine and his coauthor, Isabelle Stengers, make a related observation, saying that it appeared, during this period, that classical science "revealed to men a dead, passive nature, a nature that behaves as an automaton which, once programmed, continues to follow the rules inscribed in the program."[4] We might say that the real fear of Tennyson when faced with the demotion of man to just one more episode, and the fear of many now when faced with more extreme kinds of scientific reductionism, is not that science has proved that God is dead, but rather that science has proved that man is dead, that all we really are is a perceptual apparatus of a particular sort, destined for extinction like all other life. As one of my friends put it, "From data you have come and to data you shall return."[5]

Mention of the death of man may recall for us Nietzsche, or perhaps Lyotard or

---

3. The English collective term "Man" is used here deliberately to indicate a particular Enlightenment construction of the human condition.

4. Ilya Prigogine and Isabelle Stengers, *Order Out of Chaos: Man's New Dialogue with Nature* (New York: Bantam Books, 1984), 6.

5. I owe this quip to my colleague, the Reverend Dr. Timothy Jenkins.

Lacan, for we have arrived at an influential thesis of "postmodernism." Nietzsche's version of "the death of man," the ancestor of many postmodernist variants, is not so different from that we have discerned in Tennyson, and it goes something like this: the death of God does not mean merely the end of theism but is, in a sense, the death of any claim to absolute value, the death of any transcendental grounding of values, and the death of man as a privileged knower whose knowledge is underwritten by God. Postmodernist successors suggest that the Enlightenment "project" itself, with its pretensions to objectivity and universal truth, now stands in ruins. "Man," as a privileged knower, is dead.

As mentioned earlier, one of Lyotard's claims in *The Postmodern Condition,* a book tellingly subtitled *A Report on Knowledge,* is that this "condition" is the product of the progress of science. "Science," he states baldly, "has always been in conflict with narratives," but not able to ground itself in them.[6] Nietzsche was, he believes, correct in seeing European nihilism as the result of the truth requirement of science being turned back on itself. Following the failure of positivism adequately to demarcate the bounds of science, we can only, on Lyotard's view, acknowledge that science itself is but one more "little narrative," bounded by its own conventions. "Science," says Lyotard, "plays its own game; it is incapable of legitimating the other language games."[7] Yet a remarkable feature of Lyotard's book is that for all its putative postmodernity it employs very old-fashioned conceptions of science. The natural sciences in particular emerge as rankly positivistic, incapable of bending at all in the direction of the narratives and traditions that characterize the human life-world. On this construal, perhaps, all we can have is what Lyotard proposes — competing language games, rhetorical strategies for success, little and local narratives locked in combat.

This agonistic scenario does not seem particularly new or postmodern. In fact it looks remarkably like an epistemological variant of Hobbes's war of all against all. Is it really so that our crisis is epistemological? The purpose to my excursus from Tennyson on the "death of man" through Lyotard on the "crisis of knowledge" is to raise this question. Many voices suggest that science has been complicit with epistemological crisis. With the collapse of master narratives, the demise of ideological systems (or systems perceived as ideological), and even the implosion of scientific certainty itself, we do not know what to believe anymore. Not just on matters religious but about anything (hence Lyotard's subtitle). I wish to suggest, especially but not only from the point of view of religious faith, that the crisis conflict of our modern period is not over knowledge — that our crisis, if it is such, is not epistemological so much as anthropological and as such a crisis of hope. Our problem is not so much that advance in scientific knowledge leads to loss of religious conviction but that the suggestion (more scientistic than scientific) that the human race is epiphenomenal and human values superfluous leads to anomie and sometimes to despair.

---

6. Jean-François Lyotard, *The Postmodern Condition: A Report on Knowledge* (Minneapolis: University of Minnesota Press, 1984), xxiii.

7. Ibid., 40.

This chapter's title speaks of "the ends of man," a phrase chosen to be neatly ambiguous between two meanings, "the aspirations of humanity" on the one hand, and the "end," that is, the demise of man as conceived by Western modernity on the other. This last is what I am calling the anthropological crisis. Lyotard's "report on human knowledge" stands within the recognizably modern tradition of Western philosophy which, as Charles Taylor has pointed out, takes it as evident that a theory of knowledge will be philosophy's main contribution to scientific culture. Epistemology will make clear which knowledge claims are valid — which scientific claims are valid and, we might well add, which religious claims are valid. To a considerable extent, religious apologetics has bought into this presentation of the case.

But look at what this approach sets up. Look at its implicit anthropology. We, as knowers, address objects of knowledge that are "out there," whether these be objects of science or of theology. We are plunged immediately and almost inevitably into a definition of knowledge as "correct representation of an independent reality."[8] With this is introduced the split between the world "out there" and the knowing self "in here," the world of facts and the world of values.

The "representational epistemology" outlined above implies an anthropology wherein the knowing agent is somehow set apart from, maybe outside of, the world that is known.[9] Essential to this enterprise is the disengagement of the subject.[10] The subject is rational and objective only to the extent that it is disengaged from natural and social worlds and *even* from its own body, which can then be seen as both an object of study and a source of deception.

The disengaged or "punctual self," in Charles Taylor's phrase — rational and free, but languageless, cultureless, history-less — is an anthropological notion apparent in many of the texts of the modern period. In the twentieth century this concept of the self faced sustained attack: Iris Murdoch and Michel Foucault, Alison Jaggar, Luce Irigaray, Ludwig Wittgenstein are just some of its critics. Indeed, there would seem a remarkable consensus across theorists from a variety of philosophical traditions that only an untenable construal of knowledge can be based on this idea of the punctual, disengaged self. Notably, interest in language and in the philosophy of language in our century has convinced many of the inadequacy of any account of human knowing which does not take account of our participation in natural languages.

Now one might at first think, since science is so important a factor in the

---

8. Charles Taylor, "Overcoming Epistemology," in *After Philosophy: End or Transformation?*, ed. Kenneth Baynes, James Bohman, and Thomas McCarthy (Cambridge: MIT Press, 1987), 466.

9. This representational epistemology was, as Charles Taylor has argued, most useful to the new, mechanistic science of the seventeenth century. For Aristotle, knowledge is, in a sense, participational — in knowing the mind becomes one with the object of thought. Descartes is more interested in science as certainty and certainty is achieved procedurally. For Descartes, but not only for Descartes, rationality becomes a property of private thought rather than a vision of reality. It is achieved by a method or procedure, albeit one guaranteed in Descartes' system by a trustworthy God.

10. Charles Taylor argues this in his work on the concepts of "self" and agency in Western philosophy, *Sources of the Self: The Making of Modern Identity* (Cambridge: Cambridge University Press, 1989), and in a series of articles.

modern period, that "science" itself is naturally aligned to this anthropology of a disengaged or "punctual" self. Some early modern thinkers would have thought so. But over and against this we should note that the challenge to this anthropology has come, in recent years, as much from science as from anywhere else. In science and philosophy of science there is increasingly the conviction that the ideal agent of knowledge is not a disembodied mind, but one located in culture and history, not detached from the world but deeply attentive to it. Mary Hesse states the obvious but often overlooked when she points out that we must use "some natural language or other when we talk about the real world."[11]

This point, that science is bound up with and can only be understood in terms of human culture in general, is made with insistence by Prigogine and Stengers in *Order Out of Chaos*. It is an adjunct to their thesis that classical science (from the sixteenth century to fairly recently) — a science in which disengaged observers studied a world that was seen as essentially simple, static, and law — is a thing of the past. This conception of the scientific task was killed not by philosophers but by the progress of science itself. Nor was it only the scientists who, in previous centuries, were charmed by the notion of the model of the "punctual self" in the mechanical universe. Prigogine and Stengers suggest, with some fairness, that theologians as much as scientists favored the mechanical model of the universe in the seventeenth century. Man was, for many of them, "emphatically not part of the nature he objectively described" but rather dominated from the outside.[12] With God as guarantor of his interrogations of a mute and passive nature (notoriously rendered by Baconian science in female imagery), man could, as it were, see things from "a God's-eye view." By means of His "objectivity" he could separate fact from value, control the products of nature and also of less fully rational people as well — notably women, slaves, or "primitives," peoples of "lesser" cultures.[13] It was a most useful anthropology for the early modern West. As Prigogine and Stengers remark, "The debasement of nature is parallel to the glorification of all that eludes it, God and man."[14] (And here I would gloss "man" very narrowly.)

The interest of these remarks by scientists to me lies in the suggestion, first, that what is defective here is the anthropology (although a defective epistemology flows from it) and, second, that the defect is *au fond* theological — "man" lays claim to a "God's-eye view." If we know anything of the God's-eye view it must be that any God can have it.

Like most heresies, this one is a good theological tenet gone out of control — in this case the idea that to be in *imago dei* (construed as participating in divine rationality) means in some sense (epistemologically) to be God. It is curious that Christianity, whose central doctrine is the Incarnation, could be used to

---

11. Mary Hesse, "Science beyond Realism and Relativism," in *Cognitive Relativism and Social Science*, ed. D. Raven, L. van Vucht, et al. (New Brunswick, N.J.: Transaction Publishers, 1992).

12. Prigogine and Stengers, *Order Out of Chaos*, 50.

13. For an interesting account of the extent to which the deists' *imago dei* influenced seventeenth- and eighteenth-century philosophy see Edward Craig's *The Mind of God and the Works of Man* (Oxford: Clarendon Press, 1987).

14. Ibid., 51.

underwrite an epistemological program in which man attempts to distance himself from the human condition. In aspiring be totally "in control" while fearing we are "out of control" (to take only two examples, reproductive technology and genetic engineering) we stand at what is arguably a hope-less period of Western intellectual history — one in which we recognize that confidence in progress and control has sometimes masked arrogance and mismanagement, yet see no clear way forward.

Man is, in a certain sense, dead. The conception of man as disengaged and fully autonomous, the purely rational agent of classical science, the knower who knows from a God's-eye view — that man is dead and we are well rid of him. Yet to say that man cannot see things from a God's-eye view is not to say that we cannot see truly at all. Rather it is to admit to the human condition, as good theologians and scientists always have done. We know, as men and women, not as angels. Lyotard's mistake seems to be in saying, "If we can't say we know with absolute certainly, we can't claim to know at all" — or otherwise put, "If I can't be God, then I don't want to play." Nihilism is the reverse negative of presumption.

Hope, says Karl Rahner, is a matter of "letting one's self go." It is death to presumption. "Hope alone is the *locus* of God as he who cannot be controlled or manipulated, and so of God as such. . . . Presumption *and* despair both entail the same basic refusal to commit oneself and so to abandon oneself to the incalculable and uncontrol[l]able."[15] If you prefer your sources to be French and philosophical, rather than German and theological, Paul Ricoeur in his recent writings makes similar points about the deep religious and human value of being able to "let go."

In its openness to the future of God, hope is far from being a deadening opiate, rendering us passive and immobile in the face of our present challenges. On the contrary, hope is angry for a better world, and it is that which both commands and empowers us to trust enough "to undertake anew an exodus out of the present into the future."[16] Only with such hope are we able to surrender what is provisional in the hope of the kingdom.

Hope, in this life, has a temporal quality, and not merely in its sense of the future and its sorrow for the past. Hope, like faith and love, is a state of readiness, and hope, like faith and love, is only displayed in action. A mother or father, out of love for his or her children, washes their clothes or stops to buy the marbles that are a sudden playground necessity. While the father is doing this, he may be thinking of what to get for dinner, or something that needs to be finished at work. The mother does not always think of the children as she washes their clothes and plans their meal, and yet the love for the children flows into these actions, for she would not be doing them at all without it.

Hope in God is a little like this. It is not a transient and optimistic *emotion*. It is a readiness to act, a directedness, a commitment, a passionate practicality.

---

15. From Rahner, "On the Theology of Hope," in *A Rahner Reader,* ed. Gerald McCool (London: Darton, Longman and Todd, 1975), 235.

16. Ibid., 237.

If you hope in God's future, you do not just feel rosier about a few things, your life is changed by it.

It is perhaps fitting to end with the reflections of a scientist — another Nobel Laureate — and with a return to what might unite the poet and the scientist and point to a way forward for the rest of us. "Good research," Barbara McClintock has said, "requires a disposition to hear what the material has to say to you." This is not simply a device to fathom the reasons governing the world. "It is," as her biographer notes, "a longing to embrace the world in its very being, through reason and beyond, a capacity for union with that which is known."[17] It is not too much to describe this, in the life of a research scientist, as a religious longing. It is a desire to move beyond "mere certainty" to a reverence for the given, "a disposition to hear what the material has to say to you."

Samuel Taylor Coleridge's great poem, *The Rhyme of the Ancient Mariner,* tells a story of a sailor cursed for his gratuitous slaughter of an albatross. He is condemned to wear this dead bird around his neck as, one by one, his crewmates die around him and his ghostly ship is trapped on windless seas. The spell is broken when he sees some sea snakes and, taken out of himself for a moment by their beauty, blesses them unawares. The grace has already come, for only God can bless. The albatross falls from his neck, the fresh water falls from the sky, the winds pick up, and he is saved. He has glimpsed the glory. The poem does not lead us to believe that the sighting of sea snakes was a rare thing and the mariner fortunate to note them at a rare moment of appearance. The sea about the stricken boat may, for all we know, have been full of these creatures throughout the time of deathly still, but the Mariner, turned in on himself, could not see them, still less see that they were beautiful. The scientist, like the artist or the person of faith, believes we may on occasion glimpse a greater glory — a beauty that surrounds us but which we are too blind to see. To move toward this "given" in hope, in reverence, and with awe is a shared project of science and of faith, and the basis of an anthropology based in eschatology. In this we would seek not our own ends but the future of God, and in doing so perhaps discover what it is to be truly, fully human beings.

Note: This essay is a development of themes from my London Templeton Lecture of 1993 and my essay "The God of Hope," *Doctrine and Life* 44 (April 1994).

---

17. Evelyn Fox Keller, *A Feeling for the Organism: The Life and Work of Barbara McClintock* (San Francisco: W. H. Freeman, 1983), 199.

Chapter 7

CONTINGENT FUTURES
Imagining the Ethics of Cosmology

LARRY D. BOUCHARD

Two things fill the mind with ever increasing admiration and awe, the oftener and more steadily we reflect on them: the starry heavens above me and the moral law within me.... The former view of a countless multitude of worlds annihilates, as it were, my importance as an animal creature, which must give back to the planet (a mere speck in the universe) the matter from which it came, the matter which is for a little time provided with vital force, we know not how. The latter, on the contrary, infinitely raises my worth as that of an intelligence by personality, in which the moral law reveals a life independent of all animality and even of the whole world of sense....
                                                          — IMMANUEL KANT[1]

The problem is that the universe is expanding, and there's not enough matter to stop the expansion. After a while, no new galaxies, no new stars, no new planets, no newly arisen life-forms — just the same old crowd. Everything's getting run-down. It'll be boring. So in Cygnus A we're testing out the technology to make something new.... Sometime later we might want to close off a piece of the universe and prevent space from getting more and more empty as the aeons pass. Increasing the local matter density's the way to do it, of course. It's good honest work.
                                     —Ellie's "Father" in Carl Sagan's *Contact*[2]

Then I saw a new heaven and a new earth....
                                                          —Revelation 21:1

It may be that fruitful encounters between theology and science are historically contingent. At certain times, relations between God and nature are more easily explored than at other times. After Darwin, the view that nature displayed the orderly design of God foundered with the realization that random selection could account for the development of life. Today, however, may again be a time of convergence. Perspectives on the "close fit" between cosmic properties and physical conditions necessary for life, and on the "openness" of nature to nondeterministic modes of explanation, allow some again to recognize signs of divine creativity and

---

1. Immanuel Kant, *Critique of Practical Reason*, trans. Lewis White Beck (New York: Macmillan, 1985), 162.
2. Carl Sagan, *Contact* (New York: Simon and Schuster, 1985), 363–64; later references to this Sagan title will be parenthetical.

providence. Such discernment is not a "God of the gaps" but a matter of recognizing order and elegance, a beauty in which to see the beauty of God. Scientific discoveries yet to come will not necessarily diminish such discernment — though they may. What had looked so fine-tuned may one day appear less amazing. But if ours *is* a fruitful time for correlating science and theology, we would be wise to harvest what insights we can while the historical convergence lasts. Can there, however, be any lasting significance to such temporary convergences?

If we affirm the transcendence of our destiny with God, we will be cautious about this question. If God's hope surpasses or contradicts the ways in which we imagine the future and hope, then the physical cosmos is relevant mainly as the contingent arena for our pilgrimage with God.[3] That it will end comes as no theological surprise. But the future is always of theological concern insofar as it will be an arena of suffering and discernment. With whatever future we are given, we are also given moral responsibility and occasions of insight. Cosmology, then, bears on how theology views life and death and imagines future communities meeting suffering with works of love and discerning inquiry.

It is in the cultural sphere (where insights are contextualized by social practices and traditional categories of interpretation) that convergences between cosmology and theology may be understood and assessed.[4] We will explore three perspectives on the cosmos: that it is *pointless*, that it is intrinsically *designed for human intelligence*, and that it may *sustain other forms of life* far — but not infinitely far — into the future. The latter two are apparently "hopeful" cosmologies. But to interpret them requires placing them in the historical, cultural, and religious horizons in which we receive them. Some of these horizons correlate with the futility many feel when contemplating the futures of the earth, the sun, and the universe — as reflected in the memorable judgment of Steven Weinberg: The more we comprehend the universe, the more it "seems pointless."[5]

Our attitudes toward the far-distant future reflect, to different extents, our experiences of the past and present. Among the horizons of our times are (1) the historical catastrophes of the twentieth century, (2) the fragmentary and pluralistic character of what Langdon Gilkey calls the "late stages" of an "advanced

3. See Jürgen Moltmann, *The Theology of Hope*, trans. James W. Leitch (1965; New York: Harper and Row, 1967), 15–22; John Polkinghorne, *The Faith of a Physicist*, Gifford Lectures, 1993–94 (Princeton, N.J.: Princeton University Press, 1994), 163, 166–75; and essays by Gerhard Sauter, Janet Martin Soskice, Kathryn Tanner, Miroslav Volf, and Michael Welker in this volume. To say that the imagination is finite and fallible is not to dismiss its importance. It entails not only the projection of images in the mind, but also heightened receptivity to phenomena, expressions, and ideas and to our making novel forms out of various media. Scientific practice and theology both have their imaginative dimensions. Nothing can be believed, investigated, or made if unimagined. On relations between imagining, making, and culture, see Elaine Scarry, *The Body in Pain: The Making and Unmaking of the World* (New York: Oxford University Press, 1985).

4. "Culture" involves shareable systems of meaning, valuing, and interpreting as well as imaginative activity that can reflect upon, criticize, and transform such systems. The reflective and critical functions of culture are evident in art and literature and often in the speculative aspects of science, or what John Polkinghorne calls "metascience." See his "Natural Science, Temporality, and Divine Action," in *TToday* 55 (October 1998): 329–43, and his "Eschatology: Some Questions and Some Insights from Science," chap. 2 in this volume.

5. Steven Weinberg, *The First Three Minutes* (New York: Basic Books, 1977), 144.

scientific culture,"[6] and (3) the ethical attention now given to "otherness," "encounter," "responsibility," and "discernment." But insofar as the horizons in which we view cosmology are plural and fragmentary, we cannot describe them *in toto*. And other perspectives in culture, science, and theology invite us to reconsider one's moodiness about cosmology. What we can do is juxtapose certain fragments of literature, science, and theological reflection and then explore the spaces these juxtapositions offer us. We may hope that our juxtapositions will provide room for others to explore as well.

To these ends, Walter Miller's 1959 novel, *A Canticle for Leibowitz*, looks "back" to a nuclear war in our time and forward to centuries when science is impelled by some inevitable convergence of knowledge and sin to repeat the past. It also comments, implicitly, on the moral limits of one of our hopeful cosmologies, John Barrow and Frank Tipler's *The Anthropic Cosmological Principle* (1986). Moments from plays by Robert Lepage, Caryl Churchill, and Tony Kushner inquire into the protean nature of selves, communities, and hope after catastrophe. Finally, Carl Sagan's 1985 novel and 1997 film, *Contact*, affords a narrative that returns us to the questions of cosmology and theology with which we begin.

These works are juxtaposed for another reason, besides their millennial commentary. They help us imagine community today and the cosmic future as being enfolded in relations of appreciation and transformation, that is, in aesthetic and ethical relations. Insofar as discoveries of the cosmos can occasion experiences of awe and realizations of responsibility, and as they identify fragile resources of life and intelligence (even in different forms and under austere future conditions), then our imagining very distant futures may invite us to revise our views of nearer times. These fragments provide, then, spaces for considering how God's future, the natural future, and "the work of our hands" are disclosed in practical analogies — that is, in analogies that inherently elicit wonder and require responsibility.

I

The twentieth century was revolutionary for cosmology. Yet as astronomers verified the expansion of the universe, its ultimate fate remained in doubt. Would it expand and cool forever or would gravity eventually reverse the expansion? The answer depended on the amount and density of matter and energy in the universe, and would require new observations. By 1998 evidence favored perpetual expansion; moreover, the expansion appeared actually to be accelerating.[7] Conceivably, conclusions could shift again, but this essay recalls decades when the issue could have fallen either way. Just as modern cosmology exemplifies the reach of scientific discovery, it also illustrates its historical contingency. But the contingency of discovery is least among the reasons why cosmology may occasion

---

6. Gilkey, *Creationism on Trial* (Minneapolis: Winston Press, 1985), 165–71.

7. See Tom Siegfried's review of the issues in the *Dallas Morning News*, June 22, 1998; and James Glanz, "Cosmic Motion Revealed," *Science* 282 (Dec. 18, 1998): 2156–57.

hope or despair. More important are the historical contexts in which science is practiced and received.

One cannot imagine the fate of the cosmos — unfolding over hundreds of billions of years — apart from the fate of local worlds: of our lives, communities, nations, and planet. Our memories and continued awareness of historical catastrophes, which may themselves thwart the imagination, bear upon how we assess modern cosmology, where if incoming comets or asteroids don't doom our adventures in the cosmos, entropy surely will. Are there other images to bring to the cosmic future besides catastrophic ones? It was Carl Sagan who wrote that the big bang is our "creation myth."[8] Though Sagan was not usually warm toward religion, his use of the term "myth" here is significant. To scholars of religion and culture, myth can connote a narrative that frames, shapes, and may also transform cultural meaning, value, and expectation. Sagan was acknowledging that science does and should play such a role in shaping and transforming meaning and value in culture. All the ways in which science transforms life are part of its cultural, even religious, significance.[9]

The "hopeful cosmologies" considered here speculate on alternative futures and project visions of human transformation. Set beside the view that the universe is pointless is, first, the anthropic principle, in which the universe seems fortuitously designed for human intelligence. Later, we will contrast this vision with that of Sagan. Now, however, I wish to indicate how different versions of the anthropic principle may be seen as hopeful and also indicate how they reflect their historical horizons. The principle has not become an icon of popular culture and established science (like big bang or double helix), but there are senses in which it is a symbol that would synthesize a view of nature with a vision of human meaning.[10]

Barrow and Tipler's treatise is a multidisciplinary tome that can be read as a prose epic. Its hero is the principle itself, escaping from ancient thought and classical design arguments to lay claim to several areas of modern science. The authors portray it in three increasingly speculative forms. The weak anthropic principle (WAP) uses our own existence to explain a seemingly narrow range of conditions that emerged from the big bang. Were the universe (or at least our part of it) not so "fine-tuned" — significantly younger or older, hotter or colder, more or less dense than it is — no carbon-based life could have evolved. WAP reasonably allows us to rule out any physical hypothesis that would rule out us. The more speculative "strong" versions of the principle (SAP) are teleological;

8. Carl Sagan, *Billions and Billions: Thoughts on Life and Death at the End of the Millennium* (New York: Random House, 1997), 45–46.

9. On the cultural and symbolic functions of science, see William Stoeger, "Scientific Accounts of Ultimate Catastrophes in Our Life-Bearing Universe," and "Cultural Cosmology and the Impact of the Natural Sciences on Philosophy and Culture," chaps. 1 and 5 in this volume. See also Gilkey, *Creationism on Trial*, chap. 7, and *Nature, Reality, and the Sacred* (Minneapolis: Fortress Press, 1993). On science and technology and their interactions with ethics and aesthetics, see Jean Ladrière, *The Challenge Presented to Cultures by Science and Technology* (Paris: UNESCO, 1977).

10. See Clifford Geertz, "Religion as a Cultural System," in *The Interpretation of Cultures* (New York: Basic Books, 1973), 89–90.

they imagine how the universe might be so structured as to *require* life and intelligence to evolve. Barrow and Tipler then project an even more speculative "final" anthropic principle (FAP): once intelligence is established, "it will never die out." In the far-distant future, intelligence will fill every niche in the cosmos and will process worlds of information gathered from the distant past.[11]

By itself, the WAP alone implies a deep equivalence and openness between mind, matter, and space-time. What is amazing about nature is how far it allows *us* to understand it. The universe is an arena of suffering, surely; but it is also "home" to the species that practices the sciences, arts, and ethics that enable it to resist suffering and discover *home*.[12] Especially in its speculative versions, the anthropic future provides resources for cultivating (even on a cosmic scale) relations between energy, intelligence, and value. The future is a future of *community*: life is meaningful now, because we belong to a social cosmos yet to come. In Tipler's FAP — as a closed universe collapses toward singularity, and as information processing becomes virtually infinite — this ultimate community is said to be redemptive.[13] There is also a more subtle sense in which this proposal is quasi-religious. Barrow and Tipler frequently tell us that while their hypotheses may turn out to be false, such falsifiability only demonstrates that the stronger versions are, at least, "scientific." Thus, the reader is led to believe that a redemptive future is *scientifically* imaginable; the practice of cosmology, not just its results, becomes a reason for hope.

This hope, however, has many paradoxes. "Though our species is doomed, our civilization and indeed the values we care about may not be."[14] Everything depends on just how *soon* we are "doomed," because everything depends on seeding *homo sapiens* around enough stars to insure growth into the galaxy. The authors envisage a laissez-faire information market, which will eventually create a classless society of artificial information processors, who can survive the extremes of a colder or hotter cosmos — provided we do not annihilate ourselves in the meantime. The authors hope that our drive to explore and propagate overrides our propensities to self-destruct. They acknowledge their theory recalls discredited teleologies of progress, but also know their imagined futures could be annulled by global catastrophes. Thus, they wager on our developing technologies being cheap enough to aid in escape from the confines of this planet before the depletion of our moral as well as physical resources. They wager that human beings can outrun their limits all the way to the cosmic frontier; and before fate catches us, we will have bequeathed the future means to rescue memory and meaning.

---

11. See John D. Barrow and Frank J. Tipler, *The Anthropic Cosmological Principle* (New York: Oxford University Press, 1986), 23, 658–77. John Polkinghorne offers critiques of such "physical eschatologies" in *Faith of a Physicist*, 165–66, and in this volume (chap. 2).

12. John Archibald Wheeler, "The Universe as a Home to Man," *American Scientist* 62 (1974): 683–91.

13. Frank Tipler, *The Physics of Immortality: Modern Cosmology, God, and the Resurrection of the Dead* (New York: Doubleday, 1994), 137. The title is indicative of how the cultural authority of highly speculative science can rival that of philosophy, when the public wants its religious hopes made reasonable.

14. Barrow and Tipler, *Anthropic Cosmological Principle*, 615.

II

To envision the cosmic future as a time of creaturely transformation, with Barrow and Tipler and other visionaries, requires attending to moral as well as physical contingencies. We are hedged by sin as well as finitude; will sin prove to be our fate? Alasdair MacIntyre began *After Virtue* (1980) with a science-fiction scenario: Imagine a cultural catastrophe so great that the institutions supporting science are destroyed, and scientific knowledge is not passed on to subsequent generations except in piecemeal ways. Eventually, even the catastrophe itself is forgotten. No one understands that what bits of science they yet possess lack integrity and depth. They deludedly fit their fractured notions together and assume they have coherent knowledge. MacIntyre offered this "disquieting suggestion" as an allegory of the fragmentation of modern moral understanding, and of the autonomous individual whose normative notions are severed from the traditional practices and narratives that once contextualized them. Our only hope, he gloomily concluded, is for the wise to retreat into monastic-like enclaves and wait for a new St. Benedict to guide us through a long, dark age.[15]

This scenario recalls the premise of Walter Miller's *Canticle for Leibowitz*,[16] which also projects a future when science is all but forgotten and moral reflection survives in abbeys. Its inspiration reflects not only thermonuclear war but also the memory of World War II, for Miller participated in the bombing of a Benedictine monastery on Monte Cassino, southeast of Rome. Thus, he wrote between two catastrophes, one in the actual past and another in an anticipated future, connected by technologies of annihilation. The story takes up long after scientific knowledge was destroyed in the "Flame Deluge" and "The Simplification" — a violent reaction of many survivors against science, history, and literacy. In this era, Catholic religious orders offered sanctuary to persecuted scientists. A certain weapons technician, Isaac Leibowitz, became a priest and founded, in the western desert of North America, a religious order dedicated to preserving documents. Leibowitz himself was murdered by the Simpletons — as they called themselves — and passed into hagiographic memory. Miller's story can serve as another account of fragmentation both similar to and different from MacIntyre's.

MacIntyre's parable is part of a larger debate about the contingency of cultural narratives and signs. Do signs secure holds on the realities they signify, or do they defer to other signs, never transcending their unstable semiotic structures? For MacIntyre, the moral life depends on communities of discourse and practice, whose narratives underwrite their lives and identities. The dissolution of those narratives is to be resisted. For others, however, it can be celebrated. For what may be fragmenting are structures of injustice or dominance, and what may be discovered are a multitude of voices hitherto unheard. The metaphor of cultural

---

15. Alasdair MacIntyre, *After Virtue*, 2d ed. (Notre Dame, Ind.: University of Notre Dame Press, 1984), 1–5.

16. Walter M. Miller Jr., *A Canticle for Leibowitz* (Boston: Gregg Press, 1959); further references will be parenthetical.

fragmentation, then, works in several directions, ranging from (1) systems of signs being inherently fragmentary, to (2) cultural systems changing due to historical contingencies, to (3) framing narratives being ruptured by oppression and suffering — as in Holocaust testimony, which presses upon the limits of language to comprehend suffering.

The second vector of fragmentation is pertinent to the sciences. For Gilkey, there are paradoxes to our "advanced scientific culture." Science penetrates so many areas that few can integrate its knowledge. Having become so pervasive in society, science ceases to be a discrete culture of its own. Hybrids like "creation science" or "new age" sciences coexist with "normal science." Further, science's deepest insights into the very large, very small, and very fast are often counterintuitive, resisting integration with general knowledge, making the task of translating science daunting. The audiences for boundary-crossing books like Barrow and Tipler's will find it hard to distinguish established from speculative science.

But it is especially the third vector that is traced in *Canticle*. Miller's novel bears witness to a catastrophe that did not (has not) occurred but which ruptures present understanding from the standpoint of a realized past (World War II) and anticipated future (World War III and beyond). And it asks whether scientific knowing can but help broach into the forbidden, with moral catastrophe the inevitable outcome.

The Leibowitzian brothers have no understanding of the Memorabilia they copy, generation after generation. Brother Francis inks in the blue background of "blueprints," until he ruefully gathers that the blue conveys no information. He then spends years illuminating a manuscript from the blessed Leibowitz himself, a circuit diagram none can now comprehend. And yet, while having only allegorical legends of history before the Flame Deluge and technology comparable to Augustine's, the brothers can discern in their charred texts a beauty they hope will one day be for the good. They trust in a science they can glimpse through its aesthetic structures, an "ornamental beauty or an orderliness that hinted of meaning, as a rosary might suggest a necklace to a nomad" (146). It did not matter that the knowledge they saved

> was empty of content, its subject matter long since gone. Still, such knowledge had a symbolic structure that was peculiar to itself, and at least the symbolic interplay could be observed. To observe the way a knowledge system is knit together is to learn at least a minimum knowledge-of-knowledge, until someday — someday or some century — an Integrator would come, and things would be fitted together again. (66)

The integrator arrives six centuries later (3174 C.E.), when a renaissance is dawning and the city-state of Texarkana is enforcing its hegemony over the continent's warring clans. A brilliant scholar, or "thon," arrives to consult the Memorabilia. Thon Taddeo would like to believe his theories are original. But as he finds texts referring to Maxwell and Einstein and witnesses the light from young Brother Kornhoer's dynamo, he realizes his discoveries can be but reconstructions. Kornhoer explains that there is "no direct information about the construction of a dynamo. Rather, . . . the information is partially implicit in a whole collection of fragmentary writings. *Partially* implicit" (148). "From a few broken bits of general principles," Taddeo concludes, "we must attempt to grasp particulars. In some cases, it may prove impossible" (209). However, with the patronage of the Texarkanan military, the thon and his like do succeed. And as the abbot Dom Paulo watches the political intrigues of Taddeo, he fears that the abbey's vocation of conserving scientific knowledge only adds momentum to a perpetual cycle of violence and self-destruction.

Six more centuries pass and another abbot, Dom Zerchi, sees the fulfillment of Dom Paulo's fear. The "race of divinely inspired tool makers" has swung on its pendulum of achievement and destruction. The abbey runs on computers, the Memorabilia is on microfilm, there are colonies near Alpha Centauri, and politicians have again brought the earth to within days of annihilation. There is beauty in the way Zerchi's Gethsemane unfolds: the divine presence is encountered in the midst of destruction, while the brothers embark on a long-prepared exodus to preserve the Memorabilia. However, Miller's tale of Catholic heroism does little to dispel the cyclical doom that qualifies this view of the future. If it is humanity's "manifest destiny" to migrate to the stars, he tells us, there we shall "succumb again to the old maladies" (245). *A Canticle for Leibowitz* leaves us with a choice of hope and abandonment, which resists simple resolution.

First the hope. It is affirmed that all is transpiring in the arena of grace. Leibowitz, Brother Francis, Dom Paulo, and Dom Zerchi are, in the novel's gaze, minor lives whose works of love are part of a providential purpose; they each die aware of the grace that uplifts them. Dom Zerchi has seen his brothers depart for Alpha Centauri. He has tried to stop a mother and child, overexposed to radiation, from soliciting euthanasia. And he is hearing the confession of Mrs. Grales — a bicephalous woman, one of generations of genetic miscreants inherited from the Flame Deluge — when he senses the light of a distant explosion. Before he can rescue the ciborium from the chapel, the shock wave buries him to his chest in rubble. Fragments of the Host spill on the ground before him. And it is Mrs. Grales (not her proper head but the child-like dormant head, Rachel, now become conscious) who interrupts his silent struggle to meet death. She picks up a wafer, touches his forehead, and silently gives him communion. He tries to teach her the Magnificat, and before wandering off in the ruins babbling, "la-la-la," Rachel says one word to him, "Live" (336).

Yet the sacrament is offered as the world ends, again. The human desire to know, imagine, and make is implicated in an ancient swing of sin and destruction. The last lines revert to the opening of Genesis, as God's spirit blows and broods.

> A wind came across the ocean, sweeping with it a pall of fine white ash. The ash fell into the sea and into the breakers. The breakers washed dead shrimp ashore with the driftwood. . . . The shark swam out to his deepest waters and brooded in the cold clean currents. He was very hungry that season. (338)

III

To imagine any future, near or far, as offering time for creaturely transformation also requires imagining contingency as gift as well as danger. However, is this possible when contingency — what might but might not be, what was but might not have been — and moral evil are so entangled in history? The river in Robert Lepage and company's drama *The Seven Streams of the River Ota* (1996) flows through Hiroshima. For over seven hours, we follow story fragments of survivors and their descendants, from 1946 to the late 1990s. Their lives overlap, diverge, and interchange across generations and oceans. From the American occupation of Japan into our near future, they become entangled in chance encounters and subsequent histories. They speak in several languages, translating for us and for each other, and employ a variety of electronic and traditional media, including Japanese Gagaku music, photography, film, a scene from a farce by Feydeau, and video to convey what amount to postmodern morality plays. The focal character is Jana, a Czech Holocaust survivor who as an adult settled in Japan to learn Zen Buddhist compassion and detachment. She tells us,

> To cut the ego with the sword is the ultimate combat. The Seven Streams of the River Ota is about people . . . who came to Hiroshima and found themselves confronted with their own devastation and their own enlightenment. For if Hiroshima is a city of death and destruction, it is also a city of rebirth and survival.[17]

A generation now living anticipated theirs would be the last. But as the Cold War's apocalyptic immediacy recedes, we notice how history has been qualified by "local" rather than total apocalypses, after which — to the survivors' existential shock — life continues. As with Argentina's "Mothers of the Disappeared," memories and testimonies haunt our horizons.[18] And yet the remapping of cultural geography after the Cold War also creates novel resources for ethical awareness of the future, as evidenced in Jana's migration to Hiroshima.

The epic theater of Lepage, Churchill, and Kushner reflects an ethics of encounter and responsibility, wherein we meet other persons and communities, creatures and natural processes in relations of power, discernment, and transformation. Here, "to speak of encounter" highlights how these relations are temporal, contingent, and open to novelty. Our encounters may involve personal dramas of meeting and leave-taking, sweeping historical change, or unfolding relations with nature. "To speak of responsibility with others" highlights how our claims to "have" identities are transformed into tasks of responding to suffering and difference. Others — who suffer or flourish, and who may address me or dwell with me — are, as such, familiar. With them, I may respond to suffering and realize beauty and joy. Yet others "as other" also resist familiarity. Indeed, if familiarity is not resisted, then the very particularity of the other is too easily comprehended.

---

17. Robert Lepage and Ex Machina, *The Seven Streams of the River Ota* (London: Methuen, 1996), 1.

18. Tod Linafelt and S. Brent Plate, "Apocalypse Now and Then: Living beyond the End of the World," paper given at the annual meeting of the American Academy of Religion in New Orleans, November 1996.

To speak of discernment is to highlight how our encounters entail principles and practices rooted in many sources of understanding.[19] Our responsibilities are always interpreted responsibilities. How we interpret is informed by "who we are" and "who we may become," both by learned principles and by novel emergences in nature and history which urge us to interpret our traditions anew.

What is hopeful about the *Seven Streams* is how its images of wounded beauty, without sentimentality, elicit ethical encounter. What is less clear is how its sense of futurity resists futility. Lepage says the work originated in naive surprise upon a visit to Hiroshima. Expecting to find devastation, he saw a vibrant city. If his play follows movements of hope, it is a hope found in the discernment of human coincidence. Jana explains that "Hiroshima chose me." In search of silence, she had visited the Peace Memorial Park, and there to her surprise, "I found Prague!"

> It was the only building at the epicenter of the bomb that remained standing... and the Japanese preserved it as a symbol of the war. It was designed by a Czech architect, Jan Letzl, who lived and worked in Japan during the twenties. So for me, that metallic skeleton was like being in front of a mirror. This empty shell was myself. Me, with my illusions, and all my past on my Jewish shoulders.... So I understood that my place was here, in Hiroshima.[20]

Jana speaks to our present with courage. Within the play's centrifugal dispersion of selves into boundless relations, she urges the mutual accountability *with* and *for* others known, unknown, and yet to be. Yet these lives seem to play out before a future they are powerless to affect, as they flow toward a single, self-emptying moment. An urn of ashes is poured into the Bay of Miyajima, where the river Ota empties. We are uncertain whose ashes these are, for the survivors gathered here have all lost friends to remember. The final tableau, in which persons living and dead pass through the cloth of a single kimono, defines a space for many questions. Are these images of resignation or of resistance? Are the cutting of the ego and the cultivation of compassion ways of practical resistance or acquiescence to the ruptures the play has evoked?

Caryl Churchill's *Light Shining in Buckinghamshire* (1978) documents a time when the left wing of the English Civil War (Levellers, Diggers, and Ranters) dared believe they could, by sowing carrots on common lands, "turn the world upside down" and spur the millennial reign of God. In the penultimate scene, a cast of displaced men and women gather in impromptu critique and confession. They share bits of food and drink, and for as long as their communion transpires, "that which is of God" appears immanent among them: in their bodies, in their deeds and failures, and in the motions of time. Claxton recalls:

> When I was first a Seeker, everything shone. I thought the third age was coming, age of the spirit, age of the lily, everything shining.... Well, we know how parliament betrayed us. Then how the army betrayed us.... And then I saw even the Seekers

---

19. See H. Richard Niebuhr, *The Responsible Self* (New York: Harper and Row, 1963); Paul Ricoeur, *Oneself as Another* (Chicago: University of Chicago Press, 1992); and Adam Zachary Newton, *Narrative Ethics* (Cambridge: Harvard University Press, 1995).

20. Lepage and Ex Machina, *Seven Streams of the River Ota*, 106; ellipses in the original.

were wrong. Because while I was waiting for God, he was here already. So God was first in the king. Then in parliament. Then in the Army. And now he has left all government. And he shows himself naked. In us.

BRIGGS: We were the army of saints.

CLAXTON: Let it go. Move on. God moves so fast now.

HOSKINS:...And that's why you see men and women shining now, everything sparkles because God's not far above us like he used to be when preachers stood in the way, he's started some great happening and we're in it now.[21]

At the end, each person tells how each was forgotten and dispersed into oblivion. But they may yet impress us that their lives were strangely effective, and that as we speak of the ethics of encounter we are accountable to the hope they cultivated on a hillside in Surrey.

The horizons of resistance in Tony Kushner's *Angels in America* (1992–96) are wider than its concerns with HIV and the machinations of Roy Cohn. This diptych of plays, *Millennium Approaches* and *Perestroika*, retells the dream of America from a perspective defined by unusual juxtapositions: stories of gays, Jews, socialists, and Mormons. Among these is the infected Prior Walter, who reluctantly believes an angel has called him to be the prophetic herald of a dubious future. But other characters help to transform his vocation — including the Mormon valium addict Harper. In her delirious imagination, she wants to vacation in Antarctica, to see the hole in the ozone layer — her sign for total catastrophe.

Transformation is realized in the ways their lives cross and overlap, as in scenes where Prior and Harper inhabit each other's dreams. That we each become parts of one another in the interplay of contingency is a trope of solidarity. And this solidarity includes the dead. Kushner imagines the living and the dead joined with the future in spiritual and practical resistance. At the end of *Perestroika*, Harper's and Prior's lives are again juxtaposed. She has a dreaming epiphany while jetting across America under moonlight. At 35,000 feet, she is near the "ragged and torn" rim of ozone; it frightens her. But then, she sees,

Souls were rising, from the earth far below, souls of the dead, of people who had perished, from famine, from war, from the plague, and they floated up, like skydivers in reverse, limbs all akimbo, wheeling and spinning. And the souls of these departed joined hands, clasped ankles, and formed a web, a great net of souls, and the souls were three atom oxygen molecules, of the stuff of ozone, and the outer rim absorbed them, and was repaired.[22]

Prior survives into the 1990s. He and others enjoy debating politics in Central Park. They have seen the rise of Gorbachev and fall of the Berlin Wall and

---

21. Caryl Churchill, *Light Shining in Buckinghamshire*, in *Plays: One* (New York: Routledge, 1985), 232–33.

22. Tony Kushner, *Perestroika*, 141–42, from *Angels in America: A Gay Fantasia on National Themes*, 2 vols.; pt. 1, *Millennial Approaches* (New York: Theatre Communications Group, 1992, 1993); pt. 2, *Perestroika* (New York: Theatre Communications Group, 1992, 1994, 1996).

worry about the future of Yugoslavia. They embody the migratory spirit of Jewish immigrants and Mormon settlers. And, given the likely demographics of the Broadway cast and audience — tourists from Texas, gays from Queens, infected and healthy — they invite us into this migration toward the future. It is wintertime. The actor who plays Prior speaks beside a fountain depicting Bethesda, an angel of healing. He hopes to see it flowing in the spring, and he speaks for us who inhabit his future: "This disease will be the end of many of us, but not nearly all, and the dead will be commemorated and will struggle on with the living, and we are not going away." He bids us goodbye with Harold Bloom's translation of the Hebrew word for blessing: "More Life."[23]

IV

Can science imagine the future in terms of an ethic of encounter and dispossession, where one finds oneself so as to give and lose oneself to myriad relations and responsibilities, past and future? Carl Sagan was a veritable evangelist for science: were it as widely understood as it is used, science would become a source of critical, transforming hope.[24] His perspective on cosmology was nearly the opposite of Barrow and Tipler's. In *Contact*, he imagined the cosmos expanding forever, its island galaxies receding ever farther apart. Nonetheless, his cosmos can be construed as *with us*, though not *for us*; in nature we glimpse our own origins and, as our comprehension deepens, nature may teach us to survive and enjoy the cosmos far into the future. Sagan had little use for the anthropic principle for the same reason he eschewed religion.[25] Both contradict the Copernican principle, that there is nothing special about our place. The cosmos is special on its own terms, with "billions" of wonders, inspiring awe; we are special because we can experience awe. His take on the cosmos was materialist, his take on us a little romantic. But not being in the center also implied, for Sagan, not being alone. For if our place is not unique, then how can life and intelligence be unique to our place? As the father of Ellie Arroway says in the film version of *Contact*, if the universe is empty but for us, then what "an awful waste of space."

However, reading the novel in 1985 was perplexing. Here was the earnest, global-village atheist imagining how a maverick radio astronomer, Ellie, detects signals from the star Vega and later meets a warm facsimile of her dad on a paradisal beach among the stars. Then she deciphers evidence for a deist God (who communicates through transcendental numbers, like pi) in her computer's search protocols. Had Sagan gotten religion, or concocted a new way to debunk religion? *Contact* is more in the genre of satire than avant-garde science fiction. As a structure of action and emotion, it is also a *Bildungsroman* — a story of someone's education — and a thought experiment. Like many such tales, it asks how we

---

23. Kushner, *Perestroika*, 146; on Bloom, see Kushner's "Afterward," 154–55.
24. See Carl Sagan, "Science and Hope," in *The Demon Haunted World* (New York: Random House, 1995).
25. Carl Sagan, *Pale Blue Dot* (New York: Random House, 1994), 33–39.

would respond to extraterrestrials who want to teach us to communicate. It is a planetary *Bildungsroman*. But Sagan's more original experiment is to ask what it would be like if a religious faith — as understood by Freud — were verified. His purpose was indeed to debunk a certain kind of faith, and perhaps to appreciate another kind. But the experiment goes beyond its premises: it asks about the scope of ethical encounter and our responsibilities for, to, and with the future.

At the end of the novel Ellie and four scientists from Russia, India, Nigeria, and China ride a worm-hole transport system, or "Machine," which the "Message" from Vega has taught them to assemble (without revealing how it works). The Machine works but once. When they return with their data inexplicably erased, few believe them. So they keep their memories vivid through conversations, letters, and mutual reinforcement. The film dispenses with Ellie discovering a binary pattern, deeper in pi than any computer has gone before.[26] It also omits how the "Vegans"[27] are taking responsibility for slowing the expansion of the universe. But in both versions the Vegans wonder about the ancient ones — long departed from the galaxies — who built the transport system they now help maintain. The Vegans, like us, would like to resist fate and know more.

Sagan's views of religion were not altogether one-dimensional. To be sure, he tended to identify Christianity with fundamentalism and the seventeenth-century prelates who showed Galileo the instruments of torture. When polemical, he was Freudian as in *The Future of an Illusion*, where religion is first defined as believing in "facts" about important things one can't learn for oneself. These facts prove dubious, so Freud redefines religion as an illusion constructed out of infantile needs, wishes, guilt, and grief. In the film, Ellie believes she was partly responsible for her father's heart attack. In the novel she neglects her dying mother. So as the Vegans scan her memories and assume the persona of her father, Ellie is allowed to experience what so many long for, reunion with the dead. She knows the illusion is being assembled out of her most vulnerable desires, but it remains overwhelmingly sweet.

Even so, Sagan's polemics disclose a valuing of responsibility, adventure, and awe that he sensed cannot be reduced to a materialist vocabulary. The future will need "other sorts of myths, myths of encouragement." He reports a Talmudic story, "In the Garden, God tells Eve and Adam that He has intentionally left the Universe unfinished. It is the responsibility of humans, over countless generations,

---

26. The 1997 Warner Brothers film was directed by Robert Zemeckis, screenplay by James Hart and Michael Goldberg. It revises what is weakest in the novel — the satire of American politics and religion — but gives the story a ragged plot line and inconsistent style. Some differences from the novel are these: In the film only Ellie — not the other scientists — rides the worm-hole transport, later to be met with incredulity. So while the novel implies *community* as an analogue between science and religion, the film emphasizes "faith." Sagan's theologian, Palmer Joss, is a former carnival showman, self-taught humanist turned quasi-fundamentalist. In the film, he is more plausible as the handsome divinity school graduate who insists that while faith differentiates science and religion, science also requires acts of faith. Here, the film seems less than true to Sagan's intentions. A review in *Tikkun* 12, no. 5 (1997): 8–9, lauds it as attacking scientism, "the dominant religion of our times." The reason for this perception is the credibility given to Joss.

27. They are not really from Vega; that is where their transmitter is located.

to participate with God in a 'glorious' experiment — completing the Creation.' "[28] In *Contact*, Ellie has heard of Rudolf Otto. The *mysterium tremendum* makes one feel "utterly insignificant," but not, she says, "personally alienated." She believes "science elicits awe" and that "the bureaucratic religions try to institutionalize your perceptions of the numinous" instead of helping you perceive it "directly" (159). The truly numinous is in physical and mathematical order. The Vegans know this,[29] and the novel's gnomic last lines say that in the fabric of matter and space there is an art, a purpose, "an intelligence that antedates the universe," that anyone with "a modest talent for mathematics" may find (430).[30] What Sagan intends is unclear. It sounds like faith, but may be another exposé of (pi in the sky?) desires.

What Ellie believes in are signs that we are not alone, and here we find the ethical crux of Sagan's view of religion. Ostensibly, his interest in ethics is mainly to decry our violent ethnocentrism and ecological folly.[31] But his association with SETI (Search for Extraterrestrial Intelligence) resonates with the aesthetics and ethics of encounter and responsibility. He always said, as Ellie says (57), that a negative SETI result would at least teach us about the rarity of intelligent life and how our future is in no hands but our own. But he was not disinterested. "For me, no signals, no one calling out to us is a depressing prospect." And he wondered if, possibly, fleeting signals *had* been heard on a few occasions. They met all criteria but one, they were never detected again and confirmed. To think about it "raises goose bumps."[32]

Distant signals would symbolize a cosmos we are privileged to enjoy and love for a time — perhaps an exceedingly long time if we respectfully keep adapting and exploring. Distant signals, Sagan believed, would judge our arrogance, encourage our compassion. Our differences would pale beside the otherness of ETI, and mathematics would be revealed as the common language of creation. To receive such signals — which would be to encounter nature as a wondrous diversity of Thous[33] — would reverse the effects of Babel. In *Contact*, as the earth absorbs the

---

28. Sagan, *Pale Blue Dot*, 381–82.

29. Ellie's Vegan "father" hints that there is an intelligent pattern billions of decimal places deep in pi. This is rather silly but fits the skeptical purport of Sagan's thought experiment: a God who is real should be detectable and would communicate clearly. Ellie thinks scripture should say, "There are no privileged frames of reference," "Thou shalt not travel faster than light," "Heat and light reside in the smallest pebble," and so on (169).

30. For a serious, anthropic view of mathematics as religious, see John Barrow, *Pi in the Sky: Counting, Thinking, and Being* (Oxford: Oxford University Press, 1992), 296–97.

31. Sagan, *Billions and Billions*, especially 136–46, where Sagan considers how institutional religion and science do share common interests in issues of the environment and sustainability.

32. Sagan, *Pale Blue Dot*, 357, 365.

33. On meeting nature as "Thou" but not as a "person," see Donald L. Berry, *Mutuality: The Vision of Martin Buber* (Albany, N.Y.: SUNY Press, 1985), 1–38. (See also Gilkey, *Nature, Reality, and the Sacred*, 150.) An I-Thou relation with nature entails my being-with a natural process or creature on its own particular terms, a relation of both attentiveness and alterity. Berry criticizes the assumption that Buber's I-Thou relation is exclusively personal. Nature does not "speak" to us, but its processes and relations can solicit perception and attentions; nature is also part of our horizons of understanding, in that we are ourselves organisms and our proximate origins and creaturely limits emerged with galaxies and stars.

Message, there are many reactions, including paranoia and anxiety. But strategic arms reductions begin (the Hiroshima Accords) and everywhere there is perceived

> a new adventure for the human species, of turning a corner, of bursting into a new age — a symbolism powerfully amplified by the approach of the Third Millennium. There were still political conflicts. . . . But there was also a notable decline in many quarters of the world of jingoistic rhetoric and puerile self-congratulatory nationalism. There was a sense of the human species, billions of tiny beings spread over the world, collectively presented with an unprecedented opportunity, or even a grave common danger. . . . There was a whiff of hope in the air. Some people were unaccustomed to it and mistook it for something else — confusion, perhaps, or cowardice. (187)

V

How may we assess, in the space offered by these juxtapositions, perspectives on cosmos and community? Let us recall that the dialogue between theology and science is historically contingent. If understandings of God and nature seem to converge or diverge at certain moments, then what can be the lasting significance of the times of convergence? Let us also recall that the reception of scientific discoveries, theories, and speculations is shaped by cultural horizons. Do our violent histories irrevocably incline us to imagine near and distant futures as pointless fate? We have seen other horizons among the arts and sciences that imagine life in terms of the coincidental relatedness of others, mutual accountability, adventure, and beauty. They offer some space and time for imagining different futures through analogies with how we might encounter and enhance life today. The lasting significance of science for faith may well be in these analogies it offers for theological consideration.[34]

Few scientists any longer entertain the allegory of the starry heavens as a book or divinely wrought work of art, but some acknowledge moments when the contemplation or investigation of nature elicits an aesthetic response, or aesthesis.

---

34. Analogies are not only structures we make but relations we discover, "given" as it were, to understanding. On how the "focal meaning" and "ordered relationships" of analogy provide continuities in theology, see David Tracy, *The Analogical Imagination* (New York: Crossroad, 1981), especially chaps. 10–11. I am suggesting that cultures — and science as well — also provide analogies for theology to contemplate.

There is, of course, a long tradition of analogy in theology, which alerts us to differences between theological and scientific discourse. Science seeks to be univocal and disinterested in respect to the phenomena under view, while in theology the meaning of God entails that God is not discerned disinterestedly but through engagement — in life, history, and community. Nor can God be discerned completely, even in the scriptural and sacramental signs God authorizes. These signs are finite, and they direct us toward God in finite, fragmentary, and analogical ways. This principle is expressed in the "negative way" of speaking only about what God is not, and in the classic distinction between secondary and primary causation. Secondary causes are finite, temporal relations, to which scientific and cultural explanations apply; primary causation refers to the *whole* of those relations being ultimately dependent on God. (See Thomas Aquinas, *Summa Theologiae* 1a.3.8; and Gilkey, *Creationism on Trial*, 49, 58–61, 113–15. See also Paul Tillich, *The Dynamics of Faith* [New York: Harper and Row, 1957], esp. chaps. 3, 5, and 7.) There is no way to finally "get outside" our dependence on God nor outside of finite signs and analogies to view the "effects" of God with disinterest.

Likewise, few would say that nature is good in a normative sense, but some would report nature eliciting an awareness of interdependency that requires of us moral response. Perhaps the cosmos might be said to provide "time and space" for moral transformation.[35] Our suggestion is that the praxis of science can disclose aesthetic and ethical analogies, sometimes in conjunction with each other, and in a variety that requires discrimination and assessment.

Here we need to notice that aesthetic and ethical responses can conjoin in eschatological traditions as well. Ethically, such traditions signal a radical revisioning of the moral universe. The kingdom Jesus proclaims is a reality that breaks in on the cusp of past, present, and future — when one's world is overturned by news of God, as upon hearing the parable of the Good Samaritan. In reflection upon such a tradition, we may come to discern that the world *has been, is being,* and *will be* made new (Rev. 21:5) in ways that require our participation and responsibility.[36] Aesthetically, the extravagant images of some apocalyptic writing[37] can elicit attention both by appealing to the senses and by surpassing them: how does one "see" a "sea of glass mixed with fire" (Rev. 15:2)? The moment of aesthesis in such writing is evident in the sentence, "I *saw* a new heaven and a new earth," or when the divine presence is said to be heard, touched, smelled, or tasted.

Aesthetics as a discipline, it is true, has tended to deemphasize relations between art and other forms of experience, including moral and religious, but this formalism is unrealistic and is today often questioned. Aroused attention to form, pattern, texture, rhythm, movement, harmony, and dissonance in culture and nature may conjoin with experiences of moral and religious discernment. Such ad hoc conjunctions can promote confusion at times, but at other times new clarity, if only because aesthesis is a kind of knowing as well as feeling. The sensuous qualities of aroused perception can take one's attention beyond one's immediate interests; many kinds of responses may follow.[38]

Conjunctions of aesthetic and ethical response can cross the domains of theology and science. God is said to elicit praise (a religious-aesthetic response) and require embodied love (a religious-ethical response). We saw in Sagan patterns

---

35. See William Schweiker's "Time as a Moral Space: Moral Cosmologies, Creation, and Last Judgment," chap. 9 in this volume.

36. New Testament eschatology comprises a many-stranded tradition. The apocalyptic return of Christ may be soon expected (Mark), delayed (Luke-Acts), or already realized (John). For the historical Jesus, the kingdom of the reign of God breaks in as its proclamation overturns normative and religious expectations. We need not decide which eschatology is "truest." Rather, among these strands are times and spaces for practical discernment.

37. See Walter Brueggemann, "Faith at *Nullpunkt*," Donald Juel, "Christian Hope and the Denial of Death: Encountering New Testament Eschatology," Patrick D. Miller, "Judgment and Joy," and Hans Weder, "Hope and Creation," chaps. 10–13 in this volume.

38. While the aesthetic entails myriad forms of expression, what distinguishes it is its appeal to the senses. Thus, perceptible patterns in nature as well as art elicit aesthesis. On the aesthetic perception of "the sensuous" (*le sensible*), see Mikel Dufrenne, *The Phenomenology of Aesthetic Experience* (1953), trans. Edward S. Casey et al. (Evanston, Ill.: Northwestern University Press, 1973), 11–14. When the aesthetic is involved with other experiences (including religious and moral), various interactions can be produced, e.g., the "awe" occasioned by the "sublime" or the "numinous." See Frank Burch Brown, *Religious Aesthetics* (Princeton, N.J.: Princeton University Press, 1989), especially on the moral entailments of some experiences of art (16–19, 24–36, 145–57).

of awe and response, as if the cosmos were eliciting a sense both of wonder and of an awareness that nature both gives us a matrix for life and remains other. In cosmology, what we discern about the far-distant future may return our attentions back to nearer futures, where we search for ways to resist the oppression of the earth and enhance life among people and nature.[39] To discern the beauty and good of the cosmos requires our imaginative reception, critical understanding, and careful cultivation; so too, God's love is only discernible in our creative enjoyment and critical responsiveness to that love. Views in which the cosmos can elicit transformative discernment and praxis are views open to theological understanding and criticism.

In both the SETI and anthropic perspectives, the universe elicits sensuous awe — in its order, diversity of forms, and in its life. Both perspectives envision physically *possible* futures that admit of community. They both require this hope to be realized through respect, critical understanding, and transforming work. They know we may not survive long enough to perform this work, yet are optimistic that we will. The more speculative versions of the anthropic principle suggest that a participatory relationship between the future and life *founds* ethical encounter.[40] The speculative versions of SETI anticipate new forms of life that *might come* into ethical encounter.[41] For both, relations between life and the universe can be reciprocal. To say this much is to assent to the opening lines of Kant's confession of awe and to dissent from later lines. For moral life is not "independent of all animality and even of the whole world of sense."

There are, however, serious differences in how these perspectives give reasons for hope. Each has a different conception of the "other." The strong anthropic others are the others we *make*. They will mirror our desires and, as Tipler imagines it, will "want" to retrieve our information and emulate our souls. So they are not really all that "other" and do not deeply challenge or contradict our ways of hoping; rather, this kind of anthropic future extends to infinity our frontier expectations. Is there not something naive and narcissistic about this? That need not entirely negate it as image of hope. We *are*, after all, narcissistic sinners. Every future ever faced, every migration undertaken, was bounded by dreams and despair, idolatry and selfless giving. How would God's unexpected love and judgment be present to our narcissistic futures? Perhaps in turning sameness into unexpected otherness, as when the miscreant Rachel bids Dom Zerchi, "Live."

Sagan's others are the biological others into which we may evolve and the forms of life we may meet. It is true that the whole SETI idea could also be

---

39. See William Schweiker on "enhancing the integrity of life before God," in *Responsibility and Christian Ethics* (Cambridge: Cambridge University Press, 1995), and chap. 9 in this volume.

40. While FAP "has no ethical or moral content, it . . . is the physical precondition for moral values to arise and to continue to exist. . . . Furthermore, the FAP seems to imply a melioristic cosmos"; Barrow and Tipler, *Anthropic Cosmological Principle*, 23.

41. For Sagan, apart from the worm-hole strategy in *Contact*, the vast distances between ET civilizations means that contacts will likely be one way, or will be information exchanges taking ages to complete. That does not deter him, however, from speaking of these long exchanges as constituting the "cultural homogenization of the Galaxy," in *The Cosmic Connection* (Garden City, N.Y.: Anchor Press, 1973), 241–43.

charged with narcissism. Any plan for deciphering any anticipated message can only be a product of *our* best imagining. The intellects SETI listens for are necessarily enough like us to cogitate mathematically and broadcast on the radio frequency of hydrogen.[42] The minds Ellie hopes to detect are perhaps but slightly improved versions of her own. But the differences are telling, for their origins and forms of life will be utterly unlike our own.[43] If the anthropic future reflects our past migrations from old worlds to new, the SETI future celebrates our multicultural cities and remembers in shame those we colonized on distant shores, the demonized others, the "aliens."

To be reasons for hope, both futures require the creation of communities; that is, the imagining and making of new worlds. Both know that while Earth is our cradle, it cannot be forever home. But here, too, are differences. Not all anthropic principlists think as Tipler, but his is hope in the self-fulfilling recovery of information, which our descendants might accomplish at the Omega Point. For Sagan, by contrast, no species by itself is guaranteed a future. In *Contact*, the future is aided by strangers-become-friends, and they by other strangers, "caretakers" all (365). Everyone in the cosmos will be wondering from whence they came and where they are going. The benevolent Vegans collect dreams, music, and signs of "lovingkindness" from countless worlds (358) and try to buy us a little space and time by re-engineering Cygnus A — "good honest work."

We return to where we begin. We are taught that the first reason for reality is God's love (John 1:3) — indeed a *kenosis* or "pouring out" of God into the form of a "servant" or "slave" (Phil. 2:7), depending on how we translate it, given our histories. That the cosmos will be a slave to us is impossible; that we and the cosmos can be servants to each other is conceivable; that God will enter the suffering of slaves and servants and lift up their lives into God's life is what is promised. What can be the relation between the cosmic future, human hoping, and such a God of hope? To say there is none would contradict the doctrine of creation, and with it eschatology. For the God who "makes all things new" is also the maker of the heavens and the earth, who declares creation "good." These words authorize our search for signs and wonders of the God of hope in nature as well as culture, even as we respect the categorical differences between God's future and how we can comprehend the natural future.

There has obviously been something "Pelagian" in our comprehensions, something that risks idolizing technology and broaching forbidden knowledge. The depths of this danger are signaled in this chapter by Miller's *Canticle*. But theology ought not stop at merely identifying the naivete of views that creatures may both transform the future and be transformed. Were the analogies we receive in

---

42. Sagan, *Pale Blue Dot*, 356.

43. The forms we might evolve into on other worlds might have little more in common with us today than DNA and calculus. But Sagan is optimistic that through historical records, "they will not wholly forget the Earth" (*Pale Blue Dot*, 397). On this point, some sympathetic to the anthropic principle converge with Sagan's perspective; see Freeman Dyson on evolution in *Imagined Worlds* (Cambridge: Harvard University Press, 1997), 141–73, and his "principle of maximum diversity" in *Infinite in All Directions* (New York: Harper and Row, 1988), 298.

nature to require nothing of us — if they failed to solicit our wonder and compassionate practice — then what reason would we have to draw inferences to the God of love, the God who speaks, Thou? If the analogies were explanatory only, and offered no practical responsibilities to beings capable of intelligent love and creative making, then could we discern in them signs of God? The worst idolatry of the "god of the gaps" was its being only an explanation, not the God who beckons us enter the gaps in culture and nature to fill them with practical works of love, not the God who transforms our imaginations. "Behold, I make all things new." That nature and the imagination can collaborate in *that* transforming, negating, and creating image is a sign of God's contact with space and time and life.

Note: This essay is dedicated to Tom Siegfried, science writer and friend. Interpreting science for those of us who speak only "natural languages" is a critical, not ancillary part of scientific understanding. My adult education in science has been largely guided by Tom, though he is not responsible for this chapter's views and blunders. Nor are the colleagues represented in this volume, to whom I am also grateful. Thanks also to Wallace Alston, Robert Jenson, Don Browning, and the Center of Theological Inquiry; to Günter Thomas for his response in Heidelberg; and to Peter Ochs and Charles Mathewes for patiently reading early drafts.

Chapter 8

THE CHURCH
AS A CULTURAL SPACE
Eschatology and Ecclesiology

Christoph Schwöbel

Overcoming the Dualism of Cultures

In the twentieth century much of the cultural history in the West has been characterized by a cultural dualism, famously summarized in C. P. Snow's metaphor of the "two cultures" of scientific and literary culture.[1] At the end of the twentieth century there seem to be signs that this dualism of cultures is being overcome or, at least, that it presents itself no longer as harshly as it had at the beginning of the second half of this century. Many factors could be noted in an attempt to substantiate such an assessment of the situation. Foremost among them is the fact that science today no longer appears to be such a unified "culture" as it did to the Reid Lecturer in 1959. It has become thoroughly pluralistic, and in that has followed the tendencies toward pluralism in the literary realm that have characterized much of this century. The idea of a unified science based on a single methodological paradigm, powerfully advocated by the Vienna Circle at the beginning of this century, has long been abandoned and is today more a theme for the history of the philosophy of science than for current debate. There is a legitimate plurality of strategies of investigation and inquiry within the sciences which cannot easily be reduced to one methodological paradigm. There is also a variety of opinions adopted by scientists when they reflect on how their findings bear on the way we live our lives. Science is no longer regarded as the ultimate arbiter in all matters of knowledge. If one turns to science to consult the expert opinion one will normally not be offered one, but at least three, often widely diverging views — something that has long ceased to irritate anybody in the realm of literary culture. Pluralism has conquered the world of science so that science today is for many of its practitioners no longer such a clearly defined "culture" as it used to be, but rather a complex family of activities with rather loosely defined boundaries.

In contrast to the tendencies toward pluralism that are increasingly characteristic of the sciences, there are equally powerful unifying tendencies which affect

---

1. C. P. Snow, *The Two Cultures and the Scientific Revolution* (Cambridge: Cambridge University Press, 1959).

both formerly separate cultures. Technologically applied science has invaded every realm of life to such an extent that an article criticizing the effects of modern information technology on the soul would most likely be written on a word-processor and communicated via electronic mail to its publisher. Literary culture has come to rely on scientifically created technological subsystems that have become indispensable in the modern communication society, thereby turning the global village into an electronic reality. Increasingly, both cultures, the scientific and the literary, are forced to realize that their claims to autonomy are of a merely rhetorical nature, given the fact that they both rely on an economic "culture" that has a decisive influence on what kind of science can be practiced because it is economically feasible and how much literary culture is affordable.

When Snow contrasted the "two cultures" in 1959 he highlighted the different sets of attitudes operative in each sphere. Where the literary world appeared restricted and constrained by its adherence to traditional canons, the world of science had dreams of a new Elizabethan age; where literary culture lived, at least in Snow's picture, by a denial of the future, scientific culture seemed to be characterized by an unrestricted optimism about the future. This optimism, so characteristic for the early years of modern science, has dwindled as science has come of age. The optimistic dreams about the distant future fueled the efforts for shaping the present and the near future. This evolutionary optimism has been replaced by a deep sense of ambiguity about the future. While many still seem modestly optimistic about the near future, few seem to be able to develop much optimism for the distant future. The findings of science itself have frustrated the long-term optimism that characterized science's early years. The expectation that cosmic evolution will not lead to ultimate fulfillment but rather to final futility casts a long shadow on the search for meaning in the present. Steven Weinberg's view that "[t]he more the universe seems comprehensible, the more it also seems pointless" leads to the resigned statement that "[t]he effort to understand the universe is one of the very few things that lifts human life a little above the level of farce, and gives it some of the grace of tragedy."[2] Where science can offer no ultimate comfort when it is confronted with the ultimate frustration of its noblest aspirations it can only express this experience in literary terms. Eschatology, the questions concerning the last things, seems to be one of the fields where the walls separating the two cultures have collapsed. Which attitude should we adopt if in the end futility has the last word, at least as far as the sciences can tell us with reasonable certainty? This is a question in the face of which our membership in one of the two cultures is no longer significant. At least with regard to ultimate questions the dualism of cultures is not the last word.

Eschatological questions are concerned with ultimate meaning. That eschatology is concerned with the last things is no more than an explanation of the word "eschatology." The notion of "last things," however, contains an interesting ambiguity. Superficially, it refers to what comes last in any sort of sequence, for example, a temporal sequence. However, if we inquire, as cosmology does,

2. S. Weinberg, *The First Three Minutes* (New York: Basic Books, 1977), 149.

about the last things in the history of the cosmos, "the last things" take on an extended meaning. Then, what comes last, that which concludes the history of the cosmos, seems to throw light (or shadow) on everything that comes before it. It is the ending, as Aristotle already knew, which determines the meaning of a story. If the story of our universe will end, as science teaches us to understand, with a final scenario of utter futility, this calls the meaning of the whole story into question. There is indeed an element of tragedy here: the search for intelligibility leads to the expectation of the pointlessness of the whole cosmic history. Therefore, eschatological questions have such an enormous cultural significance, transcending even the division of cultures to which we had become accustomed.

There are very different ways of interpreting the concept of culture.[3] One of the most plausible ones is to see a culture as based on a system of signs, a way of reading reality. The basic cultural activity that is the foundation of all others is the activity of signifying something as *something*. Signification is presupposed in all cultural activities. There is a consensus among anthropologists that the use of signs is one of the distinctive marks of human beings. Humans are by nature cultural beings; they are challenged by nature to survive through cultural means, above all through the use of signs. The *homo sapiens* is therefore always the *homo significans*. Eschatological questions underline the fact that the way we conceive of the ultimate destiny of everything affects our whole system of signs; it has repercussions in every area where we use signs, it affects the whole culture. The challenge raised by the scientific expectation of ultimate cosmic futility is therefore one that affects our whole way of interpreting the world, and since interpreting the world always implies describing possibilities of action, it also affects our ways of acting in the world.

Cultural systems of signification enable us to act in the world, both by interpreting the world and by shaping the world through cultural — including technical — means. One of the most important functions of systems of signs is therefore that they provide orientation for human agents. Our capacity for orientation depends on a developed system of signs that integrates different dimensions of integration and action and so constitutes a universe of meaning. Snow's description of the situation of his time as one where two cultures are in conflict points to a lack of integration in the system of signs and therefore to an impediment for appropriate action. In order to overcome such impediments it is therefore highly plausible that an integration of ways of reading the world is called for which brings together our beliefs about the physical world, our moral convictions, and our metaphysical ways of interpreting reality.[4]

It has always been the function of religious systems of signs to offer a holistic view of reality that combines knowledge about the natural world with moral convictions and metaphysical beliefs. Just as a religious faith is a holistic faith

---

3. For a theological attempt at describing a concept of culture, cf. Chr. Schwöbel, "Glaube und Kultur: Gedanken zur Idee einer Theologie der Kultur," *Neue Zeitschrift für Systematische Theologie und Religionsphilosophie* 38 (1996): 137–54.

4. Cf. W. Schweiker's "Time as a Moral Space: Moral Cosmologies, Creation, and Last Judgment," chap. 9 in this volume.

encompassing the different dimensions of life, so religious beliefs are integrative beliefs, offering ways of integrating the different dimensions of reality by relating them to one focus that is not part of reality but transcends it. The narratives of religions are therefore narratives about beginnings and endings. They have the standard form of telling a story that starts with "in the beginning" and concludes with "when the end comes." Religious stories about beginnings and endings are always more than stories about the starting-point and the end-point of a temporal sequence. Since they are concerned with the beginning of all beginnings and the end of all ends they make an ontological point about the ultimate coordinates of the cosmos and of human life in the cosmos.[5] In theistic religions this is seen as the ontological dependence of everything there is on an ultimate ground of being and as the ontological orientation of all toward an ultimate end or purpose. It is characteristic for such religious stories that they have both a cosmic dimension and an existential dimension. In attempting to provide answers to the questions, "Where do we come from?" and "Where do we go?," they say something both about the cosmos and about personal human life in the cosmos. This demonstrates the orientational character of religious beliefs. They offer orientation by locating human beings in relation to the world and in relation to the ground and end of being, of the being of the world and of their own being, and so point to the adequate form of the relationship of human beings to themselves which finds expression in a form of self-understanding. All religions have stories to tell about humans becoming dislocated in this network of relationships by relating wrongly to the coordinates of their existence. By losing sight of their proper relationship to the ground and end of being they are displaced in all other cosmic, social, and personal relationships. The religious symbols of the Fall and the discourse of sin try to express this dislocation. By identifying the causes of dislocation, the religions have already prepared the path for ways to overcome this dislocation by relocating humans in the network of relationships. Religious stories of reconciliation, redemption, and salvation have as their theme the overcoming of dislocation by relocating humans again in the proper relationships to the source and end of being, to the world and to themselves.

    Eschatological questions are always the test case for cultural systems of signification. They confront our ways of interpreting reality with the question of the ultimate. Will the way we understand reality ultimately make sense? Eschatological questions therefore always have a religious dimension, whether they are raised in science, in the arts, or in the religions. The question of the ultimate is the point of convergence of different cultural systems of signs, of different ways of reading reality. It has far-reaching repercussions on our way of interpreting reality because, if it is the point of convergence of the cultural systems of signs, it necessarily raises the question of their relationship. Can they be integrated to form a complex but differentiated whole? And if so, what are the patterns of coordinating different ways of interpreting reality? Once again, we are confronted with the religious character of the question of the ultimate: Because this ques-

---

5. Cf. Kathryn Tanner's "Eschatology without a Future?" chap. 15 in this volume.

tion is concerned with the final outcome, the ultimate destiny of the cosmos and of ourselves, it anticipates the point where the different ways of reading reality come together, and therefore raises the question of their relationship in the present. Briefly, religious questions reach toward the ultimate, and the answers given to them have therefore a holistic impact. However, this does not imply that the religious interpretations of reality are necessarily totalitarian in character. Because the ultimate end is not yet there, because the final outcome is now only anticipated, present interpretations of reality, including religious ones, remain fragmentary in character. It is precisely the orientation toward the ultimate which concerns every dimension of reality which makes the present interpretation of reality fragmentary, open for its fulfillment when the ultimate is actualized.

This point might be conceded for religious interpretations of reality, but it might be queried whether it also applies to other interpretations of reality in the sciences and the arts. Are they not restricted to the penultimate and therefore unchallenged by eschatological questions in their restricted penultimate realms? Could the sciences not shrug off any concern with eschatological issues as transcending their sphere of operation? Two things might be said in response to this query. The first is that scientific views of the end of life on earth, the end of our solar system, and the end of cosmic history have triggered these eschatological questions. The effects of scientific investigations cannot be contained within a restricted realm of science; they affect all our ways of interpreting reality. Second, we have already seen that the answers given to ultimate questions, however tentative they may be, qualify the penultimate. This is like a reversal of the ancient maxim *ex nihilo nihil fit*: if everything comes to nothing in the end, then everything that occurs before the end is, potentially, nothing.

It is therefore not surprising that the concern with ultimate questions challenges all cultural systems of signs and raises the question of their relationship. Occasions like the turn of a century or the arrival of a new millennium provide particularly good opportunities for studying how the awareness for eschatological questions is suddenly, sometimes quite dramatically, increased and how different cultural ways of interpreting reality attempt to deal with these questions. Religious ways of interpreting reality are particularly called to task. After all, eschatological issues have always been crucial aspects of the ways in which reality is interpreted religiously. If these issues are taken up in the sciences and in the humanities the religions cannot stand aside and leave their own domain to the interpretative efforts of others.

Christianity is no exception. Eschatological questions have from the beginning played a crucial part in the Christian message. The imminent coming of the kingdom of God is a center of Jesus' message, and when he is confessed as the Messiah, the Son of the living God, the coming of the kingdom of God is so closely related to his person that he is in his person seen as the coming of the kingdom of God. The resurrection of the crucified Jesus has therefore been interpreted from the perspective of faith by Christians as the event that holds the key to answering all eschatological questions. It is precisely because the early Christians applied Jesus' own message of the coming of the kingdom of God as an unconditional gratuitous act of God, which restores and renews the old order of things by overcoming its determinative power, that they could understand the Easter message that the one who was crucified has been raised by God as the first-born of many sisters and brothers. The belief that the resurrection of Jesus holds the key for the answers that can be given to all eschatological questions like the relationship between old and new, between death and everlasting life, between destruction and futility and fulfillment, is the reason why Christianity has been from the beginning an eschatological religion. Much of the dynamic of the history of Christianity and its influence on its environment is rooted in the eschatological character of Christianity. Whenever Christianity became too settled in the present, too complacently integrated in the "old" order of things, it was reminded that Christians have no lasting home in the reality as it is now, that they are on the way toward a state that has not been reached, that they are challenged to participate in the dynamic of God's dealings with the world which have not yet reached their goal. Going back to the origin has always meant for Christianity to be confronted again with the original eschatological drive of its beginnings.

Christianity is essentially communal in character. To become a Christian has meant from the beginning to become part of the Christian community, of the church. Already in patristic times the slogan *"Unus Christianus, nullus Christianus"* was the appropriate summary of the essentially communal character of Christianity. Its communal character and its character as a personal faith are mutually constitutive for Christianity. In order to be a person one needs to be part of the Christian community, and this Christian community is always a communion of persons. This has far-reaching interpretations for the Christian interpretation of reality. It is not an individual vision of how things are, but a view of reality which is both personal in that it has the character of personal faith and conviction, and communal so that it finds expression in communal acts of worship and social action. The Christian interpretation of reality is therefore always one that encompasses the whole of reality, including the ground of being and its ultimate end, and it is liturgically enacted and translated into social action. One could also say that the Christian interpretation of reality is holistic in a twofold sense: it encompasses the whole of reality as its sphere of application; and it involves the whole person in all its dimensions in the activity of interpretation. In this sense the Christian community is a culture in a twofold sense: it offers a system of signs for the interpretation of the whole of reality; and it performs this interpretation in all forms of activity that are capable of signification or that have interpretative significance. It has therefore — for better or worse — a significant place in the cultural system of a society.

The question that is pertinent in the cultural situation of a challenge of the whole universe of meaning through eschatological questions, concretely, the challenge offered by the sciences' expectation of cosmic futility,[6] is, therefore: What

---

6. On the details of scientific prognostications of the end of cosmic evolution cf. W. Stoeger's "Scientific Accounts of Ultimate Catastrophes in Our Life-Bearing Universe," and Sir John Polkinghorne's "Eschatology: Some Questions and Some Insights from Science," chaps. 1 and 2 in this volume.

can the Christian community as it is concretely represented by the Christian churches contribute to a comprehensive interpretation of reality which takes this challenge seriously and tries to respond to it in such a way that it neither ignores it nor simply adopts it as the ultimate truth for all spheres of reality? The question can also be raised from the perspective of the Christian community: What must the Christian community contribute to the cultural conversation on eschatological questions if it wants to remain true to its being and task? In view of the urgency of the eschatological issues raised by the sciences' predictions the church is challenged from two sides, both by society and by its own self-understanding, to "be ready to make your defense when anyone challenges you to justify the hope which is in you" (1 Peter 3:15).

The Church as an Institution of the Interim

At first sight the church seems to be a most unlikely candidate for offering a cultural space where eschatological questions of ultimate significance can be discussed engaging scientists and theologians. The historical instances of the resistance of the church against new discoveries of science come readily to mind to challenge any optimism concerning the role of the church in cultural dialogue. However, if one looks a little closer at the cases of Galileo, the debates about Darwinism, and more recent disputes about creationism, a different picture seems to emerge. In the case of Galileo, the church was challenged to distinguish between the Christian faith and its doctrinal expressions and a geocentric cosmology that for a long time appeared to be a convenient correlate to a Christian view of reality. However, Copernicus's view of the universe, which Galileo defended, was itself theologically motivated insofar as he understood the universe as being created by the divine master-builder according to the best and most precise laws that can be known by the human mind, the true image of God in human persons, through rational inquiry.[7] At closer inspection the intellectual debate is therefore one between a Christian theology wedded to a (pagan) Aristotelian cosmology and a cosmology based on observation and mathematical calculation which understands itself as supporting the fundamental tenets of Christian faith. Similarly, the debate between Darwinism and some conservative Christians is at one level not a debate about religious and scientific truth but about the validity of an Aristotelian view of the natural world according to which God created nature as a fixed order of species and not as an evolutionary process. It is interesting to observe that the principle of evolution was first extended to cover the evolution of the cosmos by the theologian J. R. Illingworth on the basis of a theory of the evolutionary and gradual activity of the Logos in creation developed from the insights of the Greek Fathers.[8] When Darwinism and Christian theology and the

---

7. Copernicus's theological views are summarized in the prooemium to book I of *De revolutionibus orbium caelestium* (1543).

8. Cf. Illingworth, "The Incarnation in Relation to Development," in *Lux Mundi: A Series of Studies in the Religion of the Incarnation*, ed. Ch. Gore (London, 1889).

church came into violent conflict, this occurred because some early Darwinists like Thomas H. Huxley interpreted Darwinism as a comprehensive *Weltanschauung* intended to replace Christian faith and the church. In opposing such views some theologians employed the Bible as a manual of science to oppose the meta-scientific implications of the Darwinian theory of evolution. We have here a mutual self-misunderstanding: Huxley misunderstood Darwin's theory as a general *Weltanschauung* replacing religion (a view we would today call scientism, not science); some of his Christian opponents misunderstood the first chapter of the Book of Genesis not as a religious text but as a scientific account of how the universe and life on our planet came to be (a misunderstanding that has become programmatic in the self-description of such views as "creation science"). Above all, these conflicts are not so much examples of the warfare between science and religion or between the authority of the church and the freedom of scientific inquiry; they are examples of battles over cultural control, conflicts over claims to power, not to knowledge.

Perhaps the church may appear as a more likely candidate for offering a cultural space for the discussion of the issues raised by the sciences concerning the ultimate destiny of the universe and their implications if the role the church could play is more firmly based on its theological self-understanding. Interpreting the church theologically may be a way of pointing to the cultural role it could play.

For any theological understanding of the church, the church is, above all, an institution of the "interim," of the time between the coming of Christ and Christ's second coming, between the Incarnation and the *eschaton*. The church has only a finite permanence; as the "creature of the divine word"[9] it shares in finitude as the hallmark of all created existence. The church, therefore, appears like a bridge stretching between the life, death, and resurrection of Christ and the time when its cries of "Maranatha," come, Lord Jesus, will be answered once and for all in the kingdom of God. There are no temples in the heavenly city, no churches in the new Jerusalem, because the distinction between the church and the world will be overcome when God will be all in all. The church is finite; it has by itself and for itself no eschatological ultimacy. It has therefore no claim to ultimate authority and power. Because it hopes for the coming of the kingdom of God it lives in the expectation of its own end. Therefore the church refers in all its acts and in its whole being back to the life, death, and resurrection of Christ as its foundation and forward to the kingdom of God as its end, the fulfillment of its destiny.

This is especially characteristic for the two groups of activities that are the central marks of the church, the preaching of the gospel and the celebration of the sacraments. The gospel proclaims that the life, death, and resurrection of Jesus is the disclosure of the ultimate saving truth for the world. This presupposes that in Jesus we encounter not just an exemplary human being but the reality of God the Creator who sustains everything there is, reconciles everything that

---

9. For the interpretation of the formula, cf. Chr. Schwöbel, "The Creature of the Word: Recovering the Ecclesiology of the Reformers," in *On Being the Church: Essays on the Christian Community*, ed. C. E. Gunton and D. W. Hardy (Edinburgh: T. & T. Clark, 1989), 110–55.

is estranged from him, and brings everything to perfection. The story of Jesus is the paradigmatic story of God, continuing and pointing to the completion of God's story with Israel. The *theological* content of the *christological* story is the key to its *eschatological* significance. Because it is God who is disclosed in Jesus in such a way that Jesus must be understood as the disclosure of the reality of God, therefore the story of Jesus bears ultimate significance for the whole of humanity, indeed for the whole of creation. If the story of Jesus is to be understood as the key to the ending of God's story with creation, two points must be made about the significance of this story. First of all, God remains faithful to his creation in spite of the many ways in which human creatures contradict their Creator. Second, in reconciling those who are estranged from God and are thus cut off from the source of eternal life, God brings about the communion of creation with its Creator, and so maintains his original intention for creation, bringing about the perfect communion of the reconciled creation with its Creator and so perfecting the destiny of creation.

The first point is of particular significance for the understanding of the relationship between redemption, creation, and God's eschatological action. The gospel portrays God's redemptive action in the cross and resurrection of Jesus as the healing of the broken relationship between God and his estranged creatures. By contradicting God, by attempting to assume God's place in creation in yielding to the Serpent's promise of God-like status, as the story of the Fall indicates, human beings have cut themselves off from the source of eternal life. After the Fall their life will end in estrangement from God and they will therefore be abandoned to death as the end of all creaturely possibilities. This is the death that is experienced as being forsaken by God, the death that Jesus dies on the cross. In raising Jesus from the dead God reveals that even where all created possibilities have come to an end he will maintain his creative relationship to creation, which is not dependent on any conditions apart from God's power and which can therefore create *ex nihilo*. The resurrection of Jesus witnesses to the assertion of God's unconditional creativity over against the exhausted possibilities of created matter to maintain its life.[10] The new life that is granted to the dead Jesus by God is discontinuous with his life before the death on the cross in the sense that the risen Jesus is not the reanimated dead Jesus. Yet it is continuous with God's unconditionally creative relationship to creation. Therefore God grants continuity of identity to the one who died and has been raised from the dead. There is here an asymmetry between the pattern of continuity and discontinuity that is characteristic for created matter and the pattern of continuity and discontinuity that characterizes the being and action of God the Creator. God grants in the power of his unconditional creativity continuity where there is real created discontinuity. Thereby God maintains his creative relationship to Jesus through the discontinuity of death, which is, in terms of created continuity and discontinuity,

---

10. These remarks only focus on one aspect of the resurrection. For a fuller account of the resurrection and its significance, cf. Michael Welker's "Resurrection and Eternal Life: The Canonic Memory of the Resurrected Christ, His Reality, and His Glory," chap. 18 in this volume.

an absolute discontinuity that cannot be overcome by created means. Jesus' death is the absolute surrender of life, of all creaturely possibilities to God the Creator. It is the situation of total dependence on God's creative power, the situation of total trust. By maintaining his creative relationship to the dead Jesus in raising him from the dead and conserving his identity through the absolute discontinuity of death, God vindicates the claim implicit in Jesus' story of living in absolute and total trust in the God he called Father.

When patristic theology tried to express the ontological impact of the story of Jesus' life, death, and resurrection, one of the most successful means of conceptualizing the asymmetry between the patterns of continuity and discontinuity of created life and of the life of the Creator was to say that Jesus' human nature is *enhypostatic* in the person of God the Son. His identity is constituted through the relationship of God the Father through the Spirit to him; it is not defined like created identities through the relationship with other created identities. In this sense his humanity is *anhypostatic*; it does not have an independent center of identity distinguished from the relationship to God the Father in the Spirit. What the gospel stories narrate as Jesus' total trust in God and his obedience in freely doing the will of the Father and what the birth narratives express on a different level as his conception through the Holy Spirit are present in the model of the hypostatic union in ontological conceptuality.[11] The continuity of his identity is constituted in the relationship to God the Father in the Spirit which transcends and overcomes the discontinuity of death.

If we see the story of Jesus' death and resurrection as the paradigmatic story about God, it becomes clear that this story discloses the faithfulness of God to his creation, which grants continuity through the discontinuity of death. The hope of creation to overcome the absolute discontinuity of death is not based on an inherent capacity of creation because death is the end of all created capacities, the disruption of all relationships that can be maintained by a creature. The hope of creation is based on God's maintaining his unconditionally creative relationship to his creation. The continuity that transcends the discontinuity of death is grounded in the constancy of God's love, which brings to expression the unchangeable character of God's being.

The second point is also significant here. The reconciliation between God the Creator and his estranged creatures, which Christian faith understands to be the point of Jesus' death on the cross, is the means by which God carries out his original intention of establishing communion with his creation. From the human side, from the perspective of the human creatures who have cut themselves off from the ground and end of all being, this eschatological act is the beginning of a new creation. From God's perspective, if we may express it in this way on the basis of the story of Jesus, the *eschaton* is the fulfillment of God's original intention, actualized through the means of his reconciling act on the cross. The discontinuity of sin and alienation from God is overcome by God's remaining continuously faithful to his will which is rooted in his being.

---

11. Cf. Tanner's remarks on the hypostatic union in "Eschatology without a Future?"

The gospel has the character of a promise. This implies that what is exclusively said of Jesus in the gospel story is promised inclusively to the whole creation. The promise is based on the paradigmatic character of the gospel story. If the story of Jesus is really a story about God, and if it is the story in which God definitively discloses his relationship with creation, which is rooted in God's own being and character, the Jesus story has universal significance. As we said above: The *theological* character of the *christological* story is the key to its *eschatological* significance. Because Jesus' story discloses the character of God's relationship to his creation as one by which God maintains his relationship to creation through the discontinuity of death, this story is a promise for all. The hypostatic union of God and Christ in this way becomes the promised pattern of eternal life for the whole creation. It is important to note that the trustworthiness of the promise rests on the fact that Jesus' story is not just an example of what will happen to all creatures. Only if Jesus' story is God's own story can we trust that the pattern of his life and death will become ours. The famous statement of Irenaeus and Athanasius, "He became what we are in order that we may become what he is," only carries universal significance if it refers to God the Son. The promise of the gospel that is proclaimed by the church has as its real content God promising himself. Its content is not something other than God which God promises to give to creation, but the promise of God's own communion with creation.

Therefore the response that is called for by the promise of the gospel is faith as unconditional trust in God. It is not simply trusting that such-and-such will happen. *Whatever* happens is made dependent on God. Faith as unconditional trust in God is the absolute reliance on the creative relationship of God to his creation. It is therefore not only an epistemic attitude but an act of ontological significance. It makes explicit the utter dependence of everything created on God as the ground and end of all being. In faith Christians therefore trust that God's life-giving relationship to creation will be maintained by God even through the discontinuity of death. Christian faith is therefore based on the memory of Christ, which is appropriated in the experience of the believers as the promise that is given to them and so generates images of hope against the despair of unredeemed finitude. It is characteristic for the hope of Christian faith that it does not attempt to bypass the experience of death as the end of all relationships that can be actively maintained by human beings. Rather, it relies on God maintaining his creative relationship to his creatures in death and beyond death. The character of faith itself is exemplary for the view of reality that faith represents. It is passively constituted for human beings by the action of God the Holy Spirit in authenticating the gospel of Christ as truth about God's relationship to his creation for believers. On the basis of this passive constitution of their faith, believers are called to live the life of faith actively as a response to the gift they have received in faith. In this sense, faith is already participation in that relationship of God to his human creatures which will be perfected in the kingdom of God but which is not yet actualized in history.

The sacraments are usually seen as the second mark of the church. The sacraments do not add anything to the content of the gospel but they enact liturgically what the gospel promises. They are visible words that involve the whole human person in receiving and responding to the promise of the gospel. This can readily be seen from the two main sacraments of the Lord's Supper and Baptism. Just as the church they are interim institutions. Christians celebrate the Lord's Supper until he comes again, and baptism initiates people into the Christian community which will no longer be a distinct community in the kingdom of God. Like all acts of the church the sacraments are characterized by the twofold reference back to Christ and forward to the kingdom of God. They are therefore a tangible enactment of the eschatological tension in which the church exists as an institution of the interim.

The Lord's Supper has different points in different Christian traditions but they all correspond to the structure of relating continuity and discontinuity that we have already observed in the promise of the gospel. Where the Lord's Supper is mainly concerned with the forgiveness of sins and the assurance of God's grace, as in the Western tradition, the relationship between discontinuity and continuity is enacted in almost dramatic form. The sinner's history of sinning, summarized in the confession of sin, is disrupted by the assurance of forgiveness. The person of the sinner is distinguished from the history of his sinful actions which can be acknowledged and faced because they are forgiven. The assurance of forgiveness is the promise that God maintains his relationship to the sinner permanently so that the sinner is led on the way to eternal life. The liberation from the destructive effects of the past is a liberation for a future that is determined by God's possibilities. Again, the continuity is rooted in God's relationship to the sinner and it is maintained through the radical discontinuity of separating the person of the sinner from the effects of his actions. The restored relationship to God is at the same time the reintegration of the sinner into the community.

Where the Lord's Supper is primarily an anticipation of the communion of believers with the triune God, as in the Eastern traditions, the continuity between the eucharistic community and community in the kingdom of God is tangibly expressed in the liturgy. The eucharist is a foretaste of the world to come but one in which created persons take part not in virtue of the capacities of created life but through their anticipated participation in the eternal life of God. Eucharistic continuity is an expression of the eternal life of the Trinity which transcends the disruption of death which characterizes finite life.

The significance of the Lord's Supper for the whole created world is also expressed in the use of the finite and created matter of the elements of bread and wine as signs of the presence of Christ with the community. The logic of death and resurrection, of the continuity of divine life which transcends the discontinuities of finite created life, is in this way extended to the whole cosmos. The personal, social, and cosmic dimensions of life are brought together in the eucharistic symbolism, and the logic of divine creative continuity transcending created discontinuities is extended to all of them.

Similar points can be seen in the sacrament of baptism. Baptism is not just to be understood as the initiation of a new member into a human community of believers. It is the inclusion into community with God granted by God's grace and in this way it is the inclusion into the covenant of grace which is not ultimately determined by the death that threatens natural communities. It is significant that the act of baptism is combined with the naming of the one that is baptized. This indicates that the identity that is expressed in this name is anchored in the relationship of the triune God to this particular person. This identity carries the promise that it will be preserved by God through the discontinuity of the death of the person. Therefore this death is anticipated in the act of baptism. Participation in the death and resurrection of Christ is also an anticipation of the death of the person who is baptized and this expresses that the continuity of his or her identity is no longer based on the continuity of his or her natural life but on the relationship of God to this particular person as it is promised in the death and resurrection of Christ.

The proclamation of the gospel and the sacraments are not the only activities that characterize the church as an institution of the interim. But they provide the center for the identity formation of the church in between the coming of Christ and the kingdom of God. They make the pattern of discontinuity and continuity that is rooted in the death and resurrection of Christ explicit. From this center this logic must spread to all dimensions of the life of the church. However, the church does not exist for its own sake. The gospel it proclaims has a significance for the whole world and the sacraments it celebrates are pointers to the ultimate destiny of the whole creation. The church's dependence on God as the source of its life serves as a visible sign for the world that its hope of being granted continuity does not rest in the vital powers of created matter or in its capacities for self-organization but in its dependence on the creative possibilities of God.

This is nowhere more clearly expressed than in the church's dependence on the Spirit of God. The Spirit who in the biblical traditions is the giver of life to creation and enables creation to respond to its Creator, who is also the Spirit who mediates the communion between God the Father and Jesus, is the Spirit who creates faith in the church and is present in the church as the first-fruits of eschatological consummation. The Spirit discourse of Christian faith points to the link between the giving of life to creation, the resurrection of Jesus, and the worship of the church as a promise of the world to come. This connection is at the heart of the church's message. Paul has expressed this point with exemplary clarity: "If the Spirit of him who raised Jesus from the dead dwells in you, then the God who raised Jesus from the dead will also give new life to your mortal bodies through his indwelling Spirit" (Rom. 8:11). This Spirit-discourse identifies the link between creation, the resurrection of Jesus, and the new life that is promised in the gospel. It is the Spirit of God who bridges the eschatological tension between now already and not yet. The life that is now already promised in the gospel and celebrated in the sacraments is the life that has not yet appeared for the whole cosmos as long as the universe is bound by the "shackles of mortality" (Rom. 8:21). But it is witnessed and celebrated in the church until the coming of the kingdom of God will liberate the universe from mortality and the church will be no more because God has perfected his communion with his creation.

Conversations on the Way

We must now return to the questions we raised at the end of the first section: What can the Christian community as it is concretely represented by the Christian churches contribute to a comprehensive interpretation of reality that takes the challenge of scientific prognoses of cosmic futility seriously and tries to respond to them in such a way that it neither ignores them nor simply adopts them as the ultimate truth for all spheres of reality? From the perspective of the Christian community the question can be phrased in this way: What must the Christian community contribute to the cultural conversation on eschatological questions if it wants to remain true to its being and task?

If we start with the second question, the first thing that has to be said is that the church may not absolve itself from the task of contributing to the cultural conversation on eschatological questions. On the one hand, it is the eschatological character of the gospel of Christ that shapes the being of the church as an institution of the interim. The church could only abstain from contributing to the cultural conversation on ultimate questions if it denies its own character as existing in the tension between the coming of Christ and the full actualization of the kingdom of God. On the other hand, the message that is entrusted to the church claims universal significance because of its eschatological character. If it would withdraw from cultural conversations on eschatological questions the church would betray the universal impact of its message and turn Christianity into a tribal religion for Christians. This is not to deny that this often happens. Sometimes the churches present themselves as organizations for the pursuit of private religious interests. The inevitable trivialization of the Christian message as an individual path to salvation understood as psychological well-being often accompanies the withdrawal from the public sphere. Consenting to the Enlightenment's creed that all religion must be essentially private is perhaps one of the most serious temptations of the church in the modern situation. As our brief sketch of the character of the church can show this is a temptation that must be resisted.

If, however, the concern with eschatological questions is inscribed on the very being of the church and if the universal claim of the gospel is not denied, the church must engage in public debate about eschatological questions. This means, first of all, that it must learn to listen to findings of the sciences and to the interpretations of the cultural situation offered in the humanities. It was one of Schleiermacher's great discoveries that all statements of Christian doctrine can be conceived as descriptions of the states of human life, as concepts of divine attributes or actions, and as assertions about the way the world is.[12] If we apply this to eschatology, then the church's message must contain reference to the created destiny of human beings to find fulfillment in communion with God, to the eschatological action of the triune God, and to the ultimate destiny of the

---

12. F. D. E. Schleiermacher, *Der christliche Glaube*, 7th ed., vol. 1 (Berlin: de Gruyter, 1960), §30. "Alle Sätze, welche die christliche Glaubenslehre aufzustellen hat, können gefaßt werden entweder als Beschreibungen menschlicher Lebenszustände, oder als Begriffe von göttlichen Eigenschaften und Handlungsweisen, oder als Aussagen von den Beschaffenheiten der Welt; und alle diese Formen haben immer nebeneinander bestanden."

world. With regard to the type of statement there is a clear interface between the statements the sciences make about the final states of cosmic history and the discourse of the church about the ultimate destiny of creation. The church has far too long accepted the Kantian separation of the world into a realm of necessity investigated by science and a realm of freedom that is the domain of morality, of the humanities and religion. This has contributed to the withdrawal of the church from the public sphere and to its development into a highly specialized institution catering to private religious needs. It has also supported the tendency that many people in the church seem to be of a divided mind, accepting the findings of the sciences in everyday life, on the one hand, and consenting to the consolations of faith on Sundays, on the other, all the time hoping that the two realms should never meet. Not criticizing this attitude more severely shows a serious loss of theological nerve in the churches. If the world the Christian message talks about is the same as the world investigated by the sciences, we have to assume that the findings of the sciences have some connection to what Christians believe the world to be. Furthermore, if Calvin was right that the Holy Spirit is the source of all truth, then people in the church should approach the work of the sciences with the expectation that the Holy Spirit has not cut scientific activity altogether out of the sphere of his operation. It is the commitment to its own being and to its own message that should persuade the church to open its doors to a serious conversation with the findings of science. Only in this way can it avoid presenting its understanding of God as a "God of the gaps" left by scientific investigation. One of the first effects of opening the church's doors to a serious conversation with the findings of science could be the reintegration of the questions of natural theology into the discourse of the church. The fact that much Christian natural theology exists today in a rather loose relationship to the Christian church points not only to deficiencies in these conceptions of natural theology but more so to the inability of the church to give a place for the questions discussed and the answers attempted in natural theology in ecclesial discourse and practice.

The specific contribution the church has to make on the basis of the gospel of Christ concerns the relationship between continuity and discontinuity which is at the heart of Christian faith. The message of the death and resurrection of Christ has an ontological content if it is truly eschatological, that is, if it is the paradigm for what will ultimately happen to creation. Scientific prognoses of the future of life on earth, of our solar system, and of the universe itself force us to acknowledge the utter contingency of all created life. It has a contingent beginning and a contingent end, whether that will be the cosmological heat death or the big crunch. A universe that is allowed "to make itself" will ultimately "unmake itself" as the very forces that have shaped its existence will bring destruction to the earth, the sun, and eventually the whole universe. On the basis of the scientific accounts there is little reason for evolutionary optimism and even less hope for a continued existence of a universe left to its own regularities.

From a Christian perspective this should not come as a surprise. If there is anything specific about Christian eschatology it consists in the fact that the finitude of created existence, be it personal, social, or cosmic, is taken seriously. Everything that is created has neither brought itself into being, nor can it maintain itself in being. The Christian hope based on the death and resurrection of Christ does not deny the finitude of all created beings but transcends it. The hopes of the finite to participate in eternal life are not based on its own nature but exclusively on God maintaining his unconditional creative relationship to what he has created even beyond death. While taking the threat of utter futility seriously, Christian hope is nevertheless left neither to the noble resignation of tragedy nor to the joyless mirth of farce. The gospel of Christ promises a continuity that is maintained beyond the discontinuity of the death of finite life, a continuity that is already promised in the proclamation of the gospel and in the celebration of the sacraments.

For Christians this is not a claim that will only be verified or falsified in the eschaton. Rather, the church maintains that the same pattern of discontinuity and continuity can already be experienced here in the justification of the sinner, which makes the sinner discontinuous with his own sinful action and assures him of the continuity of God's graceful relationship to him which offers him a new beginning, based on God's forgiveness and not on the sins of the past. The church is the place where the experience of grace in the present can provide a basis for hope in the future, because the gift of forgiveness just as the gift of new life after death has the same foundation, the cross and the resurrection of Christ, and follows the same pattern of God granting continuity where created possibilities are exhausted. Every experience of gratuitous forgiveness offers vindication of eschatological hope. This is perhaps the most the church can offer in the conversations on eschatological questions.

This can also indicate what the church can contribute to a comprehensive interpretation of reality that integrates physical cosmologies, metaphysical and religious visions of reality, and ethical orientations. The gospel of Christ and the celebration of the sacraments point to the connection between the different dimensions of reality. These connections are rooted in the relationship between the creative, the reconciling, and the perfecting agency of the triune God. God's reconciling action in the cross and resurrection of Christ appears in this way as the sign of God's faithfulness to his creation and at the same time as the beginning of the consummation of all things. The church that worships the triune God can separate neither the Creator from the redeemer, as Marcionites of all ages are prone to do, nor the material from the spiritual, in Manichean fashion.

This drive for integration is rooted both in the God that is worshipped in the Christian church and in the activity of worship itself. By its worship the church interprets the world in the horizon of the gospel and the gospel in the horizon of the world in the proclamation of the gospel. At the same it refers the physical and the spiritual to God as the creator and consummator of all things in its sacramental practice. And in all the activities of worship it gives praise to the God who is the ground of all being and in the end will be all in all. The worship of the church is therefore itself an exercise in integration in referring everything, all dimensions of reality, to God, which occurs not only for the church's sake but for the world. A church that is true to the God it worships can therefore never be content with the fragmentation of reality where the material is turned against the spiritual and the moral against the metaphysical.

At the same time the integration that is proclaimed by the church in its gospel and practiced in its worship is not a closed system, a completed totality. It is precisely the eschatological character of the gospel that prevents the closed integration of the dimensions of reality from becoming totalitarian. While the promise that God will be all in all acts as the drive for integration, it also prevents it from becoming a completed totality. It must be an open integration, open for its completion by God's action in the eschaton. This is an important point because it provides the basis for the critique of ideologies as closed systems of the interpretation of reality that is an essential part of the message of the church. While the message and practice of the church necessitate the integration of the dimensions of reality, the message nevertheless must leave reality open for God's eschatological action. The drive for integration and the necessary openness together constitute the capacity of the church for dialogue with other forms of the interpretation of reality.

The contribution of the church to the cultural discussion of eschatological questions consists as much in what the church *is* as in what the church *does*. The church documents in its being as an institution of the interim the eschatological tension between an orientation toward the eschaton which is, on the one hand, not yet fully actualized and, on the other, already at work in present reality. The total dependence on God's creative love, which is the ground of hope for the future, is already the foundation of the church in faith. On the basis of what the church *is*, it practices its ministry in the proclamation of the gospel and in the celebration of the sacraments. Thereby it offers a comprehensive interpretation of reality that is both integrated by and open for God's eschatological action in the future. The ontological order of that future already informs the present being and activity of the church. Thereby the church has its being as being on the way toward the fulfillment of what it now hopes and believes.

With this interpretation of reality the church creates a cultural space for the conversation about eschatological questions. A cultural space, a perspective for reading reality, is created through a particular form of interpreting reality which draws others into conversations about the true character of reality. Because its interpretation of reality is both integrative and open the church can offer a space for interpreting reality in which many viewpoints are invited to participate. The church does not achieve this openness by lowering its own profile or by disguising its identity. It is precisely because its character and message are rooted in the gospel of Christ that it offers space for conversations. These conversations are in a very real sense conversations on the way, on the way from the present to the eschaton. They therefore participate in the dynamic of God's eschatological action. They cannot reach a conclusion in the present, but must continue until the kingdom of God is fully actualized.

The message of the gospel is not dependent on already existing public spaces, it creates them through its public character and its universal claim to truth. However, this also means that the church must be publicly accountable for its views, which thereby become publicly contestable. But what else could be meant by being "ready to make your defense when anyone challenges you to justify the hope which is in you"?

Chapter 9

TIME AS A MORAL SPACE
Moral Cosmologies, Creation, and Last Judgment

WILLIAM SCHWEIKER

Timely Matters and Human Concern

We live in a time-obsessed world. Among advanced, late-modern societies the speed of travel and communication as well as production and consumption spells an unrelenting demand for instantaneous satisfaction of human desires and wants. The rhythms of nature — the facts of light and dark, dawn and dusk — are lost in the immediacy of an electronic world. Yet, ironically, we also witness the expansion of time consciousness. Young children readily speak of the life of galaxies and stars in billions of years; we understand the evolution of our species as short-term in relation to the long geological history of the earth. The anomie and anxiety seen in contemporary cultures are due in part to the fact that our lives are rocked between the demand for the immediate satiation and a deep awareness that we seem lost in a cosmic, eternal ocean of endless time. And this ambiguity of temporality — the press of the present against the relentless stretch of time — besets the majority of people on the planet in a more urgent way. Daily demands for sustenance collide with the slow, exhausting work of cultivation, production, and distribution. Starvation and disease are demeaning deaths at the crossing of hope for relief and actual decay.

However, no one experiences time as a brute fact. Human beings endow their timeliness with meaning. We configure time — pull together the fleeting present, the ever-fading past, and the anticipated future — through memory, hope, and the narratives we tell about our lives.[1] Put oddly, people inhabit time like a space in which they must orient their lives by what is deemed worth seeking in life. If one views the future with fear, imagines that entropy, decay, or doom is the final word, then the "space" of temporal life takes on a specific color and import. Conversely, to meet the future with zest, imagination, and some confidence that genuine triumphs are possible implies a view of the world, a coloration of existence. In late-modern Western societies apocalyptic fear, say of ecological disaster, mixes and conflicts with confidence in technological progress. How are we to understand

---

1. For the hermeneutical issues involved in this claim, see Hans Weder, "Hope and Creation," chap. 13 in this volume. Also see William Schweiker, *Mimetic Reflection: A Study in Hermeneutics, Theology, and Ethics* (New York: Fordham University Press, 1990).

the eschatological mood of the day, especially as it is manifest in moral beliefs and practices? The moral worldview, or moral cosmology, configured in divergent eschatological beliefs is the subject matter of the following pages. I intend to excavate divergent strata of Western thought, specifically modern beliefs about time and ancient apocalyptic beliefs, that collide and coalesce in contemporary consciousness. The final aim of our inquiry is to show how Christian convictions about time and time's end serve to respect and enhance the integrity of life.

The theme of eschatology is of course not new in Christian moral reflection. A good deal of twentieth-century Christian ethics has been preoccupied with eschatology. Theologians looking at the New Testament found a distinctive morality in the eschatological vision of Jesus and the early Christian community. The question was "to what extent can ancient eschatological texts inform present ethics?" Three answers have dominated thought. First, some scholars held that the eschatology of the New Testament meant its virtual irrelevance for contemporary life. Insofar as the end of the world does not seem immediately at hand, then the eschatology of early Christian texts marked by the expectation of an imminent end of the world is profoundly out of step with our age. Others insisted that Christians encounter the Word of God in the present as itself an eschatological event. The command of God or the claims of Christ on life encountered in the present are, in fact, eschatological events. For these thinkers, what is unique and distinctive about Christian ethics is its eschatological meaning. Finally, there were theologians who insisted on the already–not yet character of Christian eschatology. Christ's life and teaching provide direction for Christian existence even though the final realization of the reign of God, disclosed in the resurrection, is not yet fully realized in history.

This debate in Christian ethics continues even today. Yet the confines of the debate mean that Christian moralists often fail to probe deep enough into the relation between conceptions of time and morality. Oddly enough, there is, at least in the West, a deep and surprising connection between ideas about time and conviction about the moral context of human life. In what follows, I explore the connection between time and morality in conversation with the sciences, and, thereby, cast the question of eschatology and ethics in a different key. The heart of this recasting is around the idea of "new creation" as a regeneration of conscience and its meaning for the moral life (cf. 2 Cor. 5:17; Gal. 6:15). Through the idea of "new creation" I aim to render productive the tension between modern and ancient apocalyptic modes of thought. How then to proceed? We can begin by clarifying what is meant by a moral cosmology and why it is important for the relation between science and theology from the perspective of ethics.[2]

---

2. I should note that the kind of reflection I carry out in this chapter and elsewhere is what H. Richard Niebuhr once called "Christian moral philosophy." The intention of this work is not to apply dogma to life nor to speak only to the Christian community. The purpose of this kind of ethics is to unfold the moral meaning of Christian faith as it provides insight and guidance for our lives as moral creatures, as agents. On this see H. Richard Niebuhr, *The Responsible Self: An Essay in Christian Moral Philosophy*, introduction by James M. Gustafson with foreword by William Schweiker (Louisville, Ky.: Westminster/John Knox Press, 1999).

Comparing Moral Cosmologies

There are a number of possible ways to relate the findings of the sciences to ethics. One could argue that insofar as ethics is about human conduct and the norms and values to guide relations and actions, science has little to contribute. Knowing what kind of creatures we are, the way the physical universe works, or the lessons of history does not, and cannot, tell us what we "ought" to do. However, other possibilities of relating science and ethics are possible. Some moralists argue that the sciences show us limits on human action as well as propensities and orientations that must be considered in moral deliberation. Many classical Christian and non-Christian thinkers believed that "nature" indicates what we are to be and to do. For example, a maxim basic to ancient Stoic ethics was this: live according to nature. For these kinds of ethics the findings of science, at least sciences concerned with human nature, are basic to moral inquiry.

In order to explore the relation of science and ethics in diverse cultural contexts I propose the idea of moral cosmology.[3] A moral cosmology is sets of beliefs and valuations, often tacit in a culture, about how human beings are to orient themselves rightly and meaningfully in the texture of the physical cosmos. A moral cosmology thereby configures the intersection of two other perspectives on reality, namely, physical cosmologies aimed at understanding, explaining, and controlling physical processes (paradigmatically seen in the hard sciences) and speculative cosmologies that provide frameworks of meaning about what exceeds, but includes, the domain of human behavior and natural processes (seen, for instance, in mythologies and metaphysical systems).[4] Explaining the possible entropy of the universe is the stuff of physics; asking about "God" in relation to a universe so explained and experienced vexes a speculative cosmology. A moral cosmology, conversely, articulates how human agents can and ought to inhabit a universe open to these other ways of construing the way things are.

---

3. See William Schweiker, *Power, Value, and Conviction: Theological Ethics in a Postmodern Age* (Cleveland: Pilgrim Press, 1998). For a similar argument about the importance of diverse ways of "construing the world" see James M. Gustafson, *Ethics from a Theocentric Perspective*, 2 vols. (Chicago: University of Chicago Press, 1981, 1984). My idea of a moral cosmology is also related to, but distinct from, the account of cosmogony and ethical order outlined by Robin Lovin and Frank Reynolds. See their essay, "In the Beginning," in *Cosmogony and Ethical Order: New Studies in Comparative Ethics*, ed. Robin W. Lovin and Frank E. Reynolds (Chicago: University of Chicago Press, 1985). By speaking of cosmology, rather than cosmogony, I mean to signal a broader interest in ethical order than simply its origin. For a similar idea consider the conception of "cultural cosmologies" in William Stoeger's "Cultural Cosmology and the Impact of the Natural Sciences on Philosophy and Culture," chap. 5 in this volume. Yet I think it is important to speak of "moral cosmologies" to signal the fact that every human culture is marked by basic moral convictions and distinctions necessary for human life to have meaning, worth, and direction.

4. For a summary of the religious import of current physical cosmologies see Paul Davis, *God and the New Physics* (New York: Simon and Schuster, 1983). In our time the most radical speculative cosmology, as I am calling it, is found in "process philosophy." See A. N. Whitehead, *Process and Reality*, ed. D. R. Griffin and D. W. Sherburne (New York: Free Press, 1978). For other recent attempts to provide something like a moral cosmology, see Iris Murdoch, *Metaphysics as a Guide to Morals* (London: Penguin Press, Allen Lane, 1992), and also Hans Jonas, *The Imperative of Responsibility: In Search of an Ethics of the Technological Age*, trans. Hans Jonas and David Herr (Chicago: University of Chicago Press, 1984).

However, a moral cosmology is not simply built on other perspectives. It actually helps to provide criteria for what can count in other ways of construing reality. This fact is most obviously true about so-called prescientific worldviews. Egyptologist Jan Assmann has shown that for the ancient Egyptians the world "is ambiguous and has to be constantly disambiguated by the imposition of moral distinctions." And what is more, the "moral sphere which gods and men cooperate to institute and maintain prevails over 'natural' distinctions."[5] As we will see, the same can be said of New Testament apocalyptic discourse and some forms of modern ethics. At the deepest level, my argument must focus on this decisive point about the relation between moral distinctions and the domain of intelligibility in the face of the ambiguities of life. That work is the function of a moral cosmology.

The need to clarify the world morally is easily shown. The most primordial forms of what I call *moral terror* are surely chaos and tyranny. Moral chaos, which can take various forms, is any situation where the fabric of a culture has been rend asunder such that it is impossible meaningfully to orient life. The Greek term *chaos* simply means "empty space." This is contrasted, again in classical thought, with the idea of "cosmos," or an ordered realm. Ancient themes like the fear of banishment (say, Cain's fear of being banished from God's sight) to contemporary experiences of cultural breakdown in war, anomie, and meaninglessness, all testify — mythically and experientially — to the fact that moral chaos is a genuine human terror. So too with moral tyranny. This is a situation, again taking many forms, in which there is the wrongful imposition of markers of worth such that human life becomes distorted and destructive. Racism, sexism, and other ideologies are examples of precisely this kind of tyrannous imposition of distinctions of value. While chaos bespeaks the terror of the loss of a moral space, tyranny is a terror characterized by the realization that a wrongful authority has defined one's moral universe. In each case, there is a need to disambiguate the world.

The ambiguity of life is why the conflict between good and evil is found in so many of the world's mythologies and religions. This conflict is often conceived as warring "gods" or, in apocalyptic discourse, the conflict between "ages." What is at stake is the struggle to define the moral space of life, create a moral cosmology. The struggle is imagined as suprahuman, beyond the playing field of human action; it is also, as Assmann noted, not simply a matter of "nature." This is so because what is at issue is the very definition of the context within which distinctly human action can meaningfully take place. The cultural imagination grasps how central and radical the question of defining the moral space is for human life. Worldviews breed diverse attitudes and dispositions to life: resignation, hope, courage, despair, joy. The life we actually live is given substance by an operative moral cosmology expressed in the beliefs, practices, and institutions of a culture.

The kinds of classical Christian and modern moral cosmologies we will explore

---

5. Jan Assmann, *Moses the Egyptian: The Memory of Egypt in Western Monotheism* (Cambridge: Harvard University Press, 1997), 190.

hinge on quite divergent assessments about time's content. In each of these cases, a conception of time's end has fostered a worldview in which worth is bound to norms of right and wrong conduct separated from reflection on patterns and processes in the world.[6] In a word, we will investigate outlooks that severed the connection between a moral cosmology and accounts of existence attentive to physical processes (physical cosmology). These positions insist on discontinuity, rather than continuity, between the past, present, and future morally understood and the structure of the physical universe. Inquiry into the natural world — the domain of the natural sciences — is banished from providing any valid substantive content to our understanding of the human dilemma.

In my judgment, any viable engagement with the theme of eschatology in our age requires attending to the vitalities and limits, the processes and patterns, of life. In terms of ethics this means showing how claims about the complex integrity of life in its diverse forms rightly fund concepts of moral worth.[7] The sciences have something to teach us about the possibilities and limitations on human existence, even if, as is also the case, that knowledge informs but does not determine conceptions of good and evil, right and wrong. Happily, some scientists now insist that there is a confluence between eschatological beliefs and the fact that "physical process is open to the future. We live in a world of true becoming."[8] It would seem that "reality" is not so closed or "block-like" as modern physics often imagined. And this provides room for ideas of genuine transcendence. Endorsing an integrated cosmology that traces continuity between the present and the eschaton has radical moral implications.

Eschatological reflection consistent with an integrated cosmology means that the moral meaning of Christian faith cannot be a hidden "no" to finite existence in all of its limitation, wonder, and travail. Christian faith, if it is a real power in the world, must be a radical transformation of human existence and thus a moral regeneration of life. The new creation, the regeneration of conscience, is a way to think about faith's transformation of life within an integrated cosmology. On this account, the moral meaning of eschatological faith is the love of life and love of the living God even amid the pressing facts of finitude and its limitations. The new creation is a moral transformation by God's grace that enables and empowers us to respect and enhance the integrity of life. The disposition is not stoic resignation, false consolation for a better world, or a relentless pursuit of present goods. It is a real joy.[9] This kind of joy is a realistic response to the

---

6. By the term *worth* (or *value*) all that is meant is the complex way things matters to human beings, kinds of importance. Some things are *esteemed* as ends or good in themselves; others are *assigned* importance within a scheme of other purposes. Esteeming and assigning are acts of valuation, a power that is absolutely basic in human existence and culture. The root problem of eschatology, I contend, is about the rightful power or authority to create a scale of values (what is to be esteemed, what assigned value), thereby defining the moral space of life.

7. More precisely, what is at issue here is some form of moral realism and naturalism. For a discussion of the issues and also a realistic ethics of responsibility see William Schweiker, *Responsibility and Christian Ethics* (Cambridge: Cambridge University Press, 1995).

8. John Polkinghorne, *The Faith of a Physicist* (Minneapolis: Fortress Press, 1996), 25. Also see Polkinghorne's "Eschatology: Some Questions and Answers from Science," chap. 2 in this volume.

9. The term *real joy* designates joy in the real, a yes-saying to existence, and also genuine (real)

finitude, brokenness, violence, and suffering of life without a fall into despair or the hatred of life. In biblical terms, the attitude is spoken of as delight in the Lord. Christian joy enables a proper respect and enhancement of finite existence without the temptation to demean or idolize any finite reality.

What would a moral cosmology that made real joy basic to human life look like? With that question in hand, let me turn now to comparative analysis. The analysis of modern and apocalyptic moral cosmologies is a step toward constructive claims about "new creation" in theological ethics. We are, again, excavating strands of thought that have deeply informed Western cultures.

Empty Time and the Creation of Value

While we do not often notice it, one distinctive feature of the modern West is that "time" is understood to be empty. People assume that tomorrow is neither determined, and thus going to necessarily happen in some way, nor full of some reality to which they must respond. Of course, we might imagine that at some point everything will come to an end in a cosmic crunch. But on a more human scale, most people believe, and believe heartily, that in a genuine sense they make the future. This disconnection in the contemporary mind between a moral cosmology expressed in beliefs about making the future and current physical cosmology, with its debates about a cold or hot death for the universe, is what we need to understand. To do so requires some digging into modern thought about the connection between time and morality.

Modern philosophers like Immanuel Kant noted that we cannot see or touch time. Time is not a direct object of the senses. Given this, time must be defined differently; it must be understood as a *form* of all our experiences. Whatever we do in fact experience (like the sun streaming in the window) takes place in time, but time itself is not directly sensed. "Time" is, we can say, a form for knowing anything that we in fact know. I experience the warmth of the sun in the morning. Later in the day, I can recollect its radiance and the shadows it cast across my office walls. These experiences take place "in" time, as we say. Yet time itself

---

joy, true human happiness grounded in a delight in the divine. My argument is related to but distinct from other positions that have seen the prime religious question for the moral life to focus on how we respond to the facts of finite existence. Let me mention a few. Paul Tillich spoke of the "courage to be" in the face of anxiety and he contrasted this courage to stoic resignation. Yet Tillich could hardly speak of joy. Friedrich Nietzsche did speak of joy, a "yes-saying," to reality. For Nietzsche, this "joy" was about the increase of power in self to overcome resistance. He could not imagine a joy that delights in another, say in God. James M. Gustafson insists on a piety that consents to the powers bearing down and sustaining us. Consent is an apprehension of our place in reality consigned by God. Yet it is not a zest to participate in respecting and enhancing life. While close to Albert Schweitzer's "reverence for life," my account of faithful existence is not keyed to a pessimistic cosmology. Schweitzer, after all, read too much Schopenhauer. Likewise, I do not think — but cannot argue here — that responsibility for life means that all we face are "tragic" choices when life confronts and competes with life. Tragedy there is, and enough of it for all! Yet tragedy is not the whole (moral) story. On these positions see Paul Tillich, *The Courage to Be* (New Haven: Yale University Press, 1952); Friedrich Nietzsche, *Thus Spoke Zarathustra*, trans. R. J. Hollingdale (New York: Penguin Books, 1961); Gustafson, *Ethics from a Theocentric Perspective*; and Albert Schweitzer, *The Philosophy of Civilization* (New York: Prometheus Books, 1987).

is empty. This is important. It means that the most basic form in which people organize experience is without content. Further, there are two perspectives on time so defined: clock time (the perspective of nonpersonal markers of temporal succession) and experienced time. I experience the sun "in the morning" (clock time) but can also recall its feeling later in the day (experienced time). This doubleness in how to mark time is why, for instance, the very same lecture lasting fifty minutes can be experienced by one person as dragging on boring moment after boring moment while for another the experience of the lecture might be a flash. Our experience of time is not the same as the tools — like clocks — used to measure moments.

This understanding of time as a form of experience open to contrasting perspectives has a liberating effect. It means that the way the mind organizes experience is free from the material conditions that fund, make possible, and limit human life. Neither the clock nor the lecturer determines how we experience the event. If this is so about time, then we ought to be able to explore other ways in which the mind supplies "forms" for experience. That simple but radical point is basic to much modern ethics. Immanuel Kant, one of the decisive modern moral thinkers, reformulated the golden rule (cf. Matt. 7:12; Luke 6:31) along these lines. The moral law, he insisted, is that we ought always to treat persons with respect, that is, we ought to treat others and ourselves as ends and never only as a means to some other end (say, pleasure, power, or prestige). This law given by reason is the "form" which is to direct all my actions. Whatever course of action I choose — my vocation, hobbies, whatever — must, if it is to be moral, comport with the law given by reason. The moral law is free from, but determinative of, our embeddedness in the natural order as sentient, desiring, social beings. The moral law of respect for persons is something we bring to our encounters with others. It is not found in nature or experienced like something we touch or see. It is the work of reason, giving "form" to our actions and relations if they are to be truly moral. In the terms of ethical theory, this is called "moral formalism."

One must grasp the significance of the connection between moral formalism and a conception of time as empty. The moral law is defined on purely rational grounds; it is not funded or limited by claims about the natural world or our lives as sentient creatures. Further, reason is best conceived as legislative, as a rule-giving power: "reason" legislates the forms in which any possible experience or maxim for action is to be grasped. In this way, the emptiness of time and the formality of the moral law bespeak the power of the human mind to organize its world and determine norms for action. Time is empty, but it is also a moral space: it is the space for the rule-giving work of reason. The future is open, something we make, and the only rules for our making are moral ones. The point is that, oddly enough, in much modern ethics there is a connection between how morality is understood and how "time" is defined.

This connection between empty time and rational morality combats moral terror. The moral law rooted in reason means that, at least in terms of moral principle, human life is never devoid of moral order. Moral conflict and ambiguity can be overcome because human beings all possess the same power of reason.[10] Moral tyranny is also countered. Insofar as I am acting on the moral law that my reason provides, I am genuinely free; I am autonomous. I need not bow to any power foreign to my will: the state, my parents, religious authorities. I have the grounds to criticize and revise any appeal to moral authority that challenges the rational moral law. The very formality of the moral law intertwined with a conception of time as "empty" is a bulwark against tyranny and chaos. It backs deeply held modern convictions about the freedom of conscience.

The legacy of modernity in the West is the working out of some of the ideas we have just noted. Communities embody their own moral worlds, construct their identities, because it is the linguistic forms, patterns of social power relations, histories — that is, the socially contingent "forms" of experience — that give order to experience. The moral implication of this is not hard to imagine. Moral value is not findable; there is no meaning to human existence outside our making. As Irving Singer puts it, meaning in life simply is the creation of value with respect to human needs and inclinations. And this is true even of death, the seemingly most powerful counter-example to the claim that we give form to human time. In Singer's words, "Death is so great a problem for human beings only because it intrudes upon our search for a meaningful life."[11] Here is the final triumph of the self's authority to create value as a bulwark against chaos and tyranny, even the ravages of death.

The current eschatological mood is marked by developments in philosophy and the pervasive cultural assumption, voiced by Singer, that the job of human life is about making, not finding, meaning in existence. The shared point of contact between all of these developments is that time is a moral space, but in the uniquely modern sense that it is "empty," awaiting us — as individuals and communities — to give it content. The right to create value is ours and ours alone simply because moral values — how we organize the world as a place in which we can live meaningfully — are not "out there" to be found. We must create them. This is the final triumph of the disconnection between sciences and ethics. Not only cosmic death but even individual death does not count against our power to create value. How then are we to take seriously the embeddedness of human life in the process of reality not open to our manipulation?

Full Time and the Coming of the Lord

The basic features of the moral cosmology of the modern, secular West just explored stand in radical contrast to many traditional Christian conceptions. This is most clear if we explore conceptions that bind eschatological thinking to an apoc-

---

10. This claim, we might note, is stressed by present-day Kantians like Jürgen Habermas. See his *Moral Consciousness and Communicative Action* (Cambridge: MIT Press, 1990).

11. Irving Singer, *Meaning in Life: The Creation of Value* (New York: Free Press, 1992), 71.

alyptic outlook in terms of "final judgment."[12] Take, as an example, the discourse of Mark 13:24–27 (NRSV).

> But in those days, after that suffering, the sun will be darkened, and the moon will not give its light, and the stars will be falling from heaven, and the power in the heavens will be shaken. Then they will see "the Son of Man coming in clouds" with great power and glory. Then he will send out the angels, and gather his elect from the four winds, from the ends of the earth to the ends of heaven.

This is, admittedly, extravagant, excessive discourse. Time is saturated with moral meaning. The text pictures the end-time as a cataclysmic, final judgment in which the elect will be saved. This divine is construed as moral judge; the one who rewards the righteous and punishes the wicked. Further, the point of the "final judgment" is to relieve moral ambiguity. Moral order has been established to which "nature" adheres. The "elect," while scattered around the globe, are gathered into the divine reign. The ambiguity of life is overcome by God's judgment. The discourse presents a moral cosmology under the sovereign authority of the divine, an authority that will be exercised in judgment.

The passage relates to Mark 13:3–8, in which there is discourse by Jesus on the signs before the end-time. Along with 13:14–20, the desolating abomination, the apocalyptic discourse is tied to the opening of the chapter and the destruction of the temple. And this means, of course, that the sayings about the coming of the Son of man are linked to the destruction of the ancient "Temple-State" (a social world defined by the complex relation between state and temple, king and priest). One might easily imagine that the challenge to that world by Jesus would lead to his death. The social, political, and religious reality of the Temple-State, while itself an answer to the problem of chaos, was seen as tyrannous. The destruction of Jerusalem (70 C.E.), and with it the moral universe of Second Temple Jews, is set within a wider compass, specifically a claim about the end of time. Of course, there are complex textual questions about Q, the developing discourse about the Christ, and the relation between the text and the Roman-Jewish war. All of those matters are beyond the scope of this inquiry.[13]

From a literary perspective, Mark 13 reinscribes Hebraic prophetic discourse in stressing the authority of Jesus over all the world. The vision of the Son of man is the crucial affirmation of this passage. Reflecting Dan. 7:13 — and thus, we might note, imaginatively inscribing past prophecy in future events — the text is about the coming of the Son to inherit his kingdom. In the Book of Daniel the "coming" of someone "like a human being" is toward the Ancient of Days. "To him was given dominion and glory and kingship" (Dan. 7:14). The direction of the "coming" is quite distinct. In Mark, the Son of man *comes to* the elect, from the winds, the earth, and the heavens. In this sense, his coming is not only about

---

12. For another examination of apocalyptic discourse, albeit in the Hebrew scriptures, see Patrick D. Miller, "Judgment and Joy," chap. 11 in this volume. See also his essay "Creation and Covenant," in *Biblical Theology: Problems and Perspectives*, ed. Steven J. Kraftchick, Charles D. Myers Jr., and Ben C. Ollenburger (Nashville: Abingdon Press, 1995), 155–68.

13. On the topic of the Jesus movement and Temple-State I have found helpful Burton Mack, *Who Wrote the New Testament? The Making of the Christian Myth* (New York: HarperCollins, 1995).

dominion and the Ancient One; it also draws together in a unique event domains of reality (heaven, earth, winds) and differentiates the elect from others.

A moral cosmology is thus created in terms of the Son of man. This Son of man was thought to be an individual, superhuman person possessing heavenly power and glory. His coming constitutes a new reality defined by (1) a differentiation of the elect from others, (2) the intersection of domains of reality (earth, heaven, the winds), (3) manifesting his "power and glory," (4) signaled by cosmic events (stars will be falling...), and (5) overturning the Temple-State while inscribing previous Jewish expectation into the future. To accept this cosmology is difficult for moderns! And one of the root difficulties is that rather than answering problems of chaos and tyranny, the text seems to a modern secular mindset to enact them. Nature tumbles into confusion at the Son of man's coming; the division of human into elect and nonelect could be an act of moral tyranny. Fear seems to be the only plausible attitude toward such a conception of time.

Of course, it may be, historically speaking, that much apocalyptic discourse is a defensive move to protect some threatened way of life. When a people's world is endangered, as in the Roman-Jewish war, many need to imagine a situation in which, in highly dualistic ways, the "good" are rewarded (gathered from the ends of the earth) and the "bad" punished. But that sociological observation, while pertinent, is not the whole story. We are interested in how apocalyptic discourse presents a cosmology that links time and morality. P. D. Hanson is surely right:

> Apocalyptic eschatology, then, is neither a genre, nor a socio-religious movement, nor a system of thought, but rather a religious perspective, a way of viewing divine plans in relation to mundane realities.... In its view toward the future as the context of divine saving and judging activity, apocalyptic eschatology can be seen as a continuation of prophetic eschatology.[14]

It is clear that this apocalyptic outlook is one in which all institutions and structures, religious and political, are subjected to a cosmic order of justice. More fundamentally, the order of justice, cosmically understood, is not an end (*finis*) striven for, but a fullness (*telos*) that is "coming to" earth in power and glory. The moral space of life is created from the fullness of cosmic justice, God's saving and judging acts. The future is not something people strive for and fill with meaning, it comes to the present, interrupts the course of life. This seems to answer the principal social fact that spawns apocalyptic thinking, namely, the disintegration of socioreligious structures and their supporting myths. The threat of chaos and tyranny provokes the articulation of a new moral universe. But it is a vision in which the conditions for life are reassured not through human action but by divine acts. God rules. That is the primordial fact creating the moral space of life.

---

14. P. D. Hanson, "Apocalypticism," in *Interpreter's Dictionary of the Bible: Supplementary Volume* (Nashville: Abingdon, 1976), 29–30.

Assessment of Moral Cosmologies

The accounts of time and time's end we have been exploring have helped to shape the moral outlook of Western cultures. There are profound differences and similarities between the kind of apocalyptic eschatology examined and the modern idea of "empty time." What are these similarities and differences? In each case, a conception of time and time's end is an answer to moral chaos and tyranny. The question of power and authority is taken as *the* defining fact of the moral cosmos: the power and authority of reason or the sovereignty of God. Much is at stake, accordingly, for determining the rightful or legitimate power to create the moral cosmos. Strategies for what in fact validates claims to legitimacy differ: in the apocalyptic eschatology we explored there is an appeal to a vision of cosmic justice; in modern, formalist ethics it is what, abstractly or concretely, fosters negotiation of moral differences, supports equality, and maximizes human freedom. Yet despite these differences in patterns of legitimation, our comparison has shown that two strands of tradition shaping contemporary life in the West are defined by the exercise of power to create value and moral order, legislative and sovereign power.

That is not all, however. It is also clear that despite the similarities between a modern outlook, focusing on empty time and human sovereignty in the creation of value, and apocalyptic eschatologies there are profound differences. In the Gospel of Mark the implied legitimation of Jesus as Son of man is messianic hope and a vision, rooted in the prophets, of cosmic justice. Insofar as Jesus meets that hope and enacts that vision, he is the legitimate Son of man. In terms of the modern moral vision, typically expressed by Kant, one cannot appeal to God or nature, divinity or cosmic justice, since such appeals would be heteronymous, tyrannous. The validation of the moral law must be in terms of its formal characteristics and rational necessity. While the discourse of Mark 13 was dependent for its legitimacy on an implied, if not articulate, cosmic justice, such is not the case in modern conceptions of empty time. There is no moral order outside our making time meaningful. This is the deepest implication of the contrast between full and empty time.

Comparing these moral cosmologies exposes the weakness of each. The modern conception of empty time and human sovereignty in the creation of value is a bulwark against tyranny. Yet the danger is that the human search for freedom will tyrannize its environment, since that environment has no moral standing outside of human aspiration. The modern outlook, by disconnecting morality from the whole domain of natural reality, might actually be nihilistic, a denial of finite and contingent life in order to maximize human power. Witness, for instance, the growing ecological crisis. The form of apocalyptic eschatology we explored in Mark's gospel is a bulwark against moral chaos through its implied affirmation of a larger cosmic/moral order. And yet the fissure between moral authority and cosmic order can devolve into a new form of tyranny. This possibility has, of course, actualized itself all too often within apocalyptic movements. Mark's apocalypse portrays a situation of confusion about sustaining structure of life: the sun will be dark, the moon will give no light, and the stars will fall from the sky. Ironically, a discourse that was aimed at countering moral chaos could in its zeal to assert the absolute, free sovereign judgment of God reduce all else to chaos.

I have isolated points of instability in these moral cosmologies: the modern outlook aimed at combating moral tyranny can endorse a tyrannous relation to the rest of the world; apocalyptic discourse, in no less an ironic way, seeks to overcome moral chaos and yet can lead to just that condition. These points of instability are not merely logical possibilities; they have manifested themselves in the historical legacy of the Christian movement and modern societies. Realism and modesty require that we acknowledge that a fail-safe position is beyond our grasp. Still, comparative labor does provide some direction for constructive reflection to avoid these problems.

The Time of New Creation

I have tried to show that conceptions of time are interpretive prisms through which a culture understands its moral world. Those conceptions are articulated in a variety of eschatological discourses. As a interpretive framework, any form of eschatological discourse presents a view of the world and orientation for how to live in it; it expresses a moral cosmology. Yet we have also seen, through brief comparison, that ancient apocalyptic eschatology and modern accounts are internally unstable. They too easily breed attitudes that are troubling and dangerous for actual life. The twin terrors of chaos and tyranny are unleashed when it is clear, as it surely is now, that limited resources, increasing demand, and unjust patterns of distribution mark each and every nation and culture on this planet. Indeed, the single most pressing fact of our so-called postmodern age may well be the realization that, despite technological progress, the ecosystem is limited; it is not completely malleable to our purposes. The dream of an open future and unending progress is pitifully naive. Any form of ethics that in principle undercuts the input of the natural and social sciences in our assessment of courses of action and the limits on human desire is dangerous.[15] At the same time, ancient hopes in God's coming to separate the elect from the damned, to cast the stars from their course, are problematic when they feed religious and cultural conflict or ecological abuse. The eschatological mood of our day, a mood of skepticism, despair, and even fear, clearly bespeaks a deep quest for renewal. There is a quest for the renewal of the human heart so that we might live rightly amid realms of reality that sustain and make possible life and its flourishing. New creation, as an eschatological discourse for a rich moral cosmology, might speak to the mood of the day. It might articulate for us a transformation of life. Can we make sense of this discourse?

These are, of course, complex matters. Yet two things seem important. First, we must take from modern thought the insight that forms of perception and sensibility

---

15. For example, see Stanley Hauerwas and William H. Willimon, *Resident Aliens* (Nashville: Abingdon Press, 1989).

are not simply given in what is apprehended. Human, cultural practices are at work in rendering life meaningful. But we must grasp how forms of experience are not the empty categories of "reason" but, rather, complex linguistic media that work to shape perceptions for good or ill.[16] The discourse of "new creation" is the symbolic means Christians can use to form sensibilities and understanding. The idea of new creation is bound, scripturally, to the idea of a renewal of covenant between God and humanity in the depths of the human self. Specifically, Paul writes, "Do not be conformed to this world, but be transformed by the renewing of your minds, so that you may discern what is the will of God — what is good and acceptable and perfect" (Rom. 12:2). This is linked to Paul's ideas about the "law written on the heart" and thus ideas about "conscience." In other words, the divine will resonates in the depth of human life (the "heart") and this is the condition for a "perception" of what is good and perfect. In this way, the discourse of new creation is nothing less than a "form" of experience; it is a prism through which one is to see the world. Unlike the modern turn to the formal structure of the moral law, a form that is empty and correlates to a conception of time, this form — the law written in the heart — is not empty. It is precisely a way to participate in God's good creation, to see the good and perfect, rather than a form for guiding the projection of our purposes.

Persons and communities touched by this transformation of life, this new creation, are saved from moral chaos but in such a way that the moral law — the good and perfect — is anything but tyrannous. Conscience is not some faculty of the mind or depth of existence; it is, rather, the dynamic of our lives as valuing creatures. The new creation, as God's gracious renewal of conscience, is a way of life in the world marked by a realistic affirmation of finite existence as good. This combats despair and fear without false consolation. It is a primal yes-saying to reality as God's creation. Furthermore, this renewal of mind and heart (conscience) is not simply a claim about the nature of reason; it is also about participating in the covenantal community. The transformed conscience that enables a perception of the good and perfection is not a "point" in the self; it is not the biblical version of pure practical reason! Rather, the "conscience" is a way of living in the world within the discursive, ritual, and communicative patterns of a community defined by new creation. It is a way of life in which reality is apprehended through the good and perfect.

This brings us to the second important thing to note. If we learned from modern moral cosmologies the need to explore "forms" of experience, then we can reclaim, but transform, an insight from apocalyptic beliefs about "full time." This will lend a note of realism to cosmological inquiry avoiding the impression that "new creation" is simply a matter of how we decide to interpret the world. What is at stake are beliefs about the way things are. The idea of new creation as an eschatological belief does not bespeak apocalyptic judgment wherein the stars

---

16. In this respect, constructive moral cosmological reflection is postcritical or hermeneutical in nature. On this see Schweiker, *Power, Value and Conviction*, esp. chap. 4, "Understanding Moral Meanings." A similar claim is made on behalf of a realistic biblical theology by Michael Welker, *God the Spirit*, trans. John F. Hoffmeyer (Minneapolis: Fortress Press, 1994).

fall from the sky.[17] It is, rather, about the renewal and enlivening of conscience precisely as created. Insofar as creation is more than nature, that is, it designates the bringing into being and sustaining of the right integration of diverse realms of existence (earth, wind, heaven; animals, humans, culture), then what is being renewed is not simply natural resources or how we see the world, but, rather, the human capacity to live with justice, with integrity or the right relations, among these domains of reality. The "new creation" is not about renewable resources: we cannot imagine that it can be used to endorse the ecological naivete and thirst for unending consumption that blatantly disregards the real and present limits on human activity. Rather, new creation is about a renewed "mind," a new conscience, empowered to seek the integration, establish just relations, between domains of reality so that life, with its specific finite limits, might flourish. Human beings are empowered to participate in this renewed integrity; they are enlivened by a transformed mind to be participants in God's good creation. There is continuity and discontinuity between creation and new creation.

Time is not empty; it is full. Yet the fullness of time is not linked to apocalyptic judgment; it is not about how the sovereign Lord passes judgment on the world. Better put, new creation is a judgment but one in which creation is not negated, swept away, transcended; creation is endorsed as good. Christian faith affirms our finitude and the finitude of the world as good (cf. Gen. 1:31). Wherever there are signs of dynamic integrity, the confluence of patterns and processes of life that enable the furtherance of life, then there are "signs" of God's good creation. Signs experienced by a transformed conscience are nothing else than grace. Time is not an empty form of experience; it is not the simple movement of physical reality; it is not the event of final judgment. For Christian faith, time is understood as part of the renewal of life and also as one of God's good creatures. In order to orient life rightly within God's good creation requires in the face of human violence and folly the renewal of the conscience to perceive the good and perfect. The task of human life so understood is to respect and enhance the integrity of life.

And what of the sciences, especially the natural sciences? The interpretation of "new creation" offered here, an interpretation that traces the continuities in "creation" and assigns "newness" to a regeneration of conscience, opens a new space for dialogue between the sciences and ethics. "Creation," we might say, is the domain of worth; "new" is a transvaluation of our values, how we are enabled to respond to the goodness of existence and God's transformation of patterns of life. The "new creation" is an ongoing revolution in sensibilities and attitudes.[18] Theologically stated, an adequate account of the "new creation" as the final judgment about finite life demands that we move — at long last — beyond the conflict between revealed and natural theology. It is, to use terms introduced above, a moral cosmology that mediates physical and speculative cosmologies. Like traditional natural theology, the image of new creation opens a space for

---

17. On this see, for example, Welker, *God the Spirit*, and also Jürgen Moltmann, *The Coming God: Christian Eschatology* (Minneapolis: Fortress Press, 1996).

18. On the idea of "revelation" as an ongoing revolution in human faith see H. Richard Niebuhr, *The Meaning of Revelation* (New York: Macmillan, 1941).

reflection on the patterns and processes of reality as providing some indication of God's will and way for human beings. Like standard revealed theology, "new creation" is not something we infer from the rounds of nature; it is a divine gift, a renewal of heart and mind, that cannot be achieved but only received. This vision, crossing through natural and revealed theologies as well as physical and speculative cosmologies, is consistent with the real joy that is the root and fruit of Christian life. In fact, real joy simply is the genuine freedom of the Christian to live and work within the goodness of creation.

Conclusion

The fact of the new creation means that Christians can let the sciences have their full say in any account of the nature of reality, because that reality in all its wonder and limitation will be seen as part and parcel of God's good creation. This is not to deny the obvious sinfulness, brokenness, and horrors of life; it is not to deny that Christians can and must and may work to end forms of injustice and suffering. What it does say is that Christian faith — as a form of real joy — can see through the brokenness of the world to the good that shines in reality. Is this not the moral cosmological meaning of the incarnation? Christians combat evil and injustice because life is good and a divine gift to be treasured. This is the most profound moral meaning of "final judgment." To live the new creation is to dedicate one's life to combat all that unjustly demeans and destroys life out of a profound love of life and in the name of divine goodness. It is even to love the enemy.

We are not lost in an ocean of meaningless time or awaiting the damnation of the evil. The Christian eschatological witness is that we live within the theater of God's goodness and therefore are required and empowered to respect and enhance the integrity of life. On this account of new creation, the sciences help us to understand the shape, direction, and limitations of reality and thus fund Christian moral reflection. The exploration of patterns and processes of natural and social reality are nothing other than attempts to grasp signs of God's purposes for this good creation. Those signs will give aid to providing orientation in life. And finding orientation is, of course, the principal challenge facing persons and communities.

Part 3

ESCHATOLOGY IN THE BIBLICAL TRADITIONS

THEMES OF THE END-TIME

Introduction to Part 3

READING THE BIBLE WITH "THE END" IN VIEW

Donald H. Juel and Patrick D. Miller

For Christians, thinking about life and death matters has always involved the Bible. It is probably true that in the last decades the Bible has not enjoyed as prominent a place in church and society and has thus had a lesser role in shaping contemporary imagination. While this may be an indictment of the church and its teachers, it does not lessen Christian commitment to the scriptures as a critical participant in contemporary conversation and reflection. The essays in this section seek to bring biblical perspectives to bear on the theme of eschatology.

A question that immediately arises is where one should look to find the theme. The answer depends on our perspective. In Israel's scriptures, the Christian Old Testament, there are passages whose authors most probably did not understand what they said and wrote as having to do with the distant future and whose ancient readers would not so have understood their works. Jeremiah's promise of a "righteous branch for David" (33:15) probably referred to a candidate from the Davidic line whose coming could be expected in the near future. The author of 2 Samuel and his contemporary audience probably understood Nathan's promise to David of a "seed" whose throne God would establish and whom God would call "son" (2 Sam. 7:10–14) as a promise of Solomon's birth — or at least as a promise confined to the more proximate future. Later generations, however, heard the words of both passages as a promise of a final ruler, the Messiah-King, the "branch of David who will arise at the end of days to save Israel," as an interpretation of 2 Sam. 7:14 in the Dead Sea Scrolls puts it. The New Testament understands the verses in a similar way, quoting them in such passages as Heb. 1:5 to refer to Jesus, the Messiah, God's Son.

If we read from the perspective of post–Old Testament literature, it would be fair to say that an "eschatological" text is one that is so recognized by faithful readers. For such readers, the intention of the original author and the location of a passage in its original historical setting are not determinative of a passage's meaning. That the legitimate meaning of a passage is confined to its original setting and the author's intention is a modern suggestion that is not faring particularly well in contemporary hermeneutical discussions.

The question is a bit more complex even with respect to the New Testament in its postbiblical (post–Old Testament) environment. Such promises of a "messiah" and a messianic age that faithful Jews understood as referring to a final chapter in history were applied to Jesus, the "finality" of whose ministry did not include the end of history. Nevertheless, it is fair to observe that there are major differences between the Old Testament and the New Testament when it comes to "eschatological" questions. New Testament authors, like their Jewish and Greco-Roman contemporaries, dealt explicitly with the end of the world and what they imagined lay beyond it. The resurrection of the dead, an idea not prominent in ancient Israel, had found a secure place in Jewish piety before the Christian era and, after the destruction of the temple in 70 C.E., became part of emerging "orthodoxy." Paul could write to believers in Corinth that "if for this life only we have hoped in Christ, we are of all people most to be pitied" (1 Cor. 15:19). That the world would end and that God's promises had to do with what would follow was a prominent topic in both Jewish and Christian literature.

If the first centuries of this era were characterized by confidence that God's promises included the distant future of the whole created order as well as more proximate matters, there was, nevertheless, considerable diversity among the various scenarios. Some expected the advent of a prophet like Moses, others a king from the line of David. Some apparently looked little beyond a restored kingship and a golden era; others believed the future would include the passing away of the present world and the birth of something new. Paul's reference to all creation "groaning in travail," awaiting the birth of a new age (Rom. 8:18–23), suggests he belongs with those whose view of the future may be characterized as "apocalyptic," though his argument to the Galatian churches about freedom from the law and his comment that the Lord Jesus Christ "gave himself for our sins to set us free from the present evil age" (Gal. 1:3–4) almost make it seem that "the end" has in a sense already taken place.

The difficult question is how we will read the Old Testament. Biblical scholars are unwilling simply to exclude the matter of historical location in reading biblical texts. There were clearly times in ancient Israel when speculation about the distant future and renewal of life beyond "the end" was not central to religious imagination. It is probably only in Daniel that we can speak of a genuinely "apocalyptic" view. Yet already out of the experience of exile and the subsequent history of Judaism in the following centuries, expectations for a final reign of God began to point toward a farther and universal horizon at the end of history. Still, we cannot be certain at what point thinking about the more proximate future ceased to be sufficient within the Jewish community and genuine "eschatological" reflection was born. It is unnecessary to answer the question here, but it does indicate the difficulty of identifying "eschatological" texts in the Old Testament if we are to take seriously the vantage point of its authors. The decisive question is what passages help us reflect on "the end" and how the perspective of biblical authors can challenge our experience of the world and open us to larger possibilities.

The claim of the various authors is not that the biblical passages cited are the best representatives of eschatological texts but that reflecting on these particular works is fruitful for Christian reflections on "the end."

Chapter 10

FAITH AT THE *NULLPUNKT*

WALTER BRUEGGEMANN

Ancient Israel in the Hebrew Bible/Old Testament is capable of thinking theologically about the future of the world and about the future destiny of individual persons.[1] Its preferred and most characteristic mode of thought, however, is done through critical theological reflection about the community of Israel itself, its situation in the world, its position vis-à-vis its God, Yahweh, and its future amid the vagaries of history.

I

While historical questions about the origin and character of Israel are now deeply unsettled and disputed, Israel's theological tradition is not ambiguous. Israel understands that it exists in the world as a peculiar people and as an object of Yahweh's peculiar attention precisely because of the initiatory attentiveness of Yahweh, who in sovereign power and self-giving love invests in the life of Israel. This remarkable sense of *origination in gift* is expressed in two strands of tradition.[2] First, Israel's origin is articulated in the *ancestral traditions* of Genesis 12–36, wherein Yahweh without reason or explanation addresses father Abraham (and mother Sarah) and summons them to a life of obedience as a carrier of Yahweh's blessing for the world. Yahweh's commitment to Israel, moreover, is reiterated in each new generation as a future is granted, always in the eleventh hour, with the birth of an heir who can continue the peculiar life of Israel into the next generation.

The second root tradition is the *Exodus narrative* (Exodus 1–15), wherein Yahweh intervenes decisively on behalf of an abused and suffering people. Yahweh's immense power overrides the oppressive regime of the pharaoh in Egypt and makes possible an escape from slavery with an alternative life given in a land out of the reach of the oppressive pharaoh.[3] This decisive intervention on the part

---

1. See the summary of Donald E. Gowan, *Eschatology in the Old Testament* (Philadelphia: Fortress Press, 1986).

2. See Rolf Rendtorff, "Die theologische Stellung des Schöpfungsglaubes bei Deuterojesaja," *ZTK* 51 (1954): 3–13, and, more generally, Walter Brueggemann, *Theology of the Old Testament: Testimony, Dispute, Advocacy* (Minneapolis: Fortress Press, 1997), 413–17.

3. Unlike the ancestral narratives, the Exodus tradition is deeply permeated with violence whereby Yahweh acts and secures the future of Israel. This defining violence in Israel's faith is critically explored

of Yahweh is belatedly articulated in the tradition of Deuteronomy as an act of inexplicable love: "It was because the Lord loved you and kept the oath that he swore to your ancestors, that the Lord has brought you out with a mighty hand, and redeemed you from the house of slavery, from the hand of Pharaoh king of Egypt" (Deut. 7:8). This articulation has the merit of linking the two originary traditions of Genesis and Exodus.[4]

A third, subsequent tale of origin concerns the peculiar commitment Yahweh is said to make to the *Jerusalem establishment* of temple and dynasty (Ps. 78:67–71). It is certain that Jerusalem and its theopolitical establishment are no part of Israel's self-presentation of origins. Later power arrangements nonetheless required its incorporation, and so "Zion and David" are also understood as gifts of Yahweh's remarkable and inexplicable self-giving that has the capacity to create a *novum*, to bring to be that which has no warrant except the undomesticated resolve of Yahweh. All of these traditions attest to the power of newness present in the character and resolve of Yahweh.

II

The power of *novum*, discerned in Yahweh and characteristically regarded as "unconditional," is nonetheless marked by a proprietary insistence on the part of Yahweh. That is, Yahweh is not just a giver of gifts, but has a determined and enduring intention for the newness wrought that is Israel. Yahweh imposes a will and character upon the newness that is Israel. For that reason, Moses at Sinai hears from Yahweh a loud, determined "if" (Exod. 19:5–6).[5] Israel as a people generated out of Yahweh's love is to be responsive and obedient to Yahweh who gives it life. That intention of Yahweh for Israel, moreover, is deeply and insistently ethical. For that reason, the extended address at Sinai is "Torah," direction, guidance, and instruction for how Israel is to live in the world.[6] The people of promise and of emancipation are immediately and inalienably a community under command.[7] The interface between the tradition of promise and of covenantal demand is a defining and bearable theological tension. In the actual lived life of Israel, however, that tension is not easy to manage or sustain.

---

by Regina M. Schwartz, *The Curse of Cain: The Violent Legacy of Monotheism* (Chicago: University of Chicago Press, 1997).

4. On the relationship between the two traditions, see R. W. L. Moberly, *The Old Testament of the Old Testament: Patriarchal Narratives and Mosaic Yahwism*, OBT (Minneapolis: Fortress Press, 1992).

5. On the cruciality of this moment of "if," see Martin Buber, *Moses: The Revelation and the Covenant* (Atlantic Highlands, N.J.: Humanities Press International, 1988), esp. 101–9, and James Muilenburg, *The Way of Israel: Biblical Faith and Ethics* (New York: Harper and Brothers, 1961), esp. 54–62.

6. See the definitive study of Torah by Frank Crüsemann, *The Torah: Theology and Social History of Old Testament Law* (Edinburgh: T. & T. Clark, 1996).

7. On the relation of promise and command, see Jon D. Levenson, *Sinai and Zion: An Entry into the Jewish Bible* (New York: Winston Press, 1985), and, from a Christian perspective, John Bright, *Covenant and Promise: The Prophetic Understanding of the Future in Pre-Exilic Israel* (Philadelphia: Westminster Press, 1976).

III

The "if" of Moses does prevail. It is given a classic expression in Deut. 8:19–20. The same ethical seriousness, however, is endlessly sounded and reiterated by a series of prophets. We may suppose that the prophets arise quite ad hoc and give varied voicing to the ethical urgency of Yahweh, arising no doubt from covenantal traditions but also from a felt sense of the failure of Israel. But even if their actions are ad hoc, in the final form of Israel's faith the prophets are all of a piece (see 2 Kings 17:13). All of the prophets, in sum, warned and anticipated a dire future for an Israel that refused to come to terms with Yahweh's ethical passion. No doubt the privileged in the royal arena had confidence in their own privilege and advantage, reflective of Yahweh's devotion to Israel. The "if" did prevail. The people, the monarchy, the temple, the city — all gifts of Yahweh's generosity — were swept away. The promises did not hold and could not hold, given Yahweh's ethical urgency.

IV

The great theological reality of the Hebrew Scriptures/Old Testament is the failure of Jerusalem, the end of its hegemony, the deportation of Israel, and the reality of exile, a dismal ending that was the termination of all old faith claims.[8] It is impossible to overstate the cruciality of this fissure in Israel's self-understanding. This was for Israel a genuine and profound ending, the very ending that Amos had anticipated (Amos 8:2–3). The public, institutional life of Judah came to an end. But beyond that Israel made the theological judgment that Yahweh had now abandoned Israel and had nullified all the old promises. The *political-military* experience of an ending is effectively transposed into a deep *theological* crisis.

It is this moment of failure that Walther Zimmerli terms "the *nullpunkt*" (in English, variously, "the nadir," "point zero").[9] It is the moment when Israel has two tasks that belong definitively to its faith. The first task — long practiced in Israel's Psalms of lamentation and complaint — is to *relinquish* what is gone, to resist every denial and every act of nostalgia, to acknowledge and embrace what Yahweh has ended. The task is reflected in the communal laments of Psalms 44, 74, 79, 137, and in the Book of Lamentations. Jerusalem is gone! Israel will not soon have done with its sense of loss, variously expressed as grief and as rage.

Israel's second task — long practiced in Israel's hymns and Songs of Thanksgiving — is to *receive* what is inexplicably and inscrutably given by Yahweh, to resist every measure of despair, to await and affirm what Yahweh, beyond every *quid pro quo*, now gives. The faith of Israel envisions no automatic move from relinquishment to reception; one does not follow necessarily from or after the

---

8. See Peter R. Ackroyd, *Exile and Restoration: A Study of Hebrew Thought of the Sixth Century B.C.*, OTL (Philadelphia: Westminster Press, 1968), and Ralph W. Klein, *Israel in Exile: A Theological Interpretation*, OBT (Philadelphia: Fortress Press, 1979).

9. Walther Zimmerli, "Plans for Rebuilding after the Catastrophe of 587," in *I Am Yahweh* (Atlanta: John Knox Press, 1982), 111, 115, 133.

other. Israel's poets, singers, and speakers of oracles, heard as the very assurance
of Yahweh's own voice, arise precisely in the *nullpunkt*. Here we are close to the
center of our topic and to the deepest issues in biblical eschatology. Amos Wilder
had it right, even without having seen the phrasing of Zimmerli:

> Accept no mitigation,
> but be instructed at the null point;
> the zero
> breeds new algebra.[10]

We are here at the center of the mystery of Jewish faith that receives, in Christian
perspective, its dramatic enactment in Easter. There is a "breeding," a hidden
generativity of newness, just at the zero. The "breeding" at zero is not simply
necessity. The "breeding" at zero is not only Israel's act of will for newness or
wishful thinking. The "breeding" at zero is not simply buoyant poets in their extreme imagination. Perhaps it is all of these; but beyond these is the wounded
but undefeated, affronted but not alienated, shamed but not negated resolve of
Yahweh to have a people — this people, this same people, this deported people —
as Yahweh's own people in the world.[11] Yahweh will not be "Israel-less" in the
world![12] Yahweh will be — of necessity, of Israelite insistence, of poetic imagination, of fundamental resolve — the God of Israel. And therefore, it is clear
in the canonical text of Jews and Christians, there will be a new Israel, Israel
again, Israel reloved, healed, ransomed, blessed, brought home, rejoicing — by no
claim of its own but by the nonnegotiable resolve (not yet known in the act of
relinquishment) — of Yahweh to have Israel.

The rhetoric of hope whereby Israel, in its hopelessness, must receive its new
gift from Yahweh is given in many voices. Indeed Israel requires endless generativity in order to speak the unspeakable newness from Yahweh that is beyond
explanation. Here I shall mention three voices that Gerhard von Rad has shown
to be decisive and defining.[13]

"The Book of Comfort" collects together all the hopes and possibilities of
the Jeremiah tradition (Jeremiah 30–31). The one who *scattered* in exile will
gather in homecoming like a shepherd gathers the lost, at-risk sheep (31:10).
The one who has watched *to pluck up and break down* will now supervise *building
and planting* (31:28). This is the God of "everlasting love" who "continued in
faithfulness" (31:2), who will "restore the fortunes" of Israel (30:3, 18; 31:23; see
19:14; 32:44; 33:7, 11, 26). This latter phrase, with Yahweh as subject, envisions

---

10. Amos Wilder, "A Hard Death," *Poetry* 107 (1965–66): 168–69, quoted by John D. Crossan,
A Fragile Craft: The Work of Amos Niven Wilder (Atlanta: Scholars Press, 1981), 66.

11. This resolve is forcefully expressed in the formula, "I will be your God and you shall be my
people," a formula especially crucial in the exile when most of the uses cluster.

12. In using the phrase, "Israel-less," I intend to allude directly to the Christian formulation of
Jürgen Moltmann, *The Crucified God: The Cross of Christ as the Foundation and Criticism of Christian
Theology* (New York: Harper and Row, 1974), 243: "The grief of the Father here is just as important
as the death of the Son. The Fatherlessness of the Son is matched by the Sonlessness of the Father."

13. Gerhard von Rad, *Old Testament Theology II: The Theology of Israel's Prophetic Traditions* (London: Oliver and Boyd, 1965), 263–77; see also Walter Brueggemann, *Hopeful Imagination: Prophetic
Voices in Exile* (Philadelphia: Fortress Press, 1986).

a radical reversal of circumstance wrought by nothing other than Yahweh's act of power and resolve.[14] The literature teems with verbs of planting and building and consequent rejoicing. See especially Jer. 30:12–17 and 31:31–34.[15] The deep resolve of Yahweh makes possible a new beginning in Israel, such as the shambles of exile would never have suggested.

As the corpus of Jeremiah "rolls" into Judaism, we are able to notice "futuring" that moves toward apocalyptic language, so eager is the wording to witness to a deep and real newness.[16] Indeed, the poetry just before the new covenant has it this way:

> Thereupon I awoke and looked, and my sleep was pleasant to me. (Jer. 31:26)

Is it a dream? Is it a fantasy? Or is it a future that the givenness of exile would never permit in wakeful control? It is precisely the dream that would begin to override circumstance, to invite exiles to venture out beyond where they are to where they will yet be. The new place is home beyond exile, where they have never been, a home not derivable from exile, but a new gift bred in the zero hour, conjured by poets, assured by the One who denied home and now wills it.[17]

The second large voice of newness in exile is Ezekiel, in a very different idiom. Hope and new possibility are given extended expression in chapters 33–48, especially in the vision of the new temple and its new divine presence. Here I shall mention only two specific utterances of this future-laden rhetoric. Best known is the visionary statement of "dry bones" in 37:1–14, but for being well known no less important. The key player in the encounter is the "breath" (*rûah*) that comes upon the dead carcass of Israel in the valley of death. The breath is not at the disposal of the prophet and lies beyond prophetic control or understanding. Everything waits for the inexplicable, unsummonable breath. Until it is given, the flesh, skin, and bones of Israel are as nothing, clearly a *nullpunkt*. When the breath is given, there is life anew.

End... *nullpunkt*... zero hour. And then wind... open graves. The grave is exile. The new life is restoration and homecoming (37:12–14). The grave cannot prevail when the wind comes.

---

14. On the formula, see John Martin Bracke, "The Coherence and Theology of Jeremiah 30–31," A Dissertation Presented to the Faculty of Union Theological Seminary (Richmond, 1983), 148–55, and more generally, Thomas M. Raitt, *A Theology of Exile: Judgment/Deliverance in Jeremiah and Ezekiel* (Philadelphia: Fortress Press, 1977).

15. See Walter Brueggemann, "The 'Uncared for' Now Cared For (Jeremiah 30:12–17): A Methodological Consideration," *Old Testament Theology: Essays on Structure, Theme, and Text* (Minneapolis: Fortress Press, 1992), 296–307; Hans Walter Wolff, "What Is New in the New Covenant? A Contribution to the Jewish-Christian Dialogue According to Jer. 31:31–34," in *Confrontation with Prophets: Discovering the Old Testament's New and Contemporary Significance* (Philadelphia: Fortress Press, 1983), 49–62, and more recently, Norbert Lohfink, *The Covenant Never Revoked: Biblical Reflections on Christian-Jewish Dialogue* (New York: Paulist Press, 1991).

16. William McKane, *A Critical and Exegetical Commentary on Jeremiah I*, ICC (Edinburgh: T. & T. Clark, 1986), l–lxxxiii, has contributed the felicitous notion of a "rolling corpus."

17. On "home" beyond exile, see Frederick Buechner, *The Longing for Home: Recollections and Reflections* (San Francisco: HarperSanFrancisco, 1996), and Walter Brueggemann, *Cadences of Home: Preaching among Exiles* (Louisville, Ky.: Westminster/John Knox Press, 1997).

In a very different idiom, 36:22–32 offers newness concrete and relational, but also national. Yahweh's declaration is about Yahweh's resolve for restoration (vv. 24–27). What interests us, however, is not the promise, but the ground of the promise (vv. 22–23, 32).[18] The ground of newness is nothing about Israel or even about Yahweh's inclination toward Israel. It is rather Yahweh's self-regard. In an "honor-shame culture," Yahweh has been shamed by Israel. The only way the honor of Yahweh can be recovered (along with self-regard) is to rescue Israel so that all the watching nations and watching gods can see the fidelity and power of Yahweh.[19] Israel's future is a function of Yahweh's full Godness. Yahweh is so tied to Israel (as in "I shall be your God") that Israel's future is as sure as Yahweh's self-regard and self-resolve.

In self-regard, Yahweh will make Yahweh's own name (reputation, identity) holy as it has been profaned by Israel. The future of Israel is a strategy for enacting and reasserting Yahweh's own *sui generis* quality. This motif is then unfolded in the tradition of Ezekiel in terms of holy temple, holy priests, holy city (chapters 40–48).[20] All of these holy accoutrements, however, are only functions of Yahweh's own holiness, the propelling power of Israel's future.

The third powerful voice of exilic expectation is Isaiah 40–55 that anticipates the homecoming of Israel to Jerusalem as the power of Babylonian hegemony is broken by Yahweh through Yahweh's regent, Cyrus (see 45:1). Here I shall mention only one aspect of this rich, promissory literature. Twice the poetry uses the term "gospel" (*basar*) in an intentional way to declare Yahweh's transformative presence (40:9; 52:7; see also 41:27; 60:6).[21]

The exile is understood in this poetry either as the provisional defeat of Yahweh by the Babylonian gods or, more likely, as Yahweh's willing submission to Babylonian negation as a way to enact harsh punishment upon Jerusalem. Either way, Yahweh is silent, dormant, and invisible, and Israel is alone in the world without Yahweh. Now, in this moment of poetry, Yahweh breaks the silence and is again active in the life of the world (42:14–16; see 62:1). The specific formulae of the "gospel" are "Behold your God.... Your God rules."[22] Yahweh is back in action! Yahweh is back in play! This is the same Yahweh who seemed feeble and inoperative in the face of Babylon. As exile is the end, so the gospel of homecoming is a new beginning, a "new thing." The life of Israel begins anew, made possible by the reappearance, reemergence, and reengagement of Yahweh, no longer dormant, silent, or invisible.

---

18. See Brueggemann, *Hopeful Imagination*, 69–87.

19. A close parallel concerning Yahweh's shame before the gods is voiced in Num. 14:13–19.

20. See Jon D. Levenson, *Theology of the Program of Restoration of Ezekiel 40–48*, HSM 10 (Missoula, Mont.: Scholars Press, 1976), and especially Kalenda Rose Stevenson, *Vision of Transformation: The Territorial Rhetoric of Ezekiel 40–48*, SBLDS 154 (Atlanta: Scholars Press, 1996).

21. See Walter Brueggemann, *Biblical Perspective on Evangelism: Living in a Three-Storied Universe* (Nashville: Abingdon Press, 1993), 14–47.

22. Sigmund Mowinckel has famously proposed that the formula refers to a specific liturgical enactment whereby Yahweh is made to be sovereign. See a critical assessment of the hypothesis by Ben C. Ollenburger, *Zion, the City of the Great King: A Theological Symbol of the Jerusalem Cult*, JSOTSup 41 (Sheffield: JSOT Press, 1987), 24–33.

V

The fissure of exile and homecoming in the imaginative, liturgical life of Judaism is defining. The texts of Jeremiah, Ezekiel, and belated Isaiah are the most eloquent in leading Israel — originally and in every subsequent generation — in and through exile to new life.[23] We may observe five general conclusions out of this redescribed history:

1. The turn from exile to homecoming is *lyrical, imaginative, and exuberant.* Israel fully expects that which is not in hand which it cannot see. Its hope is not reasonable, controlled, or precise. It is wildly beyond the data and cannot be held accountable to circumstance. Israel's rhetoric refuses such sober restraint.

2. Israel's lyrical, imaginative exuberance about the future it will receive from Yahweh is informed and shaped by *Israel's memory* of Yahweh's previous generosity and fidelity that dominate Israel's remembered past. Indeed, the entire past of life with Yahweh is seen as a profound sequence of *ḥasdê*, of miracles of transformative fidelity (as in Psalm 136). Israel is now able and willing to imagine the continuation of this sequence of miracles into its future, miracles that characteristically overpower circumstance.

3. The lyrical, imaginative, exuberant mode of discourse that transposes remembered miracles into anticipated miracles requires discourse that is open to *a myriad of images, figures, and metaphors.* The refusal of discipline and restraint in rhetoric dictates a pluralism of expression. No single imagery is adequate, because such a reduction would turn lyrical expectations into description and prediction, something Israel will not and cannot do.

4. The lyrical, imaginative tenor of hope refuses to be pinned down concretely. And yet these voices of possibility intend and insist that their cadences of hope pertain to *real life in the real world,* dealing with real power and real public possibility. The lyrical pluralism of hope summons Israel away from the closed world of despair sponsored by Babylon or advocated by Israel's deep guilt. Hope is a concrete summons to act in venturesome ways, not only in expectation but in defiant resistance to other construals of reality that give no credibility to Yahweh as a defining player. By situating hope in the real world, hope is not merely a passive wait upon God; it is rather a buoyant, sociopolitical, risky practice of a subversive counterlife in the world of geopolitics.

5. The utterance of hope is characteristically in the *nullpunkt.* The null point per se does not "breed" new algebra. The new algebra of life, peace, and joy is found in the hidden, determined ways of Yahweh. That is, hope is *theocentric, Yahweh-centric.* It is the irreducible conviction of Israel that Yahweh is not a victim of observed or predicted circumstance. This is an unfettered "thou" who works newness, either out of compassionate fidelity or out of uncompromised self-regard. Yahweh, so Israel imagines, is never held at the *nullpunkt.*

---

23. See Jacob Neusner, *Understanding Seeking Faith: Essays on the Case of Judaism I: Debates on Method, Reports of Results* (Atlanta: Scholars Press, 1986), 137–41.

VI

In both its depth and its lyrical buoyancy, the troping of life as exile and homecoming is decisive for Israel. It is through this troped experience that Judaism knows itself to be the at-risk, protected people of Yahweh; it is, moreover, through this troped experience that the church comes belatedly to its Friday-Sunday certitude of Yahweh and its life as the Easter people. The old slogan, "God acts in history," surely means that the community of faith characteristically attests to what it knows in and through the givenness of its own lived life, for hope from anywhere else is of only second-range importance.

But of course Israel did not linger exclusively in its reflection upon its own life. It was able, through its own life and by appeal to the great imperial liturgies all around it, to think and believe imaginatively about the life of the world... hence "creation theology."[24] When Judaism thought, believed, and sang about the life of the world, it was able to admit negatively and affirm positively in parallel to its own lived life. As exile-homecoming, with its strange texture of continuity and discontinuity, is defining for Israel, so the rubric of "creation-chaos-new creation" tells the story of the world as Yahweh's creation, wherein *chaos* may be seen as a close cognate to *exile*.[25]

Given the enigmatic grammar of Gen. 1:1–2, it is commonly agreed that creation in the Hebrew Scriptures/Old Testament is characteristically not *ex nihilo*, but it is an act whereby the creating God imposes a life-generating order upon an extant chaos, a chaos about which the scriptures themselves exhibit no curiosity.[26] The imposition of a life-giving order that makes the world a safe, joyous, peaceable place is due cause for celebration. Israel celebrates the wonder and goodness and beauty and reliability of creation even as it celebrates the wonder of its own life in the world as a gift of Yahweh (see Gen. 1:1–2:4a; Psalm 104).

The world is Yahweh's creation. It is not self-made or self-sustaining. It prospers at the behest of Yahweh. For that reason, in a context of shattering and dismay, the tradition of Jeremiah can envision the complete *undoing* of the world (4:23–26). This heavy judgment is a counterpoint to the liturgy of Genesis 1; point by point it foresees the dismantling of creation and the regression of the world into its primal chaos. Thus the "waste and void" of verse 23 is the same power of negation as "formless void" in Gen. 1:2. Everything will return to a precreation state of disorder in which the generative powers for life are not available and cease to function. The daring imagery of this poem — subsequently escalated in

---

24. See Walter Brueggemann, "The Loss and Recovery of Creation in Old Testament Theology," *TToday* 53 (July 1996): 177–90.

25. See Bernhard W. Anderson, *Creation Versus Chaos: The Reinterpretation of Mythical Symbolism in the Bible* (Philadelphia: Fortress Press, 1987), and *From Creation to New Creation: Old Testament Perspectives*, OBT (Minneapolis: Fortress Press, 1994).

26. An important exception to this interpretive consensus is Walther Eichrodt, "In the Beginning," in *Israel's Prophetic Heritage: Essays in Honor of James Muilenburg*, ed. Bernhard W. Anderson and Walter Harrelson (New York: Harper and Brothers, 1962), 1–10.

apocalyptic imagery — is as decisive and massive as any current scientific scenario of the undoing of the world.[27]

It may be that this poem in Jeremiah in the context of the late seventh century is a parabolic way of speaking of Israel. That is, the poet employs "limit language" to give voice to the radical undoing of Israel and all its lived context. The vision of world-dismantling, however, cannot be completely subsumed into or explained as the dismantling of Israel. Israel is able to ponder and contemplate the end of the world of generativity precisely because it does not confuse creation with the creator who is its only source of future.

As a seventh-century poet at the threshold of the failure of Jerusalem can envision a failed world, so a later poet, perhaps at the threshold of restored Jerusalem, can envision a restored creation (Isa. 65:17–19a). It is surely instructive that "new heavens and a new earth" are intimately connected to "Jerusalem as a joy," for Israel's imagination stays fixed upon its own homecoming. It is no doubt correct to see new creation here as a function of new Jerusalem, restored Judaism. And yet the creation imagery cannot be domesticated out of its cosmic scope.

Israel is able to imagine that as Yahweh in the *nullpunkt* of exile will fashion homecoming, in parallel fashion Israel knows that in *tôhû wabôhû*, the *nullpunkt* of a failed creation, the creator of heaven and earth can and will form a new creation that is ordered, secure, joyous, and peaceable. Israel's cosmic imagination is not of a world ordered and settled or of a world failed and ended, but of a more perfect world about to come to be, solely by the God who "calls into existence things that do not exist" (Rom. 4:17). This is indeed "hoping against hope," engaged in lyrical imagination rooted in memories of miracle but pushing beyond them in an act of hope that summons to an alternative kind of life in the world.

VII

As Israel is able to think through its own life of *exile and homecoming* to a cosmic framing of *chaos and (new) creation*, so Israel was able to think through its own life of *exile and homecoming* to a personal destiny of *trouble and new life*.

It is a truism of scripture study that these ancient texts, on the whole, did not entertain any notion of "life after death." Only two texts — Isa. 19:26 and Dan. 12:2 — seem to be clear attestations of life after death, and they are commonly regarded as quite late, cast in apocalyptic language, and influenced by the entry of Judaism into a world of Hellenistic thought. While these two texts clearly give a ground for personal hope beyond death, they are so atypical that not much of a claim can be made.

The conventional truism of scholarship — given classic theological formulation by Oscar Cullmann — has been frontally challenged.[28] First, Mitchell Dahood

---

27. Isaiah 54:10 is an important reference for our argument, because there the poetry likens exile to the flood waters of chaos.

28. Oscar Cullmann, *Immortality of the Soul or Resurrection of the Dead? The Witness of the New Testament* (London: Epworth Press, 1958).

(along with his student Nicholas Tromp), in a formidable study of the Psalms especially informed by cognates in Ugaritic, has proposed that many Psalms attest to life after death.[29] In his summary of his argument, Dahood considered "life" as "eternal life," "the future" as "future life," banqueting as an image of eternal life, beatific vision, and a summons to "awake, awake" as a summons to life after death.[30]

It is important that our discussion should take notice of the suggestions of Dahood, Tromp, and Barr. But because the dominant opinion of scholarship has not embraced their arguments, we may consider the theme of personal hope in a different mode shaped as *lament/complaint and praise*. Israel's voiced life with Yahweh, in all its intimacy, is expressed in laments and complaints. Such speech characterizes with urgency to Yahweh situations of need and then petitions Yahweh in demanding imperatives that Yahweh intervene promptly and make things new.[31] While the troubles of the Psalms seem characteristically to be illness, prison, or social isolation, the rhetoric of laments and complaints is the hyperbolic language of death, so that every need is portrayed as ultimate, as warranting Yahweh's immediate and decisive intervention (Pss. 6:4–5; 7:4–5; 13:3–4; 22:14–15).

The remarkable feature of the pattern of these poems, as Claus Westermann has made clear, is that they characteristically end in resolution and praise (Pss. 6:9–10; 7:17; 13:5–6; 22:21a–22).[32] The rhetorical structure of "plea-praise" affirms that an urgent petition evokes Yahweh's responsive intervention. Yahweh comes into the *nullpunkt* of personal life — death in a myriad of forms — and acts decisively to make a new life of joy and well-being possible. It is not necessary to follow Dahood into literalism to see that the movement of *complaint-praise* is the ground of hope for personal life in Israel. The Psalmists voice their urgent petition precisely as acts of hope, in complete confidence that when Yahweh hears and is moved to act, newness is given. It is at the nadir of human misfortune that the individual believer prays. It is toward the individual person in a variety of forms of death that Yahweh comes to give new life.

---

29. Mitchell Dahood, *Psalms III 101–150*, AB 17A (Garden City, N.Y.: Doubleday, 1970); Nicholas J. Tromp, *Primitive Conceptions of Death and the Nether World in the Old Testament* (Rome: Pontifical Biblical Institute, 1969).

30. Dahood, *Psalms III*, xli–lii. In a very different idiom and without reference to Dahood, James Barr, *The Garden of Eden and the Hope of Immortality* (Minneapolis: Fortress Press, 1993), has sought to refute the dominant categories of Oscar Cullmann, arguing that positive consideration be given to the theme of immortality. Barr's argument is not fully clear to me, because he asserts that "our story does not speak of 'life after death,'" nor about the "immortality of the soul," and "I am not opting for immortality" (19, 41). Barr's argument attends especially to Genesis 2–3 and the same Psalms and is concerned with the durability of the "soul" (*nephesh*) in a direct challenge to Oscar Cullmann.

31. See Fredrik Lindstrom, *Suffering and Sin: Interpretations of Illness in the Individual Complaint Psalms*, ConBOT 37 (Stockholm: Almqvist and Wiksell International, 1994).

32. Claus Westermann, *The Praise of God in the Psalms* (Richmond, Va.: John Knox Press, 1965). See the fuller exposition by Patrick D. Miller, *They Cried to the Lord: The Form and Theology of Biblical Prayer* (Minneapolis: Fortress Press, 1994), 55–177 and passim.

VIII

We may from our analysis draw five conclusions concerning hope in ancient Israel:

1. The three spheres of life — communal, cosmic, and personal — are practiced in parallel fashion in the faith of Israel:

> communal: exile . . . homecoming;
>
> cosmic: chaos . . . new creation;
>
> personal: complaint . . . praise.

The three negative states of *exile/chaos/complaint* are roughly synonymous, all bespeaking a circumstance without resource, seemingly beyond the reach of Yahweh's good resolve. The remarkable affirmation of Israel's text, however, is that the *nullpunkt* (exile, chaos, complaint) is characteristically transformed by the responsive initiative of Yahweh who makes new life possible where none seemed available. The triad of *exile-homecoming, chaos–new creation, despair-doxology* is defining for Israel with Yahweh. The move from point A (the negative) to point B (the new positive) is not automatic or guaranteed.

It is in between the two, at the *nullpunkt*, that Israel does its hoping. It is characteristically impossible for Israel to keep silent in the *nullpunkt* or to entertain the thought that there will be no second element of gift from Yahweh. It is this impossibility that makes Israel's hope definitional. Israel counts on a response of newness, not derived from circumstance, but from the same responsive, transformative God so thick in Israel's past circumstances of need. Thus the practices of hope for Israel, for the world, and for individual persons are of a piece.

2. The grounding of future expectation is rooted in *memories of past miracles of fidelity.* While this appeal to the past is evident in many places, it is nowhere clearer than in Lam. 3:21–23. The speaker has lost hope (see v. 18). It is memory that revives hope. And the memories that matter concern the great terms of covenantal fidelity: *ḥesed, raḥam, 'amûnah.*[33] Israel is incapable of imagining any future in which Yahweh's known and characteristic fidelity is not operative. Israel cannot imagine a communal displacement, a cosmic distortion, or a personal abandonment that lies beyond the reach of Yahweh's fidelity.

3. This reservoir of past fidelity moves Israel, in the *nullpunkt*, to offer *a variety of expressions* of hope. Here I notice only the tension between the covenantal (Dtr.) tradition of Jeremiah and the holiness (Priestly) tradition of Ezekiel. The ground of hope for Jeremiah is Yahweh's *deep love for Israel* that not only endures through crisis but is revivified in crisis (Jer. 31:20). In a very different idiom, the tradition of Ezekiel has nothing to say of such moving, tender compassion. Here it is all the *cold holiness* of Yahweh's self-regard (Ezek. 39:25–27). The wonder of hope at the *nullpunkt* is that Israel, in its urgent utterance, did not opt for one of these voicings, but knew that every voicing counts. The voicings arise in deep

---

33. On this vocabulary, see Walter Brueggemann, "Crisis-Evoked, Crisis-Resolving Speech," *BTB* 24 (1994): 95–105.

need and therefore are rich and varied, shrill and insistent, desperate and trusting. All of them count and continue to reach from Israel's need to Yahweh's ear.

4. Informed by Ernst Käsemann, Hans Heinrich Schmid has shown that the themes of justification, creation *ex nihilo*, and resurrection of the dead are already offered together as synonyms in the Hebrew Scriptures/Old Testament.[34] That insight is crucial for our argument. If we may judge that these three theological schemata are congruent with our three spheres of hope, we may see that hope in the *nullpunkt* for Israel, creation, and individual persons is all of a piece. Hope in all three spheres invites the needy and desperate to look beyond circumstance to appeal to the God who presides over the *nullpunkt*, who can move into it and through it and beyond it.

The quintessential case in Christian parlance of course is Easter. Easter, however, is no isolated event. It belongs to Israel's wide and deep practice of hope that appeals to a long recital of parallels but finally stakes everything on the unfettered "Thou" who is not in thrall to the reasonableness of any *nullpunkt*. All *nullpunkte*, in every sphere, have common properties. In the end what counts is the capacity of this "Thou" to intrude into the *nullpunkt* and override it. The theological formulae of justification, creation *ex nihilo*, and resurrection from the dead are choice ways to speak about this singular claim for Yahweh.

5. Following Hans Joachim Begrich, it is widely held that it is the "salvation oracle" uttered on behalf of Yahweh by an authorized human speaker that turns the plea to praise in Israel's complaints and laments.[35] The point is not more than a hypothesis. But it does account for a decisive turn in Israel's sense of its own situation.

According to the hypothesis, the salvation oracle has at its heart the phrase, "Fear not" (Isa. 41:10, 14).[36] The assurance, taken as Yahweh's announcement of presence, is the ground of hope and the harbinger of the newness only Yahweh can give. The *nullpunkt*, in its many forms, is enough to evoke deep and raw fear. The exile offers a fear of *abandonment*. The pressure of chaos invites fear of *obliteration*. The immediacy of death bespeaks nullification and *nonbeing*. The *nullpunkt* carries the prospect of total nullification. Into that is spoken, "Do not fear." The antidote seems modest in the face of the threat. Unless, of course, the antidote is uttered by one who is trustworthy. Everything depends upon that. The future always depends for Israel upon the trustworthiness of the One who characteristically hovers somewhere between the fear so palpably grounded and faith so fragilely embraced. It is the pivot point of hope: "Do not fear!"

---

34. Hans Heinrich Schmid, "Rechtfertigung als Schöpfungsgeschehen: Notizen zur alttestamentlichen Vorgeschichte eines neutestamentlichen Themas," in *Rechtfertigung: Festschrift für Ernst Käsemann zum 70. Geburtstag*, ed. Johannes Friedrich et al. (Göttingen: Vandenhoeck and Ruprecht, 1976), 403–14.

35. Hans Joachim Begrich, "Das priesterliche Heilsorakel," *ZAW* 66 (1934): 81–92. The theme is fully exposited in the work of Miller, *They Cried to the Lord*.

36. See the discussion of Edgar W. Conrad, *Fear Not Warrior: A Study of 'al tira' Pericopes in the Hebrew Scriptures*, BJS 75 (Chico, Calif.: Scholars Press, 1985).

Chapter 11

JUDGMENT AND JOY

Patrick D. Miller

In the middle of the Book of Isaiah, the prophetic voice moves from a series of oracles against various nations (Isaiah 13–23) to a much more comprehensive depiction of judgment and redemption (chaps. 24–27), a text that has come to be called the Isaiah Apocalypse. Such a label is deceptive, for, as one interpreter has noted, "scholars have labeled the literary genre of Isaiah 24–27 as a late post-exilic apocalyptic work, pre-exilic prophetic judgment literature, prophetic eschatology, exilic or early post-exilic proto-apocalyptic and, recently, early apocalyptic."[1] In most descriptions of these chapters, however, there is a recognition that whatever precise label is attached to the text, it presents itself as in some way speaking about God's final work, about the wrapping up of history, the judgment of the nations, and the vindication of God's purposes for Israel and all peoples. Its richness and comprehensiveness lead one to suggest that here it is possible to probe at some depth into the biblical foundations of Christian eschatology.

The material in Isaiah 24–27 is quite disparate, comprising particularly prophetic oracles and psalmic pieces (both lament and thanksgiving types). Various independent units have been brought together and often in a somewhat haphazard fashion, something not unusual in prophetic books. The scholarly investigation of this material has been preoccupied with straightening out the history and composition of these chapters, including locating them in relation to socioreligious conflicts operative in postexilic and later Judah. Unfortunately, there is virtually no consensus on most of the issues having to do with such matters. The compositional time has been set anywhere from the eighth century and the work of the prophet Isaiah down to the second century. The difficulty of locating or fixing the text is due in no small part to the flexibility of the horizon of the text temporally and spatially. Rather than seeing this as a frustrating problem, the intermixture of near and far horizons may be an important ingredient in the presentation of the consummating work of God.

Ambiguity and Poetry as the Language of Eschatology

While formal matters are generally not as significant for theological discussion as material ones, in reading these chapters to "discover" what they have to say about

---

1. William Millar, *Isaiah 24–27 and the Origin of Apocalyptic*, HSM 11 (Missoula, Mont.: Scholars Press, 1976), 21.

the last things and the end, the interpreter cannot be unaware of their form as poetry. This is, in my judgment, more important than identifying particular types of prophetic or psalmic speech within the whole, though one may do that to some extent also. The poetry of the text joins with its scarcity of historical indicators to heighten the interpreter's awareness of the *figurative* and *ambiguous* form in which the text speaks. Long ago, William Empson demonstrated that ambiguity belongs to the very character of poetic communication.[2] Elsewhere I have suggested that the poetic vehicle is a mode of speaking that is figural and nonliteral, indirect and open.[3] In a study of the nature of poetic language, Linda Waugh suggests that a "poem is to a certain degree decontextualized: it is a system of systems which is more self-contained than referential discourse. One could say that the poem provides its own 'universe of discourse.' "[4] This combination of features that belong to poetic expression — ambiguity, indirectness, figurative speech, and decontextualization — is evident in these chapters in various ways.

The separateness of these chapters has been demonstrated again and again. They do provide a kind of universe of discourse even though there are connections to the larger setting. Metaphor and simile run through the text. Ambiguity comes into play in significant ways, for example, around the language for "earth" and "city" as well as in the reference to the dead coming to life. We are thus faced with a large degree of openness of meaning, indeed multiple meanings, as to what the text says about its subject matter — even indeed as to what the subject matter is. Interpretation is required to a high degree, but finality is precluded. Referential thinking cannot be avoided in trying to make sense of the text, but the reference is not thereby pinned down and one has always to beware of slipping into literal reference in a way the text does not permit.

One may ask if it is not quite important that such a mode of speech be a part of our thinking about the eschaton. It is not the "veil" of apocalyptic I have in mind — even if this text is an apocalypse, as many suggest — for that veil is always subject to being pierced by the proper code. Poetry builds the openness and ambiguity, the indirectness of our speech, into its very being. It also creates an inherent form of continuity and discontinuity as it uses metaphor, simile, personification, and the like. What we find out about the end, therefore, is not definitive, for poetry is not definitive by nature. It is open, indirect, allusive, elusive, and possibly illusive. One might argue that poetry is the original form of eschatological speech in scripture. Perhaps it is also the final language of eschatological thinking.

What that means for a conversation with the more literal speech of science I am not sure, though two or three things suggest themselves: (a) scientific speech about the last things is penultimate, not ultimate; (b) to the extent that analogy and metaphor are prominent in scientific discourse about the end, that discourse

---

2. William Empson, *Seven Types of Ambiguity* (Harmondsworth: Penguin Books, 1930).

3. Patrick Miller, "The Theological Significance of Biblical Poetry," in *Language, Theology, and the Bible: Essays in Honour of James Barr*, ed. Samuel E. Balentine and John Barton (Oxford: Clarendon Press, 1994), 225.

4. Linda Waugh, "The Poetic Function and the Nature of Language," *Poetics Today* 2, no. 1a (1980): 72.

shares with the prophetic poetry of the Bible a formal indirectness and openness about the end; (c) scientific discussion of the last things will probably move in a poetic direction the more it speaks about such matters.

The Judgment of Earth and Heaven

The Agency or Process of Judgment

Isaiah 24–27 begins with a dimension of the eschaton that may be least amenable to scientific interpretation and analogy: an extended depiction of the Lord's judgment or punishment of earth (24:1–20) and heaven (24:21–23). The judging activity of God recurs in the passage, but the other instances seem to fit more within a near horizon of time, in relation to sometimes identifiable nations or peoples (e.g., Moab in vv. 10–12).

The judgment of heaven and earth is first of all a divine act. The description is both metaphorical — with the depiction of Earth's destruction like a drunkard staggering till he falls (24:20) — and naturalistic and personal. Earth is disfigured and dries up; people are scattered. No one is exempt from the totality of this judgment (24:1–2). Some interpreters have noted how, after the initial identification of the Lord as the subject of this activity, the description of the destruction of earth in 24:16b–20 does not point directly to divine agency but seems to depict events taking their natural course.[5] The drunkard "Earth" finally falls in its stupor. The guilty "Earth" is weighed down by its transgression so that it falls and cannot rise again.

We have in the whole a not atypical biblical depiction of events that claims the Lord's direct control and ultimate responsibility but portrays those events, at least in part, in ways suggestive of a dissolution from within, a kind of organic connection between acts and their consequences. At one and the same time, the destruction of earth is both the judgment of God (24:1, 21; 26:21; 27:1) and the working out of directions that flow out from the activities of Earth and its inhabitants. Even the transgression of the laws and the breach of the eternal covenant (24:5–6) are seen as having effects that contribute to the demise of earth, that is, pollution[6] and curse. From either perspective, the emptying and devastation of earth is not simply natural or neutral. It is both divine initiative and the outcome of Earth's choices.

Creation of Heaven and Earth
and the Judgment of Heaven and Earth

In its formulation, the depiction of the judgment in chapter 24 recalls the Lord's creative activity at the beginning. That is, the poetry of the end draws upon motifs and language from the beginning, not to describe a new creation but to

---

5. Hans Wildberger, *Isaiah 13–27* (Minneapolis: Augsburg, 1997), 503.
6. The "pollution" is in the sense of a profanation, that is, a religious pollution, but it is important that the object of this profanation/pollution is the earth.

show the undoing of the existing one by the same power that brought it into being. The reflex of creation in judgment is indicated in a number of ways:

1. The devastated earth as an arid, lifeless reality (24:4, 7) is reminiscent of the precreation state of things according to the depiction in Gen. 2:4–5, where prior to creation there was no herb or plant and no water.

2. The unnamed city destroyed at the center of this devastation is the city of "chaos" (tōhû), an intimation that it has returned to the precreation chaos (Gen. 1:2).[7]

3. The text attributes the judgment of earth and heaven to an act of God's speaking (24:3), the same impetus that brought about the creation at the beginning.

4. The opening of the "windows of the height"[8] (24:18) is reminiscent of the opening of the "windows of the heavens" together with the fountains of the great deep in the first universal judgment of humanity and the earth at the Flood (Gen. 7:11; 8:2), itself a kind of return to precreation chaos.

5. The depiction of the earth being "violently shaken" (24:19b) and of the shaking of the foundations of the earth (24:18b) uses language and imagery else-where employed to speak of God's creative work (Ps. 104:5). The language of "shaking" (24:18b) has been identified as a technical term for the final shaking of the world at the return of chaos.[9]

6. While the terminology is different, the curse that devours the earth in this universal judgment (24:6) echoes the extended experience of curse that overtakes nearly everything in God's various judgments of the primeval sins (Gen 3:14, 17; 4:11; 5:29; cf. 8:21).

7. In the scattering of the inhabitants of the earth when the Lord empties it out (24:1), one hears an echo of the primeval event of the scattering of humanity after the building of the tower of Babel (Gen. 11:1–9).

8. The drying up of the vine and the absence of wine (24:7–11, esp. v. 9) echo the Primeval History of Genesis 1–11 in that at the beginning and the end of the Noah story, he is identified as the source of wine. His name is explained as "Out of the ground that the Lord has cursed this one shall bring us relief from our work and from the toil of our hands" (Gen. 5:29). That is, the provision of wine is an important dimension of the divine provision in the stories of the beginnings. Then the story of Noah concludes by once more referring to him as "a man of the soil, the first to plant a vineyard" (Gen. 9:20).[10]

---

7. "By means of the creative work of Yahweh, the chaos was shaped to form a structured world-wide order; when the world would come to an end, then this order would sink back down into the amorphous, gloomy situation in which it existed before God intervened to separate it and arrange it. A קרית-תהו (nothing city) would thus have to be a city that had just experienced the reintroduction of the primordial chaos" (Wildberger, Isaiah 13–27, 486).

8. The term height is regularly a reference to "heaven" in this text (24:4, 18, 21).

9. Brevard S. Childs, "The Enemy from the North and the Chaos Tradition," JBL 78 (1959): 97.

10. The description of Noah as "man of the soil" specifically identifies him as representative of humanity in its vocation. In various ways, chapters 1–4 identify the vocation of the human being as tending or keeping of the soil, the ground. The primeval story thus sets the provision of wine for human relaxation as a primeval event, a manifestation of the human vocation, and a gift for the joy

9. The eternal covenant in the context of the fate of the earth, the world and its inhabitants, its breach effecting the wilting and tearing apart of the earth, takes us back to the Noahic covenant, which is where the Lord establishes an "eternal covenant between God and every living creature of all flesh that is on the earth."[11] The eschatological significance of the Noahic covenant is obvious because it is the moment in the story in which the creation is given a clear and sure future — but not an indefinite one ("as long as the earth endures"; Gen. 8:22). This unusual formulation of a broken eternal covenant and of covenantal stipulations that seem to be incumbent upon the whole of humanity suggests something of the radical character of the final judgment. The joining of the Noahic and Sinaitic covenant in this unprecedented way may be a sign of the eschatological dimension of the judgment. It is the covenant with all living flesh, the covenant of creation, that is involved. But its stipulations are those of Sinai, the covenant with Israel. There would seem to be no possible human breach of the eternal covenant, inasmuch as God initiates such a covenant. But the conjoining of the two is a way of saying that the failure to live by the Torah has eternal and cosmic implications. In other words, here is where the whole covenantal relationality is universalized and taken back to creation. This is the "breaking point" quite precisely. The failure of the inhabitants of the earth (not just Israel) to live by the laws and the statutes effects a breaking of the eternal covenant, which is not just Sinai, but the Noahic covenant, the promise of the Lord that so long as the earth remains, seed time and harvest, cold and heat, summer and winter, day and night will endure (Gen. 8:22). Since "its inhabitants" have broken the covenant, the eternal covenant is broken. Thus the provision that sustains the earth now is taken away. Breach of covenant always brings on the curse. At this point, the text is talking about sin and judgment.

The cosmic and social dimensions of covenant are thus seen to be radically affirmed in the end by the end. The seriousness of God's commitment to the world and its inhabitants is matched only by the seriousness with which God takes the violation of the statutes and laws, the breach of covenant. Such acts evoke a radical reaction that is universal and cosmic in scope. It sets underway consequences that affect the whole "earth," consequences that both erupt from within and are evoked from without. The text makes no sharp distinction between what happens and what is done.

In this text, therefore, which speaks little about new creation in a cosmic sense, the judgment is implicitly understood to be a return to the precreation status. In various ways, the universal judgment at the end is an undoing of the original creation. The connections are not precise, linguistically or otherwise. It is not simply that *Endzeit = Urzeit*. But God's activity in the end is reminiscent of the

---

of human life. (See P. D. Miller, *Genesis 1–11: Studies in Structure and Theme*, JSOTSup 8 [Sheffield: JSOT, 1978], 37–42.)

11. Once again Hans Wildberger has stated the matter succinctly and aptly: "The surprising way in which this is formulated has to have been the result of a mixing of the concepts connected with the covenant with Noah, which is an eternal covenant, and that from Sinai, which could be broken, since the premise there is that a relationship exists between partners" (*Isaiah 13–27*, 480).

way it was at the beginning. If creation has always been under the threat of the return to chaos,[12] then that now happens—but not because of God's impotence against chaos. It is the Lord's own act to undo creation. Indeed, chapter 27 concludes the depiction of the cosmic judgment with the mythic account of the Lord's slaughter of the primeval dragon, Leviathan or Tannin, a motif known from extrabiblical sources but not an explicit part of the biblical creation story.

An important further note is sounded, however, that does not simply reflect the undoing of creation and suggests more the vindication and consummation of God's creative work. As Andreas Schüle has suggested, "there is strong emphasis on the idea that the creative principle, giving shape to the new creation, is justice" (26:7–10; cf. 28:16–17). More than the divine word, "it is justice that is envisioned to become the 'inner architecture' of the new eon," a feature that is not a part of the depiction of the beginning.[13] In the midst of the people's lament in chapter 26, a juxtaposition of judgment and confidence is found: "In the path of your judgments [or "your just acts"], O Lord, we wait [or "hope"] for you" (26:8). The time of judgment is a time of expectation of the vindication of God's justice, a work of justice that is of universal scope: "For as your judgments [or "your just acts"] are (wrought) on the earth, the inhabitants of the world learn righteousness" (26:9b).

This analysis of the way the Isaianic text speaks about a comprehensive judgment "in that day" suggests some things that may belong to the discussion between scientific and theological understandings:

1. Continuity is suggested between the creative work of God and the judgment of God, at least the judgment of God that is seen to be cosmic in scope. While judgment is depicted as a disjunction, there is coherence with the creative activity of God in that similar actions happen in the judgment either as reiterations of the creative work or returns to earlier forms or states. The particulars of this account do not allow any reference beyond the poetic presentation, but the many connections to the original story suggest a sense of totality and coherence in reality. The work of God in judgment is analogous to the creative work of God. In some sense, one may speak of the continuing creative work of God in bringing things to an end. The discontinuity is in the sense of an ending. Yet throughout Isaiah 24–27, one is made aware that the end is not an end of nothingness but rather a dismantling of the present deathly existence (individual and corporate) in behalf of life, joy, praise, and the just reign of God in glory, a consummation of the purposes first begun in creation but only discerned in the whole of the story of the creation and God (see below).

The continuities between beginning and ending are suggestive of the wholeness of the creative reality that is uncovered by science, that is, of the *creatio continua* that assumes that whatever changes take place in creation and reality in the future, they will be analogous to the way in which God has carried on creation

---

12. See, in this regard, Jon Levenson, *Creation and the Persistence of Evil: The Jewish Drama of Divine Omnipotence* (San Francisco: Harper and Row, 1988).

13. Schüle's comments were made in the context of a response to this essay.

to this point.[14] Critical to the proper understanding of judgment is an awareness of its ultimately *redemptive* purpose (see below). A variety of biblical images, such as the plumbline of justice and righteousness (Isa. 28:16–17; Amos 7:7–9; cf. 2 Kings 21:13), the dirty dish washed clean and set on the shelf (2 Kings 21:13), and the refining fire (Isa. 1:24–26), suggest that God's intention in judgment is to continue the purposes set from the beginning by redoing things, by tearing down and starting over, washing clean and preparing for further use, and smelting away dross and removing alloy. The joining of judgment and creation in this text, the depiction of judgment with the language and images of creation, attests further to the one reality of God's unfolding purpose and to continuity in the whole of the divine activity of creation and judgment.

2. The text of Isaiah 24–27 is resistant to being conceived of as a scenario of the end. The juxtaposition of various forms, of words about death and life, devastation and renewal, interspersed with voices in praise and warning, which cannot be neatly laid out in a script of the end, leads the reader of this text away from the inclination to deduce out of it simple sequences in "time" as an accounting of the last things. At this point, the text is heuristic and resonates with the mathematical and physical suggestions of old and new alongside each other, of death and life not simply in an unyielding sequence.[15]

3. While not "orderly" in its presentation, therefore, this eschatological text does present us with a poetic depiction of the end that suggests a coherence of the cosmic, the sociocultural (especially in the city and the covenant), and the personal. The end has to do with all of these. It is worth noting, however, that insofar as the text talks about the new, about restoration, about life after death, it does so more in personal and cultural terms, that is, in its depiction of the gathering of the people or the elders or those lost or perishing at the mountain as well as in its focus on the defeat of death. The picture of the new is not devoid of the more physical and cosmic,[16] but that is not where the weight is.

4. In this text, human sin tends to bring about cosmic and cultural judgment.

The effects of sin are depicted as both divine activity and an undoing from within, that is, as both retribution and an organic outworking of the deeds of the earth in which acts have consequences arising from them. This raises the difficult question of how the transgressions of human beings and the "shaking" of the earth, that is, human acts and cosmic effects, can be related to each other in an intelligible fashion. It is hardly plausible to argue that the death of the solar system in the burning out of the sun or the contingent possibilities of world ending are to be seen as causally related to human acts on earth.

Yet this cosmic and human interrelatedness is so regularly a part of the biblical stories and depictions of the end that it is difficult simply to set it apart. It may be that its intelligibility is only on the near horizon. Certainly from the beginning of the biblical story, there is the continuing assumption of a consequential

---

14. See John Polkinghorne, "Eschatology: Some Questions and Some Insights from Science," chap. 2 in this volume.

15. Ibid.

16. For example, "and the face of the world shall be full of fruit" (27:6).

interface between the physical and the personal, between earth and human. This is especially evident in the 'Ādām (human being)–'Ādāmâ (ground, soil) motif in the opening chapters of Genesis. In one sense, the whole story of Genesis 2–3 is about this interaction as 'Ādām's life and being, whence and whither, are all wrapped up in the 'Ādāmâ.[17] The story is suggestive not of simple causalities but of ways in which human interaction with the physical world, the interaction of the cultural and the physical, affects both. The ecological disasters of our time arise in no small part out of the false assumption that human rule of the physical world does not have large and enduring effects upon it. Further, there are ways in which apocalyptic imagery has been most directly brought into the discussion of the end of the world precisely around the interaction of human/cultural acts (sins?) and the physical world. I have in mind the exterministic pictures associated with nuclear war, which includes effects on the natural order as well as on the culture. "Nuclear winter" is a way of speaking of the nuclear outcome. And while human activity does not bring about cosmic end in a literal sense, there may be intimations of the interaction in the way in which cultural acts are already reaching out beyond the confines of the planet that is the only habitation of human life (at least so far). Thus cosmic space is being filled with cultural objects, albeit quite slowly and not necessarily permanently.

The issue remains whether such interaction as this can be seen on the far horizon as well as on the near one.

The Redemption of Israel and the Nations in the Kingdom of God

The judgment of heaven and earth and of all the inhabitants of earth is understood in this text, however, as both redemptive for Israel and indicative of the universal reign of the Lord of Israel. The text is full of affirmations of Israel's future, from the vision of the Lord reigning on Zion before "his elders" (24:23), to the warning to "my people" to hide until the punishment of God has gone by (26:20–21), to the new song of the vineyard as under the Lord's protection (27:1–6) and Israel and Judah sprouting and blossoming (27:6), and finally to the Lord's gathering of the children of Israel and those lost in Egypt and Assyria to the holy mountain (27:12–13). Israel's redemptive future is underscored by one of the peculiarities of this text: the presence of psalmic elements, especially in 25:1–5 and 26:1–6. These are songs of praise, thanksgiving, and trust even in the face of judgment, songs that testify to the salvation of Israel.

But the text does not allow one neatly to divide the world into a world under judgment and a world redeemed. From one angle, the judgment is universal and the redemption is particular (e.g., 26:20–21). It is difficult, however, to conceive of Israel as being exempt from the transgression of Torah, the violation of statutes, and the breach of eternal covenant. And the banquet is not exclusive and in-house; it is a feast "for all peoples." The universal and the particular, the cosmic

17. I have tried to show this interaction in some detail in *Genesis 1–11*, 37–42.

and the social are joined in the announcement of God's future judgment and God's future renewal. The particular is especially sharp with regard to the temporal and the spatial dimensions of this future: It will be "in that day," an unknown but particular moment; and it will be on the holy mountain, in Jerusalem.[18]

If the judgment on that day is portrayed sharply and extensively, especially but not only in chapter 24, the redemptive dimensions of this future are also indicated by a variety of modes and images: a sumptuous banquet, the swallowing up of death, the end of tears, the gathering from afar of the children of Israel, and the perishing, the rising up of corpses, and the sprouting of Israel and Judah. Not one of these images takes over from the others or permits a kind of literalism. But their realistic depictions are suggestive for the way we think about "that day" of God's judgment and redemption. It is a dangerous time, but it is also homecoming and dinner on the grounds. It is earth-shaking, but it is also centering. It is a time when dead ones shall not live and shades shall not rise up (26:14) but also a time when the dead shall live and corpses rise up (26:19). It is a time of the withering of the world (24:4) but also of the sprouting of Israel and Judah, and the face of the world shall be full of fruit (27:6).

At two critical points, the text climaxes in announcements of the rule of the Lord — at the end of the large picture of destruction in chapter 24 and at the conclusion of the whole in chapter 27. In this regard the text is an announcement of the coming of the kingdom of God, and so its component parts are hints of the onset of that kingdom, images of what matters and the way it will be when the Lord reigns. The first instance, in 24:23, is reminiscent of the earliest historical and mythic depictions of the Lord's reign: the victory of the Divine Warrior over the enemy — whether the forces of death or the forces of Pharaoh, and they are one and the same — which culminates in the enthronement of the deity in the holy abode of God.

As at the beginning, the dwelling place of God is particular and spatial. It is not universal and everywhere. The Isaiah text echoes many other Old Testament eschatological texts and anticipates the final eschatological picture of the scriptures in locating God's presence with the people in *Jerusalem*, on *Zion*, a powerful thread of continuity with the New Testament (Revelation 21). Jerusalem is specifically a symbol for the irresistible reign of God and for the perduring presence of God with humankind. As a symbol it manifests both *continuity* and *discontinuity*:

a. Jerusalem is a realistic symbol in that it speaks of a specific city and a specific mountain, central to the history and identity of Israel — even today; but the new Jerusalem "comes down from heaven" (Rev. 21:2); and

b. Jerusalem is the place where Israel stands before the glory of the Lord in praise (24:23 and 27:13), the place of homecoming and security for the perishing, the lost,

---

18. It is the particular contribution of Donald Gowan's *Eschatology in the Old Testament* (Philadelphia: Fortress Press, 1986) to have recognized that Jerusalem is the center of Old Testament eschatology, appearing "with a prominence unparalleled by any other theme" (3).

and the exiled; but this mountain is also the place where "all the peoples" gather before the Lord (25:6–7).[19]

The actuality and the particularity as well as the continuous and discontinuous dimensions of Jerusalem/Zion are analogous to the church's claims about the particularity of God's dwelling in Jesus Christ. For there also the dwelling of God is particular, spatial, and real.[20] But, eschatologically, that particularity is also discontinuous. The Christ who comes is the same and not the same as the one who came as a part of Israel's history. The Jerusalem where God comes in glory (24:23) is the same and not the same as the Jerusalem of Israel's history. And if the images of Christ's advent and of the Lamb are a way of saying that God's dwelling is still with humankind at the end and is still personal, then Jerusalem/Zion is a way of saying that God's dwelling is still with Israel and is still cultural and spatial at the end. The conjoining of the two in the Christian vision of the end is in the vision of the city whose "temple is the Lord God Almighty and the Lamb" (Rev. 21:22). So Jerusalem is transformed into the heavenly city, the social and political center of the kingdom of God; and the Messiah is transformed into the Lamb who is enthroned with God (Rev. 21:1).

It is no easier to say what such personal and cultural continuity and discontinuity may mean for the reality of Jerusalem/Zion than it is for the coming of Christ. What John Polkinghorne has suggested about the transmutation of matter and the carryover of pattern that are indicated in the resurrection may be applicable here. One might argue that Jerusalem/Zion has been replaced with the dwelling of God in Jesus Christ, but both Old and New Testament do not let go of the cultural and communal dwelling of God in Jerusalem as the continuing dwelling of God with humanity. Thus, one may suggest that the vision of the New Jerusalem, coming down from heaven, is a way of speaking about the transformation of space as God's presence in the new creation.[21]

A Matter of Life and Death

The text before us envisions a future that is marked by life as well as death, finally by life rather than death, that is, by the end of death (25:8). To get at this dimension of the text, one must speak about the *faithfulness of God* and the consistency of the biblical portrayal of that faithfulness. From the beginning of the biblical story — and I assume that in a fundamental way the biblical story

---

19. It is worth noting that there are prophetic and eschatological texts that point to a sequence of nations/Gentiles first, and then Israel in the procession to the mountain of the Lord, for example, Isa. 2:1–5//Micah 4:1–5; Isa. 45:20–25, 59:19–20. In regard to this as well as to the eschatological salvation of the Jews in Romans 9–11 and its possible Old Testament antecedents, see Otfried Hofius, "'All Israel Will Be Saved': Divine Salvation and Israel's Deliverance in Romans 9–11," in *The Church and Israel, Princeton Seminary Bulletin Supplementary Issue*, no. 1 (1990): 19–39, and Hofius, "Das Evangelium und Israel. Erwägungen zu Römer 9–11," ZTK 83 (1986): 297–324.

20. On the connection of God's dwelling in Jesus Christ to the dwelling of God in temple space, see Karl Barth, *Church Dogmatics* (Edinburgh: T. & T. Clark, 1957), 478–83.

21. The concern for the pattern of the city in the account in Revelation 21 is an implicit echo of the earlier Old Testament claim that there is a heavenly "pattern" to the Tabernacle (Exod. 25:40).

is the human story — it is clear that this often-enigmatic God, whose wrath can and does break out again and again, this dangerous God, is not *finally* dangerous or even finally enigmatic. The Lord of Israel is bent toward the world God made, not against it, toward the human creature God created for fellowship, service, and praise. Nowhere is that more tellingly laid out than at the beginning, when the human story of sin, judgment, and curse (Genesis 1–11) ends not in an eschaton of judgment and death — a possibility specifically rejected by God after the flood (Gen. 8:21) — but in the call of Abraham and the blessing of "all the families of the earth" (Gen. 12:1–4a). The syntax of those verses is careful and indicative. The command to Abraham to "go from your land, your kindred, and your father's house" is followed by a sequence of verbal forms tying the promises that follow to the command, "Go." That is, the text is to be read as "Go . . . *so that* I may make your name great, and that I may bless you" (Gen. 12:2). The sequence of promise-blessings is to be understood as God's purpose in sending Abraham and the result of Abraham's going. They continue into verse 3, where there is a standard blessing-curse formula: "I will bless the ones blessing you; and I will curse the ones cursing you" (Gen. 27:29; Num. 24:9). In Gen. 12:3, however, the number of those blessed is *plural*, but the number of those cursed is *singular.* Blessing is expected to be the norm, curse the exception. Even more important, the purpose construction that carries through the whole promise (and is recognizable in the Hebrew verbal syntax) is broken in the curse formula (which is clearly not a purpose construction in the Hebrew). That is, Abraham's going is to accomplish the divine purpose, but only the sentences about blessing express that purpose. The sentence about possible curse does not. It is a statement about happenstance, not divine intent. The result may be translated as follows:

> Go from your land . . . to the land that I will show you, so that I may make your name great . . . and that you may be a blessing and so that I may bless the ones blessing you (and should there be somebody who treats you contemptibly that one I will curse) so that all the families of the earth may be blessed in you.

What this means is that the intention of God from the beginning is to effect blessing in a world that has come under the judgment of curse. That blessing is the purpose of the whole story of Israel. It is for the many; it is for all. And there is no divine intention to curse. That is now a parenthesis, the exception. It may happen. But the Lord of Israel is directed toward blessing and mercy, not toward curse and judgment. That is an outcome of human actions but not the purpose of God. The judgment is short and the blessing is long (Ps. 30:5 [Heb. v. 6]; Isa. 54:7–8).[22] It is on these grounds, at least, that one must understand the encompassing rubric for the end as *consummation* rather than *judgment.*[23] Both the biblical story at the beginning and what it tells us about the end are resistant

---

22. Patrick D. Miller, "Syntax and Theology in Genesis 12:3a," *VT* 34 (1984): 472–76.
23. Cf. Kendall Soulen, *The God of Israel and Christian Theology* (Minneapolis: Fortress Press, 1996), especially pt. 2.

to the reduction of God's final consummation to a judgment between vice and virtue, sheep and goats.[24]

The faithfulness of God, therefore, is at stake at the end precisely because the divine intent is so clear at the beginning. At two places in this text, the divine choice of life over death is made, despite the choices that have been made by the inhabitants of the world:

1. One is the picture of the banquet "for all peoples on this mountain" where the primary features are the provision of goodness and the end of death and sorrow (25:7–10a). The swallowing of death and of the covering or mask (25:7–8) — most likely coverings or masks of sorrow — is a reversal of the customary swallowing that Earth and Sheol and death bring about. Now it is not life that is swallowed up by death or the underworld but death that is swallowed. It is, of course, this claim that Paul reaffirms as a primary eschatological reality in 1 Cor. 15:54, where the swallowing of death comes "at the last trumpet," as it does in the Isaianic text (27:13). The banquet of life and goodness is proclaimed by the people as a salvific act that has come to those who have hoped (25:9; cf. Isa. 40:31). The banquet is an implicit celebration of the reign of God and the universal acclaim of all the peoples: "This is our God . . . this is the Lord" (25:9).

2. The second depiction of the Lord's choice of life over death is in the oracle of salvation to the people in 26:19: "Your dead shall live; their corpses rise up; the inhabitants of the dust awake and sing for joy."[25] With its mix of realism and metaphor, the text can hardly be understood except as a pointer to resurrection. Indeed, it is out of just such texts as this that the community came to know about resurrection. There is much debate as to whether this is to be understood as referring to the nation specifically or to individuals in general. Is it "resurrection" of Israel or resurrection to life of all human beings? It is surely both. The words are addressed to those who have cried out in lament in the preceding verses. But the image itself points not simply to a national restoration but to the renewal of life in its individual manifestation. The picture is not dissimilar from that of the dry bones coming back to life in Ezekiel. There, also, the scene has to do with the renewal and return of Israel, but the depiction is of the opening of "your graves" (plural), the return to life, not of some vague generality dubbed "Israel" but specifically of those persons who make up that community. If Israel's return from exile is the fulfillment of such prophecies of resurrection, then they are such in the same way that Lazarus's return from death is a sign of the resurrection that is still to come.

---

24. Cf. William Schweiker, "Time as a Moral Space: Moral Cosmologies, Creation, and Last Judgment," chap. 9 in this volume.

25. This text is to be compared with Dan. 12:2, a clearly eschatological passage: "Many of those who sleep in the dust of the earth shall awake, some to everlasting life, and some to shame and everlasting contempt" and then two verses later, "But you, Daniel, keep the words secret and the book sealed until the time of the end."

Eschatological Joy

Central to both pictures are *the sounds of joy* (25:9; 26:19). But those sounds do not occur for the first time or only at these points. The text suggests a kind of grammar of eschatological joy in its various sounds and silences.[26]

The Joy of Creation

While a reading of the familiar story of creation in Genesis 1–3 does not uncover the dimension of joy as a part of the beginning and a result of God's creative intent, there are clues elsewhere that suggest joy is a part of God's good creation. The original creation's provision of wine for human relaxation has already been noted (Gen. 5:29; 9:20). The Creator's provision of "wine to gladden/make joyful the heart" is also celebrated in Ps. 104:15. In that same psalm, one learns that the Creator has provided streams to water the trees so that the birds have a place to sing their songs, an association of music and joy that is reiterated at the end (see below). In answering Job, the Lord identifies the time of creation as a moment "when the morning stars sang for joy / and all the heavenly beings shouted for joy." Music is built into the very fabric of creation, and the joy at the end is a return to the joy of creation after that joy has disappeared in judgment.

The Disappearance of Joy in Judgment

A significant feature of the judgment and its effects is the end of joy on earth, climaxing in the announcement that "the joy of the earth has gone into exile" (24:11). This expression is a cardinal example of the poetic ambiguity that is a significant dimension of the communication of the text. The expression makes a universal claim about the judgment as manifest in the disappearance of joy from the earth — gone into exile. But it has been noted that the phrase "joy of the earth" may contain a reference to Jerusalem since that expression is explicitly applied to Jerusalem or Zion in Lam. 2:15 and Ps. 48:3.[27] The central cultural symbol of the text is itself a synonym for joy. The absence of joy is such an identifying marker for the judgment that it is mentioned several times: "all the joyful of heart groan" (24:7); "the joyful sound of the timbrel has ceased" (24:8); "the joyful sound of the lyre has ceased" (24:8); "the noise of the exulting ones (the merry singers) has ceased" (24:8); "all joy has reached its eventide" (24:11); and "the joy of the earth has gone into exile" (24:11).

The characteristic signs of the disappearance of joy in judgment are two: the *absence or bitterness of wine and beer*, those refreshments given at the beginning for the relaxation and joy of human life, and the *cessation of music*. Again, both these features are accentuated. The wine dries up; the vine wilts; no longer do they drink wine with singing; beer (sometimes translated as "strong drink") is

---

26. I would associate this joy with what Schweiker calls "real joy" in "Time as a Moral Space" (see chap. 9).

27. Dan G. Johnson, *From Chaos to Restoration: An Integrative Reading of Isaiah 24–27*, JSOTSup 61 (Sheffield: JSOT Press, 1988), 30. One is reminded also of the exclamation of the psalmist in Ps. 137:6: "Let my tongue cling to the roof of my mouth . . . if I do not set Jerusalem at the top of my joy."

bitter; and there is an outcry in the streets over lack of wine (24:7–11). So also the text repeatedly describes the stopping of the music — instrument and voice. Music, celebration, joy, conviviality, and relaxation vanish from the creation in the judgment of the earth. George Steiner has written of music:

> Music and the metaphysical, in the root sense of that term, music and religious feeling, have been virtually inseparable. It is in and through music that we are most immediately in the presence of the logically, verbally inexpressible but wholly palpable energy in being that communicates to our senses and to our reflection what little we can grasp of the naked wonder of life. I take music to be the naming of life. This is, beyond any liturgical or theological specificity, a sacramental motion.[28]

If Steiner is correct, then music, like mathematics, may represent patterns that belong to reality, providing intimations of "the existence of non-material aspects of reality."[29] As with mathematical discovery, so one can say about Bach, did he create his magnificent music or discover it?

Premature Joy

There is a premature rejoicing on the part of Israel in this text (24:14–16), to which the prophet reacts negatively (16b-20). As Hans Wildberger has put it, the prophet seems

> to want to prevent Israel from grinning from ear to ear, or possibly even stop them from enjoying the view, as the earth was about to experience incomparable destruction because of God's judgment. Initially, he simply speaks about how horrible what is going to come upon the earth will be. Israel as well, precisely Israel, was then supposed to pay attention to this message and be deeply moved, and thus was supposed to lay its songs of celebration aside.[30]

Eschatological joy is not over the destruction, not over the judgment. Joy really is absent from the judgment.

Eruptive and Interruptive Joy

At the same time, there is an interruptive joy that erupts and cannot be contained. This is reflected in the psalmic pieces in the text, specifically 25:1–5 and 26:1–6. It is difficult to place these hymns of praise at any temporal point or in any logical relation to the events of the judgment or the events of the renewal of life. They simply interrupt, the voice of the community breaking out into songs of praise. One cannot easily say which expressions of joy in the accomplishment of God's ultimate reign in judgment and redemption, in death and the renewal of life, are premature and which are not. But there is a clear movement from the end of joy, celebration, and music to their renewal. The hymns of the text are thus not only testimonies to Israel's salvation but anticipations of the eschatological choir, the voices of God's people who sing the praises of the Lord in, through, and beyond

---

28. G. Steiner, *Real Presences* (Chicago: University of Chicago Press, 1989), 216–17.

29. Polkinghorne, "Eschatology." On the relation of music and mathematics, see Steiner, *Real Presences*, 79–80.

30. Wildberger, *Isaiah 13–27*, 502.

the judgment of the universe. The fact that one cannot "locate" these hymns of praise is crucial. They are one of the continuities from beginning to end, sung now and then ("then" as both past and future) and finally.

Eschatological Joy

So it is that this joy is in some sense the final word. It has been noted above that two key places in this text depict the end as God's victory over death, as the transformation of death into life accompanied by the sounds of joy (25:6–10; 26:19): It will be said on that day,

> Lo, this is our God; we have waited for him, so that he might save us...let us be
> glad and rejoice in his salvation. (25:9)

> Your dead shall live; their corpses rise up;
> The inhabitants of the dust awake and sing for joy. (26:19)

Removal of the covering and the wiping away of tears are not a return to a kind of neutral indeterminate state. They are the turn from sadness to joy, from tears to laughter. Wine and music return — in the end. The eschatological banquet described in 25:6–10 — a text from which the New Testament draws again and again (1 Cor. 15:54; Rev. 7:17, 21:4) — is both an affirmation of the materiality and goodness of life that some of us enjoy and that others have been deprived of and an anticipation of the "enjoyment" of the "fat things" by "all" on that day.[31] In this part of the text, the "we" who speak have two locations: (1) "We" are *singers in the eschatological choir* and so find the end toward which life has been set, the praise and glory of God;[32] and (2) "we" are *guests at the eschatological banquet* where there is a final, that is, full enjoyment of the goodness of the material life God has given. Precisely here the biblical text connects with Polkinghorne's suggestion that the life of the world to come "will surely take the form of an unending exploration of the riches of the divine nature.... The old creation is a world that contains sacraments; the new creation will be wholly sacramental. Ultimate human fulfillment will be a continuing sharing in the life of God."[33] The scriptures suggest, metaphorically and realistically, that such exploration and sharing will be indeed sacramental, "dinner talk," around the table where the community receives the blessings of God and of life in God.[34]

An eschatological reading of the Psalter leads us to the same place, to praise, music, and joy at the end — all the choirs and all the orchestras of heaven and earth, with Israel leading the way, united in the praise of God (Psalms 145–50). Something of this eschatological joy, which is a real joy anticipated in so many ways but certainly in music, is suggested in two quite different secular literary contexts.

---

31. Note the repeated "all peoples" (25:6, 7), "all nations" (25:7), and "all faces" (25:8).

32. See the first question of the Westminster Shorter Catechism: "What is man's chief end? To glorify God and to enjoy him forever."

33. Polkinghorne, "Eschatology."

34. See Kathryn Tanner, "Eschatology without a Future?" chap. 15 in this volume.

In his novel *A Prayer for Owen Meany*, John Irving has the first-person narrator of the book tell about the funeral of his mother, who was killed in a freak accident. He reports about his young friend Owen, the central character of the book, singing all the hymns in a loud voice, especially "Crown Him with Many Crowns." Then he says this:

> Even later at the committal, I could hear Owen's awful voice ringing when Mr. Wiggin said, "In the midst of life we are in death." But it was as if Owen were still humming the tune to "Crown Him with Many Crowns," because I seemed to hear nothing else; I think now that is the nature of hymns — they make us want to repeat them and repeat them; they are a part of any service, and often the only part of a funeral service, that makes us feel everything is acceptable.[35]

And the fictional Mozart of Peter Shaffer's play *Amadeus* says to Salieri and Baron van Swieten in excited tones:

> I tell you I want to write a finale lasting half an hour! A quartet becoming a quintet becoming a sextet. On and on, wider and wider — all sounds multiplying and rising together — and then together making a sound entirely new! ...I bet that's how God hears the world. Millions of sounds ascending at once and mixing in His ear to become an unending music, unimaginable to us.[36]

35. John Irving, *A Prayer for Owen Meany* (New York: William Morrow, 1989), 125.
36. Peter Shaffer, *The Collected Plays of Peter Shaffer* (New York: Harmony Books, 1982), 527.

Chapter 12

CHRISTIAN HOPE AND THE DENIAL OF DEATH
Encountering New Testament Eschatology

DONALD H. JUEL

The idea of death, the fear of it, haunts the human animal like nothing else; it is a mainspring of human activity — activity designed largely to avoid the fatality of death, to overcome it by denying in some way that it is the final destiny for man.
— ERNEST BECKER[1]

All the great religions knew of the finitude of the world. Those who, according to Wisdom 2, think they should trample down the meadows and behave mercilessly because of the finitude of life are called blasphemers. We will have to give a clear account why they must not be called "realists." — MICHAEL WELKER[2]

This chapter represents a contribution to a brief but intensive conversation among experts in the sciences and in religion. One way to approach such a conversation is by sharing ideas from our various disciplines. If the topic is eschatology — an understanding of "last things," or, to use a different language, the limits of a finite universe — we can ask what each of our disciplines contributes to right and responsible thinking. What do modern astronomers and physicists contribute to the way we think about "the End"? What light does the evolution of the human brain shed on the distinctiveness of the human species as well as our tie with the rest of the created order? What bearing does such reflection have on notions of Christian hope — and vice versa? Many people live their lives within a world of "common sense" that has little to do with what is common and sensible among knowledgeable insiders in various disciplines. I presume we would agree that it is better for the public to know such matters than to remain unenlightened.

In such a conversation, one of my responsibilities as a teacher of the New Testament is to contribute some early Christian ideas about the end that will help fill out what eschatology and limitedness "mean." Chief among such notions are the resurrection of the dead and God's promise to "make all things new."

---

1. Ernest Becker, *The Denial of Death* (New York: Simon and Schuster, 1997), xvii.
2. Michael Welker, "The Theology and Science Project — The Consultation on Eschatology," conference opening remarks.

Professor Welker's opening remarks to the conference envision a more interesting and ambitious undertaking. He describes a conversation in which the
goal is not the formation of an elite community of the knowledgeable but the
shaping — or reshaping — of modern cultures increasingly distanced from life-
sustaining traditions and practices that have formed the life of the church. The
absence of God from public imagination and the attractiveness of exterministic
eschatological worldviews require of thoughtful Christians new forms of conversation and address. It is important that the testimony of the church be truthful.
It is equally important that it be plausible and engaging.

The topic of our conversation is eschatology. Ideas about the end, as Albert
Schweitzer suggested some time ago, are not just intellectual curiosities. They
shape one's attitude to the past and present as well as the future. What we
imagine life has in store for us and the creation will determine how we understand
ourselves and our place in the larger scheme of things, which will in turn have
some impact on how we invest our time and energy. Our task is to suggest ways
of testing and critiquing and deepening our ways of imagining "last things" from
the perspective of our various disciplines — and to do so in a way that takes
seriously what we believe God has to do with last things. And if we imagine that
what we are saying is truthful, we will be obliged to ask how our proposals can
be made plausible to people outside our respective disciplines whose ideas of the
future may be very different and for whose practical imagination God is of very
little consequence.

Promising Ideas

It is possible to speak of New Testament eschatology — or perhaps better, eschatologies — in descriptive terms. It is instructive, for example, to examine the
imagery with which New Testament authors picture the "last things" — images
drawn, we might say, from the "science" of the times. Striking is the consistent use
of Old Testament imagery. Equally striking is how little interest New Testament
authors have in the original meaning and setting of such biblical language and how
distinctive are the ensuing visions of the future in which Jesus is a central figure.

A regular feature of New Testament visions of the future is the enthronement
of Christ at the right hand of God. The imagery comes from two passages:

> The LORD says to my lord:
> "Sit at my right hand,
> till I make your enemies your footstool." (Ps. 110:1)

> I was in the night visions,
> and behold, with the clouds of heaven there came one like a son of man,
> and he came to the Ancient of Days and was presented before him.
> And to him was given dominion and glory and kingdom,
> that all peoples, nations, and languages should serve him;
> his dominion is an everlasting dominion, which shall not pass away,
> and his kingdom one that shall not be destroyed. (Dan. 7:13–14)

These two passages in Israel's scriptures, using the imagery of the royal court in the Ancient Near East, envision a scene in the heavenly throne room where there are two royal figures. The passages were of considerable importance to New Testament authors and the later church. Whatever their original meaning, they furnished early believers in Jesus with language by which to speak of the relationship between the "Lord" Jesus and the Lord God, and they both imagine the future in terms of the dominion both Lords will share. It is hardly surprising that the rabbis found these verses so dangerous and Christians found them so productive.[3]

Another picture of the end-time is the "return of the Son of Man," pictured with imagery from Daniel 7 and Zech. 12:10, as in Rev. 1:7:

> Look! He is coming with the clouds;
> every eye will see him,
> even those who pierced him;
> and on his account all the tribes of the earth will wail.[4]

While less common, the New Testament makes some effort to picture the world to come after Jesus' triumphant return. Jesus' parables speak of the afterlife in terms familiar from Jewish and other contemporary literature: the kingdom of God may be compared to a marriage feast (Matt. 22:1–13; Rev. 19:7–9); those who participate in the resurrection of the dead will neither "marry nor be given in marriage, but they will be like the angels" (Mark 12:25); some will reside in Abraham's bosom, while others will suffer torment in the fires of Hades (Luke 16:19–31).

Within the discipline of biblical studies, the various images can be grouped and studied for their similarities and differences from other visions of the future in the ancient world. Whatever the results of such study, many contemporary readers will find such images bizarre or quaint. The mythology needs to be interpreted, in much the same way current scientific mythology must be interpreted for those who do not understand. Its truth value must be assessed. Yet even this interpreting is only a first step. Merely observing images does little to alter notions of the future in ways that generate hope or despair. Simple statements are lacking in power and have little plausibility value. It is unlikely they will change anyone, convince anyone, instill hope in anyone. The convincing is done in a variety of rhetorical forms that include but are not exhausted by narratives and letters. Some of the forms we know from the New Testament only secondhand (i.e., worship and proclamation). New Testament literature, in other words, presumes activities within which particular notions about last things make sense and instill faith in God, which in turn produces hope. In addition to the precise metaphors

---

3. For an account of the centrality of these passages in the formation of rabbinic Judaism and orthodox Christianity, see Alan Segal, *Two Powers in Heaven* (Leiden: Brill, 1977).

4. On the use of Old Testament texts in the formation of Christian visions of the future, see Barnabas Lindars, *New Testament Apologetic* (London: SCM Press, 1961); David Hay, *Glory at the Right Hand: Psalm 110 in Early Christianity*, SBLMS 19 (Nashville: Abingdon Press, 1973); D. Juel, *Messianic Exegesis: Christological Interpretation of the Old Testament in Early Christianity* (Philadelphia: Fortress Press, 1988).

in which the future is made real, I am interested in the activities that not only "give a clear account" of our hopes for the future (Welker) but do so in a way that is convincing and moving.

My argument here takes the suggestion provided by Ernest Becker in his *Denial of Death* as a point of departure.[5] The flight from the reality of death provides a decisive clue to understanding New Testament eschatology and the history of its interpretation. At the center of Christian eschatology is the cross of Christ. While it is the promise of resurrection and the final triumph of God and the Lord Jesus that furnish the content of Christian hope, a real barrier to the birth of Christian hope is not the idea of resurrection — an idea not unique to early Christianity — but the denial of death.

Interpretation of the New Testament is a means by which people have sought to protect themselves against the reality of death — both as an experience within the Godhead and among humans. Particularly in the context of a conversation regarding the limits of the creation, a more compelling argument for hope in the God who raises the dead will take the cross of Jesus more seriously and in so doing make more difficult escape from the experience and reality of death. Reading the New Testament with such a prejudice can, I argue, make for more lively engagement with the Bible and serve as more adequate preparation for an experience of the gospel.

I have chosen to focus on gospel narratives rather than on Paul's letters, and on one gospel rather than on all the gospels, though the canon provides the larger setting within which any individual work is read. The gospels tell a story about Jesus they believe will engender hope for the near and distant future. "Endings" play a crucial role in their effort to persuade and move readers. I have chosen the Gospel according to Mark as the focus of study for a variety of reasons, not least of which is its consuming interest in the trial and death of Jesus within the context of a story that is full of promises, and its distinctive ending.

A Promising Future: Mark 13

From the first chapter, Mark's is a story about promises. Some of the promises are from the scriptures. Jesus' words to his disciples are programmatic: "For the Son of man goes as it is written of him" (14:21). On occasion the biblical citations are introduced with a formula to call attention to their scriptural status (12:10–11); on others, scriptural words are employed that can be recognized by those who know the passages (1:11; 14:62; 15:24, 29, 34, 36). John the Baptizer, the first character to be introduced in the narrative, makes his appearance in the desert "as it is written [in] Isaiah the prophet" (1:2).[6]

Characters in the story also make promises. Jesus' promises about what is to occur play an important role in the story. In particular, his predictions of his

---

5. Becker, *Denial of Death*, xvii.

6. The citation, as commentators regularly observe, appears to include words from Malachi as well as Isaiah, raising interesting questions about the use of the Old Testament in the New.

death and resurrection offer interpretations as well as foreshadowings of what is to occur in the story (8:31–32; 9:31–32; 10:33–34).

Perhaps most interesting are those promises that point beyond the confines of the narrative. In his first and only lines, John the Baptist speaks of one greater than he who comes after him. "I have baptized you with water," he says, "but he will baptize you with the Holy Spirit" (1:8). Nowhere in the story are we told that Jesus baptizes anyone. The promise points beyond the conclusion of the story. Some of the promises that drive the story on can be termed eschatological. Speaking about the kingdom of God, Jesus tells parables about seed time and harvest, of tiny seeds and large shrubs (4:1–20, 26–29, 30–32), using imagery that had become part of Israel's visions and dreams of the future. He speaks in riddles, but promises a time of clarity and openness (4:21–24).

An important moment in the story is the long pause in chapter 13 for warnings and promises about the future. While the term "Little Apocalypse" is of limited usefulness in characterizing the discourse, the chapter is surely eschatological.[7] It speaks of "the end" which is "not yet" (13:7) and of the events that will lead to the consummation of all things. The context within which discipleship is lived out will include disruption at every level of life: within families (13:12–13), religious communities (13:9–11, 21–23), nations (13:8), nature (13:8), and even in the heavens (13:24–25). The faithful will be tested by persecution from outside and temptations from within (13:9–11, 21–22). Salvation will require endurance.

The grim forecast is set within a hopeful context. The agonies of the created order are "birth pangs" (13:8). They anticipate new birth. Jesus' triumphant coming will mark the end of the old age and will provide public vindication for those who have remained faithful: "Then they will see 'the Son of Man coming in the clouds' with great power and glory. Then he will send out the angels, and gather his elect from the four winds, from the ends of the earth to the ends of heaven" (13:26–27). Why anyone should believe such a forecast — addressed not just to the disciples but to "everyone" (13:37) — depends on Jesus' trustworthiness and the faithfulness of "the Father" who alone knows the time of the end (13:32). The story must establish sufficient reason to trust the one who says, "Heaven and earth will pass away, but my words will not pass away" (13:31).

The history of interpreting the chapter does not instill confidence. Mark — or Jesus himself — may have believed that the destruction of the temple in 70 C.E. would mark the beginning of the end (13:1–8). The qualification, "But about that day or hour no one knows" (13:32), may well indicate some disappointment and adjustment in expectations as Jerusalem fell and the world did not end. Matthew and Luke, who retold Mark's story for a later generation, give evidence of further adjustments (Matthew 24–25; Luke 21:10–36).[8] Mainline Christian traditions have invested less and less in the particulars, holding at most to the promise of Jesus' triumphant return at the end. We might ask how plausible such a notion

---

7. The discourse does not assume the form of an "apocalypse," even though some of the imagery is drawn from the Book of Daniel. See my *Master of Surprise* (Minneapolis: Fortress Press, 1994).

8. Luke in particular seems to separate the events surrounding Jerusalem's destruction and the last times. The fall of Jerusalem will mark the advent of the "time of the Gentiles" (Luke 21:24).

can be even when divested of all its particulars. The question still remains: Is Jesus' word trustworthy? Can we count on anything in particular?

The Death of the King (Mark 14–15)

Having finished with Jesus' forecast, the narrative moves to the events that will mark the climax of the story.

After two and a half decades of intense involvement with Mark's gospel, I am still impressed by its unflinching attention to Jesus' arrest, trial, and death. The power of the one who bestrides the world like a colossus in the early chapters makes all the more striking the totality of Jesus' collapse. Betrayed by one of his inner circle of colleagues, abandoned by the rest — with the exception of Peter, who denies him three times with an oath — Jesus appears before the religious authorities, where he is tried, found guilty, and mocked. He is brought before Pilate where he is also tried, found guilty, mocked, beaten, and crucified. As he hangs on the cross, he is ridiculed by those executed with him (15:32) and taunted by two groups of onlookers (15:29–32). His only words, "My God, my God, why have you abandoned me?" are misunderstood by the crowd who believe he is calling Elijah (15:34–36). With that final misunderstanding, Jesus breathes his last, disappointing one last time a small group who have stayed to the bitter end, hoping for a spectacle. The story would seem to be about disappointed hopes and broken promises.

Students are often surprised to discover that in the whole passion narrative, there is scarcely a single image that belongs to the traditional language of "atonement," a conception that has provided the means by which many generations of Christians have dealt with the reality of the cross. The advantage of much theological speculation is that it can abstract itself from the particulars of the case to the rarefied atmosphere of theory. Problems can be posed ("Why did Jesus have to die?") and answered satisfactorily at a safe distance from the harsh realities of the narrative (and of life). There is no indication that Mark sought to establish such a relationship between readers and events. There are no clear signs of a "theory" by which the reading of Jesus' death becomes a satisfying experience.

There is another perspective from which the events can be read which does not require distance from the horror of humiliation and death. The story can be read as ironic. Jesus is invested and hailed as King — though by his enemies who have no idea that they are speaking the truth. Major titles for Jesus are spoken by the high priest ("Christ, the Son of the Blessed One" [14:61]), Pilate ("King of the Jews" [15:2, 9, 12]), Roman soldiers ("King of the Jews" [15:16–20]; "God's Son" [15:39]), and Jewish taunters ("the Christ, the King of Israel" [15:32]). The scriptures of Israel provide the script for the story (Psalms 22 and 69). That God's will is done — that Jesus is crowned and proclaimed King — does not deny the violence and death. On the contrary, the power of the story arises from the collision of two ideas that do not fit: kingship and humiliating death. Their uneasy union is not "explained" or resolved theoretically. The narrative depicts a world in which those who should know best know the least — for whom "Christ crucified" is scandal and folly. There is no attempt to play down the violence and horror generated by their fears and lack of insight. Experiencing the story as ironic simply suggests there may be another view of the events.

That "other perspective" is not necessarily hope-giving. The story may simply portray life as it is — mysterious, impenetrable, eluding the grasp of everyone. All depends on what God does in response to Jesus' execution. There can be good news only if Jesus' death is not the end of the story. Even a new future for Jesus is not necessarily good news. What if God chooses to repay violence with violence? How will God deal with those who are blind and deaf to the truth — and whose blindness and deafness have such terrible consequences? Answering such questions must also presume some kind of interpretive stability so that readers can have confidence in their status as insiders. By itself, irony can be destabilizing, awakening consciousness that things may not be as they seem. What is to guarantee that present readers are not as misguided as were Jesus' contemporaries? What guarantee is there that God has not simply withdrawn, abandoning interpreters to their own imaginings (Rom. 1:18–32)?

The matter is of considerable importance for appreciating the whole of Mark's gospel. Jesus has made promises at his trial — one, a promise that his judges "will see the Son of Man seated at the right hand of the Power and coming with the clouds of heaven" (14:62). That image of the Son of man coming with the clouds harks back to the climactic image in 13:26–27. At stake in reading the passion story is whether Jesus' promises are to be trusted — and because he dies, the promises must depend ultimately on "the Father," the one who alone knows the time of the end, the "my God" to whom Jesus' last cry is directed.

The Sense of an Ending (Mark 16:1–8)

With so much at stake, the ending of the gospel bears considerable weight.[9] If an evaluation of Jesus' death and his ability to deliver on his extravagant promises depends on what God does next, the story will have to offer a plausible account of Jesus' vindication. There are hopeful signs. The terse report of the women's visit to the tomb at least provides evidence that Jesus is no longer in the tomb. To know what that means, we must listen to the words of the "young man," whose testimony to the women harks back to Jesus' own words.

> Do not be alarmed; you are looking for Jesus of Nazareth, who was crucified. He is not here. Look, there is the place they laid him. But go, tell his disciples and Peter that he is going ahead of you to Galilee; there you will see him, as he told you. (16:6–7)

The invitation to go and tell, however, is unheeded:

> So they went out and fled from the tomb, for terror and amazement had seized them; and they said nothing to anyone, for they were afraid. (16:8)

---

9. I am presuming that the Gospel of Mark we are to read concludes with verse 8. I have argued the case in *Master of Surprise*, 107–10.

The ending is disappointing. The hoped-for breakthrough from the time of silence to a time of speaking does not occur. If Jesus' resurrection is the in-breaking of the end, the dawning of a new age, it appears to make no impact. Readers are left with the word of the young man. There is no proof. And when the women run away, too terrified to tell anyone what they have seen, we are left without the means of ending the story. There is no one to trust or doubt, no one whose word can be tested. There is only the fearful silence. Jesus is nowhere to be found, and whether he will appear to speak a hopeful word, what it will be, whether or not it will be for us — all are left open and unresolved.

Many presume interpretation will come to the rescue. It is surely the case, for example, that Jesus' prophecies have an important place in the story. Several times he predicts his death. On five occasions he speaks of his being raised (8:31; 9:9; 9:33; 10:33; 14:28; perhaps also 12:11, which speaks of God's vindication of the rejected stone in the words of Psalm 118). In 14:28–30, he gives a detailed prediction of what will become of his followers, including a forecast of Peter's denial and of his "preceding you to Galilee." The narrator takes pains to remind us how exactly Jesus' prediction to Peter was fulfilled. At the conclusion of the account of Peter's denial, we are told: "At that moment the cock crowed for the second time. Then Peter remembered that Jesus had said to him, 'Before the cock crows twice, you will deny me three times.' And he broke down and wept" (14:72).

We are surely expected to infer that Jesus' other predictions are trustworthy as well. The empty tomb suggests that Jesus' prophecies of resurrection and vindication are as trustworthy as of his death and rejection. The young man's announcement, "as he told you," harks back to a whole narrative of promise and fulfillment, anticipating a continuation of the story with more promises and fulfillments continuing to "the end."

Yet the ending is disappointing nevertheless. The multiplication of conclusions in the history of the Markan text[10] and the continuing efforts of commentators to imagine another conclusion provide evidence that the lack of a satisfying ending is problematic — intellectually, emotionally, and finally theologically. Closer attention to the text only makes matters worse. The women run off, too terrified to say anything to anyone. The reason, we are told, is that "terror and amazement had seized them." There is a passive sense, reminiscent of the comments that the disciples' hearts had been hardened (6:52; 8:17). The language does not locate the solution of the women's or the disciples' plight in the realm of human will and action. Deliverance will require being acted upon.

The problem for readers is that we are left with insufficient resources to resolve the story at least so that we can experience the ending as confirming and satisfying. Jesus never makes an appearance. That he returned to his place at God's right hand would not be good news without some sowing of seeds that promised a harvest in this world. If hearts are hardened, who will give them new life? If the women are seized by terror and amazement, who will release them? Jesus remains silent. And there is no formal passing of the baton even though

10. Ibid., 109.

successors have been prepared — no breathing the Spirit into the disciples and giving them the power of the keys (John 20:21–23). There is no one left in whom to invest confidence. Not even the narrator makes a final appearance to assure us that the story ended properly, as the later additions to the gospel attempt.

That places readers in a strange position. Some commentators argue that the ending is a "device" intended to awaken readers to the urgency of proper discipleship. Readers, so the argument goes, must add the "amen" to the story themselves. Its resolution lies in our hands. We must prove faithful where the disciples and the women failed. That is a strange argument, however, in a story that has repeatedly emphasized the inability even of insiders to see and understand. At the conclusion of the gospel, the disciples have fled; even a visit to the empty tomb and the testimony of the young man do not transform the little circle of women. And those most suited to be authorized interpreters — the religious and the legal experts — make their decision about Jesus convinced that they know the truth and that their rejection and execution of him are not only in the public interest but constitute fidelity to God.

Readers alone can appreciate the irony that the leaders have no idea where and how God is at work. What is to say that contemporary interpreters may not be as far from the mark? What hermetic guarantees are there that we know "the mystery of the kingdom of God" — particularly when so many disagree in their interpretations? Who knows with any confidence that he or she is included in the good soil destined to be productive (4:3–20)? Who can say that he or she is among the elect — that the blessings of "eternal life" are assured? Readers are given no access to the requisite data. It is only Jesus who is in a position to speak such words — and in Mark, at least, Jesus is unavailable for interrogation.

One of the most stimulating reading partners I know is Frank Kermode, whose books *The Sense of an Ending* and *The Genesis of Secrecy* have enriched my appreciation of the literature of the New Testament immeasurably.[11] Kermode is a good reading partner principally as a challenger of interpretations. Students generally have no defense against his erudition and his deftness with texts that he employs against traditional interpretations. Particularly in his *Genesis of Secrecy* he offers his opinion about the ability of the gospels and their interpreters to make an argument on which one might build a life. His comments about engagement with Mark might well be directed to our whole interpretive enterprise. I quote them in full because of their appropriateness to our task:

> What is the interpreter to make of secrecy considered as a property of all narrative, provided it is suitably attended to? Outsiders see but do not perceive. Insiders read and perceive, but always in a different sense. We glimpse the secrecy through the meshes of a text; this is divination, but what is divined is what is visible from our angle. It is a momentary radiance, delusive or not, as in Kafka's parable. When we come to relate that part to the whole, the divined glimmer to the fire we suppose to be its source, we see why Hermes is the patron of so many other trades besides

11. Frank Kermode, *The Sense of an Ending* (New York: Oxford University Press, 2000), and *The Genesis of Secrecy: On the Interpretation of Narrative* (Cambridge: Harvard University Press, 1979).

interpretation. There has to be trickery. And we interpret always as transients — of whom he is also patron — both in book and in the world which resembles the book. For the world is our beloved codex. We may not see it, as Dante did, in perfect order, gathered by love into one volume; but we do, living as reading, like to think of it as a place where we can travel back and forth at will, divining congruences, conjunctions, opposites; extracting secrets from its secrecy, making understood relations, an appropriate algebra. This is the way we satisfy ourselves with explanations of the unfollowable world — as if it were a structured narrative, of which more might always be said by trained readers of it, by insiders. World and book, it may be, are hopelessly plural, endlessly disappointing; we stand alone before them, aware of their arbitrariness and impenetrability, knowing that they may be narratives only because of our impudent intervention, and susceptible of interpretation only by our hermetic tricks. Hot for secrets, our only conversation may be with guardians who know less and see less than we can; and our sole hope and pleasure is in the perception of a momentary radiance, before the door of disappointment is finally shut on us.[12]

For Kermode, an encounter with Mark's gospel is an eschatological experience. It is an experience of the end — an end that marks not the consummation of all things but the termination of hope. Though something may have happened to Jesus after he was placed in the tomb, it has little to do with us. While there may be secrets, even a divine radiance streaming from the story, it is and will remain beyond our grasp. When it comes to interpreting a story as simple as Mark's, we cannot find an Archimedean point from which to pry open the story's secrets.[13] There is no rock on which the wise may build. There is only the closing of the door at every level of life to which we have access. The desire to construct "an appropriate algebra" may be therapeutic, but it is finally a denial of death. There is no theory by which to evade the reality of the cross. Interpretation can provide no rescue. There will be deliverance only if God raises the dead. Yet readers are left at the mercy of a God who for most people is absent or silent.

This is one of the arguments the New Testament makes, most pointedly in its Pauline form. There is no "making sense" of the cross in such a way as to absorb it into a system of thought that removes its sting. It remains foolishness (1 Cor. 1:18–25). In Jesus' cross we encounter the limit of our calculations.

"Yes, but..."

There can be no denial of death. The gospel is the "word of the cross." As a word that takes the reality of finitude and death seriously, it respects the experience of contemporaries who respect the reality of death and finitude. The cross of Christ is "eschatological," however, not only because it does not evade death. It is an experience of the last things most especially because God does not allow

---

12. Kermode, *Genesis of Secrecy*, 144–45.

13. The image is used by Richard Bernstein in his *Beyond Objectivism and Relativism* (Oxford: Blackwell, 1983) to portray what he terms the "Cartesian anxiety" that drives modern culture in its search for stability.

the cross to be the last word. The testimony of the New Testament is that God raised Jesus from the dead, and in so doing opened a new possibility for the whole created order.

That Jesus was raised from the dead may be as unsettling as the reality of his death. For some, it will be the most unsettling of all. That is surely what frightened the women. They at least were prepared to deal with his death. They came to the tomb to pay their respects. What they discovered is that they could not count on the one thing most certain about life. Jesus was no longer dead. "He is not here, he has been raised," they learned. And they were terrified. There was nothing available within their ordinary experience on which they could rely. If they did not have Jesus to grasp and hold, they also discovered that he could not be sealed away safely. It could be argued, in fact, that there is a group for whom the greatest and most unsettling surprise is that God raises the dead. I have argued elsewhere that it is precisely the prospect of "something more" that interpreters like Kermode seek to head off in providing closure in their own engagement with Mark. The closed door with which Kermode concludes his study of Mark — an image he borrows from Kafka — turns out to be thrown open by the One who will not allow such premature closure.[14]

How to speak of resurrection requires artfulness. The mark of theological wisdom is knowing when and how to speak of such matters in a way that avoids an escape from the reality of death — and that prevents closing off the future to new possibilities for those who take strange solace in the finality of death.

"Given for you"

Speech that engenders hope must issue in and arise from a kind of discourse that includes address. Narrative is not such a rhetorical form. Readers may imagine that the promises in the story are for them, but there is no way to know, and interpretation is of no help here. That God raises the dead must be a reality that can intrude into closed futures and bound imaginations of real people. This is precisely the direction of some suggestive passages in the gospel itself, the first of which is a single verse: "the good news must first be proclaimed to all nations" (Mark 13:10). Proclamation in this case is direct address in which someone speaks for God to particular people, not just an audience in general. For good reasons Christian tradition has stressed the "living voice" of the gospel and not chosen to rely on written words.

To this promising verse we may add a few others, from the account of Jesus' last meal with his followers:

> While they were eating, he took a loaf of bread, and after blessing it he broke it, gave it to them, and said, "Take; this is my body." Then he took a cup, and after giving thanks he gave it to them; and all of them drank from it. He said to them, "This is my blood of the covenant, which is poured out for many. Truly I tell you, I

---

14. Juel, *Master of Surprise*, 119–21.

will never again drink of the fruit of the vine until that day when I drink it new in the kingdom of God." (14:22–25)

Mark's gospel, together with the rest of the New Testament, invests a great deal in particular activities through which God frees bound lives and gives birth to hope. The claim that God refuses to accept death as the final word is made in light of a history of divine activity centered in God's raising the crucified Jesus from the dead. Crucial is how that reality becomes effective through the medium of human systems of signs that address particular people in their particular settings. In the worship of the church, where the risen Christ is present in the spoken word and in the sacraments, generations of Christians have testified that God gives birth to hope against hope.

Taking that testimony seriously suggests some limits for theological discourse: it cannot itself solve the problems it identifies.[15] The reality and finality of death cannot be dispelled by arguments. Only God can raise the dead. Death's hold on our imaginations will yield only to God's action that is available to us now only in the form of a promise. The promise assumes the form of discourse that we normally call proclamation or preaching through which God actually gives life and gives birth to hope. Such hope springs not from interpretive schemes but from a word that must be spoken to us from outside — finally, from God. That such words are spoken and do give life is reason for confidence that death and futility are not the end. That such words can be spoken in ordinary human systems of signs is an indication that the world subject to futility is still vulnerable to the intrusion of a God who raises the dead.

An Afterword

I confess that I am most taken by those within the natural sciences who find their probings and discoveries theologically ambiguous at best. I am most sympathetic with those whose increasing sense of the limits of the universe leads to a feeling of emptiness. What the Christian tradition has to offer is not an easy word but the gospel of the crucified and risen Christ. Mark's narrative embodies that message with a starkness that seems remarkably appropriate to such an experience of life. I am also aware that outside Mark's gospel there are narratives and letters and an apocalypse in which the language of joy and praise is far more prominent. It is important that we read in the context of the canon and the broader tradition of the church.

I am likewise impressed by the Bible's invitation to thoughtful discipleship. While taking death seriously, the New Testament nevertheless makes extravagant claims about what may be known: "But, as it is written, 'What no eye has seen, nor ear heard, nor the human heart conceived, what God has prepared for those who love him' — these things God has revealed to us through the Spirit" (1 Cor. 2:9–10).

---

15. This is one of the arguments forcefully made in Gerhard Forde's *Theology Is for Proclamation* (Minneapolis: Fortress Press, 1990).

We are invited to explore the "breadth and length and height and depth" (Eph. 3:18) in our own languages, expanding and reshaping our imaginations by reflecting on the imagery in which the end comes to life for us. Christian tradition has everything invested, however, in the character of the one who makes promises. Is God, as God can be known and experienced, trustworthy? The plausibility of any genuine future must depend on the God who raises the dead — a God whose gracious activity is tied intimately with the history of Jesus of Nazareth and is now located in spoken and visible words, in the "word of the cross" which we proclaim until the Lord comes. The testimony of the church and individual believers that that word gives life is not to be despised. Whether or not those promises are ultimately plausible to our contemporaries and are to be trusted — whether or not there is something beyond the reality of death and the end of the created order — is, of course, something that remains to be seen.

Chapter 13

HOPE AND CREATION

Hans Weder

The following reflections concentrate on the subject of eschatology in a particular aspect. Eschatology is thought of with respect to the relationship between the world and the kingdom of God on the one hand, and to the relationship between natural science and theology on the other. Religious hope, which is the practical and present approach to eschatology, has not fallen from out of the blue; rather, it is nourished by earthly experience. Although hope is hoping for a reign that differs from this world in a qualitative way, although it is hoping for a reign of truth, it is still living in the reign everybody knows, in the reign of reality accessible to everybody. Hope is not based on the trends and possibilities of reality; it is indebted instead to the creativity of God. But since God is seen as the Creator of the world, hope still has an intimate relationship precisely to this reality. I shall try to focus on some essential traits of the relationship between hope and reality, to be more precise, between hope and creation. This will be done from a New Testament perspective. Many New Testament texts have as their subject hope and its relation to everyday experience, and there is some evidence for the assumption that in the New Testament we can observe a process of the purification of hope.

Theology is the methodological and hermeneutical reflection of what faith gives us to think; one subject of theology is the kingdom of God, the reign of true life. Natural science is concerned with the description and explanation of the universe, the reign of real life. But in our religious tradition knowledge of God does not exist without knowledge of the world (and knowledge of the self). That is why theology, trying to grasp the knowledge of God that faith has given, has an indispensable relationship to natural science, describing the function and the structures of the world. Thus theology is vitally interested in the dialogue with natural (and social) science. This dialogue has to supplement the well-known and often practiced reception of philosophical ideas in contemporary theology.[1]

---

1. Some remarks on epistemological aspects of the dialogue between science and theology would be inevitable at this point. They can be found in the introduction of the present volume, or in a study in German language: H. Weder and J. Audretsch, "Kosmologie und Kreativität. Theologie und Naturwissenschaft im Dialog," *TLZ* 1 (1999): 48–60.

Hoping against Hope: Eschatology in a Universal Context

Hope is the particular way in which the ultimate becomes present. Hope is in this sense realized eschatology, eschatology that has entered the present. In the New Testament texts we can observe the process of the purification of hope, a process that provides manifold clues to the issue of our dialogue. The word *elpis*, "hope," derives from everyday language and keeps the contact to that language throughout the New Testament. This contact to everyday language is vital for the religious use of the word *hope*. One of the prominent motives for hope in an everyday sense of the word is the experience of things that have been reliable. Hope is not man's movement toward the future; it is his present reliance on things that promise a good future. Insofar as hope may be a characteristic of human beings, it is not based on human power and action, but on things that have turned out to be reliable.

This aspect is underlined and clearly worked out by the theological reflection of hope. Hope has an intimate relationship to faith, and faith is at the center of an anthropology that describes humans as relying upon alien forces, upon forces that are not at the hand of man. Further, faith is not confidence in the things of the world, it is confidence in God. Faith does not rely on the creature, it relies instead on the Creator of whom it is reminded by the creature. And yet, faith perceives that Creator *in the creature* (the created order, in which we discern divine energies, included). The creature, then, must bear some traits that can remind us of the Creator. And thus hope is not independent of the creatures that one encounters in the world. And it is not independent of the results and notions that natural science produces. Through faith, on the ground of which hope exists, hope has an *indirect relationship to the things of the world*. And that is why the results of scientific research are not directly relevant for religious hope. They rather are indirectly relevant. This indirect relation will be clarified later.

In the context of eschatology, hope bears a relation to the ultimate. The ultimate, the new eon, the kingdom of God, the realm of true and eternal life, belongs to the domain of the Creator, not to the field of the creature. This hope thus relates to the point of finitude, to death, to the end of the world. Finitude is a positive presupposition of Christian hope. So hope cannot, per definitionem, be directly infected by the notion of finitude put forward by natural science.[2] Finitude never has been an evidence against true hope, since true hope does not rely upon the forces of the finite, but rather on the power of infinity. That is the innermost reason for the process of the purification of hope that takes place in the New Testament.

It belongs to that process when the Gospel of Luke can speak of hopes being disappointed as a positive event. Herod's hope to see a sign done by the Messiah is disappointed by Jesus.[3] This is a necessary disappointment belonging to the

---

2. Cf. J. C. Polkinghorne, *Belief in God in an Age of Science*, The Terry Lectures (New Haven: Yale University Press, 1998), 20–23; see also his "Eschatology: Some Questions and Some Insights from Science," chap. 2 in this volume.

3. Luke 23:8ff.

positive work of Christ. It means being saved, so to speak, from the power of futile hope. In a similar way the disciples at Emmaus tell of their hope for Israel's political "redemption"; this hope has been disappointed bitterly by the crucified.[4] This sort of hope *must* be disappointed, because it prevents the disciples from perceiving the risen One[5] who is the true living Savior, who brings a redemption from the political play of power as such and not only from the hostile powers. It is not by accident that both pieces of evidence mentioned are cited in the context of the cross. Jesus' way to the cross brings all kinds of hope into a fundamental crisis, and since then only that kind of hope is valid that proves true in view of the cross, the cross as a sign of finitude, even for the son of God. By narrative means Luke shows the way from illusion to hope in the face of the reality to which death and finitude essentially belong.

The clearest purity of hope is achieved in the Pauline letters. First it is worth mentioning that Paul makes a distinction between hope related to secular life and hope that remains valid in the face of death: "If for this life only we have hoped in Christ, we are of all people most to be pitied" (1 Cor. 15:19). Though there is no doubt that hope has its relevance for present life, too, this relevance is based on the fact that hope reaches out in a life differing qualitatively from the present life. Hope is relevant for human life only if it is valid as well for human death: the hope for resurrection from the dead, which has its evidence in the resurrection of Jesus.[6] As far as hope, therefore, remains within the possibilities of the world, it has not yet reached its purity or truth. Purity is achieved as soon as hope concentrates on the reality of God.

In the Letter to the Romans this receives some further reflection and is given systematic coherence. Abraham was "hoping against hope, he believed that he would become 'the father of many nations,' according to what was said, 'So (numerous) shall your descendants be.'"[7] In this text two concepts of hope clash together: the normal concept of hope that relies on the possibilities of the world, a hope that is grounded on trends and lines of development within the realm of the visible, and the hope that is based on the creativity of God, on the realm of the invisible. Abraham believed against that hope that is based on the estimation or assessment of trends and probabilities. He was able to overcome this (ordinary) hope, because his faith was directed toward God, the creator of the universe, as well the creator of the possibilities of the universe. Abraham heard the word of promise; he heard it as a word of God. The idea of divine promise can be interpreted as a symbol of the promising character of life itself. The divine promise makes explicit what could be grasped as an implicit, a deep dimension of life. The word of promise can be interpreted as the message that can be perceived by a thoughtful glance at the universe. Faith is defined as confidence in that word, confidence in the creativity of God, a creativity of which one can have a presentiment in view of the creatures. As faith in the creativity of God (Paul

---

4. Luke 24:21.
5. Cf. Luke 24:25–26, 33–35.
6. 1 Cor. 15:20–22.
7. Rom. 4:18.

draws a parallel between the resurrection of Christ, the justification by faith, and the creation of the universe; cf. Rom. 4:17 and 4:3) Abraham's faith became pure hope, hope against hope, reliance on the creator of the universe and on the One resurrecting from the dead. This hope is pure insofar as it does not rely on trends and possibilities of the world. But still it cannot exist without having in mind the universe, this monument of God's creativity. This pure hope aims to the unexpected, to a future beyond any expectation, but a future that is reached only through death and finitude.

The same sort of critique is expressed by Paul in Rom. 8:24–25, where he contrasts hope for what is seen with hope for what is not seen: "For in hope we were saved. Now hope that is seen is not hope. For who hopes for what is seen? But if we hope for what we do not see, we wait for it with patience." In the second phrase *hope* is used in the sense of "content of hope" (*Hoffnungsgut*): the content of true hope is not what lies before everybody's eyes. In respect to things that can be seen, it is not hope that is the adequate relation, but perception. One needs not hope for things one is able to see. The adequate counterpart of hope is the invisible, the invisible deity and power of the creative God. This creativity cannot be perceived by human eyes, because it is something totally other than the world accessible to the senses. This creativity is rather perceived by faith that takes the creation as a monument of the Creator. Faith is, consequently, the nourishing ground of hope. To be sure, hope does not just hope with no particular goal. Through faith it is related to the visible. Since faith is the perception of God, achieved by a thoughtful perception of the given reality, hope has — in the eyes of Paul — two pieces of evidence within the present secular world: the first one is the experience of Jesus not being overcome by death, the second one is the visible fact that the universe exists instead of nothing. These two pieces of evidence are in fact brought together into one: pure hope is related to the pure God (*spes purissima in purissimum deum*),[8] whose nature is to create things for life out of nothing and to call the dead into life.

In the already quoted passage of Romans 8 our attention is drawn to another dimension of hope, its effect on the approach to the present. If hope concentrates on the invisible, it provides for human patience, a patience that consists in waiting for the invisible (the future of God). Thus hope provides for a relaxed relation to the present. If there were no hope, the realm of the visible would have to bear the burden of bringing true life. The visible, then, would be heavily weighted and in fact overloaded with the ultimate. "It's now or never" would be the approach to the world, and the secular things, human relations, goods of the earth would all be consummated by this approach that overloads the world by far. Patience, on the other hand, implies a distinction between the ultimate, which cannot be absolutely present in the world, and the relative. This distinction implies that a human being who hopes receives from the world that which it can provide, and leaves perfection to the future of God. This relaxed relation to the present would

---

8. Cf. P. Bühler, "Kreuz und Eschatologie. Eine Auseinandersetzung mit der politischen Theologie, im Anschluss an Luthers theologia crucis," HUT 17 (1981): 148–54.

be, I think, of utmost ethical relevance, too. If the moral space could be viewed as relative, without becoming indifferent and trivial at the same time, this would be an excellent basis for a humane behavior. I leave this point to further elaboration (New Testament eschatology contains quite a lot of clues to find a relaxed and yet adequate relation to the present).

In this brief sketch of the process of hope being purified in the New Testament, we have seen that hope, although it relies on the creativity of God alone, does not forgo the reality of the world, especially the traces of creation within the admixture of the universe. At this point a dialogue between natural science and theology might prove quite fruitful. Following the hints given by Paul, we start by looking at the everyday experience of life as possibly containing traces of creation. If we think of Christmas, for instance, we probably realize that every birth of a child brings something new into the world and is therefore a trace of creation and a piece of evidence for hope. If we think — to give another example — of the Holy Spirit, we probably realize that every illumination or flash of inspiration is a trace of that alien force making life alive. If we finally think of the step from cross to resurrection, we probably realize that every experience of being raised out of the depths — be they spectacular or insignificant — is a trace of creation. We could conclude, then, that the generation of the new is the secular concept that must be related to religious hope.

And thus the question is whether natural science can possibly identify such a concept. It indeed can, for instance in astrophysics. A star — to give an example — is generated out of accidental fluctuations of clouds of interstellar gas.[9] The new that is generated cannot be derived from the old, the generated star is new in the sense that it is an unpredictable event, a surprise (in theology we call this contingency). It is also new in the sense that old matter has been transformed into a new structure; the old is still a part of the new, but it has not remained the same in the process of generation. The new does not occur everywhere, it occurs at particular places under particular conditions of disequilibrium (*Ungleichgewicht*).[10] The new is not generated arbitrarily, but nevertheless spontaneously. This can be observed in all systems that are controlled by self-organization. So we can state that the generation of the new is, in fact, a typical and characteristic pattern of the developing universe.[11]

To describe the relation between a religious and a scientific perception of the universe, let us turn to the concept of metaphorical relationship.[12] The following phrase can be imagined and taken as a model: "The generation of the new is God's work." Were this phrase to be understood as conceptual language, it would exclude a scientific description, which for methodological reasons is constrained to the secularity of the universe. It would mean that the generation of the new

---

9. See A. Benz, *Die Zukunft des Universums, Zufall, Chaos, Gott?* (Düsseldorf, 1998), 22–24.

10. See ibid., 129.

11. Benz points out that this development is frequently brought forward in jumps (discontinuously) and is therefore not a predictable or continuous one. See ibid., 130–31.

12. As to the formal description of a metaphorical relationship see the preface of this volume, and Audretsch and Weder, "Kosmologie und Kreativität," 54–60.

can only be explained by using the word *God.* To understand the phrase literally is, according to the preliminary remarks on a proper hermeneutical procedure, not adequate. It is far better to understand it as a metaphor bringing together two phenomena that could not be brought together literally. This metaphor is correctly understood when one keeps in mind that there is a qualitative difference between the work of God and the generation of the new. The nature of God's work is, according to fundamental religious insights, to create things out of nothing.[13] The generation of the new is, according to scientific research, that something new and unexpected comes into being by a process of transformation of the old.

The semantic value of the mentioned phrase understood as a metaphor operates by a fundamental tension between subject and predicate. It is the tension between creation and transformation. This tension cannot be overcome; it is, on the contrary, necessary for the semantic value of the phrase. One important moment to be contributed to the dialogue between theology and science is to strengthen the described tension by clarifying the difference between creation and transformation. This is as well a contribution to a sensible religious language.

There is, to go a step further, a reciprocal action between subject and predicate, between the generation of the new and the work of God. This reciprocal action can be described as a process of mutual disclosure.

The generation of the new, to begin with, discloses the work of God as transcending the predictable, since the new appears as a surprise, as unpredictable (even if nothing other than the natural laws are at work in those processes), and as opening the space of the future (like the basic openness of the cosmic process, which for that reason can only be described when it already has taken place). These properties (they could be easily multiplied) are not mere *illustrations* of God's work, they are in fact *interpretations.*[14] They must bear to a certain extent the claim to truth of the religious concept, work of God. They are not mere pictures or signs for something totally different, they are in fact the anchoring of the work of God within the world of experience. These properties may serve as an interpretation of the religious ideas of qualitative novelty and of a future that is not just a continuation of the present. They interpret the religious notion that it is God's nature to free human beings as well as all things of the universe from their being bound to the past.

To estimate the significance of this element of the metaphor, we can ask what difference it makes whether the basic openness of the universe already mentioned exists or not. In a clockwork universe, too, religious hope would be possible; but since there would not be even a single clue for the possibility of the new, one would have to hope for the radical end of everything (as it was in fact the case in apocalyptic systems) in order to produce space for a new and true eon (and there would be no evidence for that hope in the present age); the old age must end ontologically as well as epistemologically. In view of the pattern of the generation

---

13. Cf. E. Jüngel, "Das Entstehen von Neuem," in *Wertlose Wahrheit: Zur Identität und Relevanz des christlichen Glaubens,* Theologische Erörterungen III (Munich, 1990), 132–50.

14. Cf. E. Jüngel, "Paulus und Jesus, Eine Untersuchung zur Präzisierung der Frage nach dem Ursprung der Christologie," HUT 2 (1986): esp. 135–39.

of the new, hope is in a different situation: it may take the coming into existence of the new as a trace of a newness that goes beyond worldly novelty in a qualitative sense, yet still has a family similarity with the new that is generated by the cosmic process. So it makes a decisive difference for the concrete shaping of hope if the universe is gifted with the unpredictable new or not.

The predicate "work of God," on the other hand, discloses the generation of the new as a process whose meaning goes far beyond the particular cosmic development. The predicate discloses this process as a trace of creativity; it discloses a secular process as having a meaning in respect to the ultimate. This disclosure allows us to perceive not only the new and its generation, but also the creator of that generation, God. It allows a faith that entails a hope for the ultimate that is invisible and at the same time at work in the realm of the visible. And, to sum up this point, in exploring this mutual disclosure, much work has to be done in an improved dialogue between natural science and theology. Each approach can keep its own shape and inclinations (science need not become pious, theology need not become atheistic), and still they are related to each other in a fruitful way.[15]

It is the nature of a metaphor that it gives something to understand as something; it shows something as something else; in our example, the metaphor gives the generation of the new to be understood as a work of God. It is of utmost importance that this process of new understanding has no logical necessity whatsoever. The becoming of the new can quite well be understood just as becoming of the new. The predicate does not replace the secular understanding, it tries to deepen it instead. And this deepening can only be effective when compulsive logical strategies are avoided. The mere existence of a scientific interpretation of those processes provides for avoiding the compulsive. The deeper understanding put forward by the metaphor is an *offered* understanding, not a *forced* one. The offer it makes opens at the same time an open space, a space for human freedom (this is in fact the same space that is opened up by the unpredictability of self-organization processes). This freedom is absolutely vital, because the Christian gospel cannot exist without the free consent of the human addressee. Religious insights, at least in the Christian tradition, belong to those truths that are immediately destroyed when they are administered with compulsive power (this has not always been kept in mind by theologians and rulers). The space of freedom opened by our metaphor is in itself a trace of God's creativity, whose nature it is to free from old boundaries. So the space of freedom is created by metaphorical language; nevertheless, the addressee is offered a particular interpretation. He is not put in a situation of the deliberate, where he is facing nothing; he is, on the contrary, moved into the direction of God. The metaphor can be taken as a model of cooperation between natural science and theology: it is the task of natural science to prevent theology from compulsive strategies, and it is the task

---

15. Cf. W. Pannenberg, "Theologie der Schöpfung und Naturwissenschaft," in *Mensch und Universum. Naturwissenschaft und Schöpfungsglaube im Dialog*, ed. J. Dorschner and M. Heller (Regensburg, 1995), 148–50.

of theology to remind natural science of the freedom to deeper interpretations and to prevent it in this way from the temptation of reductionism.

The hope for the ultimate is nourished by faith in the creativity of God, and faith cannot exist without perceiving the creatures as traces of creation in the midst of the secular mixture of the universe. The shape of the phenomena of the world is not indifferent to faith and consequently to hope. Thus hope is intimately related to the notion of reality as achieved, for instance, by natural science.

Hope beyond Death: Personal Eschatology

In the following remarks I shall concentrate on the personal aspects of eschatology, that is, on the hope for a life that comes beyond earthly human life. This is — in a Christian theological perspective — not a life after life[16] but rather a life after death. The Christian concept of resurrection, which has risen in the context of early Jewish eschatological insights,[17] cannot think of an eternal life that has not undergone death. Thus, finitude (death) is at least a necessary presupposition of eternal life, if not an important element of it in the sense that a pure eternal life can only come after death as the end of any human fight against truth and purity.

The early Christian model for this insight was given with the resurrection of the crucified Christ. Various attempts were made to exclude the bitter reality of Christ's death, especially in gnostic circles of the second century A.D. As far as the real humanity of Christ was respected, as was the case in the New Testament texts (cf. 1 John 4:2), death as the real end of his life was to be included into the faith in Christ. The life he had been given after his death was the unique work of the creative God alone. There was no substance within the earthly person of Jesus that was able to persist through death. The life of the risen Christ had, then, a quality that differs in a qualitative way from any earthly life. The most predominant difference is the character of eternity, that is, of not being subjected to finitude anymore (not only in the temporal sense of the word). As a consequence of Christology, the Christian eschatological concept of life after death had an extremely positive relationship to finitude. The qualitative newness of eternal life cannot do without the radical end of temporal life.[18] This implies a specific and positive understanding of finitude.

---

16. Cf. R. A. Moody, *Life after Life: The Investigation of a Phenomenon — Survival of Bodily Death* (Harrisburg, Pa.: Stackpole Books, 1975).

17. Hen(aeth) 39:7–8; 51:4–5; 4 Es. 7:97, 125; *Apoc. Bar.* 51.3.

18. In a particular way this idea is treated by the concept of the paraclete in the Johannine community, who can only come because and after the first paraclete, Jesus, had died (parted); cf. John 14:16–17, 26; 15:26–27; 16:7–11, 12–15; R. E. Brown, "The Paraclete in the Fourth Gospel," *NTS* 13 (1966/67): 113–32; G. Johnston, *The Spirit-Paraclete in the Gospel of John*, MSSNTS 12 (Cambridge, 1970); H. Weder, "Evangelische Erinnerung. Neutestamentliche überlegungen zur Gegenwart des Vergangenen," in Weder, *Einblicke ins Evangelium. Exegetische Beiträge zur neutestamentlichen Hermeneutik, Gesammelte Aufsätze aus den Jahren, 1980–1991* (Göttingen, 1992), 196–98; A. Dettwiler, *Die Gegenwart des Erhöhten. Eine exegetische Studie zu den johanneischen Abschiedsreden (Joh 13,31–16,33) unter besonderer Berücksichtigung ihres Relecture-Charakters*, FRLANT 169 (Göttingen, 1995), esp. 181–89, 203–7, 286–92, 298–304.

Finitude characterizes life as described by natural science. One might even say that the emergence of individual life was made possible by the invention of death.[19] The evolutionary process of developing higher forms of life was only possible on the basis of dying individuals. In this respect the Christian hope for eternal life implies no contradiction to scientific insights. It is, on the contrary, relying on the presupposition of finitude, for any concept that implies infinite parts in a human life dissolves the true hope, at least partly. The true faith in the creativity of God entails the assumption that there is nothing infinite in a human being, for eternal life exists and consists merely grace to God. It is a life out of death.

There is, of course, a substantial difference between the scientific description of life as finite and its religious perception. What is described by natural science as a finite being is perceived by faith as a creature. To be a creature implies finitude, to be sure, but it draws the attention at the same time to the creator of finitude. It perceives finitude as a work of a creative alien force. Both aspects are combined in the New Testament use of the Greek concept of *sarx*, "flesh."[20] Every living being is flesh, and as flesh it is finite and a creature at the same time. Thus the finitude described by natural science is given a deeper dimension by Christian religious interpretation: what is just finite in a secular perspective is understood as a creature in a religious perspective.

At this point another metaphorical phrase can be imagined and taken as a model for the dialogue between theology and science: "The finite is a creature of God." Again, this phrase must not be understood as conceptual language. Within the scientific construction of reality the possibility of naming something a creature is excluded for epistemological reasons. But again, if the phrase is understood as a metaphorical predication, subject and predicate interpret each other mutually. And an important epistemological demand to the theological interpretation of the finite as a creature is that it must not contradict the scientific description (which might as well be an interpretation). Finitude, to begin with, can be scientifically described as having absolute limits. A finite individual exists within certain limits that cannot be overcome. Due to the finitude of resources and the limitations of reproducibility the individual cannot live forever. This finitude discloses an important aspect of the nature of creatures. It is the aspect of being limited, which is a necessary implication of being created. The aspect of finitude makes sure that any creature differs in a qualitative way from its creator. While the creator is free to create, the creature has been given a definite and vulnerable form like an earthen vessel (2 Cor. 4:7).[21]

---

19. "Death moves exhausted organisms to another phase of the cycle of nature and allows potentially more successful combinations of genes to supplant them. Death, therefore, is one of nature's ways of improving life; it provides a changing stage on which natural selection can try new experiments in evolution." "Death," *Encyclopedia Britannica* 16 (Chicago, 1985), 1030.

20. Cf. 2 Cor. 4:11; 2 Cor. 10:3; Gal. 2:20; Phil. 1:22; see also R. Bultmann, *Theologie des Neuen Testaments*, UTB.W 630 (Tübingen, 1984), 233–35.

21. Cf. Chr. Wolff, "Der zweite Brief des Paulus an die Korinther," ThHK 8 (1989): 88–92; T. B. Savage, *Power through Weakness: Paul's Understanding of the Christian Ministry in 2 Corinthians*, MSSNTS 86 (Cambridge, 1996), 164–69.

The predicate, on the other side, has an interesting relation to the subject of the phrase. To be a creature implies with necessity to be limited. The predicate explains, then, and confirms an essential quality of the subject: its limitation. But the term *creature* looks at limitation not quite in the same way as the scientific description does. While the latter is confined with the limit as such, while the latter looks toward the border merely from within the area that is limited, the former sees the limit as a border between immanence and transcendence, so that it discloses the limited area as neighbor of a wide and free country beyond the border.

Scientific statement and theological interpretation differ essentially in their perspective on the border: scientifically, the border is seen as a one-side border, so to speak, while the border theologically is seen as relating this side to the other side. Consequently, seen as a creature, a limited individual hints to the creator who has given the limits and who is awaiting the creature beyond its limits. The scientific view of finitude is ambivalent: it can serve as an argument for the nothing, as an argument for the annihilation of the finite being beyond its end, but it can serve as well as an argument for creativity, as an argument for the re-creation of the creature beyond its end. This ambivalence is essential for scientific descriptions, unless they have become reductionist. In interpreting the limited being as a creature, theology does not contradict natural science, but rather enriches it by disclosing a deeper dimension of being finite. The concept of finitude is deepened by the religious concept of creativity. But still, finitude is a positive presupposition for an eternal life that is created afresh by the same creator who has created the finite one.

The stressing of a strict difference between earthly and eternal life brings up the problem of continuity. If there was no continuity whatsoever between both lives, the New Testament idea of an "eternal life" would be proven wrong, since it is not confined to the absolute future but rather reaches from there to the present life before death. Not only this, but also there would be no reason at all to speak about eternal life in a sensible way. If worldly experience were not to contain any clues for eternal life, nothing can be said about it; it would remain an empty fantasy. If there were no continuity, there would be no possibility of grasping the life to come. At the same time discontinuity is essential, due to the qualitative newness of eternal life. The problem then arises of how to think together continuity and discontinuity.

The solution to this problem may lie in a paradoxical interplay of continuity and discontinuity. This interplay can be studied by investigating the Pauline distinction between "psychic body" (*sōma psychekon*) and "pneumatic body" (*sōma pneumatikon*).[22] "It is sown a natural body, it is raised a spiritual body. There is a natural body, and there is a spiritual body" (1 Cor. 15:44). A first glance at this Pauline word makes clear that "body" is the element of continuity, while "natural" and "spiritual" are the elements to mark discontinuity. Paul speaks about the

---

22. Cf. F. Altermath, "Du corps psychique au corps spirituel. Interprétation de 1 Cor 15,35–49 par les auteurs chrétiens des quatre premiers siècles," BGBE 18 (1977): 20–37.

gap between time and eternity, and at the same time of that which overcomes or survives that gap. Paul's idea is rather remarkable seen against the cultural background of his time. Mainstream anthropology would locate the gap just the other way around: while the soul would have been seen as the surviving substance, the body[23] would have counted for the finite part, the gap between time and eternity. The remarkable difference of Paul's idea to the mainstream anthropology points to an interesting view of continuity and discontinuity. In Pauline anthropology *body* does not mean the material part of a human being, but rather the whole person (consisting of material body, soul, and spirit).[24]

The gap itself is due to the idea of resurrection, which is the opposite of any idea of personal development toward eternal life or survival of the gap. The step from here to now is not a human step, it is rather a step caused by God alone, by his creative activity. The time to come is for Paul a time of redemption from any limitations, troubles, and pressure of human life.[25] For this reason the transition from the natural body to the spiritual one is to be understood as liberation from all limitations of the body or the person. To be a natural body means to exist under the conditions of the earthly life, to be stressed by earthly calamities, and to be limited at the same time. To be a spiritual body means to live as a personality that is created by divine creativity and formed by the spirit. To be a body means for Paul that human beings live fundamentally in a relationship; they are in relation to themselves, to the world, and to God.[26] Bodily existence is an existence that is — at its best — rich in relationships. The more relationships, the more alive the life. The fundamental relationship, to be precise, is a peaceful one. And in this respect the natural body differs from the spiritual body. The natural body is limited by natural conditions; these limitations are — due to sin — felt as a big provocation to fight against them. The limited human being keeps fighting against its limitations and this fight diminishes the peaceful relationship; it prevents human beings from living as a body, as a person. The conditions of earthly life are, to add another dimension, of such quality that human relationship is hindered and limited. This prevents a human being from being truly alive.

Paul stresses the moment of discontinuity between this life and the life to come. Still he draws our attention at the same time to the moment of continuity, the moment of being a body in both realms. Eternal life as well is somatic, personal, rich of relations. Death is the definite end of a person as natural body. There is

---

23. With regard to the New Testament concept of body see H. Weder, "Leiblichkeit. Neutestamentliche Anmerkungen zu einem aktuelle Stichwort," in Weder, *Einblicke ins Evangelium*, 219–38.

24. Concerning Paul's understanding of body, cf. E. Schweizer, "sōma ktl.," *TWNT*, 7 ed. G. Kittel (1964): 1057, 1064, esp. 1063; Bultmann, *Theologie*, 193–203.

25. Compare 1 Cor. 15:42–43: the gap between corruption and incorruption, between dishonor and glory, between weakness and power; Chr. Wolff, "Der erste Brief des Paulus an die Korinther," ThHK 7 (1996): 406–7; G. D. Fee, *The First Epistle to the Corinthians* (Grand Rapids, Mich.: Eerdmans, 1987), 784: "The first three sets of contrasts are intended to describe the essential differences between the 'naked seed' and 'the body that is to be' (v. 37); that is, despite the verb 'sown,' they are not intended to describe the 'dead body' that is buried, but to contrast the present body with its future expression."

26. 1 Cor. 6:12–20; Rom. 12:1; Bultmann, *Theologie*, 196–200.

no bridge from this life to the next. In death all human relations come to an end, at least insofar as those relations have their origin in the human person. Death is the end of all human possibilities, the end as well of all relations people can have out of themselves. But it is not the end of God's possibilities and power. In this respect death is at the same time the point where God's power can act in an unlimited way. When human power comes to an end, even the power to fight against God, there is no human resistance left against any relation. It is the point where God will create a new relation to a human being and where this human being becomes a spiritual body, a person, whose peaceful relation to God is no longer impeded either by the limitations of earthly life or by the powerful transgressions of sin. It becomes a body, a relational being, not something totally different from its earthly existence, but a true body, because it is determined by God's creative relation alone.

The bodily nature of life, to sum up, is the moment of continuity, which allows at the same time for radical discontinuity. The discontinuity is given by the radical difference between natural existence, which is characterized by relationships that are limited for various reasons, and spiritual existence, which is filled out with peaceful relations. Both aspects, the natural and the spiritual, can be experienced in present life: although limited, there are fundamental relations that make life alive, the fundamental relation to a mother or to a community of language; although difficult to perceive, there is the alien power of spirit to be sensed, which is the principle of life in the whole universe.[27] The continuity is given by the bodily nature of life, the relational structure (*Beziehungsstruktur*) of existence. A body is a human being insofar as it exists in and as an interactive being, interactive with the world, with itself, with God. The aspect of interactivity draws our attention to a fundamental structure of life: the structure of the interplay of particular entities or parts building a whole and consequently improving its complexity.

At this point there is again a possibility (not to say a necessity) of the dialogue with natural science. The natural body is — in Paul's perspective — characterized by relationship and interplay. And although the hope for eternal life rests on the transcendent reality of the spirit, this hope depends on the relational structure of present life. This structure must be accessible to natural science. The question is whether or not relation and interplay are universal patterns of life. One could mention the capacity "of performing a number of such functions as eating, metabolizing, excreting, breathing, moving, growing, reproducing, and being responsive to external stimuli"[28] (the "metabolic"[29] character); one could mention the biochemical definition of "living organisms as systems that contain reproducible hereditary information coded in nucleic acid molecules and that

---

27. Cf. Cicero, *Nat. D.* 2.7.19, 8.22, 11.29; and the Stoical understanding of spirit (*pneuma*); see, e.g., G. Verbeke, "Geist," *HWP* 3, ed. J. Ritter (Basel, 1974), 158–62; cf. also John 6:63; S. Schulz, "Das Evangelium nach Johannes," *NTD* 4 (1987): 111; E. Schweizer, "πνευμα," *TWNT* 6, 436, 5–443.

28. "Life," *Encyclopedia Britannica* 22, 985, although this physiological definition is not quite sufficient.

29. Ibid. (there are again some exceptions).

metabolize by controlling the rate of chemical reactions using proteinaceous cat-
alysts known as enzymes"[30] (the "genetic definition" of life as a "system capable
of evolution by natural selection").[31] The processes of both evolution and natural
selection are to the greatest extent made possible by relations (both to the following generation and to the natural environment). Finally, one could mention the
thermodynamic distinction between open and closed systems. While the universe
as a whole is thought of as a closed system "steadily moving toward a state of
complete randomness, lacking any order, pattern, or beauty," life is understood
"as an ordered system," living systems as "not closed but rather open," which
increase "their order at the expense of a larger decrease in order of the universe
outside."[32] So the moment of building up complexity seems to be highly characteristic for life.[33] And higher complexity always means a more intensive interplay
between more elements and a more relational existence. The contribution of
natural science is to concrete the relational[34] nature of life and to deepen the
understanding of improved complexity.

The contribution of a theological interpretation of life deriving from the insights concerning eternal life, on the other hand, does not contradict a natural
scientific description, it rather enhances or enriches the latter. Eternal life concentrates on the relational character of life, a character that will be realized in
a fully unlimited manner in eternity. By this concentration it stresses the importance and deeper meaning of relationship in natural life; it encourages the
cultivation of this relationship, which is steadily threatened either by the calamities of nature or the selfishness of human beings. The hope of eternal life implies
a qualitative difference from natural life, and at the same time it rests on traces
of the eternal that can be perceived in the realm of natural life. One of these
traces is the relational structure of life, another is the alien force that makes life
live, in a religious language: the life-giving spirit.

Hope for Perfection:
The Relation to the Experience of the Imperfect

It is highly characteristic of the teaching of Jesus that it contains many parables, especially parables of growth. Although one could explain this fact by the
predominance of agriculture in Jesus' world, there seems to be more in it. The

---

30. Ibid. (although this definition is again not fully satisfying).

31. "Life," 986.

32. Ibid. One has to bear in mind that a good deal of scientific controversy exists about details of
this. Exactly in what sense is the universe closed, when it might at the same time be infinite? There
are further tricky questions relating to the thermodynamics of large-scale gravitating systems (remarks
by J. C. Polkinghorne).

33. The following example may illustrate this point: "Human beings are ambulatory collections of
some cells" ("Life," 986). Even if this should not be all that can be said about human beings, it is
quite enough to prove the complexity and relational structure of life.

34. To the fact that there is much relationality in the physical world as well as in the biological,
cf. the paper of J. C. Polkinghorne, "Eschatology: Some Questions and Some Insights from Science,"
in this volume.

phenomenon of growth is indeed very particular and promising for religious interpretation. It is again a field quite appropriate for a dialogue between theology and science.

To begin with, the basic structure of parabolic speech in the teaching of Jesus is sketched in the following remarks.[35] The parables belong to metaphorical language; their underlying structure is: a subject, that is, the kingdom of God (which in some cases is not explicitly mentioned), is combined by a copula with a story telling a regular or interesting process within nature or human life. In the case of the parables of growth, the metaphorical predication brings the kingdom of God together with the secular phenomenon of growth. The semantic value of these parables can only exist as long as the fundamental discrepancy between growth and the kingdom of God is kept in mind. The secularity of the story is not at all compromised by its use as a metaphor for the coming of the kingdom, and yet it is able to interpret the realm beyond the world. The fundamental tension between the phenomenon of growth and the kingdom of God is indispensable to the success (happiness)[36] of the parable. This fundamental tension is intensified when the parable is interpreted within the framework of an interdisciplinary dialogue. Theology stresses the heavenly character of the kingdom; natural science enforces the secular nature of the story that interprets the kingdom.

The parable of the self-growing seed may be taken as a good example for studying the metaphorical impact on the dialogue between theology and science (Mark 4:26–29):

And He said:
A "The kingdom of God is as if
  B a man should scatter seed on the ground, and should sleep by night
              and rise by day,
    C and the seed should sprout and grow,
      D (he himself does not know how).
      D For the earth yields crops by itself: first the blade, then the head,
            after that the full grain in the head.
    C But when the grain ripens,
  B immediately he puts in the sickle,
A because the harvest has come."

As can be readily noticed due to the graphic presentation of the parable, it is structured by an interesting symmetry.[37] If one looks at the subjects of the elements, one can observe a meaningful play of changing subjects. In the first element, the kingdom of God is subject; it is present in the form of being "as if"; in the parallel phrase at the end, the harvest is subject, a standing metaphor for the kingdom of God in the state of fulfillment (marked by the letter A). In the second element the

35. Cf. H. Weder, *Die Gleichnisse Jesu als Metaphern. Traditions- und redaktionsgeschichtliche Analysen und Interpretationen*, FRLANT 120 (Göttingen, 1990), 58–98.

36. In regard to the happiness of speech acts, cf. J. L. Austin, *How to Do Things with Words* (New York, 1975), 12–24.

37. Cf. H. Weder, "Metaper und Gleichnis. Bemerkungen zur Reichweite des Bildes in religiöser Sprache," *ZTK* 90 (1993): 392.

man is subject; his action is sowing, sleeping by night and rising by day, leading a life without pain and sorrow. In the parallel phrase later on, this subject's action is putting in the sickle, harvesting (marked B). In the third element the seed is subject, is sprouting and growing, while in the parallel phrase the same seed has become grain that is ripening (C). Then follows a sort of interjection (the only verb used negatively): the center is the earth, which yields the crops by itself (D).

This remarkable concentric structure reveals much of the intended meaning of the parable. The central position is held by the earth, to be more precise, by an earth producing fruit by itself. On the level of the secular story of the parable it is the earth that makes the growing seed become ripening grain, and makes the sower a harvester. With respect to the parallel elements on the outmost circle (A), one is probably allowed to assume that it is again the productive earth that makes the kingdom, which has been existing in the form of "as if," to be the kingdom existing in the form of perfection. If this were so, this parable could be read as an indication of the relation between the present world and the coming kingdom. The outmost circle of the concentric structure deals with hope: that which is present in a metaphorical or symbolic shape may be hoped to be present in perfection at the end of time. The inner circles of the concentric structure deal with everyday reality, with phenomena that can be understood by everyone. The outmost circle deals with future perfection; the inner circles deal with present imperfection. The phenomenon of growth is the central point, causing the seed to bear fruit, causing the sower to be a harvester, and — probably — leading the parabolic presence of the kingdom of God, as it is evoked at the beginning of the parable, to its final perfection symbolized by the image of the harvest. The interjection then functions as a means of underlining the mystery of the fruit-producing activity of the earth.

The world of growth is indeed imperfect. Everyone knows that no one could behave in the way of this sower.[38] In the world of the story he sows at the beginning, and then he lives day by day, night by night, without any sorrow, fully trusting in the power of growth. He lives in a fully relaxed way. In the real world he would have to work very hard for his grain; he would have to fear storm and pest destroying the yield of his fields. It is exactly this discrepancy between the world of the story and reality that is used by the parable to persuade and to give reason for hope.[39] Although everyone knows that in the real world the fruit is threatened by manifold evil forces, everyone should have known at the same time that there is in fact a power of growth that provides for fruit and harvest. The

38. The fictional moments of the parable provoke a new description of secular reality. This new description is no mere contradiction to reality but rather a clarification of it (against W. Harnisch, *Die Gleichniserzählungen Jesu. Eine hermeneutische Einführung*, UTB.W 1343 [Göttingen, 1990], 164–66, who describes the alternative between reality and possibility too much in the sense of a contradiction between the bad reality and the good possibility).

39. J. Fischer, "Kausalität, Kontingenzerfahrung und christlicher Glaube," in Fischer, *Glaube als Erkenntnis. Zum Wahrnehmungscharakter des christlichen Glaubens* (Munich, 1989), 11–15, esp. 13, points out that the notion of the faith consists of two components, of a particular way of experience and of a creative perception of it; cf. H. Weder, "Wirksame Wahrheit. Zur metaphorischen Qualität der Gleichnisrede Jesu," in Weder, *Einblicke ins Evangelium*, 151–81.

story does not lie; it rather reduces the complexity of everyday experience to a central, important point: the existence of growth. The story is told as if the sower would live in a perfect creation. This is the parable's way of making a difference between world and creation. The world is that which anybody has before his eyes, a realm of labor and danger; the creation is that which can be sensed by a heart sensitive to the mystery of everything, a power on which hope can rely.

The parable does not just draw a realistic picture of the world, it rather discovers its deep dimension; it discovers the acting principle[40] that keeps the world alive and is at the same time responsible for its existence. World and creation are not separated like two totally different realms without any relation to each other. Creation is perceived and identified by a poetic approach to reality as a mystery occurring within the admixture of the world, as an alien force to trust in. In the present case, the difference between world and creation is made by isolating the phenomenon of growth, which reminds of creation, even in the midst of a world of pain and threat. The way this parable describes the world's mixture yields many clues for making a differentiation between creation and world without separating them in a gnostic or Manichaean way. Both the distinction and the relation of creation and world open a space for manifold interactions between theology and science, between a religious view of the world and everyday experience.

The parable does not identify growth with the kingdom of God. The parable's semantic value can only exist on the basis of a difference between growth and the coming of the kingdom. But still it alludes to an intimate relationship between growth on earth and the perfection of the heavenly kingdom. Both processes, the process of growth and the process of perfection, seem to belong to the same realm of creativity. It might be permissible to grasp the relationship by Wittgenstein's concept of family resemblance (*Familienänlichkeit*). In the way that members of a family are particular beings with different natures, but still can be identified as belonging to the same family by their resemblance, so growth and the kingdom of God may belong to the same realm, religion identified as God's creativity. The parable may serve as an example of how cosmology is approached in a religious context, or as a model of how the hope for perfection is related to the imperfect present world. Hope reaches to the invisible, but is at the same time grounded on visible experience. A religious approach to cosmology identifies the creative force in the midst of the admixture of the world; it reduces the complexity of this admixture to one decisive moment, the moment of growth, a symbol of creativity, the ground that sustains life and hope.

The basic metaphor ruling this parable could be described as follows: The kingdom of God is the fruit-producing earth. It gives another occasion for shaping more clearly the dialogue between theology and natural science. To know more about growth helps to understand more precisely the phenomenon to which the kingdom of God bears a family resemblance. The phenomenon of growth can be described scientifically as a process of increasing complexity. Sunlight, for in-

---

40. Cf. I. U. Dalferth, "Schöpfung — Stil der Welt, 17–18" (unpublished manuscript).

stance, is "utilized by plants to construct complex molecules from simpler ones."[41] In this respect the phenomenon of growth, typical for the productivity of the earth providing for the essentials, seems to contradict the universal tendency toward entropy.[42] This contradiction can, of course, be explained and ruled out by the assumption that open systems like organisms increase their complexity at the expense of the universe outside. But this explanation cannot deny the fact that there is a steady building-up of higher complexity. This seems to be a characteristic of the universe, too, and this can be taken as an argument for hope: what hope is hoping for, perfection, cannot be seen, but what can be seen, processes of increasing complexity, may mean more than what comes to one's eyes. They may be seen as evidence of a creativity that is truly promising.

Another interesting feature of growth is self-organization. Self-organization means that an organism does not develop just by trial and error; it is able to "choose" more promising possibilities and paths to higher evolution instead. Even if one resists any teleological interpretation of this fact, it is very interesting and most significant for the understanding of life. This principle of self-organization seems not to be confined to the processes of life-evolution; according to chaos-theory[43] it is a universal principle, at work in the whole. Self-organization is defined generally as the development of a system toward order that is independent of particular original conditions.[44] Out of what appears to human perception as a total disorder, ordered structures emerge, structures of a much higher complexity than before. This phenomenon has to be combined with the total unpredictability of the developing process of the universe. "Most of what we have to deal with in macroscopic physics is *intrinsically* unpredictable. Yet the future options are contained within certain limits (strange attractors)."[45] The idea of an attractor makes it possible to bring a certain aim-orientation (*Zielorientierung*) together with causality. Causality no longer excludes the emergence of the unpredictable, and the unpredictable can well be described (after its emergence) by causal regularities. (It should be noted that in this respect the once fundamental difference between nature and history is diminishing: historical events cannot be predicted, although they can — once they have occurred — be described by laws, or at least regularities of becoming; the more the universe is understood as a singular process of development, the smaller the differences between nature and history.) The phenomena of self-organization and attractors stand for an open future that is still not deliberate. Some sort of aims seem to be laid down in the whole process, which give it a certain promising direction (until the emergence of human

---

41. "Life," 986; concerning the immense and complex field of biological growth, cf. the article, "Biological Growth and Development," *Encyclopedia Britannica* 20, 408–87 (plant development, 426–37).

42. See P. Davies, *Cosmic Blueprint* (London, 1987), who makes a distinction between the optimistic arrow of developing higher structures in contrast to the pessimistic arrow of thermodynamics.

43. See Polkinghorne, *The Faith of the Physicist* (Princeton: Princeton University Press, 1994), 25–26.

44. See Benz, *Zukunft des Universums*, 170: "Unter Selbstorganisation versteht man die Entwicklung eines Systems zu einer Ordnung, die unabhängig von speziellen Anfangsbedingungen ist."

45. Polkinghorne, *Faith of the Physicist*, 25 (italics mine).

mind to grasp this somehow free and ordered nature of the universe). Some sort of structure or information seems to exist and to guide the processes of evolution.[46] These phenomena are indeed accessible to theological interpretation.[47] Openness and self-organization of the universe can become a metaphor for the freedom that will be realized in the kingdom of God; the existence of attractors, strange as they may be, can become a metaphor for the orientation toward the ultimate goal, the kingdom of God, a realm of highest complexity and order and of freedom most universal. If there is openness in the universe, there is the possibility to hope for the best. If there is an attracting order in the universe, there is the possibility of ultimate perfection.

As far as the hope for perfection is grounded by the parable on the nature of the imperfect, this hope is per se interested in getting to know more about that nature. If the coming of the kingdom is related with the worldly process of growth, the insights of natural science are immediately relevant for faith and hope. Although there is no proof to justify faith and hope, there is some evidence accessible to everyone. Quite an amount of evidence, among it the existence of growth, can be increased quite considerably when one expands one's knowledge about the fundamental characteristic of the universe. And some important traits of the universe, on the other hand, gain depth and significance when they are taken as religious metaphor.

Conclusion

Hope, the practical and concrete approach to eschatology, has not fallen out of the blue; it rather is nourished by earthly experience. If so, hope is well advised to expand its knowledge of that experience as intensely as possible. Theology as the reflection of faith is well advised to seek a dialogue with science. But unlike the natural theology of past generations, for which natural phenomena and therefore the findings of science were of direct and immediate theological relevance, the dialogue suggested here is modeled on the metaphorical process. Unlike in natural theology, where nature is not left to its secularity, in a metaphorical use of nature it may keep its worldly character. This is so because the qualitative difference between subject and predicate is essential for any semantic value; in a religious metaphor the fundamental distinction between world and kingdom of God is necessary and even of hermeneutical advantage.

The process of the purification of hope that we can observe in the New Testament leads to a hope grounded on faith (instead of trends and tendencies in reality); this faith, however, is faith in God's creativity, a creativity that left its traces in the created world. Natural science comes in here, because it can help to

---

46. This may be compared with the physical idea of a quantum vacuum, which "contains" nothing except information or structures; cf. J. C. Polkinghorne, *The Particle Play: An Account of the Ultimate Constituents of Matter* (San Francisco, 1979), 70–75; Audretsch, *Physikalische Kosmologie II*, 100–103.

47. Polkinghorne, too, thinks it perfectly possible "to go on to use it (sc. the unpredictability of the universe) as the basis for an ontological conjecture. This asserts that actual physical reality is subtle and supple in its character; that physical process is open to the future" (*Faith of the Physicist*, 25).

identify such traces of creativity: the generation of the new, for example, which is a fundamental property of the universe. The generation of the new can be metaphorically related to the creative activity of God. The generation of the new turns out to be an *interpretation* of God's creation of qualitative novelty; to see in that generation a work of God means to enrich its understanding in the direction of the ultimate.

Religious hope for a life beyond death is indebted to the somatic nature of life, a nature that accounts for the radical discontinuity between the present life and the life to come and at the same time for the moment of continuity. The new life of unlimited relationship has the end of the natural body as necessary presupposition, but, still, the hope for unlimited relationship rests on the relational nature of life, which allows for a hope that perceives the Creator's activity as creating relations even where they have totally vanished. The concept of this relational nature of life can be grasped much better if fundamental insights of natural science are taken into account: the natural body of any living organism is characterized by relation and interplay. This very nature, seen as a metaphor for the relational character of eternal life, may be an interesting reason for hope, for the hope in the ultimate liberation of the body to become a true body, a true personality, with unlimited and not endangered relations to God, to the universe, to itself.

The coming of the kingdom of God, finally, is related by the parables of Jesus to the phenomenon of growth. This is perceived as another trace of creativity, which nourishes faith in the creative God. There is a family resemblance between the creative process of growth and the creativity of the kingdom to come. The phenomenon of growth points to two fundamental conditions of the universe described by natural science: the process of building up higher complexity in open systems and the openness of the universe, which is protected from chaotic deliberacy or chaotic indefiniteness by strange attractors and the capacity to self-organization. Although the world to come cannot be grasped as a prolongation of this universe, although this universe is bound to finitude, its openness, ordered by attractors, may be seen as a metaphor of a freedom so attractive that it allows hope for the final creation of a new and free world of everlasting peace.

Part 4

ESCHATOLOGY IN THEOLOGY AND SPIRITUALITY

HOPE AND ETERNAL LIFE

Introduction to Part 4

REALISTIC ESCHATOLOGY

Michael Welker

The five contributions in this part of the book offer five different, yet comple-mentary, perspectives on a realistic eschatology. This means that they contribute to a theological eschatology that is well aware that it does not merely deal with a reality that can be grasped within the boundaries of materialistic naturalism alone. This means, above all and in a positive way, that all contributions are aware of the fact: eschatological realities have to stand in both discontinuity and continuity to realms and forms of experience related to material nature, if they are supposed to make sense to the natural and cultural sciences and if they want to stay attuned to important strata of the biblical witnesses. A theological eschatology does not mean travel and traffic in hyperreality.

Gerhard Sauter focuses on the Christian hope and the biblical notion of "hope against hope." This hope is not just optimism but a "transfiguration of our inten-tionality," based on the hope of resurrection. It is a complex "alliance with life." In the biblical traditions, hope affirms God's promises of justice, of peace, of rest, of knowledge. Sauter deals with the difficulties to affirm and to awaken this hope in personally and existentially desperate situations. Christian hope is not just a mental attitude, but a given reality, which overcomes, as he argues, the ambi-guity of self-identification and despair. Sauter examines the great alternative in current Western cultures: the consolation that "life goes on," which often seems to be "more realistic" but which — not least under the impact of the natural sciences on eschatological moods — breaks down as a convincing alternative to hope. Sketching the great impact of this breakdown on our cultures (the spread-ing of the idea of being deceived by faceless powers and the many consequences of this in mentalities of distrust) Sauter presents Christian "hope against hope" as the alternative to facing a faceless fate. From another angle Kathryn Tanner examines future-oriented, this-worldly eschatologies and their problems with sci-entific end-time scenarios. She shows that an eschatological concentration on "the ongoing redemptive relation to God that holds for the world of the past, present, and future" could relativize the predominant future orientation of mod-ern eschatologies and their current preoccupation with cosmic finitude. On the basis of a broad spectrum of biblical insights she offers new perspectives on the understanding of "life in God." She shows how this leads to a reevaluation of "death" and "life" and to a realistic understanding of "eternal life": "Eternal life

infiltrates, then, the present world of suffering and oppression, to bring life, understood as a new pattern or structure of relationships marked by life-giving vitality
and renewed purpose." Tanner carefully examines several theological, political,
and ethical concerns that ask to hold on to the future-oriented eschatology and
warn against a too-simple spiritualization of God's eschatological gifts. She shows
that an eschatology out of joyful recognition and gratitude for the life in God
we are given strengthens rather than weakens the ethical and political struggle
against "injustice, exclusion, and impoverishment, which make up the realm of
death." This eschatological reorientation will not only strengthen those who have
the power to work for the better in this life. Even to the suffering and the victim-
ized, so Tanner argues, the awareness that this innerworldly realm of death does
not have the power to disconnect creatures from the life in God will give greater
strength than the traditional future-oriented eschatologies.

"What remains of our lives when we die? ... Where are the dead?" From the
perspective of a strongly future-oriented eschatology Jürgen Moltmann asks these
burning questions. He examines classical theological answers that tried to give a
meaning to death and argues that death should be seen "as a fact which provokes
grief over transience, and longing for the eternal life of the future world." He
critically examines religious and philosophical ideas about the "immortal soul"
and theological and philosophical attempts to develop other concepts of "immortality." Moltmann argues that notions of immortality that abstract from God's
eternity and God's life and the participation in it remain unconvincing and empty.
He examines three eschatological concepts developed in Christian and other religious traditions which try to grasp God's relation to the dead after death: the
purgatory, the resurrection at death, and the reincarnation. He points out that
any valid eschatological concept of life after death has to account for the "completion" of "the life of those who were unable to live and were not allowed to live:
the beloved child dying at birth; the little boy run over when he was four; the
sixteen-year-old friend torn to pieces by a bomb as he stood beside you ... and all
the many people who have been raped and murdered and exterminated." Over
against "traditional societies" modern societies have lost a whole world of forms
that allowed people to live in a community of hope shared by the dead and the
living. Moltmann does not simply argue for a retrieval of the eschatological mentalities of traditionalist societies. But he argues for a "culture of remembrance"
that tries to do justice to the dead and seeks to give room for their "second
presence." Only this culture of remembrance could free a "culture of narcissism"
from an endemic loss of hope and its destructive impact on culture, ethos, and
personality.

Miroslav Volf wants to concentrate his investigation on the eschatological
transformation of the physical and cultural dimensions of human beings. He wants
to explore the transition from this present world ("in which human beings are
caught in the net woven of the consequences of their physicality's transience
and of their cultural productivity's sinfulness") to the state of freedom in God's
"new world." He argues that the grand eschatological themes — the resurrection
of the dead and the last judgment — address precisely the transformation of

the physical makeup and cultural matrix of human life. Volf develops his own contribution in a critical evaluation of Jüngel's, Pannenberg's, and Moltmann's dealing with these eschatological themes. Volf is highly sensitive to "eschatological moves" that just offer translations of earthly states of affairs into conceptual or even rhetorical realms. Thus he insists, for example, that the problem of death cannot be adequately addressed via the notion of taking up time into eternity. He argues for an eschatological honesty that does not override our life and time under the conditions of finitude and sin by conceptions of an all-integrating totality and infinity. Nor can eschatology just offer visions of restitution without judgment and transformation. Eschatology has to conceive of a "post-mortem change," as Volf puts it, of "the resolution of the problems within the sphere of cultural productivity; without it past cannot be redeemed and history cannot be set aright." Eschatology that has to take life after death seriously has to conceive the resurrection of the body as an aspect of the comprehensive *transformatio mundi*. This embodiment of our lives and world in the time, space, and matter of a new creation (John Polkinghorne) is "thinkable only as human beings' undiluted enjoyment of God, of one another, and of their environment in a new world of perfect love." Volf's insistence that a "realistic eschatology" cannot give up on a salvific transformation of this world and our lives beyond our dwelling on earth raises the question of what theological means help us to reach out to this realm and not to lose the eschatological credibility and realism. Volf himself points in the direction of Christology and trinitarian theology in order to face resurrection, divine judgment, and the eschatological transformation of finite lives under the power of sin. In order to gain ground for such eschatological claims Michael Welker investigates the New Testament resurrection accounts and asks for the reality of the resurrection. He shows that a diversity of witnesses opens up a field of tension between the palpability of the resurrected body and the mere appearance of the risen one. This spectrum of witnesses makes it very clear that the resurrection is not just a physical reanimation. Even the palpable encounters are followed by the acknowledgment of a theophany — and by doubt. Nowhere in the Bible is the pre-Easterly Jesus simply welcomed back. But what reality has the "glorified" or the "spiritual" body of the resurrected that the New Testament witnesses speak of? Pointing to the phenomena of "cultural memory" (Jan Assmann) and of what he calls "canonic memory" Welker claims that the knowledge of Jesus' resurrection is as little an illusion as the discovery of justice or of mathematics. Cultural and canonic memory is a real power that shapes remembrance, experience, and expectation. It is rooted in a reality and generates reality. The resurrection of Jesus Christ brings forth this reality-grounded and reality-shaping memory in which the fullness of Christ's person and life becomes present. "In this canonic memory which is only one dimension of faith and of the working of the Spirit — although a most important one — the resurrected Christ, in the fullness of his person and in the fullness of his pre-Easter history, brings his presence to bear." Proclamation and Holy Communion become central forms of celebrating and experiencing this presence of the resurrected Christ, although many elements and events of his life can ignite the canonic memory. The "eternal life" that becomes palpable in the life of the resurrected Christ with its orienting, judging, healing, consoling, strengthening, ennobling powers is presented by the New Testament traditions in a twofold way. It encounters us in an "eschatological complementarity": as a life that guides our lives in the merciful transformation of earthly life into eternal life; and as a life that reveals the difference between earthly and eternal life to us. This "eschatological complementarity" generates different styles of eschatological memories, experiences, and expectations. The adequacy of these styles to the presence of the resurrected Christ, their intelligibility, their coherence and consistency, their spiritual, theological, and ethical fruitfulness, and their eschatological realism are explored in the discourse of science and theology.

Chapter 14

OUR REASONS FOR HOPE

Gerhard Sauter

Toward the Theological Context of Justification (*Begründungszusammenhang*)[1] of Christian Hope: Different Characters of Hope

You may know the story of the two frogs who have fallen in a mug of fresh milk. One frog is very pessimistic, its situation seems to be past hope. It thinks, "There is no way out of the mug. I will die sooner or later. It might be better to resign just now and to give up all hope." And it is drowned. The other frog is optimistic and full of hope. It does not think at all but it struggles as much as it can — and after trying to trample during the whole night it transforms the milk into butter and jumps happily out of the mug.

To which religion do these two frogs belong? Maybe the first one is an old-fashioned German Lutheran frog, concerned about the sinful weakness of all creatures, especially of frogs. Perhaps it speaks a short prayer begging for a ladder that God can put into the mug. But there is no ladder; therefore it takes its misfortune fatalistically. The other frog might be a good American Presbyterian frog, confident that if it struggles powerfully God will support it. And it works!

Unfortunately this nice story is much too simple — it is simply a success story told by the frog who survived. But usually we do not just fall into a mug of milk. And sometimes, if we trample, we put our feet on others who are less able to stamp their feet. Hope is not identical to optimism, and being deprived of hope is not at all times linked with a pessimistic attitude. And if you want to associate God with one of these two types, you get in trouble, unless you are ready to identify God's acting with sheer success.

Therefore, let us ask more seriously: Do we have reasons for hope? For what kind of hope? What is the character of hope according to Christian faith? And how is this character conceptualized? Later we shall try to compare this character with some scientific perspectives, and the way they affect our concepts of life and death, with our views of the future of our world.

Do we have reasons for hope? If we search for an answer in the Bible, we might be surprised.

---

1. Concerning the term "context of justification," see Gerhard Sauter, *Eschatological Rationality: Theological Issues in Focus* (Grand Rapids, Mich.: Baker Book House, 1996), 182ff.

On the one hand, there is the sentence of wisdom, similar to the proverb "hope springs eternal in the human breast": "As long as there is life there is hope" or (according to the New Revised Standard Version, 1989) "Whoever is joined with all the living has hope" (Eccl. 9:4), but on rather ironical grounds: "for a living dog is better than a dead lion." That is the same for all living beings; humans are no exception. But on the other hand, Job laments — and this is much more characteristic — "For there is hope for a tree, if it is cut down, that it will sprout again, and that its shoots will not cease. Though its root grows old in the earth, and its stump dies in the ground. . . . But mortals die, and are laid low; humans expire, and where are they?" (Job 14:7–8, 10). Humans are sharply, we might even say hopelessly, distinguished from the nature that will endure by the emergence of new entities out of disappearing ones. Job observes an essential difference, even linguistically: A tree can be cut or otherwise destroyed, but all humankind will die; their finitude is much more radical. They expire when the spirit God had given them has been taken away. One might argue that this skepticism is linked with the growing individualism within the text of the Old Testament: some kind of self-reflection or even self-confinement that is unable to see further than to the limits of individual life — a temptation caused by the gradual but rapid decay and destruction of social relationships of the Jewish people in the time when the prophets proclaimed God's will for demanding, among others, the common good. But if we look closer, we notice that the inability to console oneself with the thought that one is part of nature and its enduring creative power is deeply rooted in the witness to God the Creator.

To understand oneself as creature means not to trust in the promises of nature, not to rely on the creative power of dying and becoming. Job's cry of despair does not arise from any insight into human mortality. It is not an expression of that fearful question, "What shall I become when I die?" The context of Job's lament is the search for God's righteousness, expressed in the question, "How am I to live so that God will judge me as 'righteous' and affirm my life? This affirmation would not be limited by my death. But without God's righteousness there is no real hope for me."

The search for reasons for hope and the character of hope becomes more urgent when human beings renounce their confidence in the rather obvious, regenerating powers of nature. The focus is now shifted toward creation and God's faithfulness to it — as it is expressed in God's covenant with Noah, for example. *To cling to God's faithfulness means to receive hope.*

How this may happen, we learn from the story of Abraham. He received God's promise of numerous offspring. Yet he could not be certain of this future as long as he looked at his own and his wife's age, that is, at their natural capacity to procreate. In asking, "Who will be my heir?" Abraham locked himself up within himself, nurturing the depressing perspective of bequeathing his possessions as well as the promised blessing to his slave. (Maybe this is an allusion to an adoption — that would at least appear as a solution, however a solution of Abraham's own choice.) But God called Abraham to leave the hopeless circle of his self-centered struggle for a future. God asked him to leave his tent, the place of his lonely self-reflection. God placed Abraham in the open. He not only reaffirmed his promise to Abraham, he also gave him a hint to help him grasp something of the extent of that promise. "'Look toward heaven and count the stars, if you are able to count them.' Then he said to him, 'So shall your descendants be'" (Gen. 15:5). Counting the stars: that is as impossible as counting the sand at the seashore. But every attempt to count these involves the one who is asked to do so in the incalculable wonder of God's creation and its mystery. Thus, Abraham was confronted with his Creator, who placed his creature into his creation by being faithful to his promises. Abraham was placed within the reality that God created and for whose further existence he stood. Abraham believed, found the reason for his confidence, and learned how to hope in a silent way by being anchored within this reality. And this "the Lord reckoned . . . to him as righteousness" (Gen. 15:6 — a first glimpse of the reward that is promised to him).

The Apostle Paul will read this story as the disclosure of hope against hope[2] created by God "who gives life to the dead and calls into existence things that do not exist" (Rom. 4:17). Abraham's faith will be proved again by God's commandment to sacrifice his son — and the angel will tell him that God had provided a proper sacrifice (Gen. 22:14).

Hope is based on God's promise, inseparable from his power to create the future and give hope. Therefore, hope means trust in the good that God has promised and provided. This is the reason for the unmistakably very positive character of hope in the biblical languages. Hope is rootedness in God's promise and through it a deeply rooted confidence in God's providence. Hope in this strict sense, related to humans, is related to the good God gives to them, as responsible, answering, and acting beings, able to reflect on their being in space and time — in the given space and time.

God is the God of hope (Rom. 15:13) in the same sense as he is the God of peace (Rom. 15:33). He gives hope and peace, and he justifies by communicating his justice. Facing this, God's judgment implies that there have been times and spaces without hope, that is, times and spaces missing links with God's purposes. So we are addressed in Eph. 2:12: "Remember that you were . . . without Christ, being aliens from the commonwealth of Israel, and strangers to the covenants of promise, having no hope and [being] without God in the world." Of course, this statement is false in an everyday sense. All people have some kind of hope. But from an ultimate Christian standpoint, those without Christ were without hope.

Here, hope is an unexpected gift, not a given fact of human nature, and therefore has an exclusive positive meaning. If it *were* some basic, inherent feature of human life, hope would be conceived as intentionality. Intentionality is the capacity or, perhaps stronger, the urge to stretch oneself out into the mixed possibilities one can imagine. Intentionality may be an undeniable fact of human life, since, as humans, we do relate to our future as an uncertain field of possibilities. The

---

2. Gerhard Sauter, "Hope — the Spiritual Dimension of Theological Anthropology," in *Spirituality and Theology: Essays in Honor of Diogenes Allen*, ed. Eric O. Springsted (Louisville, Ky.: Westminster/ John Knox Press, 1998), 101–11, esp. 106ff.

Greeks, for example, knew much about this ambiguity, as indicated by the myth of Pandora: The future holds good and bad, and therefore produces either hope or fear. Yet, intentionality is not at the core of that hope which is given to us "through the resurrection of Jesus Christ from the dead" (1 Pet. 1:3). Therefore, we ought to distinguish between intentionality and hope. But how are they related to one another? It cannot be sufficient to state that they are incompatible and leave it at that. We have to ask how the specific hope that we receive affects our more general intentionality. Hope is a transfiguration of our intentionality; it liberates it to conceive God's purpose and to consent to divine providence.

Hope, therefore, is focused on the resurrection of Jesus Christ. It is the risen Christ who gives us hope. The fact that he is present with us is the source of our hope. Now, we have to be careful, because even this can be mistaken. We may be tempted to say, "Christ has overcome death, therefore there is hope beyond death even for us." We have to pay very careful attention to the difference between this sentence and the first one: the *risen* Christ is the one who gives us hope. The risen Christ is the one who claims to be with us now. The fact of his presence is why we can claim to be hopeful.

In this sense, hope is to be understood as the hope of resurrection. It is a hope that comes to life and stays alive within the presence of the risen Christ. Understanding hope in this sense we are pointed to the expectation of God's acting — the acting of God who is the Creator and who affirms Godself as the Creator by calling Jesus Christ to sit at the right of God the father. Their community is the reason why Christ is present with us. Which is to say: their community is the reason of our hope. This was and is the starting point of the doctrine of the triune God which is the explication of the foundation of the hope of Christian faith.

Conceptualization

Hope and Creation

Hope emerges from God's creative acting: it cannot be against God's creation and God's creatures. Creation and hope are bound together. In this sense we can say that there is hope in creation, for it is wherever the Creator pronounces judgment on what he created. And the very essence of this judgment is God's righteousness — a very verifying, positive intention.

Even though the hope of which we want to speak here is not identical with intentionality, as stated above, and, even though hope is not just an integral feature of human life, we ought to ask in which sense hope is related to our beings as creatures. The claim that there in fact is a relation between hope and creation can be recognized as anti-Marcionite. Hope is, in fact, in alliance with life: the same who gives life also gives hope; however, we may continue to misunderstand both.

This hope is involved in dramatic changes that cannot destroy the confidence in God's truthfulness but do raise suspicions regarding any simple conception of continuity. Christian theology has to balance this dialectic of change and steadfastness, expressed especially by the term *transfiguration*. Hope is, so to speak, the

In-between of God's promises and our various expectations: a transfiguration of expectations and visions, even wishful thinking.

Being a creature means to be repeatedly, continuously dependent on the presence of the creative God. In this sense, there is in fact a certain familiarity between hope and creation. One could say that being a creature means to be given a reason for hope — and to give reason for hope. But we must keep in mind that being a creature means to be subject to dramatic changes, because it is dependency on divine redemption that enables humans to live, act, interact, and hope as creatures.[3]

T. S. Eliot says in the first of his *Four Quartets*, "Burnt Norton," in my beginning is my end — and, in my end is my beginning.[4] Eliot speaks of a darkness into which we must enter in order to experience history. Otherwise reconciliation with the past is impossible. Hope is hope for healing, for the redeeming grace, which brings the confused and distorted past to an end in such a way that there is a new beginning.

This beginning will be a kind of departure, an awakening and a leaving behind. In a prayer it is said, "every moment of our existence becomes a departure point, a leaving everything to follow you."

The Risen Jesus Christ: The Coming One

We encounter God when we encounter God's promises; that is, we do not encounter God, but God encounters us. In Jesus Christ, God meets us along our way just as the risen crucified Christ confronts two of his disciples on the way to Emmaus (Luke 24:13–35). This story can be read as a paradigm for what it means to be faced by God in his promises. God steps into our lives and makes us recognize his will: the will of a living God who in his holiness is a free God. This is where eschatology finds its proper subject: the perception of the living God who by his promises discloses a way that we can go without being clear about where it may lead us and without being given any means to measure distances. Hope, then, is more like the day-to-day life-saver which is given to us according to our present needs; it is more the extent of clarity that emerges when the fog is lifting. In hope God gives us glimpses of his will and purpose, yet he withholds from us that overview-perspective that we as human beings wish to acquire: the intimate knowledge and control of what God intends to do, perform, and fulfill.

When we speak of the presence of the risen Christ, we say that he is the same yesterday and today. What kind of identity do we claim for him? It is the identity of he who gave his life in a way that appeared meaningless and without promise, without a view to any further impact. Christ's identity was formed through a change that had its roots in God's faithfulness. God did not forsake him who remained obedient to God's calling and walked his way to the bitter goal that

---

3. Cf. Miroslav Volf, "Enter into Joy! Sin, Death, and the Life of the World to Come," chap. 17 in this volume.

4. T. S. Eliot, *Four Quartets* (New York: Harcourt Brace, 1943), 7: "Or say that the end precedes the beginning, / And the end and the beginning were always there / Before the beginning and after the end."

seemed to be no consummation at all. His presence is the momentum "between" his coming and vanishing from humans' sight, when their eyes were opened (Luke 24:34). The character of his presence gives us hope and assures us in the same manner that God may not forsake us as the work of his hands.

According to the Emmaus story, this presence is a *redeeming* force, redeeming the traumatized past that the disciples of Jesus could not grasp, staring only at their expectations for the salvation and glorification of Israel, which were based on their understanding of the coming of Christ as prophet and Messiah. The risen Christ gives them just a glimpse of the hidden new creation rooted in divine necessity: "Was the Messiah not bound to suffer thus before entering upon his glory?" (Luke 24:26). Redemption includes the coincidence of facts with this *passivum divinum* and, therefore, with God's creativity which establishes the new creation as community with Christ (2 Cor. 5:17). "Perhaps we can say that the doctrine of redemption, the declaration of our hope, provides specifically Christian content to the Christian doctrine of divine creation" — "the declaration of the *goodness* of God's creation is a statement not merely of memory, let alone of 'observation,' but of hope"[5] (see the context of 2 Cor. 5:17).

There is even God's hope: We are his hope because we are expected, like the prodigal son (Luke 15:11–32). God waits patiently and tirelessly for the transfiguration of human expectations to the confidence in God's promise and creative acting. God expects us to leave room for God's redeeming activity. On this hope rests our hope.

Jesus Christ, the crucified and risen, represents and presents the life of hope in God. Hope includes the confidence that we cannot be separated from Christ and the character of his power. We live in his presence.

Memory and Hope

A whole new set of questions arises here. What evidence do we have of the presence of Christ? How does his presence affect God's promises that kept alive the hope of Israel? These promises are passed on to us by the way in which God affirmed them in the death and life of Jesus Christ: the promises of justice (given by justification), of peace (by redeeming our distorted past and uniting Jews and Gentiles, creating the unity of the church; Eph. 2:14, 16), of life (by sharing the new life of Christ with his body, the church), of rest (in intensifying unrest by the perspective that "a sabbath rest still remains for the people of God"; Heb. 4:9, having peace with God; Rom. 5:1), of knowledge (by being known by God; 1 Cor. 13:12). We may call these affirmations of God's promises the areas of evidence of hope.

This evidence shapes the service of the church, its liturgical memory and hope. It is not produced by the practice of the church. The time in which we live is marked by the character of God's promises — in remembrance of Jesus' death

---

5. Nicholas Lash, "Production and Prospect: Reflections on Christian Hope and Original Sin," in *Evolution and Creation*, ed. Ernan McMullin, University of Notre Dame Studies in the Philosophy of Religion 4 (Notre Dame, Ind.: University of Notre Dame Press, 1985), 286.

until he comes again: "For so often as you eat this bread and drink the cup, you proclaim the Lord's death until he comes" (1 Cor. 11:26). "Until he comes" means not, or not only, a certain time-space. The coming of Christ will bring the memory of his death without ending his presence. Therefore we call upon his coming: "Maranatha — Our Lord, come!" (1 Cor. 16:22).

How do we recognize this evidence of hope in our lives? There may not be just one opportunity.

Some time ago my daughter was seriously ill. One morning when I called her in the hospital, she said, "Papa, I am really empty. There seems to be no future, and I cannot hope any more." What could I answer, having studied eschatology for many years, in just one short and simple sentence or two? Finally I said, "Hanna, there is hope within you. Just don't withhold or suppress it." Then she asked, "Papa, is that true?" I only could answer, "I don't know, but only in this hope I can trust."

Was this answer sufficient — at least helpful and encouraging? Afterwards I doubted it. Didn't my answer to my deathly ill daughter's question sound all too reserved? When I said, "I don't know," didn't it seem as if I wanted, out of pure intellectual honesty, to take back what I had so confidently said in the first sentence? Can we really not know that for which we hope? Or do we avoid the truth claim when we compare knowledge and trust and only express confidence?

Perhaps I should have said, "If you can't hope now, I'll hope for you!" But was it really possible to say that? Can someone really hope for another (in the place of another)? Can we encourage others in their situation of hopelessness with what we consider to be "our hope" and maybe also as our common hope? Can we speak for the hopelessness of others, even if we think it is only subjective? If I emphasize the certainty of my hope in order to help another person hold onto this hope, to help them up out of the abyss of his hopelessness, can I "bridge over" this hopelessness? Or should I want to jump into this emptiness with them?

In hindsight I see that I spoke differently about hope in the two sentences that I said to my daughter. First about the hope that is in you according to 1 Pet. 3:15, a hope that we should not suppress when we receive the hope that God implants in us. Second, about the hope that I cannot secure in advance, that has a good look at the conditions of life, and that then can grow — or die, and, if it pleases God, in this way can be awakened to new life. Martin Luther said that this hope leads across "into the unknown, the hidden, and the dark shadows, so that he does not even know what he hopes for, and yet he knows what he does not hope for."[6] The hope that is in us is God's presence in Jesus Christ, embedding and surrounding us in many ways, even in the presence of the needy, the hungry, the desperate, the imprisoned, the dying (Matt. 25:40). The hope in us is Christ among us, Christ the crucified and resurrected, to whose continuity and discontinuity, identity and nonidentity, our life will be conformed

---

6. "Scholion," Rom. 8:24, in *Lectures on Romans*, ed. Hilton C. Oswald (St. Louis: Concordia, 1972), 364, vol. 25 of *Luther's Works*, 55 vols., ed. Jaroslav Pelikan and Helmut Lehmann (1955–); *Luthers Werke*, Kritische Gesamtausgabe, ed. J. K. F. Knaake et al. (Weimar: Böhlau, 1883ff.), 56:374, 14–17.

as old and new life. This Christ intercedes for us; he even stands in for us in our hopelessness and speechlessness. This is the paradoxical evidence of hope against hope.

Now how can we express a certainty regarding our hope which shows that hope is not an illusion? To be hopeful means not to yield to the sensation of emptiness, but to get in touch with something that is real. This can be experienced as a confrontation. On the one hand, sometimes all the possibilities that I cling to, which are within my reach, are torn into pieces, and I am forced to see something beyond myself. This is not a smooth continuation of my daily attempts to build up my own identity and future, to transfer myself into an imagined time and space. The reality that then confronts me is significantly not my own; neither is the confrontation at my own disposal. Rather it is God's promise that opens up a new horizon of perception. On the other hand, the sensation of emptiness itself may be an illusion, resulting from my resistance against anything that could possibly divert me from my desperation. The "objectivity" of hope as the given reality overcomes the ambiguity of self-identification and desperation. This victory of hope over both is called faith.

Now, let us stop for a moment in order to make some methodological remarks. I started with some biblical testimony of the character of hope: stories we were engaged in. Then I explained conceptual propositions consistent with other grounds of theology and areas of evidence. With these grounds we try to address everyday experiences. Now we have to face the scientific notion of finitude as negation of self-referential evolutionary optimism.

Making the Conception of Future
More Precise in Dialogue with Sciences:
Eschatology and Cosmology — Eschatology and Creation

We can only conceive of finitude in contrast to infinitude. How do we form those perceptions of finitude? They probably arise from a distinction from perceptions of never-ending processes. On the other hand, we cannot have a knowledge of *the* end. Normally we do not really know what it means for something to come to an end.

The story of Jesus Christ is a paradigm for something that comes to an end and comes to a new beginning. This story forms our perception: Christ's resurrection is not a new stage in the circle of life. Rather, the life of the risen Christ wholly depends on God's judgment on his existence. This leads to a different meaning of "end." Our perception of the story of Christ, according to our judgment of the meaning and goal of life, comes to an end. God's judgment interferes with our own. The perception of this judgment is identical to the discovery of the New beyond finitude. Thereby our sensibility for finitude as ending is increased, but it is different from any fear of extermination.

How does this insight challenge prevailing concepts of finitude and infinitude? Let me start with two alternative visions.

"Life goes on"

Natural sciences tell us the world is finite, but as long as there is life, there is hope. "Life goes on" is a valuing of the finite, which is to be maintained alongside our awareness that the world is finite.[7]

We may find comfort in the fact that we are not alone on earth. We may be mortal, but there have been people like us before us who left their marks in history, and there will be people like us yet to be born who will weave the threads that we spun in our lives into the great world-web that we call "life."

The world will continue, even though our own being may be finite: there are times in our life when we are more aware of this fact than other times. We may ignore it for a while. Then again, when it occurs to us that a person who is close to us or we ourselves have to die, it may hit us out of the blue and we feel rather rudely awakened. Still, we can usually calm ourselves with the idea that something will continue. Something like the family history or, broader, the history of humanity. By this perspective we nourish the feeling that we are in good keeping with the chain of being of which we are only a small part. What matters stretches itself out beyond the horizon of where we stand.

This commonsense wisdom of "Life goes on" has been backed up by the sciences, for example, with the following observation: "Permanency does not require that no *change* occurs and change does not constitute an ending."[8] Every ending is only relative, compared with the urge to continue in other forms or substances of life. The finitude of individuals is hopefully embedded in the duration of the world with the answer, "I have to die — but life goes on."

In this sense past generations were able to confront their knowledge of their generations' finitude with the confidence that their engagement for a shared history will still remain. And this confidence was to them a source of hope.

Whenever we look at the world's finitude, the knowledge of which is brought to us through natural sciences, we may cope with and process this knowledge by confining ourselves to social history. This can converge with a religious perspective, as exemplified by Chander McCuskey Brooks (1905–89). Brooks was a distinguished scientist and, for 1987–89, a fellow of the Center of Theological Inquiry. In 1971 he was asked to preach at the 150th anniversary of the French Creek Presbyterian Church in West Virginia, where his ancestors lived. Brooks entitled his sermon "The Quest for That Which Has No Ending." In this sermon, he points to the self-sacrificing efforts of the founding members of the congregation and of those who followed. They had to make their living in a rough country and under great trouble — but so they did, simply because they wanted to pass life on to the next generation. Generally, they lived without a perspective of personal success or of noticeable improvement. Chandler Brooks concludes

---

7. Cf. William Stoeger, "Scientific Accounts of Ultimate Catastrophes in Our Life-Bearing Universe," chap. 1 in this volume.

8. Chandler McCuskey Brooks, "The Quest for That Which Has No Ending," in *French Creek Presbyterian Church: A Memorial to the 150 Years of Service of the French Creek Presbyterian Church*, ed. Lois M. Pinnell (Parsons, W.V.: McClain Printing, 1971), 127.

that these people ought to be remembered because they help us keep alive our sense for life and responsibility.

Brooks concludes:

> *Do not fear the future.* It will not inflict on us more than we can bear if we seek the help of God which [Brooks does not say "who"] is within and which surrounds us in others who are travelling our way.
>
> *Let us not fear death.* It is but the embrace of our fathers. No one can be taken completely from us if we hold him in our love. Death is a gathering, a return to the beginning, not an ending. Those who built this church 150 years ago believed that somehow men could belong to God and find immortality in him. We too can face the future with this faith that *we* can become a part of that world which has no ending.[9]

Now, the sentence "Life goes on" is at least ambiguous. For it can also be understood as an expression of the total lack of hope. The flavor of hopelessness can be discovered now and then. It expresses itself by allowing that life goes on just as "the show must go on." If we listen carefully, we may hear as much resignation and cynicism as some reluctant confidence.

Somehow, a sentence like "Life goes on" shows how human beings give up in the face of death — and at least one element of this capitulation is a yet stronger commitment to life. Besides, the dead seem to place the living under the obligation to continue, to keep the flame of their life and hopes burning. And in the same manner those who live live their lives more or less with the perspective to oblige the next generation. Therefore, Chandler Brooks's sentences, and their evocative imagery, are open for interpretation: "the embrace of our fathers" can evoke a feeling of belonging and embeddedness as well as a feeling of oppression.

We have to consider the ambivalence of a hope that rests on the perspective of a continuum of which each of us is a part. Regarding this ambivalence, do we have a right to recommend a hope to others, if it does not go beyond the perspective that somehow things will continue? However *we* may respond to this question, it will depend on the answer whether we will fear or welcome the disruption of such a hope.

Ending or Completion? Finitude as Total, Hopeless Ending?

The confidence that life goes on — that in time there will be no limits to the continuance of the world — has been disrupted by natural sciences also. We have to learn that there is no scientific justification of hope. All long-term predictions seem to be clearly contradictory to hope:

> Every prognosis we have, be it for living things, planets, stars, galaxies or the universe, finally amounts to disintegration: the sun will cool off, the earth will be lost in space, and even the matter of the universe will radioactively decay. Therefore, there is no hope which can be backed up by natural sciences.

---

9. Ibid., 131.

With these words Arnold Benz advertises his book *The Future of the Universe: Chance, Chaos, God?*[10]

Recent theories of cosmology agree that the world will come to an end either by slowly, yet certainly, going cold — or just the other way: by progressive warming up and burning. The result seems to be the same: extermination. Or can the conception of an open universe, which may be consistent with those predictions, support hope? As far as our planet is concerned, a much more imminent ending is conceivable — be it by the many self-destructive dealings of us humans, or by destruction from space — by the collision with a gigantic meteor, for example. Yet the general perspective of decay and disintegration has a paralyzing impact on the imagination, since it does not allow for any perspective beyond destruction, and we need such a perspective for our acting.

There is a politically destructive effect of this fear. It often converges with another rather widespread attitude: distrust in politics, lack of confidence in the information given to the public, and the suspicion that those pieces of information that really matter are held back by the unknown few who are in power. It is the suspicion of average citizens that they are continuously deceived by those who more or less secretly rule the world and manipulate the exchange of information. The idea of being deceived by faceless powers gives rise to another idea — the notion of some power of history, which may be human, superhuman, or inhuman, yet can never be localized, and always conceals itself. This is the characteristic attitude of contemporaries who are very much impressed and influenced by the flood of information — and who grow more and more suspicious that they are repeatedly told the wrong stories. This loss of confidence often appears in conjunction with an imagination that is transfixed by the end of the world. This is a contemporary way of facing finitude — reflecting a cultural concern.

These terrifying visions contradict the ambivalent attitude that is expressed in the commonsense statement "Life goes on." The former, familiar pillars of hope, such as the feeling of embeddedness in one's family, nation, or some "mission," are now crumbling away. Negative cosmological theories destroy the illusion of being and remaining a tiny part of a whole that, in terms of its continuing existence, I can take for granted. With this illusion I also lose the goal of integrating myself into a wider context. This goal of integration did justice to both the need for affirming and for overcoming oneself. Both needs appear pointless when the permanence of the world is denied. Now it is an emptiness that lurks at the borders of our daily dealings with life: the emptiness in which humanity is not only off-center, but also without any measures, not to speak of human measures. It is the emptiness of the Unknown and Inconceivable, of stars, galaxies, black holes, unpredictable meteors, and inevitable catastrophes. Seemingly in alliance with the predictions of scientific cosmology are the "science fiction" myths of a popular culture. Maybe the question of whether there is extraterrestrial life is a contemporary expression of human beings' amazement about themselves and their extremely improbable and extremely endangered existence. By looking for another

---

10. Arnold Benz, *The Future of the Universe: Chance, Chaos, God?* (Düsseldorf: Patmos, 1997).

"intelligence," human beings may be hoping for a possibility of confronting their own improbability with some measure of certainty.

Perhaps the theological phrasing of the *creatio continua* (the continuing creation) can be seen as in relation to this attitude. When theologians speak of the conservation of creation they explicate what they mean by speaking of God the Creator. They also reject any tendencies toward Deism, which sees the activity of the Creator as confined to some distant time at the beginning of the world's history. Yet, there is even more to the theological idiom of *conservatio*, conservation, and *creatio continua*. It is also a statement about the nature of creation and the character of creatures. Both are seen as highly threatened, persistently surrounded by the danger of annihilation.

Thus, the visions of destruction to which we are pointed by recent cosmology only highlight the very realistic sense of immediate dependence which is expressed in the term "continuing creation," where creation is understood in the meaning explained above. The world as we know it is not in and of itself capable to resist destruction. It may be ready for radical changes but it is not ready to be exposed to chaos without any remaining structures.

Therefore there is a double meaning of "end": Creation is that which keeps the universe from ending and brings it to its end. Creation may be finite — yet it is kept from simply dropping out of existence. Ever since Augustine, Christian theology tried to express both. To this purpose it applied the terms "creation," "conservation," and "new creation," and thereby intended to develop a sense for finitude that does not confine itself to historical relativities.

What Is to Come? Rather, Who Is Coming?

Nowadays there is a rising contrast between reality as it can be overlooked by the individual and a cosmos whose measures can no longer be comprehended, but only technically expressed. There is furthermore a contrast between those things that we can do and those things that are done to us from outside, which includes the popular idea of the "extraterrestrial" as the perpetrator of these things.

The mere idea that one day life on Earth will be brought to an end by some cosmic catastrophe is more terrifying than the traditional ideas of the last judgment — even if one considers the fear of ending up on the wrong side of the final division. What is so terrifying about the new visions of destruction is that it all happens without someone who faces us, who confronts us. There is no other, there are only those who are left to destruction. What does this idea do to the many problems and responsibilities with which humanity has involved itself, problems that may go beyond our various abilities to handle them, yet are still associated with a sense of responsibility and obligation? And now, what does the idea of a sudden global destruction do to our involvement in our "global village" and to our fragile structures of meaning? The idea may hit us like a blow from outside of ourselves — yet not from God. This is the vision of total meaninglessness. Here, nothing more is left to be said to us.

We may feel reminded of Blaise Pascal's sentence, "The silence of the infinite spaces makes me shudder."[11] Against this sense of horror, Pascal finds the order of reality by asking for the reasons of another order — an order that is shaped by the presence of Jesus Christ, which means: a perception of Christ as the coming One.

Neither the decay of the world nor one's own death can be integrated into one's daily attitude to life. The media culture, however, seems to be infatuated by these visions of global destruction. We have only to remember some of the more recent movies. There is a genre of movies and serials on TV which plays with the idea that extraterrestrial and nonhuman powers — intellectual beings who may have nothing in common with human beings — gain power over the earth to work toward its destruction.

How is the attitude of the two rather vague concepts of finitude cited above, in relation to infinitude, related to the hope that is expressed in the story of Christ and which emerges from his story? For instance, what if one sees the question "Is there extraterrestrial life?" as a substitute for the quest for God, in whose coming we trust, just as we are assured of his presence. We may not know what is to come, but we have a new sensitivity for him, who is the coming One. This sensitivity affirms a hope that enables us to face the very limited time-space we call "our today."

"If I knew that tomorrow the world would end, I would still plant an apple tree today." Even though this sentence is only mistakenly ascribed to Martin Luther, it is very deeply related to hope and the reasons for hope. It shows that the basis for our hope in faith is neither confidence in the future consequences of responsible acting on the stage of history, nor is it confidence that nature will prevail. On the contrary, to do what needs to be done today is a vivid expression of hope against hope. More than this rather humble perspective is not requested of us, but, if one carefully considers it, this *is* in fact a lot! Hope also includes the ability to renounce the wide perspective of some unlimited overview and to hold on to something much more specific — in a broader, multidimensional context that God alone knows, that he will provide and redeem through the risen Christ.

---

11. "The silence éternel de ces espaces infinis m'effraie." Blaise Pascal, *Pensées*, ed. Léon Brunsvicg, fragment 206, edition de Ch.-M. des Granges (Paris: Garnier Frères, 1961), 131.

Chapter 15

ESCHATOLOGY WITHOUT A FUTURE?

Kathryn Tanner

The best scientific description of the day leaves little doubt that death is the end toward which our solar system and the universe as a whole are moving. Our sun will one day exhaust its fuel, annihilating life on planet Earth. The universe will either collapse onto itself in a fiery conflagration or dissipate away its energy over the course of an infinite expansion. On the face of it, such end-time scenarios conflict with the future-oriented, this-worldly eschatology of most contemporary Christian theologians. If the scientists are right, the world for which Christians hold out hope ultimately has no future. Hope for an everlasting and consummate fulfillment of this world is futile: destruction is our world's end. As one theologian prominent in the contemporary dialogue between theologians and scientists starkly formulates the problem:

> [If] the law of entropy has the last laugh and the cosmos drifts into a state of irrecoverable equilibrium...then we would have proof that our faith has been in vain....Our faith is allied with our hope, and our hope is based upon the promise...that a new creation is coming by the grace and power of God....The upshot of this is that at the present time we will have to base our eschatological hope on specifically theological resources, not scientific ones.[1]

As this quotation suggests, one strategy of response to an apparent conflict between scientific prediction and theological hope for this world's future is for theologians to contest the finality or completeness of scientific description of the world's end. Science accurately depicts the fate of the world left to its own devices; what it leaves out of account is the influence of God's working to divert, or overcome, what one could legitimately expect to occur simply from the world's own principles of operation. Thus, a theologian might maintain that the world will not come to the dire pass scientists envision because of the ongoing influence of a good, life-affirming God in world processes generally. Or, a theologian could claim that the world will be led beyond the destruction to which it does indeed come of its own accord by a God who, as Christians affirm of their Creator and Redeemer, can bring something from nothing, and life from death. God might indeed use the old world's destruction, as the scientists describe it, as a purgative means to

---

1. Ted Peters, *God as Trinity* (Louisville, Ky.: Westminster/John Knox Press, 1994), 176.

a new heaven and earth beyond the reach of the old world's own capacities; the destruction of the world becomes in that case a kind of world crucifixion that signals the death of death by way of divine power.

By taking this sort of strategy of response, a future-oriented, this-worldly eschatology escapes any direct challenge from scientific end-time scenarios. These scenarios or the reasoning that leads to them is simply incorporated, with suitable theological modifications, within the same barely modified eschatological perspective from which the theologian started. The basic shape of the eschatological perspective remains the same. At most, scientific prediction of a dire future encourages the trend in contemporary Christian eschatology away from optimistic assessments of what one can expect from natural processes apart from God's help. The consummation of the world is not brought about by the world. A gap exists between the results of world processes and the world's consummation, a gap to be bridged by a God with the power to reverse those results, the power to bring what is otherwise absolutely unexpected into existence — say, a world that knows neither loss nor suffering.[2] Or, a grace-motored continuity, rather than a continuity of purely natural processes, spans the world as we know it and the world to come: the world moves without any great interruption to its consummation but it does so only in virtue of divine powers not its own.[3]

Besides this eschewal or qualification of evolutionary accounts of the world's end, the incorporation of scientific description within a future-oriented, this-worldly eschatology simply redirects theological interest to certain aspects of the usual story of the world's end. Taking their cue from what scientists try to describe — the nature and workings of the world — theologians in dialogue with science are inclined to try to describe, often with the help of scientific categories, the nature of the transition to the world to come, and the new character of that world. Does, for example, that transition, or the world to come, involve spatial and temporal processes comparable to the ones scientists describe? Is that transition, or the world to come, constituted and formed at least in part by the interactive agencies of finite creatures in something like the way the present world is? Despite the fact that God's working brings about what nature cannot, do natural processes or some sorts of natural occurrence (say, instances of exceptional novelty) provide hints about the character of God's own working? What must the world to come be like if it is really our world transformed — that is, does science set certain minimum conditions for the new world's remaining our world? In the world to come, what features of the world might account for its being an everlasting world of perfect fulfillment, a world without death, suffering, loss, or the tragic competition for goods that sets one creature against another? These preoccupations are, I think, amply demonstrated in this volume.

---

2. See the work of Jürgen Moltmann for such a view, e.g., his *The Coming of God* (Minneapolis: Fortress Press, 1996).

3. For this viewpoint, see, e.g., Karl Rahner, "Immanent and Transcendent Consummation of the World," in his *Theological Investigations*, vol. 10, trans. David Bourke (London: Darton, Longman and Todd, 1973), 273–89.

There is, however, another possible strategy for responding to the apparent conflict between scientific end-time scenarios and theological hopes for the future of this world. This strategy does not directly contest the adequacy of scientific description on its own terms, and therefore allows the apparent conflict between theology and science to pose a greater challenge to theological understanding. This strategy of response — the one that I pursue as a thought experiment in this chapter — asks what a Christian eschatology might be like if scientists are right that the world does not have a future. Is it really the case that such an end is simply incompatible as it stands with Christian hopes for this world? Might not there be something that theologians can say directly to address that eventuality? Might not there be a Christian hope that can cope with and make sense of the end of things that scientists describe?

This sort of response to scientific descriptions of the end-time would do for eschatology something comparable to what many theologians in the history of Christian thought have already done for the doctrine of creation in response to scientific (and philosophical) accounts of the world that conflict with Christian descriptions of a beginning of things. In response to that conflict — say, in response to a philosophical deduction of the world's eternality — theologians did not always feel the need to attack the adequacy of the philosophical argument; instead, they often simply dropped the importance in the account of creation of an insistence on a beginning to things. In so doing, a new account of creation was offered in which the world is the creation of God whether it has a beginning or not and whatever the process of its origination. In the case of a conflict between eschatology and scientific description, one would think that one could, similarly, reinterpret the common contemporary outlook on eschatology so that it holds whatever the final state of the world, as scientifically described. A Christian eschatology would have no more stake in whether or how the world ends than a Christian account of creation has in whether or how the world had a beginning (say, by means of a big bang).

One might suspect that such a reinterpretation of Christian claims would mean Christianity's relinquishing its hold on cosmic questions. Such questions would be turned over to the scientist (or philosopher), leaving Christianity without a say on matters that concern this world. Again, however, the comparable case of creation does not bear this worry out.

Belief in creation can, it is true, be spiritualized as a way of avoiding conflict with scientific descriptions of a beginning of things — say, by reducing the import of creation to a psychological, purely human, and private matter. For example, creation might mean nothing more than a sense of the uncanny, of the irretrievable importance of the moment, and of being disposed by a force beyond one's control.[4] When reinterpreted to avoid conflict with scientific and philosophical descriptions of the beginning of things, creation can, however, continue to concern this world and its relation to God, as the classic example of Thomas

---

4. See Rudolf Bultmann, "The Meaning of Christian Faith in Creation," in his *Existence and Faith* (London: Hodder and Stoughton, 1961).

Aquinas's effort to reinterpret creation in the face of the best Aristotelian science of his day makes clear.[5]

In a move that is typical for most modern theological struggles with scientific description of the world's beginnings, creation for Thomas is detemporalized, one might say, so that it becomes a relation of dependence on God that everything that exists enjoys in every respect that it is. Such a relation of dependence holds whether the world has a beginning or not. This irrelevance of the question of beginnings suggests nothing otherworldly, subjective, or acosmic about the account of creation being offered. To the contrary, it is the very irrelevance of that question of beginnings that guarantees the cosmic comprehensiveness of the account. If being created means to depend on God, the world that is created is not just the world of the beginning but the world as a whole, across the whole of its duration however long or short that may be, whether with or without a beginning or end.

If one were to reinterpret eschatology in a similar fashion so that considerations of the world's end are no longer of paramount concern, presumably the consequences might also be similar to what one finds in the Thomistic case. The consequences would be, in other words, not an otherworldly or spiritualized eschatology that leaves concern for this world behind (say, by the reduction of the content of the claim to human attitudes toward the world), but a more comprehensively cosmic eschatology. Such an eschatology would be comprehensively cosmic in the sense that its preoccupations would not center on the world of the future but on the world as a whole and on an ongoing redemptive (rather than simply creative) relation to God that holds for the world of the past, present, and future. What might drop out, then, in response to a conflict with science is not the this-worldly, cosmic character of Christian eschatology but simply its predominantly future orientation.

Can, however, Christian hopes do without preoccupations concerning the world's future? With the loss of those concerns for the future, hasn't too much been lost? If Christian eschatology does not offer specifically future hopes, what might motivate action to bring in a better future for humans and the planet? Without expectations of a world to come, what disturbs complacency concerning the world as it seems to work now? Without hopes for the future of this world, what can Christian eschatology do to alleviate despair in the face of present injustice and suffering? What is to prevent the sense that all our efforts to better the world are simply futile?

To put the same set of worries another way, hasn't perhaps too much of a modern scientific viewpoint been conceded by the strategy of response I am exploring? What is to prevent such an eschatology from being coopted by the exterministic cultural concomitants of a belief in cosmic death? Christian eschatology in that case would simply confirm the untoward contemporary understandings of world, self, and community which scientific predictions of the world's end already

---

5. See Thomas Aquinas, *Summa Contra Gentiles* (Notre Dame, Ind.: Notre Dame University Press, 1975), book 2.

play into and foment: (1) a nihilistic sense of the futility of efforts to improve the human situation and conditions of the planet — what's the difference if everything's to end in some cosmic crunch? — and (2) an irresponsible, simply self-interested focus on goods that can be had in the moment without much expenditure of effort. The Bible gives shocked expression to such a view of the moral space of human life:

> They said to themselves in their deluded way: "Our life is short and full of trouble, and when man comes to the end there is no remedy; no man has ever been known to return from the grave.... [C]ome then, let us enjoy the good things while we can, and make full use of the creation, with all the eagerness of youth.... Down with the poor and honest man! Let us tread him under foot.... For us let might be right!" (Wisd. Sol. 2:1, 6, 10, NEB)

Thesis

My explorations, then, of an eschatology for a world without a future will have to have two parts. I will first, of course, need to lay out the basic shape of such an eschatology. But I will also need, in a second step, to explain the main options such a position affords for obligating and inspiring action to further the flourishing of human beings and the planet. How are hopelessness in the face of present trouble, complacent inactivity regarding suffering and injustice, and irresponsible self-concern to be avoided? In short, absent a vision of this world to come, what motivates and helps sustain action in history for a better world over the long haul? This second part of the project is to make clear, then, how my reinterpretation of contemporary eschatology does not bring with it the loss of eschatology as political theology, the loss of active, socially committed challenge to structures of oppression, injustice, and ecological devastation that is so much a part — and rightly so — of many contemporary eschatologies.

I

As was suggested when discussing the eschatological parallel to modifications in Christian accounts of creation, what I seem to require is an account of a salvific relation to God that undercuts the religious importance of the question whether the world will end. Most generally, I need an account of the world's relation to God as Redeemer that lessens religious interest in what the world is like considered independently of that relation. Specifically at issue is the world's continuing to exist or ceasing to exist, and whether one can lessen the impact that either scenario would have for a salvific relation that the world enjoys with God.

life death

Several biblical moves relativize the religious significance of the difference between biological life and death (or life as existence and death as cessation of existence). We might follow them up in our own efforts to reinterpret Christian eschatology.

widening the circle

First, there is the dominance, particularly in the Old Testament, of a wider (so-called metaphorical) use of "life" and "death," where life refers to fruitfulness and abundance, longevity, communal flourishing, and individual well-being, and death is a catch-all for such things as suffering, poverty, barrenness, oppression, social divisiveness, and isolation. According to these more extended senses of life and death, one can be dead while alive; death enters into the course of life as the threat of such things as sickness, impoverishment, and lack of fulfillment. One can also enjoy a death that imitates life — in old age, surrounded by one's posterity. "Your descendants shall be many and your offspring as the grass of the earth. You shall come to your grave in ripe old age" (Job 5:25–26).

A second, similar sort of relativization of the difference between biological death and life is suggested by Old Testament passages in which "life" and "death" seem to refer to the way one lives or dies, in particular whether one lives (or dies) for God (and for others). One lives, in this sense, to the extent one dedicates one's life to the God who is the source of life in all its extended senses, to the extent that one keeps faith with a relationship with God by maintaining the form of life that relationship with God requires. All the goods of life — in our first, extended sense of the term "life" — are blessings that stem ultimately from relationship with God. To die is to break with this life-giving, blessing-bestowing relationship with God and the covenant it forms; to live is just to place oneself willingly and joyfully within it. "I have set before you life and death, blessings and curses. Choose life that you may live, loving the Lord your God, obeying him, and holding fast to him; for that means life to you and length of days" (Deut. 30:19–20). One can and should hold fast to God, whatever the dangers and vicissitudes of life; in this sense one enjoys a gift that cannot be lost, a blessing of life that survives every trial and tribulation, every threat, that is, from the forces of death. Whatever the adversity, one can take comfort in the fact that "Yahweh is my portion and my cup" (e.g., Ps. 16:5), "my refuge" (Ps. 73:28); indeed, in such circumstances it becomes clear the way in which "thy steadfast love is better than life" (Ps. 63:4).

But can the relations with God and neighbor that spell life be sustained across the fact of biological death? (Spiritualizing that relationship, in the way the last biblical quotation suggests, can only go so far; it is therefore an ultimately unsuccessful way of relativizing the difference between life and death.) Doesn't death disrupt one's relationship to the life-giving powers of God? "I shall lie in the earth; you will seek me, but I shall not be" (Job 7:21). "For the grave cannot praise thee, death cannot celebrate thee; they that go down to the pit cannot hope for thy truth" (Isa. 38:18). To what extent, then, does our second sense of life in relational terms genuinely relativize the difference between continued existence and its cessation?

For the Old Testament the worry I am now raising primarily concerns the effect of biological death on an individual's relation to God. The death of individuals may be final for them but not for the community, which continues to exist in relation to God. Thus, a single generation of the community might be cut off from God and suffer a grievous downturn, but presumably there might still be hope for the next.

Despite a sense of the finality of death for the individual him/herself, worries about individual mortality are, moreover, quelled in the Old Testament by a more primary concern for the community and by a sense of the dead individual's continuing existence for it — through offspring or communal memory.[6] So the finality of his own individual death is softened in this way by Jacob on his deathbed: "Behold, I am about to die, but God will be with you, and will bring you again to the land of your fathers" (Gen. 48:21). One can participate beyond one's death in the ongoing life of the community through one's children, but even "eunuchs . . . shall receive from me something better than sons and daughters: a memorial and a name in my house" (Isa. 56:3–5).

This sort of response to the irrevocability of personal death is lost, for us, however; with scientific descriptions of the end-time, all human communities, along with the cosmos itself, seem to suffer as irrevocable a death as any individual person. The problem posed by personal death, in short, is now simply writ large for us. Are there biblical perspectives, particularly Old Testament ones in which the finality of personal death is assumed, that might be of help here in discussing a relation to God unaffected by death, perspectives on personal death that might be extended by us to the whole of the cosmos marked for death?

Old Testament passages suggest, first of all, that the dead are not cut off from God because God is the Lord of both life and death. Death is a sphere within God's power, God's reach, and therefore (one presumes) the dead are not lost to God. "The Lord gave and the Lord taketh away; blessed be the name of the Lord" (Job 1:21). "There is no god beside me; I kill and make alive; I wound and I heal" (Deut. 32:39; also, e.g., 1 Sam. 2:6–7). Therefore, "where can I go from your spirit? Or where can I flee from your presence? If I ascend to heaven, you are there; if I make my bed in Sheol, you are there" (Ps. 139:7–8). In keeping with such ideas, maintaining a relationship with the God who gives life would not seem to require the destruction of death (as a more apocalyptic outlook requires). Death does not have the power to separate one from God. Such a confidence, without the development of any explicit ideas about life after death, may underlie Psalms 16, 49, and 73. Thus, in a context where literal death seems to be at issue ("those who are far from you will perish; you put an end [to them]"), the psalmist exclaims, "my flesh and my heart may fail, but God is the strength of my heart and my portion for ever" (Ps. 73:26).

"Eternal life," in some New Testament senses of that, might develop this suggestion that not even death can separate us from the love of God and others. "Neither death, nor life, nor angels, nor rulers, nor things present, nor things to come, nor powers, nor height, nor depth, nor anything else in creation, will be able to separate us from the love of God in Christ Jesus our Lord" (Rom. 8:38). There is a life in God (in Christ) that we possess now and after death. Ante- and post-mortem do not, then, mark any crucial difference with respect to it. Death makes no difference to that life in God in the sense that, despite our deaths, God maintains a relationship with us that continues to be the source of all benefit. Even when we are alive, we are therefore dead insofar as we are dead to Christ. Separation from Christ (and from one's fellows in Christ) is a kind of death despite the apparent gains that might accrue to one in virtue of an isolated, simply

---

6. See Lloyd Bailey, *Biblical Perspectives on Death* (Philadelphia: Fortress Press, 1979), 58–59.

self-concerned existence. Eternal life, moreover, is one's portion or possession despite all the sufferings of life and death in a way that should comfort sufferers of every kind of tribulation. In all the senses of death, including the biological, we therefore live even though we die if we are alive to Christ. "If we live, we live to the Lord, and if we die, we die to the Lord; so then, whether we live or whether we die, we are the Lord's" (Rom. 14:8).

This understanding of eternal life follows the Old Testament suggestion, then, that all the goods of life ("life" in its extended senses) flow from relationship with God (the second biblical sense of life in relationship). The effort to turn away or separate oneself from God has, in this understanding of things, the force of death, broadly construed. (It is literally the effort to unmake oneself.) Eternal life as *life in God* is a way of indicating this priority of the second biblical sense of life as relationship with God. It is also a way of specifying a character of relationship with God that might survive death. If the world, human society, and individual persons have the life of relationship with God beyond the fact of their deaths, one might say they live *in* God and not simply in relationship *with* God. Eternal life means a deepened affirmation that one's relation with God is not conditional; it is not conditioned even by biological death or the cessation of community and cosmos. The Bible maintains that God remains the God of Israel and the church, remains the God of the world that God creates and of all the individuals in it, whatever happens; the idea of eternal life is simply a way of continuing this affirmation of God's loving and steadfast faithfulness across the fact of death.

While continuing and consummating God's faithful commitment to the creature's good as that is manifest in creation, eternal life is itself a greater gift (and brings in its train greater gifts) than the relationship with God that creatures enjoy simply as creatures. The evident unconditionality of eternal life marks one such difference. With eternal life it becomes clear how relation with God as the source of all benefit cannot be broken by either sin or death (in all its senses, including the biological); relations with a life-giving God are maintained unconditionally from God's side. Whatever might happen, God remains faithful to a life-giving relation to us and empowers us, through Christ, for faithfulness, too. The relationship is also unconditional, then, in that what we should be in it — the image of God's own relationship with us — is maintained or shored up from God's side (in virtue of the free favor and mercy of God in Christ) despite our own failings, sufferings, and sin. In the relationship of eternal life, God sets us in and upholds our position in relation to God, whatever we do, whatever happens to us. Despite the fact of human failing, faithlessness, and death, we *are* alive in God.

Eternal life is not the same sort of relationship as the rather external one that exists between God and creatures: our very identity as creatures is redefined so as to be essentially constituted by relationship with God. Separation from God is now impossible for us in a way that was not before for us simply as creatures. The very meaning of this new identity is that our dependence upon God for our existence is now complete: we essentially *are* that relationship in a way that simply being creatures of God does not entail.

The model for this aspect of life in God is the incarnation. Jesus is the one

*eschatol,
Xpology*

who lives in God, the one who is all that he is as a human being without existing independently of God, the human being whose very existence is God's own existence — that is the meaning of the hypostatic union. Otherwise expressed, in Jesus God becomes the bearer of our very acts and attributes. As a result, the powers and character of Godself shine through those human acts and attributes — giving Jesus' acts and attributes a salvific force (e.g., so as to overcome and heal the consequences of sin) and eventuating in the manifest glorification of Jesus' own human being in the resurrection. By grace — by virtue, that is, of a life-giving relationship with Jesus — we enjoy something like the sort of life in *imitatio Xpi* God that Jesus lives. We (and the whole world) are to live in God as He does, through Him. In short, there is an approximation to the hypostatic union that the world enjoys through grace, most particularly after the world's death, when it becomes undeniably apparent that, like Christ, the only existence we have is in and through God.

So understood, eternal life promotes a more spatialized than temporalized eschatology. At the most fundamental level, eternal life is ours now as in the future. It is therefore not directly associated with the world's future and not convertible with the idea that the world will always have a future or further time. Here the eschaton cannot be primarily understood as what comes from the future to draw the time of this world ever onward. It is not especially associated with any particular moment of time (past, present, or future), and therefore such an understanding of the eschaton has no stake in any reworked theological account of temporal relations in which a coming future is given primacy over present and past times.

Besides the fact that it is not temporally indexed in any of these ways, eternal life is also spatialized in that it suggests a living *in* God, a kind of placement within the life of God. Since there may come a time when the world no longer exists, this placement in God cannot be equated with God's presence or placement within the world.[7] A kind of indwelling of God in us is, however, a consequence of life in God. In imitation of Christ, we live in God and therefore the life we lead has a kind of composite character to match our new composite personhood: God's attributes become in some strong sense our own; they become part of our very sense of self.

Eternal life is also understood in spatial terms so as to become a realm or sphere. Eternal life is a kingdom of God, comparable to an Old Testament sense of righteousness as a new pattern of relationships to which the righteous commit themselves. Eternal life is a new "power-charged area, into which men are incorporated and thereby empowered to do special deeds."[8] This realm of eternal life is not otherworldly, either in the sense of becoming a part of the picture after death — that is, in the sense that one enters into it only after death — or in the sense of marking a spiritualized, merely personal attitude to events of this world. Instead, eternal life exists now in competition with another potentially

---

7. This seems to be the case for Moltmann.

8. Gerhard von Rad, *Old Testament Theology* (New York: Harper and Row, 1962), 1:376. See also 388.

all-embracing structure or pattern of existence marked by futility and hopelessness — the realm of death, in the broadest biblical sense. One exists in this realm
of eternal life now and it extends as far as that other realm of death does, under
which, as Paul says, the whole created universe groans (Rom. 8:22). Eternal life
infiltrates, then, the present world of suffering and oppression, to bring life, understood as a new pattern or structure of relationships marked by life-giving vitality
and renewed purpose.

Eternal life is a present reality, we possess now, in an unconditional fashion,
life in God as a source of all good and need not wait for death to pass from the
realm of death to that of life. "He who hears my words and believes . . . has eternal
life; he does not come into judgment, but has [already] passed from death to life"
(John 5:24). This does not mean, however, that the full consequences of that
entrance into eternal life are evident immediately. Not yet manifest in a world of
suffering and tribulation are the full consequences that follow from the decisive
fact of eternal life, already ours. A world of blessings is the expected effect of life
in God, and therefore life in God permits no simple spiritualization of God's gifts.
We and the world are to exhibit all the good consequences of life in God as the
signs or manifestations of our entrance into it. "We . . . have crossed over from
death to life; we know this, because we love our brothers. The man who does
not love is still in the realm of death" (1 John 3:14–16, NEB). Eternal life is not
ours then in a way that suggests there is not more to come in manifestation of
it. This "more," however, is the world's living out or adequate reflection of what
is already the case: that is, this "more" is a life with others that properly reflects
what follows from life in God, a life in God that has already been granted to us
irrevocably from God's side and that exists irrevocably as an empowering source
for all the goods of life in its extended senses. After the world's death, when we no
longer exist as independent beings apart from God, there must be some different
and greater manifestation of such goods in the life we continue to live in God.

The model for the life-affirming consequences of life in God is an account of
the way the saving effects of Jesus' life and death are enabled by the incarnation.
All that Jesus does and "enjoys" for the sake of life throughout the course of His
life and death in a world of sin (healing, delivering, blessing, dying for our sakes) is
a consequence of his life in God qua incarnate Son of God. What Jesus does and
what he suffers are the unfolding of the meaning of life in God (i.e., the meaning
of incarnation) as that power for life enters into and struggles to overcome a
world of suffering, exclusion, and despair. The more that is to come in our lives
and the world's — the end of the host of death-dealing consequences of sin — is,
similarly, an unrolling or reflection during the time of the world (and after it) of
what life in God should bring with it — life in the entirety of its connotations.

Are, however, the goods that properly manifest life in God compatible with
the finality of death? Must not literal death be part of the realm of death that
eternal life works to overcome? I suggest the contrary by modifying the usual New
Testament understanding of eternal life to bring it into conformity with an Old
Testament recognition of death as the end — not just for individual persons, but
for humanity and the cosmos. But what exactly would this mean?

One thing it suggests is that death may be overcome without requiring the end of mortality. With the Old Testament one can affirm that what is to be gotten rid of is bad death — premature, painful, community-rending death. Death itself, however (in the sense of temporal cessation, in the sense that each of us, the species, and the planet have a limited duration), is a simple fact of existence, a concomitant of the finite constitution of things as we know them.[9] We are made from the dust and therefore return to the dust (Gen. 3:19): "We must all die; we are like water spilt on the ground which cannot be gathered up again" (2 Sam. 14:14). As a natural fact about the created world, death could indeed be considered one of the goods of creation. Developing such an idea, one might claim, for example, that the definition of human character requires temporal finitude: If we were never to die, would we be anything in particular? Might not each moment of personal decision lose its character-forming significance if there were always to be a next one?[10] As the Bible suggests, "So teach us to number our days that we may get a heart of wisdom" (Ps. 90:12). Certainly on the viewpoint I am developing, death (as cessation) can be made good. Even Isaiah's vision of the new heaven and earth seems to envision not the end of death but its betterment: "Behold, I create a new heavens and a new earth. . . . No more shall there be in it an infant that lives but a few days, or an old man who does not fill out his days, for the child shall die a hundred years old" (Isa. 65:17, 20). Claiming that mortality itself is to be escaped, in a world where, if the scientists are right, the very principles of the universe devolve toward death, suggests Manichaeism. The world seems to be working naturally (certainly before, that is, the entrance of human sin) in a way that runs contrary to God as a source of the good.

This sort of account of the overcoming of mortality is not sufficient, however. For one, it does not adequately address the fact of lives that are not made good before death, and of deaths that are in no sense good. If death is simply the end of everything, how can one maintain the expectation of life in God as a fountain of goods in the face of all those creatures whose lives are short and brutish and whose deaths are cruel? In the second place, if we exist in God despite our deaths, the very idea of eternal life suggests some sort of overcoming of mortality itself. But what sort of overcoming of mortality is this if death remains a creature's good and natural end?

The key to intelligibility here is not to think of our mortality being overcome independently of our life in God. One does do this — one does think of the overcoming of the creature's mortality independently of life in God — when one focuses, as most contemporary eschatology does, on the character of the creature in itself pre- and post-mortem and on the overcoming of mortality as a change

---

9. In principle, perhaps, eternality (in some senses of that) is not incompatible with finitude, with being a nondivine creature. The fact of the matter, however — following contemporary science rather than, say, an Aristotelian one in which some things (e.g., stars and planets) are eternal — is that all organized structures are prone to fail. The world as we know it seems constructed in a way to ensure temporal finitude.

10. Suggestions like these are developed by Eberhard Jüngel, *Death — The Riddle and the Mystery* (Philadelphia: Westminster Press, 1974), and Karl Rahner, *On the Theology of Death* (New York: Herder and Herder, 1961).

[handwritten margin notes at top: "• Tanner seems to use "immortality" + "resurrection" interchangeably? • is her notion "dualistic"? | too individualistic"]

in its intrinsic constitution with the transition between the two. This makes eternal life the return of creatures, after the hiatus of death, to something like the existences they had before, but now in a form no longer susceptible to death. Although creatures in such a contemporary eschatology might be said to be living in God, independently of that relation they seem to have become immortal themselves.

Avoiding this way of discussing the overcoming of mortality, one can say, instead, that after death (as before death) we are taken up into the life of God as the very mortal creatures we are. It is only in God that we gain immortality; considered independently of this relation to God we remain mortal. We are immortal pre- and post-mortem only in virtue of our relation to an eternal God. Immortality is not, then, granted to the world in the form of some new natural principles that prevent loss or transience; instead, God's own animating eternity shines through or suffuses the very mortal being of those who hold their existence in God. We do not, then, leave our mortal lives behind after death, as if our deaths (and sufferings) have been simply canceled out, replaced by a new immortal version of ourselves — no more than the resurrected Christ appears as someone who is not also visibly the crucified. It is the crucified body that is glorified to immortality in the resurrection of the body. This immortality is properly considered ours, despite the fact that we remain mortal in and of ourselves, insofar as, living in God, we are no longer our own but God's. A new identity is in this way given to the world. Not in the form of a new version of one's old nature (considered in itself) but in the transition from an old self-enclosed identity to a new one that is constituted by an intimate relationship between who we are (and have been) and the God who offers to mortal creatures something that remains properly God's own.

[handwritten margin notes: "(1) what about eternal damnation" / "also immortal but not in relation to God!!" / "this is true even before death, from before birth (Jn 1:4)"]

Clearly, something may also happen *to* our mortal lives in God, post-death. In God, after its death, the world and everything it has ever contained may really receive as their own intrinsic properties of the blessings of life in God that were perhaps always blocked in the pre-mortem world by forces of sin and death — those forces that are no more in God. Immortality may be a gift that creatures cannot receive in themselves without the loss of creaturehood (or the loss of particular identity), and therefore they may have it only in relation to God; but clearly many other gifts stemming from life in God can be received in a way that genuinely transforms the creature's own nature considered in itself — healing replacing a broken woundedness, joy replacing sorrow, justice replacing trials and woes. The life that continues to receive such gifts after death is, however, a life of the world redefined so as to be inseparable from God.

II

How does the eschatology I am developing stimulate action for the better in this life? It might not seem to do so, for a number of reasons. Because eternal life is an unconditional, already realized possession, nothing we do is necessary to bring it about or to sustain it; this might suggest (erroneously, as I shall argue) that action is not obligated in any way *by* life in God. The present possession of eternal life might also seem to compensate for all other disappointments in a way that would simply reconcile us with them; even when matters could be improved by human action we would not see any need to do so because we already have all that we need simply in virtue of life in God. Finally, hope that sustains action in the face of obstacles and disappointment seems shattered by the world's eventual end; and thereby hope for the future of the world itself seems gone as the primary spur to present action.

While on the viewpoint I am developing one need not deny that the future will be different from the present, criticism of the present is not fueled primarily by the difference between present realities and what one expects the future to bring. Instead, criticism of the present is prompted, and complacency about it prevented, by a recognition of the disparity between the realm of life and the realm of death as those two realms or powers wrestle for supremacy in the here and now. One is led to see the way the world currently runs as an insufferable, unacceptable affront, not by the disparity between the present and God's coming future, but by the utter disjunction between patterns of injustice, exclusion, and impoverishment, which make up the realm of death, and the new paradigm of existence empowered by life in God as a force working in the present. In short, complacency is ruled out not by a transcendent future but by a transcendent present — by the present life in God as the source of goods that the world one lives in fails to match.

Action is the proper response to take with respect to a world that is not the way it should be, because, although human action does not bring about life in God (that is God's unconditional gift to us), human action of a certain sort is what life in God requires of us. Only one way of living in this world — living so as to counter suffering, oppression, and division — corresponds to life in God, achieved in Christ. Life in God is not inactive then. Life in God sets a task for us: to be a holy people and in that way demonstrate through the character of one's deeds what it means to be God's own people. Eternal life calls for a certain way of living as a sign of one's willing entrance into the realm of God's life-giving being. This is a kind of unconditional imperative to action in that life in God remains an empowering source of our action for the good, whatever the obstacles and failing of Christians. The imperative to act is also unconditional in that it is not affected by considerations of success. Irrespective of the likely success of one's action to better the world, one is obligated to act simply because this is the only way of living that makes sense in light of the fact of one's life in God. This is the only possibility for us given our reality as God's own. Without primary concern for the consequences of one's actions, one acts out of gratitude for the life in God one has been given; one acts out of joyful recognition that a certain course of action is part of those good gifts that stem from a special relationship with God. In this way, nonmoral forms of appreciation and response inform a Christian sense of obligation.[11]

---

11. Something like this is also suggested by William Schweiker in "Time as a Moral Space: Moral Cosmologies, Creation, and Last Judgment," chap. 9 in this volume.

In another sense, action is a conditional imperative as well; one is also acting in an attempt to bring about a world that more closely matches the one that life in God should bring. Although eternal life is not conditional on our action since it is in a primary sense already achieved through God's action in Christ, the blessings in the world that should naturally follow from it are yet in some significant sense conditional in the world as we know it. Blessings flow from life in God but their egress from that source can be blocked by sin, understood as the effort to turn away from relations with God (and one's fellows), the One from whom all goods flow. In this life, action that accords with the life-giving forces of God runs into the obstructions posed by our world as a realm of death — forces promoting impoverishment, suffering, exclusion, and injustice. One is called to act to counter such forces in the effort to bring in another kind of life.

This action cannot, moreover, be delayed in hopes of more propitious circumstances to come. Action is present-oriented and therefore realistic. One must work with what one has and that means figuring out the present workings of the world, with, for example, the help of the physical and social sciences, in order to intervene as best one can. Action has an urgency, moreover; every moment counts. As scientists describe it, the world does not have an indefinite extension into the future; nor will a second chance for action come again by way of a future reinstatement of the world now suffering loss.

Failure to have success is not a reason for despair. Certainly, if our action is not primarily motivated by hopes for success, the failure of those hopes is no cause to give up the fight. But to the extent our hopes *are* for the furthering of God's blessings through our own action, those hopes can be sustained even in the most dire and hopeless of circumstances; one can continue to hope in God, and specifically in God's gift of eternal life, since that is not conditioned by those circumstances or by our own failure because of them. The motor of blessings and of our own action to promote them — eternal life — is something already achieved without us, not something our action brings about, and therefore our hopes in it are not subject to disappointment when our actions fail to have the effects we desire. A hope, then, to counter despair in the present comes not from the idea that God Himself is the coming future; but from the fact that despite appearances to the contrary in a world of sin, God has in fact already assumed our lives in Godself. What draws our action and the world ever onward is not a future running ahead of us but a steadfast and unshakable rock (Christ) as the source of that movement, the fund and fountain of an ever-expanding movable feast.[12] On the basis of the fact that in Christ we already have all we need to do so, on the basis of the fact that through Christ's mercy even now we live in God as Christ does, we can hope to have done our part before the end of time.

---

12. See Gregory of Nyssa, *Life of Moses* (New York: Paulist Press, 1978), 243–44: "here the ascent takes place by means of the standing. I mean by this that the firmer and more immovable one remains in the Good, the more he progresses in the course of virtue.... [I]f someone, as the Psalmist says, should pull his feet up from the mud of the pit and plant them upon the rock (the rock is Christ who is absolute virtue) then the more steadfast and unmoveable...he becomes in the Good [and] the faster he completes the course."

Indeed, we can continue to hope in the world's (and our) progress after that end comes, but this is no hope in the world in itself, for that world ends (and has already ended); it is a hope in the world whose new identity essentially means nothing other than life in God.

Conclusion

It may be helpful, in concluding, to use the question of continuity and discontinuity to help clarify the distinctiveness of my position vis-á-vis others in this volume. First of all, on the question of continuity and discontinuity between the old world and the new my position is different from others in not formulating the issue in terms of temporal sequence. Old and new are found together in the world we know — that is the continuity. The discontinuity is expressed in the primarily spatial terms of a disjunction between competing spheres, that is, there is only a partial overlap between the new world and the world as it presently exists. Or the source of the new (life in God) is already fully realized — that is the continuity between life in God and the world as we find it. The proper effects of life in God are yet to be fully manifest — that is the discontinuity. Second, the issue of continuity and discontinuity is not focused on the point of transition between literal death and life — personally, communally, or cosmically. Instead, the issue is raised on a much broader level. Continuity amounts to the faithfulness of God's relations with the world across all the disruptions of death, suffering, oppression, and loss, from the beginning to the end of time. Discontinuity amounts to differences in the character of those relations in their creative and redemptive respects over the same span. Third, issues of continuity and discontinuity between the old and new world, on my way of looking at things, do not involve primary interest in these worlds and their internal constitution considered independently of their relation to God. Fourth, as an issue of personal identity, continuity and discontinuity for me do not concern aspects of created existence that remain (to insure identity) over and against those that change (the discontinuity between this world and the putative one to come).[13] Instead, the whole of the world is what is carried over into life in God; and it is as a whole that the world's identity is reconstituted, as nothing other than life in God.

These differences in the way continuities and discontinuities between old and new creation are discussed highlight the discontinuities between my own position and others in this volume. A more fully developed account of eternal life would, however, draw out the similarities — and also allow for greater incorporation of scientific description within my own position. Thus, while I have used the incarnation as a primary model for eternal life, there is no reason why models from science could not be used as an aid toward understanding what incarnation involves. Science might provide models comparable to those of glowing iron or the soul-body relation that theologians down through the centuries have used as

---

13. See John Polkinghorne, "Eschatology: Some Questions and Some Insights from Science," chap. 2 in this volume.

starting points for discussing the odd relationship between humanity and divinity in Christ. Furthermore, a full description of eternal life would involve not merely the effort to capture the character of the relationship per se but the consequences of it for human life. Part of the task, in short, would be to imagine the echaton, in which eternal life would come to full flower in the gift of all goods. As I have said, we should expect that some aspects of human existence in this life will be altered in and of themselves. While I, following much of the theological tradition from which I work, would not be especially sanguine about our abilities to say exactly how they will be changed, scientific descriptions could offer suggestions here about alterations to the internal constitution of things — their new matter and energy. Some aspects of human life, as I have emphasized, will not be altered in themselves but only in and through a relationship with God; they will be altered themselves only as they have been redefined so that a relationship with God is part of their very identity. On these matters, it makes sense to incorporate — as it stands within an account of the new life that follows from life in God — scientific description of the world as it is. Thus, in my account of the eschaton, it is the very mortal body as scientists describe it that takes on the immortality of God as it lives in God through Christ.

Chapter 16

IS THERE LIFE AFTER DEATH?

Jürgen Moltmann

Is Death the Finish? Is There Life after Death?
Why Do We Ask? What Are We Asking About?

What remains of our lives when we die? That is the question we ask when we pause in the midst of life's "ever-rolling stream" and search for the thing that sustains us. Where are the dead? We ask about their future when we stand at the grave of someone we love, and when we mourn the people who were the joy of our lives; for when they die, our love of life dies, too. So where are we going? Do we await anything? What awaits us?

What lasts? Does anything last at all? Of course we are overwhelmed by this question when we feel the cold breath of death — our own death, or the death of people we love. When people are in the grip of a serious illness we say that they are fighting for their lives. If they win, life is given back to them and they are as if new-born; if they lose, they vanish away, like all the other things that once made their lives what it was. Death seems to us final — the finish — gone — nevermore.

But this is not just the question we ask about death at the end of someone's life. The question is always already with us. It is the question about time; for "our days are soon gone and we fly away," as Psalm 90 laments. We cannot hold on to a single moment, even if, like Goethe's Faust, we long to say, "O tarry a while, thou art so fair." For we ourselves cannot tarry. The lived moment passes, and we pass away, too, "in the twinkling of an eye." Nothing remains, for time is irreversible, and what has once become the past can never be brought back. The future we hope for and for which we work will, if our hopes for it are fulfilled, become our present, and our expectations will then become the experiences we longed for. But every present passes, and what is past never returns. Expectations become experiences, and experiences turn into remembrances, and remembrances will in the end become the great forgetting that we call death. Yet something in us rises up in protest: "Is that all this life has to offer?"

When we ask about a life after death we are always asking at the same time about a meaningful, livable, and loved life before death. For what could a life after death mean for us unless there can be a fulfilled life before death which we affirm?

In the first part of this chapter we shall look at a number of religious and philosophical ideas about immortality, considering them in the light of the central question: what remains of life, what endures? In the second part we shall discuss various ideas about eternal life, viewing these in the light of the central question: where are the dead? It is true that our question is: "Is there life after death?" But what we know about that does not belong to the sphere of scientific knowledge about "what is" and over which we can dispose — about phenomena that can be experienced, and provable facts; it belongs to the other sphere of the knowledge that sustains existence, knowledge that gives confidence in life and death, and courage to live a life that is transitory, and which confers the consolation that makes it possible to survive. We shall test ideas in this sphere against the consequences they have for this life here and now, and for the way we face up to death, our own death and the death of other people.[1]

Why Do We Die? Does Death Have Any Meaning?

The experience of death is always secondary. Our primary experience is life. First comes the love for life, then pain over the loss of people we love. The way we live and the degree to which we deeply affirm life decide how we experience the deadliness of death. If we lose all interest in life, then death becomes a matter of indifference, too. But if we love life, we experience death as a hostile and annihilating power. Terrifying and mysterious, death stares us in the face. Why death? What is the meaning of death? If it is simply part of life, because it is the temporal end of finite existence, and because every life on this earth oscillates in the great cycles of "die and become," then we have to accept it, and there are no more questions we can ask. But if it is experienced as the destruction of a beloved life, then love rises up in rebellion against death and does not ask just about the meaning of this particular death; it calls death itself in question. Love wants to live, not die, to endure, not pass away. The life of love is "eternal life," so as long as we love we shall never accept death.

If we try to take our bearings from the Bible, we discover that the various biblical traditions do not offer any doctrines with abstract concepts for life and death. What they offer are testimonies about life with the living God. In the theology of the Christian church, however, two views developed:

> Death is the result of original sin.
>
> Death is the natural end of finite human life.

I believe that these two theses are not incompatible, and I should like to put forward a solution, before going on to discuss the hitherto-unconsidered problem of violent death.

Death and Sin

Death came into the world through sin. Original sin was followed by hereditary death. The Church Fathers all followed the Pauline-Augustinian doctrine, which held that because of the link between act and destiny, death is the inescapable

---

1. Cf. Jürgen Moltmann, "Eternal Life: Personal Eschatology," in his *The Coming of God: Christian Eschatology*, trans. Margaret Kohl (Minneapolis: Fortress Press, 1996), 47–128.

punishment for the sin of human beings. Through the Fall (Genesis 3), the creaturely mortality of the first human beings (*posse mori*) becomes death as their
inescapable fate (*non posse non mori*). Beforehand they *could* die. Afterwards they
had to die.[2] The universality of death proves the universality of the Fall of humanity. If sin is of the human being's own making — a deliberate turning away
from the living God — then death as the consequence of sin is not merely the
person's temporal end. It is his or her eternal end, too. Physical death is followed
by eternal death. And eternal death is the name given to final and irrecoverable
exclusion from fellowship with the living God.

As the church's doctrine developed, a distinction was made between three
deaths, or forms of death, as the consequence of original sin:

> the death of the soul (*mors spiritualis*);
>
> the death of the body (*mors corporalis*);
>
> eternal death (*mors aeterna*).

In people's experiences of dying and death these three forms of death are inter-
woven. In dying, the soul in its God-forsakenness feels God's wrath, and in its
fear of death suffers the death of the soul. Eternal death is heralded by the death
of the body. Fears of death grow into fears of hell. Immediately on the death
of the body, the soul stands before God's eternal "Judgment Seat" and receives
the verdict. In eternal death, the soul then suffers the eternal torments of hell,
where there is no way out, and no longer any hope. As we can see from hymn-
books and the church's literature on *ars moriendi* — the art of dying — this idea
about "death as the consequence of sin" imposed on the dying all the terrors
of the last judgment, and heightened the natural fear of death into the fear of
hell. Limitless feelings of guilt were a heavy load that accentuated the torments
of death, torments from which the church's means of grace and its consolations
were supposed to relieve the dying.

Death and the Earthly Life

The death of the body is the natural end of earthly life. Exceptions apart, and
leaving aside some Christian groups that were termed heretical, it was the Liberal
Protestant theology of the nineteenth century which for the first time disputed the
causal connection between sin and eternal death on the one hand, and physical
death on the other, cutting loose the end of earthly life from the religious interpretative framework of guilt, judgment, and punishment. According to Friedrich
Schleiermacher, the assertions of Christian doctrine do not have to do with the
nature or constitution of the world; they are related simply to the consciousness
of the believer.[3] But that means that physical death is not in itself an evil; it is
an evil only in the human awareness of death, and it is a divine punishment only
in the human consciousness of guilt. Insofar as the awareness of death draws up

---

2. Augustinus, *Enchiridion*, 105–7.

3. Friedrich Schleiermacher, *The Christian Faith*, trans. H. R. Mackintosh and J. S. Steward from
the 2d ed. (Edinburgh, 1928; repr., Philadelphia, 1976), 75.

the balance sheet of a life that has gone wrong, death will be subjectively viewed as the consequence of these wrongdoings. Consequently we shall be redeemed through God's grace not from death itself but from the fear of death resulting from guilt. "The death of the soul" and "eternal death" are terms for the loss of fellowship with God which begins with sin. But neither has anything to do with physical death, and hence nothing to do with the process of dying itself either.

In spite of his anti-Liberal theology, Karl Barth followed Schleiermacher at this point: "Finitude means mortality" and "death in itself" is the natural end of limited human existence.[4] If through faith in God's grace people are freed from the fear resulting from sin and from the fear of death, they will also be freed for "a natural death." Their finite life is "eternalized" in the memory of God: that is their redemption, not physical resurrection and the abolition of physical death.

If, according to the first view, death came into the world only through *sin*, then we have to restrict this to the death of human beings, for the death of animals, the dying of trees, and the extinction of the dinosaurs can hardly be traced back to human sin. That would be a negative self-deification of human beings by way of an immense and presumptuous arrogation of guilt. Not every death in the world can be traced back to human sin. And on the other hand, the angels "who sinned" (2 Pet. 2:4) will have remained immortal.

If, according to the second view, finitude always and everywhere means mortality, then here too we have to make a qualification. Angels are presumably immortal, although they are finite beings; and stones and other lifeless matter cannot be called mortal, even though these things are finite. Biologically speaking, death came into the world together with sexual reproduction.

If, in contrast to both these views, we do not start from *the origin* of death (whether that be the Fall or finitude) but take as starting point *the future* of redemption in the new creation of all things — then, out of the remembrance of Christ's resurrection, we see emerging on this horizon of expectation a new world in which "death will be no more" (Rev. 21:4), since as "the last enemy" of God and of life it will be "destroyed" (1 Cor. 15:26) through the divine power of resurrection, and will be "swallowed up" in the victory of life (1 Cor. 15:55). So, in the new creation of all things, it is not just death as the consequence of sin or the fear of death as the outcome of our consciousness of guilt that will be overcome. The mortality of creation-in-the-beginning will be overcome too, so that a new, immortal creation comes into being (1 Cor. 15:53–54). This means that the death of the living must be seen neither as "sinful" nor as "natural," but as a fact that provokes grief over transience, and longing for the eternal life of the future world.

Violent Death

If we now consider *violent death* — murder, death in war, and mass annihilation through atomic, biological, and chemical weapons, or death through starvation

---

4. Karl Barth, *Church Dogmatics*, III/2.632–39; Eberhard Jüngel, *Death: The Riddle and the Mystery*, trans. I. and U. Nicol (Edinburgh, 1975), 120.

because help is not forthcoming — then we shall see the relation between human sin and physical death in a more differentiated way. Sin is not just a turning away from God; it is also an act of violence against life. Because people have an awareness of death, death can be used as a threat. Because their awareness of death is linked with fear for their lives, they can be blackmailed. Tyranny is always based on the threat of death and is administered by way of mass murder.

The sin of organized violence lives from the fear of death of those who are oppressed, and is a covenant with death against life. Today more people die through organized violence than through murder and war — and this organized violence takes the form above all of "economic death." "The murder of millions through administrative methods has made of death something which people never before had to fear in just this fashion," said T. W. Adorno.[5]

The death of the mass victims of violence is not a consequence of their "sin," nor is it a natural death. It is suffered crime. The blood of the victims "cries out to high heaven," and it is not just persons that are accused; it is the unjust structures of organized violence, too. These are signs of the bestial empires that rise up out of chaos, as they are pictured as doing in Daniel 2 and 7. They will be overcome only by the humane kingdom of the Son of man. His kingdom will be eternal because it is not based on injustice but on justice and righteousness. If that redeeming and enduring kingdom of the Son of man belongs to the victims of the human empires of violence, then their cries are already the judgment on the perpetrators of violence here and now. "The silence of the peoples is the judgment passed on tyrants." The Son of man crucified in the name of the Roman empire with its rule of violence has become one of the victims, so as "to seek that which is lost."

What Remains of Life?

We are familiar with very old religious ideas expressed in the pictures of early peoples, where the immortal soul of a human being is shown departing from the body after death, leaving that body behind as a lifeless corpse, while the soul returns to its eternal home in a heaven beyond earth. The ancient Egyptians imagined the soul as a bird, with the human face of the dead person. Elisabeth Kübler-Ross found strikingly many butterflies in the pictures painted by children in Auschwitz. In medieval pictures, the soul enters the body before birth in the form of a tiny human being with angel's wings, so that after the person's death it can fly away and return to heaven. Obituary notices often cite a famous verse written by Eichendorff:

> And so my soul
> spread wide her wings,
> flew through the silent lands
> as if she flew towards home.

---

5. Theodore W. Adorno, *Negative Dialectics*, trans. E. B. Ashton (New York, 1973), 362. Cf. also Phillipe Ariès, *Geschichte des Todes* (Munich, 1980).

That is a lovely picture even though the "as if" in the last line suggests a romantic unreality. Every prisoner knows the longing that the free flight of a bird awakens, the longing for "the broad place in which there is no cramping."

But what do we mean when we talk about the soul as the part of our life that is immortal? Do we mean the immortality of the unlived life, or the immortality of the lived life?

According to our philosophical tradition, which goes back to Plato, the human soul is essentially and in substance immortal.[6] Death does not kill it. Death merely divides the immortal soul from the mortal body, which then lies there, a lifeless corpse. For all those who loved that body, with its senses and passions, death may be a reason for grief. But for the soul, death is the greatest feast day on the way to freedom in its own world of Ideas. Because it is immortal, it only occupied this mortal body as a guest, or as if in a prison.

Let us now turn to the question: why is the soul immortal, while everything else in us is, after all, mortal? The answer is a simple one, even if it is not universally familiar: the soul cannot die because it was never born. Because it was there before the child's birth, it will still be there after the old man or woman has died. Its life after death is its life before birth as well; for its "eternal life" is beyond the birth and death of this life. But if the soul is never born and cannot die, it has nothing in common with the physical, sensory world of this life of birth and mortality. It is in its substance immutable, always the same, incapable of suffering and hence incapable of happiness, too. In the sense of what we call "life" or "livingness," the soul is lifeless. To put it epigrammatically, what is meant by the immortal soul is not the immortality of the lived life; it is the immortality of the life that has never lived.

But if that is true, then this doctrine of the immortal soul offers us no answer to the question: what remains of life? And yet the consciousness of "possessing" an immortal soul gives people serenity and imperturbability in the ups and downs of life, and makes them indifferent toward life and death. Self-transcendence and the self-irony that prevents one from taking oneself too seriously: those are their virtues. We find this not merely in the philosophy of the Greek Stoics, but in the Indian Bhagavadgita as well.

> It is neither born nor does it die,
> as it once was, so it remains,
> unborn, immortal.
>
> He who is steadfast in joy and pain,
> remains himself at every hour,
> ripens for immortality.
>
> He who renounces all desire,
> from selfishness and longing free
> walking this earth,
> he enters into tranquil peace. (II.15–71)

---

6. Plato, *Phaedo*, trans. D. Gallop, World's Classics (Oxford, 1983).

Perhaps there were closer links between Greece and India than we have any idea of.

But when we talk about the soul today, do we really mean these attributes of untouchability? When we talk about an "ensouled life," we mean the wholly and entirely living life, not the life that is unlived. We mean a life that is open, able for happiness, and capable of suffering, a life full of love. If we say that a mother is "the soul of her family," we certainly do not mean that she is the part of the family which nothing can touch. We mean that she keeps her family together, and makes it a living entity. So I should like to understand "the soul" in a different way from Plato.

Human life is entirely human when it is entirely living. But human livingness means being interested in life, participating and communicating, and affirming one's own life and the life of others. This vital interest is what we call love of life. It expresses itself in a life that is wholly and completely lived because it is a life that is loved. Our "soul" is present when we give ourselves up to something completely, are passionately interested, and, because love makes us strong, do not hold life back but go out of ourselves. But if we go out of ourselves we become capable of love, and also capable of suffering. We experience the livingness of life — and at the same time the deadliness of death. But how can we really give ourselves up to this life, with its conflicts, its happiness, its disappointments and pains, if we do not put more confidence in this love for life than in transient time and death? The real human problem is not the dualism of an immortal soul and a mortal body; it is the conflict between love and death.

Can this loved, ensouled, and mortal life be immortal? This obvious contradiction is resolved if, instead of ascribing immortality to a substance like the Platonic soul, we see it as a relationship of the whole person to the immortal God. Ever since its beginnings, Christian theology has worked on this transformation of the idea of immortality. Let me mention some different stages and aspects.

In both the Old and New Testaments, immortality is always postulated of the divine Spirit (*ruach, pneuma*) which gives life to us and to all the living. "Into thy hands I commend my spirit," prays the dying Jesus according to Luke (23:46), using the words of Ps. 31:6, the Jewish evening prayer. Christian poets have taken up this idea, Paul Gerhardt among them.[7] One hymn-writer calls the Spirit "the seal of immortality." Another writes:

> Breathe on me Breath of God,
> so shall I never die,
> but live with Thee the perfect life
> of Thine eternity.

According to biblical ideas, this Spirit, who is the giver of life (*spiritus vivificans*), is a divine relationship out of which life and the blessing of life proceed. What divine relationship?

---

7. "Kann uns doch kein Tod nicht töten, / sondern reit / unsern Geist / aus viel tausen Nöten."

Human beings are created to be the image of God on earth. That is to say, God puts himself in relationship to these created beings in such a way that they become his mirror and reflection, and the response to him. If God is God, his relation to his human image cannot be destroyed, either through the antagonism and recalcitrance of human beings or through their death. Only God could dissolve the relationship to his creatures into which he has entered, if he were to "be sorry" he created them, as the story about Noah and the Flood tells.

But as long as God holds fast to this relationship to human beings, to be made in the image of God remains the inalienable and indestructible destiny of human beings. If this were not so, the powers of time and death would be mightier than God. For human beings, what results from the special relation of God to them is called life, soul, or "spirit."

This certainly does not mean "spirit" in the sense in which we often use the word. The Hebrew word *ruach* means the energy and force of life. It fills the whole lived life, which means a person's whole life history from birth to death, everything we mean when we use a person's name. "Fear not, for I have redeemed you; I have called you by your name, you are mine." So we say in the words of Isa. 43:1, at a sick bed, or standing before a grave. But what is meant by a person's name? Surely not just that person's disembodied soul or soulless body, but rather the whole configuration of the person's life in space, and the whole history of his or her life in time. If this living configuration is called by name, then as a consequence our whole life becomes immortal in God's relation to it. As mortal, transitory men and women, in the immortal and intransient fellowship with God we ourselves remain immortal and intransient. How can we conceive of this?

The American process theology of A. N. Whitehead and Charles Hartshorne calls this remaining in relationship to God *objective immortality*.[8] It is not just that God affects everything; everything has its effect on God, too. People are not just created by God. They themselves, for their part, also make an impression on God. It is not just we who experience God. God "experiences" us, too. The "experience" that God has of us remains existent in him even when we die. Our life in time is transitory, but we have an eternal presence in God. The history of our lives is fleeting. We ourselves forget quickly. But for God that life history is like a book of life in which his experience of our lives remains eternally in his memory.

This idea about an objective immortality in God's eternity is still not in itself a consoling idea. Would we really like to be reminded to all eternity of everything we have ever said, done, and experienced? But according to the Psalms in the Old Testament, God's memory is not a video of our lives, recorded from heaven and played back to all eternity. It is a merciful, healing remembrance that puts things to rights. "Remember me according to thy mercy," and "remember not the sins of my youth." It is the shining countenance of God's love which looks at us, not the cold, impersonal lens of a monitor set up by a state security authority.

---

8. Alfred North Whitehead, *Process and Reality: An Essay in Cosmology* (New York, 1941), 523, 532.

God's relation to human beings which makes these human beings come alive is also termed *dialogical immortality*. "The one to whom God speaks, whether in wrath or in grace, that one is surely immortal," said Luther.[9] This idea has the support of many theologians. People remain God's conversation partner, even if they do not listen. Even death cannot alter that. But if they do listen, their whole life becomes a responsive existence: they respond, and make themselves responsible. If that is correct, then death is the boundary of our lives, but not the boundary of God's relationship to us. In that relationship, our death is rather a gateway or connecting door, a transformation on our side. The speaking, calling, and ultimately redeeming relationship of God to us endures.

Finally, there is in faith an experience in fellowship with Christ which leads to a *subjective immortality*, and a positive hope of resurrection. This is the experience of being in the divine Spirit a child of God's. "All who are led by the Spirit of God are children of God," says Paul. As God's children, they belong to God's family and lineage and, by virtue of hope, already participate here and now in the eternal life of God's future world. In the Spirit of the resurrection, they already, here and now, experience that eternal life as eternal livingness in love.

So let us sum up: what remains of life?

We have two impressions. On the one hand, we cannot hold fast to anything, not even ourselves: everything passes; naked we came into the world, naked we shall leave it. Death is the finish.

But, on the other hand, nothing is lost at all. Everything remains in God. Before God, with God, and in God we mortal beings are immortal, and our transitory life remains intransitory. Our life as we experience it is temporal and mortal. But as God experiences our life it remains eternally immortal. Nothing is lost with God, not the moments of happiness, not the times of pain. "All live to him" (Luke 20:38).

Where Are the Dead?

That sounds like a speculative question, but that is not the case. Where do we really experience death? At the end of my own life, what I experience is dying but not death, because I do not survive my death on earth. But when the people I love die, I experience their death, for I have to survive that death, mourn their loss, and go on living in spite of it. Life is good, but to be a survivor is hard. This means that what we experience ourselves is dying, but in other people we experience death. The question "where are the dead?" is an important question for us personally, because it is a question about the community of the living with the dead, and is important for a life in their presence.

I remember what was for me a painfully embarrassing situation. Ernst Bloch had just died. He was a neighbor of ours, and I went over at once to speak to his wife. She came toward me and simply asked, "Where is he now?" His body was still

---

9. Martin Luther, *Genesisvorlesung* (1535–45), WA 43, 481. See also Joseph Ratzinger, *Eschatologie: Tod und ewiges Leben* (Regensburg, 1977).

in the house. For the moment I was without an answer. But I have learned that this "where" question is important for the people left behind, because without an answer they cannot hold fast to fellowship with "the beloved person" (as Bloch's wife called her Ernst).

Let us now look at three ideas about the life of the dead, submitting them to a critical question: do they strengthen the love of the living for the dead?

The Doctrine of Purgatory

This is unknown in Protestant circles or among people without any church connections. In an examination, one Protestant theological student answered my question about purgatory by saying that he supposed it was hell for Catholics. The dogmatic starting point for the development of the idea of purgatory can be found in a declaration made in 1336 by Pope Benedict XII.[10] He rejected the idea that the dead sleep until the resurrection at the Last Day. After their own personal death, Michael Schmaus explained, everyone is immediately judged, confronted by God with the whole truth about the life they have lived, in the light of what they themselves know; they become their own judge. Many people have experienced something like this in near-death situations: their whole life passes before them in quick motion, in a flash. If someone dies in faith in Christ, his or her sins are certainly forgiven, but the consequences of sin remain. They have not yet been expiated through temporal punishments. Life before death is a continual repentance, and life after death is continued as a similar process of purgation and purification. This process is purgatory. It has nothing to do with hell — on the contrary. To put it in modern terms, in death the believing soul experiences the presence of God as light and fire. The light of the eternal love draws it to God — the fire of eternal love burns away everything that is in opposition to God and that cuts the soul off from him. Some people who have stood at the threshold of death tell of visions of light and fire like this. The basic idea of the doctrine of purgatory can be found in Christ's promise that "the pure in heart shall see God." Consequently, the purification of the heart must be continued until the contemplation of God can take place — the *visio beatifico*, or beatific vision.

In the world of religious ideas, heaven and hell are terminuses, the end of the road. But the idea of purgatory permits God's history with a person to continue after death. That is why Dante writes in his *Divine Comedy* (1319): "Beloved son, let thy hope rise," whereas over the gate to hell are written the words: "Abandon hope, all ye who enter here." In Dante, purgatory lies on a mountain of purification, with seven stages, a mountain that reaches from earth up to heaven.

Can the living do anything for the "poor souls in purgatory"? A tenet of faith says that in Christ the living and the dead are a great communion. It is a "penitential community." So if someone acquires an indulgence — a remission of the punishment for his or her sins — that person has the right to ask God to pass

---

10. J. Le Goff, *Die Geburt des Fegefeuers* (Stuttgart, 1984); Michael Schmaus, *Katholische Dogmatik* IV/2, 2d ed. (Munich, 1941), 151–73.

on to the dead the remission of punishment that has been granted. But the most efficacious help is the Mass for the dead.

Protestant criticism of the notion of purgatory is familiar. As we all know, the Reformation began with Luther's attack on Tetzel's trade in indulgences, an advertising slogan for which has come down to us: "The moment that the money rings, the soul from purgatory springs." In the Smalcald Articles, Luther criticized the "fair-ground trafficking in purgatorial Masses," and Calvin called purgatory a "pernicious invention of Satan"; for both Luther and Calvin proclaimed that what Christ has done is sufficient for all our sins, so there is no need for the souls of the dead to perform anything additional for their salvation, by enduring punishment.[11] But with their criticism the Reformers were attacking only the concept of penance and the "penitential community of the living and the dead." They were not criticizing — though they were not, of course, unaware of the fact — the idea that God's history with human beings continues after death. Nor were they calling in question the community of the living and the dead in Christ.

The Doctrine of the Soul's Sleep

A second idea, which we find in Luther and in modern Catholic theology, is the doctrine of the soul's sleep or resurrection at death. Luther conceived the state of the dead as a deep, dreamless sleep, removed from time and space, without consciousness and without feeling. In this concept he did not think so much from here to there, as from there to here. When the dead are raised by Christ "on the Last Day," they will neither know how long they have slept nor where they are. We shall rise "suddenly" and shall not know how we came to die, or how we have passed through death.

> As soon as thy eyes have closed shalt thou be woken, a thousand years shall be as if thou hadst slept but a little half hour. Just as at night we hear the clock strike and know not how long we have slept, so too, and how much more, are in death a thousand years soon past. Before a man should turn round, he is already a fair angel. (WA 37.191)

The theological reasoning is as follows:

> Because before God's face time is not counted, a thousand years before Him must be as it were but a single day. Hence the first man Adam is as close to Him as will be the last to be born before the final Day. For God seeth time, not according to its length but athwart it, transversely. Before God all hath happened at once. (WA 36.340)

When Luther calls death a sleep, this does not mean that he is drawing a veil over the brute fact of death. What he means is, first, that death has lost its power over human beings, and, second, that it is not the last thing that awaits us. Both affirmations presuppose Christ's resurrection from the dead, for with that, death

---

11. Martin Luther, *Widerruf vom Fegebeuer* (1530), WA 30, 2:360–90; Johannes Calvin, *Institutio Christianae Religionis*, III, 5, 6.

surrendered its power to Christ. It still has its "form," as Luther says, but no longer its power.

How long does the soul's sleep last — what the hymn calls "death's dark night"? Luther does not reply with projections drawn from the time of the living and extrapolated on to a continued existence of the soul. He finds expressions for God's time: "suddenly, in a moment." The Last Day is "the Day of the Lord," so it is not just the last day; it is "the day of days," the time of the eternal present. How long will it be, from the hour of our own death until the dead are raised into the eternal kingdom? Just "an instant." Where are the dead now, in terms of our time? They are already in the world of the resurrection. "Today" — not "in three days," not "at the Last Day" but "today you will be with me in Paradise," says the dying Christ to the man dying on the cross beside him.

Karl Rahner and other Catholic theologians have taken up this idea about "resurrection at death." The ecumenical *New Book of Belief* of 1973 (*Das Neue Glaubensbuch*) says, "Individual resurrection from the dead takes place with and at death." Unfortunately, in his first declaration as cardinal, Joseph Ratzinger, through the medium of the Congregation for the Doctrine of the Faith, rejected this idea, for it makes indulgences and Masses for the dead superfluous, and therefore runs counter to the practice of the church.

Reincarnations

This brings us to the much discussed question about possible *reincarnations.*[12] Do we live only once on this earth, or are we reborn many times?

Although a soul that cannot die cannot be born either, from time immemorial the notion of an immortal soul has often been linked with ideas about the transmigration of souls, and their reincarnation in new forms of life. Everything that lives comes into being and passes away. Why should it not come into being again afresh? If we cease to look at our own lives, but consider life's great cohesions in the community of human beings and the community shared by all the living, then the notion of the eternal return appears quite normal, and the idea that a life is unique and original seems actually something out of the way. Plato and Plotinus, Lessing and Goethe particularly were all attracted to the doctrine of reincarnation, and the new age movement has taken it up as well. So I should now like to compare the old and new doctrines of reincarnation with the biblical — that is, Jewish and Christian — philosophies of life.

1. Every doctrine of reincarnation sets the individual life in the wider community of the generations and of all the living. All are related to all others. Do not kill an animal — it might harbor your mother's soul! Do no living thing an injustice — in the next life you could be that same living thing! If we see the souls of human beings, animals, and plants within the great cohesion of the world soul, then all live together in an ensouled cosmos. The Abrahamic religions, in contrast, have linked their conviction about the counterpart of a personal God with a belief in the uniqueness of the human person, and the individual life that

---

12. Cf. Hans Küng, *Eternal Life?*, trans. E. Quinn (London, 1984), 81–94.

can never be brought back. People are not just "part of nature" (as the United Nations' Earth Charter says). They are an image of the invisible God, too. In this relationship to God they are above the patterns and cohesions of nature. Before God, every human person is an original, not a replica, and God never clones. From this follows the respect for the individuality of every life, and the uniqueness of the lived moment.

From the biblical standpoint, those who believe in reincarnation must be asked whether their doctrine does not very considerably reduce the number of existing souls. Surely the claim to have already lived several times, or to have been reborn again and again, means a tremendous ousting of other people from their own lives? I remember seeing the film in which a Tibetan lama dies, and the monks look for the reincarnation of his soul. They find it in a little Chinese boy, and revere him accordingly. The boy can no longer live his own life, for he is no longer himself.

From the standpoint of the doctrines of reincarnation, the Abrahamic religions must in their turn be asked whether the personal elevation of human beings above nature, with its warp and weft, does not destroy the community of the living on earth, and whether it is not responsible for the ecological catastrophes of the modern world. That leads us to a synthesis: as persons before God, people are part of nature; and as part of nature they are persons before God. Their unique character as the image of God does not cut them off from nature, but merely describes their particular task within nature. Persons are not individuals. They are social beings, and live in community with each other, in the community of the generations, and in the community of creation. It is quite possible to mediate fruitfully between the Western understanding of person and the Eastern understanding of nature — not only possible, but vitally necessary. The critical questions lie elsewhere.

2. Every doctrine of reincarnation is faced with the question of how it can hold fast to the soul's identity in the transmigrations of the forms of life which that soul assumes. If I am reborn as a human being, I must be able to preserve my soul's human identity. If I am reborn as an animal, or if I once died as a tree, this identity cannot be preserved. It passes away with the human form of my life. If I have the impression that "I have been here before," I must be able to recognize myself in that past form of life. My "I" or self cannot be mortal. But if my "I" is part of this life, I shall not be able to recognize myself again, however often I am reborn. And according to ancient Indian teaching, the soul does not really "migrate." The Bhagavadgita certainly says

> As a man casts off his worn-out clothes and takes on other new ones,
> so does the embodied [self] cast off its worn-out bodies and enters new ones.
>   (II.22)

But if the soul is without individuality, it is not a determining subject that can migrate or change its clothing. So in Buddhism the idea of a "transmigration of souls without a soul" was thought through further:

> Is the one who is born again the same as the one who departs, or different? Neither the same nor another. . . . One appearance emerges, another disappears, yet they all

range themselves to each other without interruption. In this way the final constitution of the consciousness is attained neither as the same person nor as another.
(Milinda Panha)

That is a typical Asian "neither-nor," in place of the "either-or" of Western
thinking.

3. According to ancient Indian teaching, the reincarnations belong to the
wheel of rebirth; and according to the teaching about karma, they are the requittal
for good and evil acts in a former life. They are the materialized consequences of
sin, so to speak. According to Western spiritism and new age teaching, they belong
to the evolutionary principle of the modern world. The doctrine of karma maintains that there is an inexorable and inescapable link between act and destiny:
"The person who steals corn will become a rat" (and "You have made your bed—
now lie in it"). No power in the world can break this link, and no God either. But
in the Western interpretation, reincarnations are supposed to give us "a second
chance," so that we can do better next time, as Elisabeth Kübler-Ross believes.
"Little by little we climb higher and higher up the ladder of progress until we
reach the stages of perfection," taught the Spiritist Alan Kardec.[13] There is thus
a contradiction between the Eastern and the Western judgment of reincarnation;
for the one it is retribution, for the other a chance.

The biblical religions recognized a karma, too, one that spans generations:
"The fathers have eaten sour grapes, and the children's teeth are set on edge."
This is proverbial wisdom: "He who sows the wind will reap the whirlwind." But
what is special and new in the biblical traditions is the principle of grace, which
breaks through the general chain-linking act and destiny, setting it aside and
invalidating it: "His grace is new every morning." "He who forgives all your sins
and heals your infirmities" is himself the power of life that breaks through the
laws of karma and destiny, and replaces retribution by a new beginning.

Finally, this also means that the cosmic law of karma cannot be pressed into
service to explain the disabilities, illnesses, or suffering of the present, tracing
them back to the guilt of the sufferer's forbears. The dead of Auschwitz: what
karmic guilt are they supposed to have expiated? The dead of Hiroshima: what
karmic retribution are they supposed to have suffered?

The Future of the Spoiled and Curtailed Life

Much in our lives remains unfinished. We began something, but did not carry
it through to the end. We tried to make a plan for our lives but the plan was
spoiled. Life was promised us, and the promise remained unfulfilled. How can a
life here ever be "complete" or "successful"? However we may imagine eternal
death or eternal life, it can surely not mean the eternalization of our unsuccessful
beginnings or miscarried attempts at life. It is impressions of this kind which make
us think about an ongoing history of God with our lived lives and which give us

---

13. Elisabeth Kübler-Ross, *On Life after Death* (Berkeley: University of California Press, 1991);
Alan Kardec, *Das Buch der Geister* (Freiburg, 1987).

the feeling that the dead are still not at rest. Whether the idea be purgatory or the transmigration of souls, the feeling remains: I must or shall again come back to this life so as to set right the things that have gone wrong, pay off the debts, heal the pains, and complete what was never completed.

But it is not just the harsh caesuras in the story of our own lives which make us ask about a life after death. I think of the life of those who were unable to live and were not allowed to live: the beloved child dying at birth; the little boy run over when he was four; the sixteen-year-old friend torn to pieces by a bomb as he stood beside you, a bomb that left you unscathed; and all the many people who have been raped and murdered and exterminated. Of course their fate can be of great importance for other people, but where will their own lives be "completed"? Where and how will they find "rest"?

The idea that for these people their death is the finish would surely plunge the whole world into absolute absurdity; for if their lives had no meaning, have ours? The modern notion about a "natural death" may be appropriate enough for members of the affluent society, with their life insurances, who can afford a death in old age. But in the countries of the Third World most people die a premature, violent, and by no means affirmed death, like so many people of my generation who died in the Second World War. The idea of an "eternalization of the lived life" does not take in the people who were not able to live or were not permitted to do so. So do we not have to think the thought of an ongoing history of God with the spoiled and curtailed life, if we are to be able to affirm life in this ravaged world and to love it in spite of all its cruelties?

I believe that God will also complete the work that he has begun with a human life. If God is God, even violent death cannot stop him from doing so. So I believe that God's history with our lives will go on after our deaths, until that completion has been reached in which a soul finds rest. According to theological tradition, this is not as yet "the kingdom of God," nor is it yet "the life of the world to come"; it is a kind of "intermediate state" between the life that has died here and eternal life there. An intermediate state of this kind is presupposed by the doctrines of purgatory and reincarnation, but the idea of a great divine Judgment also gives a name to something between our death and eternal life. I do not believe in the necessary performance of penitential acts in a purgatory. Nor do I believe in a great and final divine criminal court of justice. For me, God's judgment means the final putting to rights of the injustice that has been done and suffered, and the final raising up of those who are bowed down. So I conceive of that "intermediate state" as a wide space for living, in which the life that was spoiled and cut short here can develop freely. I imagine it as the time of a new life, in which God's history with a human being can come to its flowering and consummation. I imagine that we then come close to that well of life from which we could already here and now draw the power to live and the affirmation of life, so that the handicapped and the broken can live the life that was meant for them, for which they were born, and which was taken from them.

For that reason I do not believe that we ought to compare that life with a sleep, as Luther did. We should rather, like Calvin, think of a great "waking and watching of the soul" after death, with which it "perceives" its healing and its completion, and "experiences" its rebirth for the life of the future world.[14] Those whom we call the dead are not lost. But they are not yet finally saved either. Together with us who are still alive, they are hidden, sheltered, in the same hope, and are hence together with us on the way to God's future. They "watch" with us, and we "watch" with them. That is the community of hope shared by the dead with the living, and by the living with the dead.

I think all this not for selfish reasons, neither for the sake of a personal completion nor in the interests of a moral purification, but for the sake of the justice which I believe is God's own concern and his first option.

A Community of the Living and the Dead?

Ideas about a life after death are not only important for the dying and the dead. They are also important for the living, who see themselves as "coming after" or as the "surviving bereaved." These ideas express the relationships of the dead to the living and of the living to the dead, and influence the life led in remembrance or forgetfulness of those who have died.

In the traditional societies of Asia and Africa, but in the old village communities of Europe, too, the cult of one's dead ancestors guarantees a continual presence among those who have come after them. One can sometimes even talk about an "ascendancy" of the forebears over their descendants. These forebears are not dead, in the modern sense of no-longer-existent. They go on existing in the kingdom of the spirits and are spiritually present to the living. This belongs to the spiritist feeling for life which is the archaic foundation of all religions. Ancestors can torment their descendants through their unrest, or bless them through their peace. Those who come after must at all events live and work in the presence of their ancestors, and see that they are given the necessary veneration, as the long family registers in the Old Testament and the long ancestral tablets in Korea prove. The dead must receive justice; otherwise they find no peace and do not allow their descendants to live in peace. Every decision that is of importance in life must be made in the face of the sequence of ancestors, and in the face of several coming generations, because it does not touch merely the people living in the present, but forebears and descendants, too.

In modern societies, individual consciousness has pushed out the ancient collective consciousness of the sequence of generations. This has turned the relationships of the living to the dead upside down. Those who are dead are simply dead and no longer exist as "ancestors." If they are no longer present, they will be forgotten, or the distressing remembrances of them will be suppressed, so that the living can go on living their own lives undisturbed. People need not pay any attention to their ancestors, for these no longer have any influence on their lives. So in modern societies the living acquire ascendancy over the dead. If there is to be a community, it cannot proceed from the dead, but must start from the living.

---

14. Heinrich Quistorp, *Die letzten Dinge im Zeugnis Calvins* (Gütersloh, 1941), 89–102.

But first we can observe a quite unusual suppression of the awareness of death and the remembrance of the dead in a society that no longer reveres the old with their wisdom but keeps its veneration for youth: "Forever young!" Mourners have no public status anymore, periods of mourning are no longer respected, mourning rituals are forgotten. In the big German cities the number of "anonymous burials" has risen sharply in recent years, and already amounts to 25–50 percent of all burials. The body is burnt, the ashes are scattered, "and no one knows the place thereof." In the great cities, the districts where people live and the cemeteries where the dead lie are now far apart, and families no longer live together in a single place, so the graves can neither be visited nor cared for.

Of course, in modern society, too, people are tormented by pain over the death of those who belong to them and are overwhelmed by grief over their loss; but in pastoral care and counseling we ask less about what happens to the dead than about what is going to happen to the living after their loss. They are the ones left behind and, after the experience of death, are trying to regain the courage to live. But they do not find this courage for life by suppressing memories and by forgetting the dead, but only together with these things. When we do not fill up the gap that their death has torn in our life through some substitute, but leave it unfilled, if we go on missing them, we remain bound to them and they to us.

Once we understand their death not as a farewell but as their transformation into that other world of God's and that other life which we call eternal life, we experience their presence in our life as a kind of "second presence." In this strange "second presence" the dead do not bind the living to themselves but let them go free, although the living know that they are still bound to those who are gone. That is why the survivors do not have to forget the dead in order to be able to lead their own lives.

If modern men and women cannot return to the cults and rituals of traditional societies, they will find their own individual forms of mourning and fellowship with the dead. In the hospice movement a new culture of dying is growing up, and in the self-help groups of mourners new forms of life are also developing, in fellowship with the dead through the mutual comforting of those involved. In his Beatitude Jesus said, "Blessed are they who mourn, for they shall be comforted" (Matt. 5:4); so mourners belong to Jesus' people, and the community of Jesus also belongs to the mourners. They will intervene personally for the right to mourn and for the strength to endure grief, and will fight against the public "culture of narcissism," with its public suppressions of the awareness of death, and of grief and mourning, for these suppressions make modern life sterile and incapable of love.

If in their worship Christians celebrate the presence of Christ who "is the Lord both of the dead and of the living" (Rom. 14:9), then they are worshipping in communion with the dead, too. When in the worship of the Latin American base communities the names of "the disappeared" and the martyrs are read out, the congregation responds with the cry, "*Presente.*" They are present, and we sense our fellowship with them and their fellowship with us.

The forms given to grief, and lives shaped for a new community between the living and the dead, have a further meaning still, in the conscious formulation of the generation contract. Earlier, this seemed a matter of course. It was part of the sequence of generations in families. Today it must be deliberately formulated, because it is continually broken by present generations. Because of the huge load of public debt, the present-day generation is living at the expense of generations in the future. This is easy enough, because those who have not yet been born have no lobby in the present. But the compensatory and equalizing agreements between present and future generations are only one side of the generation contract, which spans the times. The other side is the community of those who come afterwards with their forebears. Anyone who forgets the rights of the dead will be indifferent toward the lives of those to come as well. Without a "culture of remembrance" that tries to do justice to the dead, there will also be no "culture of hope" that will open up a future for our children.

Chapter 17

ENTER INTO JOY!
Sin, Death, and the Life of the World to Come

MIROSLAV VOLF

Introduction

In the short essay "Speculative Beginning of Human History," undertaken, as he puts it, "for the sake of mind's relaxation and health," Immanuel Kant told the story of the emergence of human freedom. Having noted a raging conflict within a human being "as [a member of both a] moral species and a natural species," he argued that from this conflict "arises all true evil that oppresses human life and all vice that dishonors it." His diagnosis of the human predicament suggested the character of the cure. The plague of evil and the stain of dishonor, which are, as the Fall itself, necessary for culture to develop, will be removed only when culture "so perfects itself as to become a second nature."[1] Or so Kant argued, projecting the solution to the problem, in a typically modern way, onto a future fashioned by the history of human progress.

We need not explore here the ways in which the conflict between a human being as a member of moral and natural species, as Kant portrays it, might be inadequately set. The apparent dualism, for instance, between "instincts" and "reason," between "the guardianship of nature" and "state of freedom,"[2] on which both the diagnosis and the cure are predicated in this text is, arguably, mistaken.[3] Adjusted appropriately, however, a certain fundamental duality in human beings remains. We are both animal beings and, broadly conceived, moral beings — cultural producers, we might more accurately say, so as not to lose sight of the morally neutral aspects of free human activity. This duality, which is incompatible only with purely physicalist accounts of human nature, signals the emergence of humanity out of mere animality.

If this duality is characteristic of human beings, the crucial question is whether, as Kant thought, the relation between the realms of physicality and cultural pro-

---

1. Immanuel Kant, "Speculative Beginning of Human History," in Kant, *Perpetual Peace and Other Essays on Politics, History, and Morals*, trans. Ted Humpherey (Indianapolis: Hackett Publishing, 1983), 49–59, 54.

2. Ibid., 53.

3. Kant himself seeks to mediate between the spheres in *The Critique of Judgment*. See John H. Zammito, *The Genesis of Kant's Critique of Judgment* (Chicago: University of Chicago Press, 1992), 342–46.

ductivity lies at the heart of the fundamental problem of human existence. If so, then possible resolutions of the tension between these two realms — for example, "second nature" as a result of cultural development (Kant) or retreat from culture and return to "nature" (Rousseau) — are possible ways of pursuing the solution for the fundamental problem of human existence. Alternatively, one could locate the problem less in the conflict between the two realms, and more in the specific character of each of the realms. If so, then whatever needs to happen *between* the two realms, the solution for the human predicament will not be found until one attends to the specific problems *in* each of the realms.

To a large extent, the basic problem of eschatology concerns precisely the ques-tion of the relation of the physical and cultural dimensions of human beings. This is to be expected since, theologically, the human predicament revolves around the phenomena of mortality, which is so intimately related to the character of human physicality, and of sin, which has largely to do with cultural productiv-ity. If it is true that Christian eschatology restates the doctrines of creation and salvation in the mode of consummation, then a key anthropological and hamar-tiological problem is bound to emerge as a key eschatological problem. A cursory look at standard Christian eschatologies confirms this inference. Arguably, two central eschatological themes — the resurrection of the dead and the last judg-ment — address precisely the physical makeup and cultural matrix of human life. The centrality of these two eschatological themes suggests that, for the Christian tradition, ultimate human fulfillment is thinkable only if we attend to the spheres of physicality and cultural productivity.

But what does it take to attend to the two spheres adequately? The same questions raised earlier in relation to Kant's diagnosis and proposed solution must be raised in relation to Christian eschatology. Will attending to either physicality or cultural productivity take care of the other? If not, what is the nature of the relation between the two spheres with respect to the transformations that need to happen in each? In this chapter I will explore the themes of the resurrection of the dead and the last judgment as two complementary aspects of what I call "the eschatological transition."[4] I am interested in the character and interrelation of these two "gateways" from the present world of sin and death to the coming world of everlasting life and love.

In the essay to which I referred, Kant's topic was the emergence of humanity from animality (which for him, as for many thinkers in the idealist tradition who followed him, coincided with the Fall).[5] He narrated speculatively "the transition

---

4. In *Loci theologici*, Johann Gerhard, one of the most important post-Reformation Lutheran schol-ars who offers an extensive treatment of the doctrine *De novissimis*, distinguishes six last things, two that destroy the old (death and the destruction of the world), two that bring about the new (resur-rection and the last judgment), and two that explicate the new (heaven and hell). The category of the "eschatological transition" in the present text occupies systematically the same place as Gerhard's middle two last things that bring about the new.

5. For a brief account of the interpretation of the Fall in German idealism, see Odo Marquard, "Felix Culpa? Bemerkungen zu Einem Applikationsschicksal von Genesis 3," *Text und Applikation: Theologie, Jurisprudenz und Literaturwissenschaft im Hermeneutischen Gespraech*, ed. M. Furhmann, H. R. Jauss, and W. Pannenberg (Munich: Wilhelm Fink Verlag, 1981), 53–71; Christoph Gestrich, *The*

from the raw state of a merely animal creature to humanity, from the harness of the instincts to the guidance of reason — in a word, from the guardianship of nature to the state of freedom."[6] My topic is, in a sense, the obverse of his — not the primal fall, but the final transformation. I will explore the transition from this present world in which human beings are caught in the net woven of the consequences of their *physicality*'s transience and of their cultural productivity's *sinfulness* to a state of freedom in God's new world of life and love. But instead of offering a philosophical proposal, as the great Kant did, I will, more modestly, try to clear the ground and draw the contours of a foundation for a theological edifice.

Given that a person reflecting on the eschatological transition must keep casting side glances on both what the transition is *from* and what the transition is *to*, the breadth of my topic is enormous. But my purpose is limited. I will try to specify how the eschatological transition *must be thought of* if the eschatological consummation is to be properly explicated so as to fit core Christian persuasions and yield a compelling vision of human ultimate purpose and true happiness. Others in this volume[7] will address the question whether the claims one *must* make in order to think adequately theologically about the eschatological transition *can* in fact be *plausibly* made, given what humanities and natural sciences tell us about the nature and destiny of human beings.[8] If the plausibility of the notion of the

---

Return of the Splendor in the World: The Christian Doctrine of Sin and Forgiveness, trans. D. W. Bloesch (Grand Rapids, Mich.: Eerdmans, 1997), 92–128. On the influence of Kant's interpretation of the Fall see Christine Axt-Piscalar, *Ohnmächtige Freiheit: Studien zum Verhältnis von Subjektivität und Sünde bei August Tholuck, Julius Müller, Søren Kierkegaard und Friedrich Schleiermacher* (Tübingen: J. C. B. Mohr, 1996), 158.

6. Kant, "Speculative Beginning," 53.

7. See John Polkinghorne, "Eschatology: Some Questions and Some Insights from Science," chap. 2 in this volume.

8. The problem of plausibility is a major one, and in the West increasingly so, not only for the cultural elite but also for the wider population. According to statistics from 1992, in most parts of Europe well below 50% of the population embraces a belief in life after death (Denmark 26%, Germany and France 38%, Spain 42%, for instance) (see S. Ashford and N. Timms, *What Europe Thinks: A Study of Western European Values* [Aldershot: Dartmouth, 1992], 40). For the United States, the numbers are significantly higher, 71% according to statistics from 1980–81 (see George Gallup, *Religion in America, 1935–1985* [Princeton, N.J.: Gallup Report no. 326]). In the contemporary intellectual climate, one therefore needs to show not simply that a given account of the eschatological transition makes sense, but that the *idea of such transition itself* is plausible, even to argue that the exploration of its plausibility is not a futile and misguided effort. Any notion of the eschatological transition assumes that the world is open to the "beyond" and "after," however understood. Today, both the possibility and the desirability of an afterlife have been called into question. For scientifically trained people today, "beyonds" and "afters" belong to the imaginative worlds of fairy tales; the sciences seem inhospitable to these notions. As William R. Stoeger points out in this volume, "from all the indications we have from the neurosciences, biology, physics, astronomy, and cosmology, death and dissolution are the final words" (see "Scientific Accounts of Ultimate Catastrophes in Our Life-Bearing Universe," in this volume). Moreover, important intellectual currents during the past two centuries have not only denied the possibility of "beyonds" and "afters," but insisted that these notions are anything but innocent. For Karl Marx, Christian expectation of the eschatological fulfillment of history distracts from our work on its historical fulfillment (see Karl Marx, "Toward the Critique of Hegel's Philosophy of Law: Introduction," *Writings of the Young Marx on Philosophy and Society*, trans. Loyd P. Easton and Curt H. Guddat [New York: Anchor Books, 1967], 249–51). For Friedrich Nietzsche both the expectation of the eschatological fulfillment and efforts toward historical fulfillment are forms of nihilism toward life in its ambiguities (see Friedrich Nietzsche, *The Antichrist*, trans. H. L. Mancken [New York: Knopf, 1920]). For Nietzsche's poststructuralist heirs like Gilles Deleuze, any talk of eschatological or

eschatological transition is in doubt, does it follow that the exercise in which I am about to engage is, in Kant's words from "The End of All Things," a futile "doting on the beyond," unfitting "for an intellectual inhabitant of a sensible world"?[9]

I don't think so. One should keep in mind that reflection on the "beyond" is always already reflection on the "sensible" world and its inhabitants, and reflection on the great transition from the present world to the world to come is always already reflection on many small transitions within the present world. Groping and unsure of itself, as thought inescapably becomes when it stands tiptoe to reach toward the eschatological heights, it nevertheless seeks to grasp something that is as essential to flesh and blood human beings as their daily bread — the character of their ultimate purpose and true happiness. If this is the case, then reflection on the eschatological transition, provided it is plausible on its own terms, may serve at least as an invitation to natural sciences and humanities to inquire whether their accounts of human and cosmic destinies are complete.

How should the spheres of physicality and cultural productivity be related in the eschatological transition? I will answer this question by trying to overcome deficiencies of the three most significant recent proposals that thematize the eschatological transition. I will engage Eberhard Jüngel, for whom "the last judgment" as the final justification of sinners is the central eschatological event, Wolfhart Pannenberg, for whom "the resurrection of the dead" as the integration of individuals and humanity into God's eternal present takes on that role,[10] and Jürgen Moltmann, for whom the last judgment and the resurrection of the dead are two sides of the eschatological transition, one turned toward history and the other toward eternity. I will use their thought to revisit from different angles a set of partly overlapping issues and "spiral" myself toward my own position.

The Final Justification

The Last Judgment as the Final Justification

Eberhard Jüngel's proposal about the eschatological transition finds its most sustained though not final expression in his *Death: The Riddle and the Mystery*.[11] There he builds on a widely accepted distinction between death as a natural

---

historical fulfillment conjures up images of totality and closure, homogenization and dualization, all of which are deemed inimical to the flourishing of the concrete and the particular (Gilles Deleuze with Fanny Deleuze, "Nietzsche and Saint Paul, Lawrence and John of Patmos," in Gilles Deleuze, *Essays Critical and Clinical*, trans. D. W. Smith and M. A. Greco [Minneapolis: University of Minnesota Press, 1997], 36–52; cf. Catherine Keller, *Apocalypse Now and Then: A Feminist Guide to the End of the World* [Boston: Beacon Press, 1996], 15–16).

9. Immanuel Kant, "The End of All Things," in Immanuel Kant, *On History*, trans. L. W. Beck, R. E. Anchor, and E. E. Fackenheim (New York: Bobbs-Merrill, 1963), 69–84, 74.

10. Of course, Jüngel does not disregard fully the resurrection of the dead, nor does Pannenberg exclude the last judgment, yet each privileges the one over the other.

11. Eberhard Jüngel, *Death: The Riddle and the Mystery*, trans. Iain and Ute Nicol (Philadelphia: Westminster Press, 1974).

phenomenon and death as a curse.[12] Following Karl Barth,[13] Jüngel construes the distinction to imply more than that, as a natural phenomenon, death is a necessary implication of human finitude. Death also places a "salutary limit to life."[14] Hence it is not death that poses a problem for life; rather, it is life, as we live it, that "makes a radical problem of death." More precisely and somewhat poetically, "the shadow cast by death (over human life) is no more than the haunting primordial shadow, now extended and magnified, which our life casts upon our ending."[15]

A life lived in a breach of the relationship with God makes death into a curse, argues Jüngel. In biblical terms, human sin gives death its sting (1 Cor. 15:56).

Once Jüngel has made the distinction between the curse of death and natural death, and defined the problem of death not as the problem imposed on us by our physicality but created by us as sinful cultural producers, he has cleared the path toward a particular eschatological solution. He can safely put aside the belief in the resurrection of the dead understood as a form of belief in life after death, and place the full weight on the theme of the last judgment, the "resurrection" serving merely as its formal condition. What is raised at "the end" is not a human being who is a psychosomatic unity convincingly in communion with God "for ever."[16] As Barth, on whom Jüngel heavily leans, puts it, one day we "will only have been."[17]

Instead, what is raised is a human being's *lived life* as an object of God's eternal perception. We will be raised in that our *past* will be "in God who himself is life." Our "person" will then be nothing but "our *manifest history*."[18]

It is ultimately not human beings who settle *how* they shall have been, but God. As we shall be known in God's judgment, "this is how we shall have been."[19] In and of itself, such divine knowledge would not be hopeful were it not for the fact that it will liberate lived lives from sin and open them up to their yet-unrealized possibilities.[20] For this divine knowledge at the end is identical with

---

12. Friedrich Schleiermacher introduced into theology the distinction between death as a natural phenomenon and death as a curse (*The Christian Faith*, trans. H. R. Mackintosh and J. S. Stewart [Philadelphia: Fortress Press, 1978], 75).

13. Karl Barth, *CD*, III/2, 553–72.

14. Jüngel, *Death*, 91. See Barth, *CD*, III/2, 629ff., esp. 625.

15. Jüngel, *Death*, 75, 74.

16. For Jüngel, the resurrection of Christ in no way reverses the withdrawal of Christ that happens in his death; it rather confirms it. It looks backward rather than forward (see Eberhard Jüngel, "The Effectiveness of Christ Withdrawn: On the Process of Historical Understanding as an Introduction to Christology," in his *Theological Essays*, trans. with an introduction by J. B. Webster [Edinburgh: T. & T. Clark, 1989], 214–31, 231; cf. John Webster, "Jesus in the Theology of Eberhard Jüngel," *Calvin Theological Journal* 32 [1997]: 43–71, 63–65). Put differently, Jüngel lacks a robust doctrine of Christ's ascension and therefore misconstrues the doctrine of Christ's resurrection (on ascension see Douglas B. Farrow, *Ascension and Ecclesia: On the Significance of the Doctrine of Ascension for Ecclesiology and Christian Cosmology* [Edinburgh: T. & T. Clark, 1999]). On the absence of human post-mortem conscious relation with God in Jüngel's thought, see also Ivor J. Davidson, "Crux probat omnia: Eberhard Jüngel and the Theology of the Crucified One," *Scottish Journal of Theology* 50 (1997): 157–90, 187–89.

17. Barth, *CD*, III/2, 632–33.

18. Jüngel, *Death*, 120, 121.

19. Ibid., 121.

20. See Eberhard Jüngel, *God as the Mystery of the World: On the Foundation of the Theology of*

the justification of the godless. The last judgment is the final justification.[21] Since justification and its completion in the final judgment will take care of life wrongly lived, they remove the sting of death.

Jüngel has located the eschatological transition primarily into the sphere of cultural productivity (though he himself would argue that justification and the last judgment ontologically define human beings!).[22] No transformation happens in the sphere of physicality; physicality is simply left behind. The move is predicated on the belief that a wrongly lived life casts a dark shadow on death, but not the other way around. I will argue later that matters are more complex; death (and the nature of physicality that leads to death) casts a shadow on life just as a wrongly lived life casts a shadow on death. Consequently, death itself needs to be overcome, not just its sting removed; human ultimate fulfillment requires a temporally and spatially lived everlasting life. Anthropologically, this line of thought presupposes that finitude does not imply mortality,[23] and that the desire for an everlasting life need not be egotistical.[24] Here I want to make two points about Jüngel's account of the eschatological transition in the sphere of cultural productivity. First, I will argue that his account, though basically accurate as far as it goes, is incomplete; second, I will try to show that, as it stands, and even more when necessary adjustments are made, his account presupposes a robust notion of life after death and therefore requires that attention be paid to the eschatological transition in the sphere of physicality.[25]

Final Justification, Final Reconciliation

I can leave aside here the important question about whether one should understand the last judgment as the completion of justification or of sanctification.[26] Whichever path we take, Jüngel is certainly right not only in grounding the es-

---

the *Crucified One in the Dispute between Theism and Atheism*, trans. Darrell E. Guder (Grand Rapids, Mich.: Eerdmans, 1983), 215 n. 58.

21. In "The Last Judgment as an Act of Grace" Jüngel explicitly describes this redemption of the past as "the *completion* of the *iustificatio impii*"; correspondingly, the resurrection of the dead is "their *glorification unto judgment*" (*LS* 15 [1990]: 389–405, 401). Conceptually, a distinction has to be made between raising of the past and its redemption; the one would correspond to what traditionally was thought of under category of the resurrection of the dead, and the other to the last judgment. But since for Jüngel this raising of the past takes place as raising of the redeemed past, it is appropriate to describe his position, at least as expounded in *Death*, as "eschatological transition as the final justification."

22. John Webster, *Eberhard Jüngel: An Introduction to His Theology* (Cambridge: Cambridge University Press, 1986), 91, 102.

23. See Wolfhart Pannenberg, *Systematic Theology*, trans. Geoffrey W. Bromiley (Grand Rapids, Mich.: Eerdmans, 1998), 3:560.

24. If one argues that the belief in life after death is as such egotistical (Jüngel, *Death*, 120, echoing, it would seem, Ludwig Feuerbach, *The Essence of Christianity*, trans. George Eliot [New York: Harper and Brothers, 1957], 170–84), one might as well argue that a person's desire to live past the present moment, which is to say a person's desire to live at all, is egotistical, too.

25. I am assuming in this text that human beings are irradicably physical beings and that any meaningful talk about life after death must include a transformation of physicality.

26. In a formal response to this paper, Gregor Etzelmüller, building on Schleiermacher's reflections and on a reinterpretation of Karl Barth, rightly suggested that it may be better to conceive of the last judgment as the completion of sanctification rather than of justification.

chatological transition in "the proposition that he who judges is he who has been judged in our place,"[27] but also in making the *past* its object. But, for Jüngel, dealing with the past — the lived life — is the *sole* content of the eschatological transition. In a sense, the thrust of this chapter is an extended argument that exclusive concentration on the past is a mistake. But it is a mistake of excess, not that of missing the mark. "To redeem the past... that alone do I call redemption," remarked Nietzsche rightly in *Thus Spoke Zarathustra*.[28]

No ultimate fulfillment is possible if the past remains unredeemed; an unredeemed past will keep every present (and future) unredeemed. The eschatological transition cannot therefore be only about being given a fresh beginning, but must also be about having all of one's failed beginnings, middles, and ends redeemed.

The question, however, is whether the last judgment conceived of as justification is adequate to deal with the problem of the past.[29]

Soteriologically, justification concerns the individual person. To propose justification as sufficient to accomplish the eschatological transition is to assume that sin is *only* an individual matter and that dealing with sin adequately does not require an interhuman process. But *is this* not to misconstrue the nature of both sin and salvation? Precisely as sin against God, sin is committed in a multidirectional and multilayered interaction *between* people, an interaction with both diachronic and synchronic dimensions. It manifests itself, for instance, as "the monstrous injustice of generational succession,"[30] in which later generations "exploit" the sufferings of earlier ones as well as suffer the consequences of their misdeeds. Sin also takes *the* form of conflict between persons and communities in which violence, injustice, and deception are the order of the day and in which the weak suffer at the hand of the strong and today's victims often become tomorrow's perpetrators.

If sin has an inalienable social dimension and if redemption aims at the establishment of the order of peace, as Jüngel rightly claims,[31] then the divine embrace of both the victim and the perpetrator (justification) must be understood as leading to their mutual embrace. Persons cannot be healed without the healing of their specific socially constructed and temporarily structured identities. Because past interactions of persons — whether direct or mediated via social institutions — shape their identities, their common past cannot be healed if one circumvents the participation of these persons in the healing. Dealing adequately with sins suffered and committed can only be a *social process*. If those reconciled with God are not to remain unreconciled among themselves on account of their unreconciled pasts, and if history is therefore not to remain unredeemed, the final justification

---

27. Jüngel, "Last Judgment as an Act of Grace," 395.

28. Friedrich Nietzsche, *Thus Spoke Zarathustra: A Book for Everyone and No One*, trans. R. J. Hollingdale (London: Penguin, 1969), 161.

29. On the following see Miroslav Volf, "The Final Reconciliation: Reflections on a Social Dimension of the Eschatological Transition," *Modern Theology* 16 (2000): forthcoming.

30. Oliver O'Donovan, *The Desire of Nations: Rediscovering the Roots of Political Philosophy* (Cambridge: Cambridge University Press, 1996), 287–88.

31. Jüngel, "Last Judgment as an Act of Grace," 397. Cf. also Jüngel, *Death*, 122.

will have to be accompanied by the final social reconciliation — not, of course, as an independent human activity, but as the interhuman dimension of the activity of the God who, as Luther puts it, "does not work in us without us."[32]

Justification, Reconciliation, Human Agency

Even more basic than whether Jüngel's account of the cultural dimension of the eschatological transition is complete is the question whether he can plausibly explicate the last judgment as the final justification, given his understanding of the resurrection of the dead. In soteriology, the "objects" of justification are always persons, never their done deeds or lived lives. In fact, the doctrine is predicated on a clear distinction, though not separation, between person and work. For if the *work* — the lived life — were justified, Christ would be indeed "a servant of sin" (Gal. 2:17), though in a different sense than intended by the Apostle. In the New Testament, works are an object of negative or positive *judgment* (1 Cor. 3:12–15); they are never objects of *justification*. Jüngel maintains, however, that on the Day of Judgment God will justify *lived lives*, not alive persons. Persons will not be declared just and transformed; their lived lives will have been just because they will have been known by God to have been just.

If the analogy with more traditional soteriology holds, this will not do. The only appropriate object of the final justification is not the lived life, but the human person as a subject of that lived life and recipient of God's grace. The doctrine of justification presupposes *continued life and agency* of human beings precisely in the passivity of their being justified. So does the last judgment, understood as justification. Jüngel would probably respond that the person is anthropologically constituted by the act of justification. "We *are* now as God knows us to be."[33] That brings, however, creation and justification in such proximity that it becomes unclear "who" it is that is engaged in sin and therefore "who" it is that needs to be redeemed. Sin is then an actual impossibility and justification becomes unregarded with *creatio ex nihilo*.[34] But that is implausible. A coherent doctrine of justification presupposes *continuity* of persons in creation and redemption, as well as their creaturely *agency*; the passivity of the justified sinner must be the active passivity of a creature.[35]

Jüngel's formulations in "The Last Judgment as an Act of Grace," published some twenty years after *Death*, seem to concede the point about the need of agency. The persons judged will be able "to recognize sin as a power condemned

---

32. Martin Luther, *Luther's Works*, gen. ed. Helmut T. Lehmann (Philadelphia: Fortress Press, 1972), 33, 243. Elsewhere I have suggested that the act of what I have called "eschatological non-remembrance" is in fact an act of God's grace in us: "Enveloped in God's glory we will redeem ourselves and our enemies by one final act of the most difficult grace made easy by the experience of salvation that cannot be undone — the grace of nonremembering" (Miroslav Volf, *Exclusion and Embrace: A Theological Explication of Identity, Otherness, and Reconciliation* [Nashville: Abingdon Press, 1996], 138).

33. Jüngel, *Death*, 121 (italics added).

34. Ronald Spjuth, *Creation, Contingency, and Divine Presence in Theologies of Thomas F. Torrance and Eberhard Jüngel* (Lund: Lund University Press, 1995), 63–67.

35. For a critique of Jüngel along these lines see David Kelsey, "Two Theologies of Death: Anthropological Gleanings," *Modern Theology* 13 (1997): 347–70, 361–62.

to perdition," "affirm" their justification, and "distance" themselves from their sin forever, or even make the impossible choice of self-destruction, indeed "manifestly delight" in it. Similarly, since God can "redeem those already redeemed . . . from willing their own ruin," the last judgment can be described as "the therapeutic event."[36]

The change from the use of exclusively passive verbs to describe the final justification in *Death* to the presence of active verbs in "The Last Judgment" would at a substantive level require a change in understanding of the resurrection of the dead. For there to be recipients of the final justification, they have to be raised to a life after death. This may have been implied in the cryptic remark in *God as the Mystery of the World* that in eternal life "my person as the subject of my life" is not set aside.[37]

If the last judgment understood as justification requires the continued life of a person as "a subject of one's life," final human reconciliation does all the more, since it is thinkable only as a social process. However we conceive of the relation between divine and human action in the final justification and the final social reconciliation, human participation is an essential precondition of the eschatological transition. To have participation, however, one must conceive of life after death in such a way as to allow a person to do and become something, rather than "only be what he was."[38]

The last judgment conceived of as the final justification presupposes persons as active recipients of divine grace; the final social reconciliation conceived of as the redemption of the past presupposes persons as channels of that same grace toward others. Both presuppose the resurrection of the dead as the inception of a "new" life of the very persons who lived the "old."

We leave our critical engagement with Jüngel's work with two conclusions about the eschatological transition, one related to the sphere of cultural productivity and the other to the sphere of physicality. First, though it is accurate to understand the last judgment as fundamentally rooted in God's grace, it is not sufficient to think of the eschatological transition in the sphere of cultural productivity as the final justification (or the final sanctification). We must stress more robustly its social side by developing something like "the final social reconciliation." Second, to deal adequately with the problem of death, one cannot remain exclusively within the sphere of cultural productivity. We must move into the sphere of physicality — not only to be able to address the problem of death as a problem in its own right (as I will argue later), but also to be able to address the problem of sin. Without an afterlife, neither final justification nor the final social reconciliation is possible.

---

36. Jüngel, "Last Judgment as an Act of Grace," 403, 404, 401.

37. Jüngel, *God as the Mystery of the World*, 215 n. 58. In the same text Jüngel claims that all possibilities, the missed ones and the concealed ones, will be revealed to the individual as "the *subject* of his lived life" (215 n. 58, translation mine). Since it appears in the context of the argument in favor of the positive valuation of perishability and since it is introduced as a clarification and not as a correction of his former views, it may not be right to treat this formulation as representing a retreat from his position in *Death* about post-mortem life.

38. Jüngel, *Death*, 115.

But how should we think of the "resurrection of the body" so as to respond adequately to the problems of mortality and sin? Wolfhart Pannenberg has offered an important proposal in this regard.

Taking Up of Time into Eternity

Manifestation of Totality in Eternity

Unlike Jüngel, Wolfhart Pannenberg clearly distinguishes between finitude and mortality. Death is not an implication of human finitude; rather "sinners' nonacceptance of their finitude . . . delivers them up to death."[39]

It is crucial to understand properly this "nonacceptance." In contrast to the mainstream of the Protestant tradition, Pannenberg takes the most fundamental dimension of sin out of what I have called the sphere of cultural productivity and weaves it into "the *natural conditions* of our existence."[40] At the most basic level human sin has to do with the interrelation between finitude and temporality. Not that Pannenberg valorizes temporality only negatively. The "independence for which God has destined his creatures, and especially among them his human creatures, needs time as the form of their existence."[41] Yet in the inescapable brokenness of our experience of time "temporality is of a piece with the structural sinfulness of our life" (3:561).

We are sinners because we experience the reality of the world always from the perspective of a given "now" (and "here") and in relation to the center of our ego, rather than living as "the self, the finite totality of our existence" (3:563).

The separateness of the moments and the structure of our ego combine to qualify human life always as self-centered. "In the self-relation in which it (ego) experiences itself each moment as the center of the world, it is always defined as *amor sui*" (3:562).

As Pannenberg presents it, the precise nature of the relation between "the separateness of the moments of time in the process of our experience of time" and "the structure of our ego that is the site of our experience of time" remains somewhat unclear (3:562). Are the two parallel, or does the one condition the other? Though he sometimes makes it sound as if the structure of the ego conditions a particular experience of time, it would seem that the human inability to manifest "at each moment of the ego the self, the totality of our life" (3:563) is more fundamentally tied to the fact that the ego is part of a temporally structured creation. Such a strong link between sin and temporality is the hamartiological obverse of Pannenberg's account of the construction of meaning. The meaning

---

39. Pannenberg, *Systematic Theology*, 3:561.

40. Wolfhart Pannenberg, *Anthropology in Theological Perspective*, trans. Matthew J. O'Connell (Edinburgh: T. & T. Clark, 1985), 107. See Svein Rise, *The Christology of Wolfhart Pannenberg: Identity and Relevance*, trans. Brian MacNeil (Lewiston, N.Y.: Mellen, 1997), 228ff.; Hannas-Stephan Haas, "*Bekannte Sünde." Eine systematische Untersuchung zum theologischen Reden von der Sünde in der Gegenwart* (Neukirchen-Vluyn: Neukirchener Verlag, 1992), 63–179.

41. Pannenberg, *Systematic Theology*, 3:580 (subsequent references in the text).

of individual events in a person's life depends on the totality of that person's life, and the meaning of that totality itself depends "on the totality of all events and reality that can be the object of experience" (3:590).

Since totality is unthinkable without "the end," the end of a person's life and the end of history are presuppositions of every individually experienced meaning. Hence the claim that eschatological completion is impossible "without an end of time."[42]

Pannenberg's accounts of meaning and of the human predicament have committed him to a particular way of understanding the eschatological transition. To reach the "totality," the succession of separated moments of time will have to be overcome and the end of human lives integrated into their identity. This is precisely what happens with the taking up of time into eternity. Ultimate fulfillment does not require securing the continuity of persons' beings along a line; indeed, such securing would amount to locking them into nonredemption. Instead, their "essence" — "the totality of their manifestation in the form of simultaneity" — must be preserved "in God's eternal present."[43]

"Preserved," of course, in a particular way. For the entry of eternity into time does not simply affirm life, but also *judges* it. Since the moments of human life, when ringing together in the eternal present, would, on account of their contradiction, produce "shrill dissonance" (3:610), human beings must undergo "purging and cleansing" by the "fire of judgment" (3:619). With "all the heterogeneous admixtures, perversions, and woundings of their earthly existence" removed (3:606), human beings will become "selves" made eternally whole.

In Pannenberg's account of the eschatological transition as a single and integral event,[44] the resurrection has primacy. The last judgment is one of its aspects, albeit a central one; the last judgment as the entry of eternity into time makes possible resurrection as the taking up of time into eternity. Rather than thinking of the resurrection in neutral terms as merely a presupposition of the last judgment, he thinks of it as salvation, as participation in God.[45] The last judgment, which serves to turn the disharmony of the raised totality of life into harmony, is a "medium" of the resurrection.[46] The critical question about Pannenberg's notion of the eschatological transition is whether it is adequate to understand "resurrection-cum-judgment" as the taking up of time into eternity.

---

42. Ibid., 3:587. Cf. Thomas Freyer, *Zeit, Kontinuität und Unterbrechung: Studien zu Karl Barth, Wolfhart Pannenberg und Karl Rahner* (Würzburg: Echter, 1993), 263–82.

43. Pannenberg, *Systematic Theology*, 3:606.

44. See Pannenberg, "Die Aufgabe christilicher Eschatologie," *ZTK* 92 (1995): 71–81.

45. Pannenberg, *Systematic Theology*, 3:566ff.

46. Presumably a third element — in addition to the last judgment and the resurrection — would have to be introduced if the last judgment is to be an aspect of the resurrection. It is the initial element of "making all the moments of life ring out in the eternal present" which allows judgment as "purging" (or judgment as "destruction") to take place (Pannenberg, *Systematic Theology*, 3:620). This unthematized element plays structurally a similar role in Pannenberg's proposal, as did the neutral form of the idea of the resurrection in the tradition which he rejects.

Personality, Temporality, Sin

At the most basic level we have to inquire whether the notion of preservation of the totality of a human being's manifestation in God's eternal present is intelligible. Even if one takes into account the purging that occurs through judgment, it is not clear how it would be meaningful for such a totality to be preserved. Consider the extraordinary density of what actually constitutes our moment-to-moment life, with all the multiplicity of thematized and unthematized experiences and impressions, including the presence of remembered pasts and expected futures. If place will be left in God's eternal present "for what is distinct in time,"[47] as Pannenberg claims, wanting to ensure that eternity be not understood in antithesis to time, then the totality of *such lived moments* in their temporal sequence will have to be preserved. But is this plausible? And could a person raised in this way recognize him- or herself? It would seem that raising of something *less* than the totality would be required. But if so, what would happen to the question of meaning, which in Pannenberg's account requires totality?

But even if Pannenberg's account of the resurrection were plausible, would it be desirable? As Kant has argued in "The End of All Things," if one postulates "life" while asserting that time has ceased, "such a life, if, indeed, it may be called life, must seem equivalent to annihilation."[48]

Pannenberg is, of course, aware of the difficulty. He argues, however, that "the problem of linking the thought of an end of time with that of life, including eternal life, disappears...when we consider that *God and not nothing is the end of time.*"[49] But does it disappear? In God or not, a life of human persons must be lived *by them.*[50] Any imaginable form of life lived by a human being entails time and change. Even contemplation does, as Kant rightly noted. For contemplation presupposes reflection, and reflection "can only occur in time." Without time and change, "the final thought, the last feeling will remain stationary in the thinking subject," and nature together with the person "will grow rigid and petrified."[51] If Kant is anthropologically right, Pannenberg is eschatologically wrong. His understanding of the divine new creation is flawed because it has the feel of the Rodinean account of artistic creation, in which the object of art must be "withdrawn from all chance,... lifted out of time and handed over to space" to "become lasting, capable of eternity."[52]

---

47. Pannenberg, *Systematic Theology*, 3:595.

48. Kant, "The End of All Things," 78.

49. Pannenberg, *Systematic Theology*, 3:593–94.

50. The questions of God's temporality and the temporality of human beings in consummation are related but distinct. The view that God is totally outside of time does not commit one to the view that human beings in consummation will be outside of time. After all, if the eternal God has created a temporally structured universe and relates to it, why could that same God not continue to relate to a temporally structured universe in the state of the eschatological consummation? (see Brian Hebblethwaite, *Heythrop Journal* 20 [1979]: 58–62, 61). The argument for eternal life as totally outside of time cannot therefore be an argument from God's eternity, but must be an argument from the character of human beings and the demands of their ultimate salvation.

51. Kant, "The End of All Things," 78.

52. Rainer Maria Rilke in a letter to Lou Andreas-Salome (August 8, 1903), *Letters of Rainer Maria Rilke, 1892–1910*, trans. J. B. Greene and M. D. H. Norton (New York: Norton, 1969), 119. Pannenberg

Pannenberg's citizens of the world to come seem statue-like eternal repositories of their lived lives because he has linked intimately the problem of sin with the problem of temporality. For a human being, to be in time is to be a sinner. The price of this position is too high, however. If my argument above is correct, the consequence is the transmutation of death from the wages of sin into a consequence of the *liberation* from sin. For as long as there is sin, at least there is life because there is time; as soon as sin is overcome, life must have ended — at least the only kind of life that is imaginable as the *life of a human being*.[53] One will either have to give up the idea of ultimate fulfillment or conceive of the human predicament in such a way that it may be exacerbated by (a particular experience of) temporality but that it is not inextricably bound with temporality.

Community and Contentment

More than just a restatement of the doctrine of bodily resurrection, the taking up of time into eternity secures for Pannenberg two important aspects of the eschatological transition in the sphere of cultural productivity. The first has to do with the relation between individual and communal dimensions of salvation. Though aware that they have to be thought together, tradition has never found it easy to think them in fact together. Offering his own solution to the problem, Pannenberg writes, "God is the future of the finite from which it again receives its existence as a whole as that which has been, and at the same time accepts all other creaturely being along with itself." Since in the eternal God all is simultaneous, this "acceptance" of all other creaturely beings will include all human beings across time and space. Thus, Pannenberg claims, "an unrestricted actualizing of the unity of our destiny as individuals with that of humanity as a species" will be achieved.[54]

From my perspective, Pannenberg's notion of "acceptance of all other creaturely beings" is significant. Structurally it plays a role similar to interhuman reconciliation in my proposal. Unlike Jüngel, Pannenberg does not thematize only what happens *to* individual human beings in the eschatological transition, but also what happens *between* them. He is both clearly aware that *relationships* need to be restored rather than simply individual human beings purged and rightly implies that this restoration cannot simply *happen to* them. Rather, it must be, in a carefully qualified sense, *done by* them; each must "accept all others."

Yet Pannenberg squanders a good deal of this important insight by connecting the notion of "acceptance" to the idea of the taking up of time into eternity. For come the last judgment, Pannenberg *lacks acting human beings* who could

---

himself rejects the idea that the eternal presence equals spatialization of time (see "Providence, God, and Eschatology," in *The Whirlwind in Culture: Frontiers in Theology. In Honor of Langdon Gilkey*, ed. D. W. Musser and J. L. Price [Bloomington, Ind.: Meyer-Stone Books, 1988], 171–82).

53. Timothy Bradshaw raises rightly the question of the subject of the life in eschaton: "Again the question as to *who* knows God even at the eschaton is an embarrassing one because it seems that the *totality of human historical consciousness* subsumes the individual" (*Trinity and Ontology: A Comparative Study of the Theologies of Karl Barth and Wolfhart Pannenberg* [Edinburgh: Rutherford House Books, 1988], 271).

54. Pannenberg, *Systematic Theology*, 3:607.

do the "accepting," because the taking up of time into eternity has interrupted the continuity of persons' existence on the time line and "closed" them into the totality of their lives. Since the end of life is the end of time, the activity of "acceptance" of all creaturely reality and even that of "self-distinction" from other creatures and from God, which Pannenberg ascribes to the "citizens" of the world to come, can only stand for what *God* has done *to* them and *with* them. For the act of "acceptance," as indeed any other act, presupposes time.

Second, the taking up of time into eternity is meant to secure the experience of both meaning and contentment. Pannenberg's account of meaning, on which much depends not only in his eschatology but also in his project as a whole, is too complex to be addressed adequately within the confines of this text.[55] I will engage here only the related question of contentment. Pannenberg leans heavily on Kant's argument about the end of time in relation to contentment. Though the idea of the end of time "transcends our cognitive capacity," Kant argues that it is "closely akin to reason in a practical respect." The practical reasonableness of the end of time is predicated on the impossibility of contentment without the end of time.

> [Man] cannot (even in the consciousness of the immutability of his disposition [to progress in doing good]) unite contentment with the prospect of his condition (moral as well as physical) enduring in an eternal state of change. For the condition in which man now exists remains ever an evil, in comparison to the better condition into which he stands ready to proceed.[56]

Kant's argument presupposes that, at least for a human being, change always occurs on a linear "progress–regress" axis, and that even under the assumption of a steady progressive movement discontent inevitably results on account of comparison between what was before and after a given stage. Hence the ultimate purpose can only be a state in which movement has come to rest.

It is possible, however, to think progressive movement and contentment together. One only has to postulate, as Gregory of Nyssa did, that "by enjoying what is more worthy" the memory "of inferior things is blotted out" since "at each stage the greater and superior good holds the attention of those who enjoy it and does not allow them to look at the past."[57] If one is unpersuaded, one can argue plausibly that change need not be progressive/regressive, and movement need not be linear. The movement can also be cyclical (as in Nietzsche's notion

---

55. For explication of his position, see Wolfhart Pannenberg, *Theology and Philosophy of Science*, trans. F. McDonagh (Philadelphia: Westminster Press, 1976), 206–24, 326–45. For a critique see Gerhard Sauter, *The Question of Meaning: A Theological and Philosophical Orientation*, trans. Geoffrey Bromiley (Grand Rapids, Mich.: Eerdmans, 1995). For a response see Wolfhart Pannenberg, "Meaning, Religion, and the Question of God," in *Metaphysics and the Idea of God*, trans. Philip Clayton (Grand Rapids, Mich.: Eerdmans, 1988), 153–70. Cf. also David Patric Polk, *On the Way to God: An Exploration into the Theology of Wolfhart Pannenberg* (Ann Arbor, Mich.: University Press of America, 1989), 76–81 (from the perspective of process thought); Harvey W. White, "A Critique of Pannenberg's *Theology and Philosophy of Science*," SR 11 (1982): 419–36 (from the perspective of Wittgenstein's philosophy).
56. Kant, "The End of All Things," 78–79.
57. Gregory of Nyssa, *Song of Songs*, trans. Casimir McCambley (Brookline, Mass.: Hellenistic College Press, 1987), 128 (PG 44, 885D–888A [Commentarius in Canticum canticorum]).

of the "eternal return")[58] or kaleidoscopic (as a child's play may be described). In both of these later cases, change entails neither gain nor loss, and is compatible with contentment.

Within a state of *achieved* ultimate purpose, change is thinkable. Ultimate fulfillment is, therefore, compatible with temporality. Indeed, I want to argue that *ultimate fulfillment is not only compatible with temporality but also unthinkable without it*, partly because any intelligible notions of both reconciliation and contentment in fact *presuppose* change. Whatever the virtues of the notion of the taking up of time into eternity, its inadequacies are major: with the erasure of temporality in the "life" of the world to come, it takes away the possibility of communal peace and personal joy.

Two conclusions from my critical engagement with Pannenberg's thought are important as building blocks for my own constructive proposal. First, he rightly suggests that the problem of death is a fundamental problem in its own right, whose solution requires change in the fundamental conditions of human existence which does not leave the embodied and temporarily structured life of human beings behind; the life as lived must be made whole. Second, against Pannenberg I have argued that the problem of death cannot be adequately addressed via the notion of taking up of time into eternity. This proposal in fact reinforces the problem of death rather than solving it because a life without time and change is unthinkable as a genuinely human life.

But how should we think of this post-mortem life and change? How should we think of the eschatological transition so as to be a transition *to* such a life and change? Critical discussion of Jürgen Moltmann's thought will help us with a way to proceed.

Transformation and Eternalization

Time, Space, and Their End

Jürgen Moltmann embraces the thought of post-mortem change — to a point. In analogy to his suggestion in *The Coming of God* to see the millennium as the completion of history,[59] in his text for this volume he undertakes to rethink the classical doctrine of purgatory with the purpose of ensuring the completion of individual human beings. The negative backdrop of the proposal is the experiences of damaged and partially lived lives. He writes,

---

58. See Friedrich Nietzsche, *The Gay Science* (with a prelude in rhymes and an appendix of songs), trans. Walter Kaufmann (New York: Vintage Books, 1974), frag. 285, 341; Nietzsche, *Thus Spoke Zarathustra*, "The Convalescent." Cf. Karl Löwith, *Nietzsche's Philosophy of the Eternal Recurrence of the Same*, trans. J. Harwey Lomax (Berkeley: University of California Press, 1997); Günther Abel, *Die Dynamik des Willens zur Macht und der ewige Wiederkehr* (Berlin: de Gruyter, 1984), 187–374. Nietzsche argues for eternal return by noting that in infinite time a limited number of possibilities must repeat themselves. The argument is unlikely to be correct, but the notion of eternal return itself is not self-contradictory.

59. Jürgen Moltmann, *The Coming of God: Christian Eschatology*, trans. Margaret Kohl (Minneapolis: Fortress Press, 1996), 192–202.

I believe that God's history with our life will continue after our death until that perfection is attained in which we will find rest and the joy of eternal life....I imagine, therefore, the intermediate state as a broad place where there is room for life, in which all that is now broken and disturbed can freely unfold. I imagine an "intermediate time" in which the history of God with an individual can develop and come to completion.[60]

This post-mortem history of God with a person takes place before the last judgment, at which, according to Moltmann, God will condemn and annihilate all sin and evil and liberate "Godforsaken" evil-doers "from their deadly perdition through transformation into their true, created being."[61]

Not giving up entirely post-mortem change is the advantage of Moltmann's proposal over against Jüngel's and Pannenberg's. True, when describing post-mortem human beings in *The Coming of God* Moltmann privileges terms that suggest passivity ("lived life," "Gestalt"). This could suggest that, like Jüngel in *Death*, he offers but a variation on Karl Barth's position, which shies away from ascribing agency to post-mortem human beings. However, the proposal about purgatory, in which he builds on Calvin's idea that those who have passed away are "awake," indeed that their blessedness is "always in progress" before the judgment day,[62] is predicated on such agency. Moltmann is thus not forced to the awkward position of thinking about the final transformation of human beings by God's grace without persons as receptive agents of that transformation. He would also be able to incorporate into his notion of the eschatological transition the indispensable but neglected dimension of interhuman reconciliation.

For Moltmann, however, post-mortem movement and change have a temporal limit. After God's judgment, "which puts things to rights," comes God's kingdom, "which awakens to new life."[63] The character of that "awakening" — the nature of the resurrection and the *transformatio mundi* — determines both the meaning of the "new life" and the adequacy of Moltmann's proposal about the eschatological transition. Consider the following summary:

> If God himself appears *in* his creation, then his eternity appears *in* the time of creation, and his omnipresence *in* creation's space. Consequently temporal creation will be transformed into eternal creation, and spatial creation into omnipresent creation.[64]

"Awakening to new life" is the transformation of temporal and spatial into eternal and omnipresent creation and therefore entails the "end of time" (succession of moments) and the "end of space" (distance), as the titles of the sections in which Moltmann treats these matters state. Why the end of time and space, one may wonder? Because temporal and spatial creation are capable of sin and death. But

60. See Moltmann, "Is There Life after Death?" chap. 16 in this volume.

61. Moltmann, *Coming of God*, 255.

62. John Calvin, "Psychopannychia," in *Tracts and Treatises in Defence of the Reformed Faith*, trans. H. Beveridge (Grand Rapids, Mich.: Eerdmans, 1958), 3:414–90; cf. Heinrich Quistorp, *Calvin's Doctrine of the Last Things*, trans. H. Knight (Richmond, Va.: John Knox Press, 1955), 87–92.

63. Moltmann, *Coming of God*, 255.

64. Ibid., 280.

"redemption can only mean that with sin itself the potentiality for sin has also been surmounted; otherwise redemption would not be final."[65] Since they leave the potentiality for sin open, temporality and spatiality emerge as *deficiencies* whose overcoming demands the end of time and space.

The question of the finality of the eschatological consummation is a crucial one. Any notion of eschatological transition, which could not secure the finality of fulfillment, would be flawed. What the early Marx noted with respect to communism applies even more to the eschatological consummation: "Sein vergangenes Sein wuerde die Praetention seines Wesens widerlegen."[66] But should one affirm the end of time and space in order to secure finality? Moltmann himself is rightly unwilling to give full force to the affirmation. Though the chronological time will end, aeonic time, whose content are the gathered moments of meaningfully lived time, will remain, he argues.

Yet there is a tension in his account of time and space in relation to the life of the world to come. I will limit myself here to my main concern, the problem of time. He describes the time of the world to come, on the one hand, as aeonic *eternity* (as distinct from God's absolute eternity), which entails the simultaneity of past and future and absolute presentness. On the other hand, he describes it as aeonic *time*, in which reversible and symmetrical circular movement takes place.[67] The affirmation of the eternity of creation and creatures and, therefore, the end of time is needed to secure the "finality" of the consummation. The affirmation of (aeonic) time is needed to secure the "eternal livingness" of the citizens of the world to come. Moltmann has not shown how one can affirm both. Simultaneity of past and future of creatures seems incompatible with a reversible circular movement,[68] and even if these were compatible in principle it is not clear how they would be compatible in human experience of time.

I want to argue that the tension evident in Moltmann's account of the consummation is unnecessary. It ought to be resolved by giving up the notion of the end of time and space. Quite apart from the fact that the exegetical base of this

---

65. Ibid., 307.

66. Karl Marx, *MEW* Erg.Bd. I, 536.

67. Moltmann, *Coming of God*, 291, 282, 295.

68. To show that for creatures (which is of whom aeonic time and eternity, as distinct from God's absolute eternity, are predicated) reversible circular movement is compatible with simultaneity of past and future it is not enough to point to the obvious fact that on a circular line what is ahead is also what is behind. For Moltmann the circle is not stationary. If I understand him correctly, aeonic *time* and aeonic *eternity* are predicated of one and the same creatures, which requires that we think the circular movement and simultaneity of the past and future *together*. Moltmann has not shown, however, how the two can be conceptualized together. On the one hand, if the circle is moving, then it would seem that a given point would always reach a given position either after or before another point would. On the other hand, simultaneity of the past and future would require that the order of earlier-later relations not obtain and the circle stand still. To have circular movement and simultaneity of the past and future one would need to show that a point on the moving circle could be at a given position at all times. Alternatively, one could shrink the circle to a point. In either case one would have eternity but not time. Things are even more complicated if the aeonic time is to take up in itself "all (historic) times," which are supposed to "return" as transformed and transfigured. Such taking up seems to require sequencing, either temporal or spatial. If temporal, one will have movement, but not simultaneity; if spatial, one will have simultaneity, but not movement.

notion is nonexistent,[69] there is one excellent reason for doing so. If God's giving time to creation is constitutive for the act of creation, as Moltmann claims, then the end of time would mean the destruction of creation. The same holds true for space.[70] If Moltmann insists on the end of time and space, he will have to contend with the charge that his proposal entails not only "the end of nature," as Catherine Keller objected in *Apocalypse Now and Then*,[71] but the end of creation in *any* meaningful sense. To have "eternal livingness," we must think the eschatological transition in a way that allows for the continued life of human beings and other creatures.

Transformation and Innocence

The "end of time and space" strategy for ensuring the finality of the consummation is flawed quite apart from whether or not it amounts to the destruction of human beings along with the rest of the creation. It seeks a "metaphysical" solution to the problem whose source is best located in the broad domain of collective "cultural productivity" (though not simply in the related but more limited domain of the individual's will).[72] To the extent that human beings are transient bodily beings, the eschatological transition will have to involve a transformation of the very stuff of which they are made, even, as Moltmann puts it, "a transformation in the fundamental conditions of the world itself."[73] For transience, which human beings experience as death, is an enemy at the end of life, whose menacing and violence-inducing presence casts a dark shadow on the entirety of life. Similarly, though the fact that cultural production takes place under limited resources is ultimately not a sufficient explanation of human sin, it nonetheless exacerbates significantly human sinfulness by nudging human beings into conflicts. Ultimate fulfillment of human beings is thinkable only in a realm of "finitude beyond transience" — as a life in which space and time are uncontestedly and prodigiously given to human beings and in which plenitude reigns.

---

69. Moltmann appeals to Rev. 10:6 to support the notion of the end of time and to Rev. 20:11 to support the notion of the end of space. Neither will do. Rev. 10:6 is properly translated as "There will be no more delay" (NRSV) or, as David Aune suggests, "There will be no more interval of time" (*Revelation 6–16* [Dallas: Word, 1998], 567). Moreover, it would be odd for a text that speaks about the "him who lives forever and ever" (v. 6) to announce the end of time, and more significantly, would contradict presuppositions for v. 7. As far as Rev. 20:11 is concerned, if the statement "The earth and the heaven fled from his presence, and no place was found for them" implies the end of space, then the statement "Then I saw a new heaven and a new earth" (21:1) implies "new space" rather than "omnipresence."

70. So rightly Wolfhart Pannenberg, "Anbrechende Zukunft. Jürgen Moltmann's Eschatologie," *EvK* 29 (1996): 76–78, 78.

71. Keller, *Apocalypse Now and Then*, 18.

72. For a more complex understanding of sin that includes but is not reducible to actions of the individual's will, see Michael Welker, "Warum Moral und Medien der Sünde gegenüber hilflos sind. Gedanken im Anschluss an 1Kor 2,1–10," in *Sünde. Ein unverständlich gewordenes Thema*, ed. Sigrid Brandt, Marjorie H. Suchocki, and Michael Welker (Neukirchen-Vluyn: Neukirchener Verlag, 1997), 189–94, 192. If one were to locate sin exclusively in a person's will, one would have an excessively ethicized theology of sin which would be unable to give an adequate account of sin as *power* over a person.

73. Moltmann, *Coming of God*, 272.

The transformation of the fundamental conditions of the world should not be, however, conceived of as destruction of the "potentiality for sin" but as the creation of the *possibility for innocence*. Unless such a transformation is to destroy the possibility for life along with the possibility for sin, one would need more than a transformation of the fundamental conditions of the world to reach the state *non posse peccare*. To the extent that human beings are embodied cultural producers and therefore free agents, the finality of their fulfillment cannot be secured completely by the alteration of the conditions of their existence or of anything located outside their wills (unless, of course, one robs them of life and therefore of the possibility of sinning). If at all, the finality of the consummation will have to be secured in the "space" *internal to human wills*. The eschatological transition must be thought of as divine liberation of the human will, which, as a result, wills only the good.

Though the good does not require the presence of evil to be good, the *consciousness* of the good *as* good always implies knowledge of evil and therefore opens up the possibility of actually doing evil. It would therefore seem that one should conceive of the divine liberation of the will as translation into a state of *new innocence*, a state that is, from the internal perspective of the citizens of the world to come, beyond good and evil. Seen from outside, however, the possibility of doing evil would be at hand, though not subjectively perceivable as a possibility and therefore not available for execution. Though theoretically possible, evil would then be practically impossible. A possibility of committing evil would have been made impossible by the love of God flooding the person's heart. Entry into the state of innocence would thus be the final reconciliation of persons with themselves and their own strivings.

How then can the reconciliation of persons with themselves and with others be achieved? Put in Kant's terminology from the beginning of this chapter, change needs to take place both in the sphere of "nature" (physicality) and "culture" (cultural productivity). To advocate change only in one sphere, as Kant did, is to lock human beings in nonredemption. It takes a new "body" and a new "heart" for human beings not always to stand "at the edge of an abyss" on account of their freedom,[74] but to think and do the good unfailingly in freedom.

Temporality and Deep Eternity

The questions of time and change in the world to come are intimately related to the resolution of the problems of transience and transgression in the establishment of the reign of plenitude and innocence. I submit that the problem of time for human beings is not the experience of the sequence of separate moments of time, not the absence of totality or of total simultaneity of past and future. Instead, it is the experience of the *conflict* of times in the overlap of times at any of our given

---

74. Kant, "Speculative Beginning," 51, describing the uncertainty and anxiety before the infinity of possibilities opened up by transition from the rule of instincts to the sphere of freedom.

presents. Our present is not at peace with our past and future.[75] We feel anxiety about what we expect and carry the burden of what we remember, and are thus robbed of an unattenuated joy in the present.

If this is right, then we should think of the time of the world to come not as the "fullness of time," but as "reconciliation of times." The difference lies precisely in the refusal of closure, which the term "fullness" suggests.[76] For joy to be complete, there is no need for the Boethian "whole, simultaneous and complete possession" of life,[77] as not only Moltmann but also Pannenberg and Jüngel maintain.[78] Indeed, such total simultaneity and total possession would make joy impossible. Joy lives from the *movement in time* qualified by unperturbed peace between past and future in all presents. Since the riddle of time in many ways overlaps with the riddle of life,[79] the joy of such peace between times can follow only on the heels of the reconciliation of *all things* (Col. 1:15–20) — reconciliation between human beings and God, reconciliation among human beings themselves, internal reconciliation within human beings, and reconciliation of human beings and the nonhuman environment.

The ultimate salvation as experience of peace and joy depends both on radical transformations in the spheres of physicality and cultural productivity and on these transformations respecting continuity of creatures' being on the time line. Consequently, the eschatological transition must be conceived of in such a way that in the state of consummation creation remains in a qualified but important sense *creatio mutabilis*. For the joy that "wants eternity"[80] is predicated on change, as I have argued earlier. But how should we understand this change as a precondition of the ultimate fulfillment in the world to come? The formal framework must be the irreversibility of life and the corresponding unidirectionality of time. But what content should we put into this formal framework?

In the moral domain, one should understand change in the world to come simply as *continuation* in the unthematized good. The idea of continuation, especially when grounded anthropologically in what may be described as "satisfied insatiability,"[81] would mean a free movement of all which creates a kaleidoscopic succession of equal because incomparable joys in each. This movement of human

---

75. So rightly Robert W. Jenson, *Unbaptized God: The Basic Flaw in Ecumenical Theology* (Minneapolis: Fortress Press, 1992), 145. Discussions with him have helped me formulate my own notion of the reconciliation of times.

76. "Fullness of time" in the New Testament does not suggest an end and therefore a closure but stands for temporal coming of the opportune circumstances for the divine eschatological act in Christ (Mark 1:15, Gal. 4:4, Eph. 1:10).

77. Boethius, *De Consolatione Philosphiae*, V.6.4 9 (*Aeternitas igitur est interminabilis vitae tota simul et perfecta possessio*). Pannenberg points back to the roots of this concept in Plotinus (*Enneads* 3.7) (cf. *Systematic Theology*, 1:403–6).

78. Eberhard Jüngel, "The Emergence of the New," *Theological Essays II*, ed. John Webster, trans. Arnold Neufeldt-Fast and John Webster (Edinburgh: T. & T. Clark, 1995), 35–58, 54.

79. See Löwith, *Nietzsche's Philosophy*, 163ff. (in the context of the discussion of Otto Weninger's essay "Unidirectionality of Time").

80. Nietzsche, *Thus Spoke Zarathustra*, "The Drunken Song."

81. See Thomas Boehm, *Theoria, Unendlichkeit, Aufstieg. Philosphische Implikationen zu* de Vita Moysis *von Gregor von Nyssa* (Leiden: E. J. Brill, 1996), 256–64.

beings, in which eternal "life" would coalesce with eternal "rest," would participate in the eternal movement of divine love and would therefore be a form of exchange of gifts in which the other does not emerge as a debtor, because she has already given by having joyfully received, and because, even before the gift has reached her, she was already engaged in a movement of advance reciprocation.[82] Though circularity would be present in this exchange, there would be no need to close the *movement of all* into a grand circle, whatever its magnitude. For it would be precisely the *open* play of difference in plenitude, innocence, and love that would make the world to come a joyous "world without end" — a world in which the lived life in communion with God and the whole creation has itself become, in all its dimensions, its own never-ending end.

In the cognitive domain, however, one should understand change in the world to come as *progress* in knowledge of God and creation. On account of the infinity of God, argued Gregory of Nyssa persuasively, the state of perfection is one of unlimited progress — a suggestion that he, mistakenly I believe, understands also as moral ascent. As I have already indicated, Gregory has a way of warding off the kind of argument against progress in the blessed state which Schleiermacher raised and which is analogous to Kant's argument for "the end." "Dissatisfaction with what is present," Schleiermacher argued, "naturally goes along with the expectation of something better yet to come."[83] But in Gregory's more plausible view, the superior perfection erases memory of the inferior.[84]

A given character of change entails a given character of the experience of time. From a perspective *outside* that world without end — from our present perspective — its life must be described as everlasting. Though correct, the term "everlasting" would, however, still be inadequate to describe what is going on inside. For "everlasting" life is understandable only in opposition to "passing" life, and an "unending" world is conceivable only in opposition to the idea of the "end" of the world. But just as the goodness of the world to come is internally beyond the distinction of good and evil, so its everlastingness is beyond the distinction between "everlasting" and "perishing." Hence, internally, the "world without end" would be the world in which even the thought of the end, and therefore also the thought of "no end," would be absent. Borrowing from Nietzsche the term but not the content, I would like to call the experience *unthematized* because reconciled temporality is "deep eternity"[85] — the depth dimension of the linearity of everlasting life.

In my last section ("Temporality and Deep Eternity") I have already moved significantly beyond critical engagement with Moltmann's thought to a sketch of my own proposal. Before concluding the chapter, it may be helpful to sum up insights gained from the critical engagement with Moltmann. First, post-mortem

---

82. Miroslav Volf, "'The Trinity Is Our Social Program': The Doctrine of the Trinity and the Shape of Social Engagement," *Modern Theology* 14 (1998): 403–23, 412–13.

83. Schleiermacher, *The Christian Faith*, 163.

84. Gregory of Nyssa, *Song of Songs*, 128.

85. The content of the idea of deep eternity as explicated in this paragraph I owe to the conversations with my research assistant, Ivica Novakovic.

change is an essential precondition for the resolution of the problems within the sphere of cultural productivity; without it past cannot be redeemed and history cannot be set aright. Second, dealing with these problems — addressing the question of human sin — cannot take place simply at the level of fundamental conditions of human existence (such as proposing the end of time and space). Though transformation of the fundamental conditions of human existence — resurrection of the body conceived as an aspect of the comprehensive *transformatio mundi* — is essential, the change needs also to take place in the space internal to human wills. Third, resolution of the problems of death and sin in the reign of peace in plenitude and innocence is the precondition for the experience of redeemed temporality.

Conclusion

In conclusion, let me pull together four crucial aspects of the position about the eschatological transition that emerged in the course of my argument and that lie scattered in my debates with Jüngel, Pannenberg, and Moltmann, especially as they touch the character and the interrelation of the required transformations in the realms of physicality and cultural productivity.

First, ultimate fulfillment is unthinkable without continued life of human beings after death. Eschatological transition entails, therefore, that they be, as John Polkinghorne has argued, "embodied in the 'matter' of the new creation" and "located in its 'space' and immersed in its 'time,' "[86] as well as that the time, space, and matter of the new creation be so prodigiously given to human beings that they suffer no want and death no longer reigns. With the threat of death and scarcity removed, the pressure to conflicts between human beings would be eased and thus one important source of evil in the sphere of cultural productivity removed.

Second, ultimate fulfillment is thinkable only as human beings' undiluted enjoyment of God, of one another, and of their environment in a new world of perfect love. Eschatological transition entails that evil in human history be finally and unmistakably exposed and judged, that the evil-doers themselves be transformed by God's grace, so that they can be freed from all evil, reconciled to one another, and thus reach the state of new innocence. Without such a change in the sphere of cultural productivity human beings would turn even the prodigiously given time, space, and matter of the new creation into a scarce good around which conflicts would rage.

Third, ultimate fulfillment requires reconciled temporality.[87] In a world in which "what is mortal" has been "swallowed up by life" (2 Cor. 5:4) and in

---

86. John Polkinghorne, "Eschatology: Some Questions and Some Insights from Science," chap. 2 in this volume.

87. The two previous comments together (one about the new physicality and the other about new cultural productivity) should also be explicated in terms of a redeemed spatiality. Only such redemption of space would make the redemption of time possible. The image of a restless pilgrim, whose time is short, entering the celestial city to find the final rest — the image that has profoundly shaped the Western sense of time — suggests a linkage of the two. Being "at home" in space is a precondition of reconciled temporality.

which innocence and love reign, there will be nothing in the past to resent or repent of and nothing in the future that would have to be achieved or avoided. Every present will be saturated with a joy that is undiminished by the thought of its possible end, and so one will be irretrievably "lost" in the depths of eternity with no desire for anything but this very lostness.

Fourth, the eschatological transition can be understood neither as an apocalyptic discarding of the old world and creation of a new one *ex nihilo* nor as a holistic integration of "everything" into a "totality." Rather, the eschatological transition must be ultimately understood as the final reconciliation of "all things," grounded in the work of Christ the reconciler and accomplished by the Spirit of communion, as the process by which the whole creation along with human beings will be freed from transience and sin to reach the state of eternal peace and joy in the communion with the Triune God.

I hope to have shown that some such eschatological vision not only grows out of basic Christian persuasions but is also internally consistent and eminently desirable. To show that the vision is also intellectually plausible, one would need to develop it systematically in dialogue with humanities and sciences.

Note: I am indebted to Ivica Novakovic, a research assistant *extraordinaire*, for thinking along with me about the matter and form of this text. The comments of the members of the consultation on Eschatology and Science for which the text was written were invaluable, including the formal response to the text by Gregor Etzelmüller. I wrote the text as a member of the Center for Theological Inquiry, Princeton, New Jersey, where I benefited from comments of my fellow members, and as a Pew scholar.

Chapter 18

RESURRECTION AND ETERNAL LIFE

The Canonic Memory of the Resurrected Christ,
His Reality, and His Glory

MICHAEL WELKER

There is perhaps no topic that seems less suited for the dialogue between theology and the so-called exact sciences than the topic of the resurrection. At least in the contemporary cultural, intellectual, epistemological, and theological climate of Western societies, the reality of the resurrection strikes most people as located, at best, at the farthest edge of any reality that corresponds to the standards of rationality, experience, and technical reproduction set by the sciences. It seems that this particular "reality" can only be introduced in contrast to, or in negation of, all scientifically trustworthy forms of reality. It seems to be a counter- or hyperreality that science, when confronted with it, cannot but trace back to the realms of fantasy, dreams, or even pathological individual or psychosocial phenomena.

This chapter wants to challenge this opinion. It will confront the exact sciences and the forms of common sense (that claim to derive their standards of knowledge, experience, certainty, and truth from the sciences, particularly from the natural sciences) with the reality of the risen Christ, as it can be grasped through the biblical witnesses.[1] It will attempt to describe this reality and the participation in it. Finally, it will try to grasp the nature of "eternal life," a life that is embedded in finite natural and cultural life processes, but which transcends this embeddedness, because it is not bound by, or subjected to, their forms of transmission and reproduction.

Doing this we want to test the duality, on the one hand, of scientific certainties and truth and, on the other, of religious certainties and truth. In order to face the

---

1. On the whole, it is amazing how resistant the belief in resurrection, or at least the tolerance of the church's insistence on that belief, has been despite the severe doubts and attacks on it since the Enlightenment. Cf. only for Germany the scandal-causing publications of David Friedrich Strauss, *Das Leben Jesu* (Tübingen: Osiander, 2. Aufl. 1837), 657ff.; Rudolf Bultmann, *Neues Testament und Mythologie. Das Problem der Entmythologisierung der neutestamentlichen Verkündigung*, Kerygma und Mythos, Bd. 1 (1948), reedited with an introduction by Eberhard Jüngel (Gütersloh: Gütersloher Verlagshaus, 3. Aufl. 1988); and Gerd Lüdemann, *Die Auferstehung Jesu. Historie, Erfahrung, Theologie* (Göttingen: Vandenhoeck, 1994), and Lüdemann, "Zwischen Karfreitag und Ostern," in *Osterglaube ohne Auferstehung? Diskussion mit Gerd Lüdemann*, ed. Hansjürgen Verweyen (Freiburg: Herder, 1995), 13ff.

reality of the resurrected Christ and of "eternal life" (which is offered to creation by the reality of the resurrected), we do not start with the presupposition of any specific form of a metaphysical duality, or an axiomatic split between two realities, no matter what terms might be applied (e.g., natural/supernatural).

On the whole, this chapter wants to show that in dealing with the reality of the resurrection, it is possible — on the basis of the biblical witnesses to the resurrection — to go a long way with the conditions of certainty and rationality set by the exact sciences. It is possible to describe the reality of the resurrection in such a way that the recognition and knowledge of this reality can turn into a meaningful challenge to the nontheological sciences, even if they have difficulties in rising to this challenge within the boundaries of their epistemological and experimental procedures.

The Reality of the Resurrection

Three groups of New Testament texts promise more specific information on the resurrection: (1) the traditions of the empty tomb; (2) the texts that connect the witnesses of the resurrection to appearances of light; and (3) the traditions that connect the witnesses of the resurrection with direct personal encounters in the manner of appearances. What do these traditions tell us about the resurrection?

Since the traditions of the empty tomb were supported by both the Christian and the Jewish sides, although for different reasons, most researchers grant them a "historical basis." It is, however, clearly seen that in themselves they offer no basis for bearing witness to the resurrection of Jesus. The witnesses that maintain that the tomb was empty *in principle* admit of four different interpretations:

1. The tomb was empty because the pre-Easter Jesus was in fact physically reanimated and had gone to a place initially unknown. This is the interpretation on which those skeptical of the resurrection mostly concentrate.

2. The tomb was empty because the corpse had been stolen and decayed at an unknown place. This is very important to Gerd Lüdemann, a New Testament scholar, who raised a public scandal by his writings: "The factual statement of Jesus' decomposition is to me the starting point of all further work on the questions in the context of his 'resurrection.' "[2]

3. The tomb was empty because a removal, a withdrawal of an unimaginable kind, had taken place.

4. The tomb was empty because an empty tomb had been mistaken for the real tomb. This is a possibility only occasionally considered by a few interpreters.

All these interpretations have in common that they emphasize the fact that *the empirically perceptible body of the pre-Easter Jesus was, at least for some time, withdrawn.* All the imaginable interpretations of the empty tomb — from the dry empirical ones (theft of the corpse or the confusion of the tombs) to the

---

2. Lüdemann, "Zwischen Karfreitag und Ostern," 27 (see n. 1); translation M.W.

magical and supranaturalistic ones — have in common that they do not offer any material for judicial autopsies.

The experience of the withdrawal of the pre-Easter body is not a sufficient condition for the belief in the resurrection. The empty tomb *in itself* — and here not only almost the whole history of interpretation, but also the biblical traditions themselves agree — does not create a well-founded belief in the resurrection. Even the appearances of the angel or the young man or men at the empty tomb with the message, "The Lord has risen!" do not yet lead to the spreading of the knowledge of the resurrection.

The first biblical reactions to the empty tomb and the appearances of messengers/a messenger or an angel in or at the tomb are fear and silence (Mark 16), the worry or the public rumor that a theft of the corpse has taken place (Matthew 28; John 20), or the belief that the claim of the resurrection was mere talk of women (Luke 24).

The second group of witnesses to the resurrection (particularly Paul) speaks of light appearances and thus completely excludes the idea of a merely physical reanimation of the pre-Easter Jesus. Important academic theologians such as Wolfhart Pannenberg wanted to trace back *all* the witnesses to the resurrection to such appearances of light and thus tried to evade the difficult problem of the confusion of resurrection and physical reanimation.[3] For at least three reasons they voted for the historicity of the appearances of the resurrected: (a) because of the wide time-span in which they took place; (b) because of the fact that in a disciplined way, so to speak, the appearances remain centered on Jesus' resurrection and do not proceed to an enthusiastic expectation of general resurrection as would, according to Pannenberg, have corresponded to the eschatological moods of the time; (c) because of the mutual support of the experiences of Jesus Christ's appearance and the traditions of the empty tomb which probably originated independently.

However, the seemingly elegant limitation of the appearances of the resurrected to light appearances is problematic since these appearances alone do not explain in any way why and how the relation to the person Jesus became evident and clear. More modestly, one should start from the fact that *among* the resurrection appearances were *also* appearances that in no case referred directly to a mortal real person, but to a phenomenon of light from the heights, from heaven. It should be noted that among the various appearances of the resurrection were ones that *at any rate* excluded any confusion with ideas of a physical reanimation. This, however, is not the case in the third and most complicated group of appearances of the resurrected.

The third group of texts is not only offensive to modern thought and feeling. At first glance these texts seem indeed to start from a notion of the reanimation of Jesus. But at closer inspection they all contradict the impression that the

---

3. W. Pannenberg, *Grundzüge der Christologie* (Gütersloh: Gütersloher Verlag, 6. Aufl. 1982), 96, cf. 85ff.

resurrection was a mere reanimation. They bring before us a strange embodiment and real presence.

On the one hand, it is said: The resurrected meets the witnesses palpably. He is *palpably perceived* by them with eyes, ears, and hands. Matthew 28:9 says that the women who meet the resurrected touch his feet. Luke 24:30 tells us that Jesus breaks the bread for the disciples who lie at table with him. According to Luke 24:39, Jesus asks the disciples to touch his wounds. In John 20:27 this is said to the skeptical Thomas. Particularly pointedly, Luke 24:41ff. emphasizes, "And while they still disbelieved for joy, and wondered, he said to them, 'Have you anything here to eat?' They gave him a piece of broiled fish, and he took it and ate before them."

On the other hand, these texts make it very clear that the resurrected is and remains *an appearance*. In direct connection with the emphasis on the palpable presence of the resurrected they acknowledge: *The resurrected is an appearance.* Mark 16:12 reads, "he appeared in another form." Mark 16:14 and other texts refer to the surprising and unmediated appearance among the disciples who lie at table. Repeatedly, several texts say expressly that the first witnesses to the presence of the resurrected find faith as well as *no faith*. It is said that even some of those who are directly confronted with the appearance of the resurrected *doubt* it. Matthew 28:17 for instance tells us that the disciples see the resurrected and worship him. But it is also explicitly stated, "but some doubted." Correspondingly, Luke 24:36 reads, "As they were saying this, Jesus himself stood among them. But they were startled and frightened, and supposed that they saw a spirit."

As I have shown elsewhere,[4] many biblical texts try to express this complicated identity of the resurrected Christ with the pre-Easter Jesus by, on the one hand, highlighting the *palpability* of the presence of the resurrected Christ and by, on the other hand, emphasizing that this presence is the presence of an *appearance*. Among a number of accounts, the Emmaus story (according to Luke 24) is the most graphic example. It states that the eyes of the disciples who encounter the resurrected Christ were kept from recognizing him (Luke 24:16). It says that when they sat down, the resurrected Christ took bread, blessed and broke it, and gave it to them. Then their eyes were opened and they recognized him. But already in the next sentence the text explicitly states: And he vanished from their sight! (Luke 24:31).

After the opening of their eyes to the presence of the resurrected Christ, he vanishes from sensual visibility. But instead of bemoaning this and complaining about a "spooky" event, the disciples now recognize retrospectively that they had a feeling for the presence of the resurrected even before their eyes were opened by the ritual act in table fellowship. They say to each other: Were not our hearts burning within us, while he was talking to us on the road, while he

---

4. Welker, "Resurrection and the Reign of God," in *The 1993 Frederick Neumann Symposium on the Theological Interpretation of Scripture: Hope for the Kingdom and Responsibility for the World*, ed. Daniel Migliore, *Princeton Seminary Bulletin*, Supp. no. 3 (Princeton, N.J., 1994), 3–16.

was opening the scriptures to us? (Luke 24:32). And then they bear witness to the resurrection before others.[5]

In a variety of ways, the accounts of the resurrection that deal with the personal encounters contradict an impression that the resurrection only restores the old pre-Easter liveliness and embodiment of Jesus of Nazareth. "Resurrection" — this does not mean: The dead Jesus stands up again and leaves his tomb as if nothing had happened. The resurrection of Jesus does not simply lead to a continuation of an earthly life that was only interrupted. It is no re-entrance into the life lived before his death. The resurrected does not live on with his disciples and his fellow persons in the same way that they live together and deal with each other. Nowhere does the Bible have a person say, "Good that you are back again, Jesus!" The touch of the resurrected is rather experienced as a revelation of God, as a theophany. The disciples and the women fall down before him. "My Lord and my God," exclaims the disbelieving Thomas. And again and again it is said: But some doubted. So what kind of reality is this new life and this new embodiment?

By maintaining the disturbing connection between palpability and appearance of the resurrected, the witnesses to the resurrection emphasize: The reality of the resurrection is more than a simply natural event. This reality concerns the human species more deeply, it is more powerful than merely natural events. Here we deal not only with the earthly person who could be crucified and killed. Here we encounter the resurrected Christ who has overcome death. Here we have before us not simply an earthly person who can only be present in one place and time. Here we meet with the resurrected and elevated Christ who can and does reveal himself in diverse forms and in surprising ways at many places. This reality of the resurrection is no illusion, no product of the fantasy. It is borne witness to by many men and women, and in many different contexts of experience. All the witnesses refer back to the historical Jesus and the fullness of his life. They all refer to his past and to his future.

The knowledge of Jesus' resurrection is just as little an illusion as the discovery of justice or of mathematics. This event, however, is not only the discovery of a new order and a new truth, but here the person and life of Jesus bring their influence to bear. The pre-Easter person and the pre-Easter life here continue in a new way. From the outside perspective one could speak of a cultural-historical event. The pre-Easter Jesus is transcended and yet remains true to himself. The biological body is not restored. The biblical texts speak of a "glorified" body or of a "spiritual" body. The person and the life that the pre-Easterly body bore now look for and find in the witnesses to the resurrection a new body as bearer of Jesus' earthly historical existence. But how can we make it clear that this is not the result of a sudden psychotic and faked change of opinion, of counterpropaganda or a contagious fantasy?

The resurrection of Christ is not a mere reanimation of the pre-Easter Jesus. In no case do the biblical witnesses give the impression that the post-Easter

---

5. The Gospel of John also follows this "logic of the resurrection." John 20:19 and 20:26 emphasize that Jesus comes and stands among the disciples when the doors were shut.

Christ lived together with his disciples or with other persons in the same way that the pre-Easter Jesus did. Although they claim that there is both identity and continuity between the pre-Easter and the post-Easter Jesus Christ, they point to a complex identity and continuity that need to be unfolded. This continuity is not just the continuity of an earthly physical existence, realized at several space-time points of intersection.

It is important to see that the encounters with the resurrected Christ as witnessed by the scriptures take different forms, from visions of light to the appearance of a person with all the impressions of palpability. It is important to see that the biblical texts do not try to smooth over the problems connected with this presence. They describe the fear, the doubt, the derision, and the disbelief connected with this reality. They state that the resurrected Christ revealed himself "in another form" (Mark 16:12). They stress the improbability of these encounters by underscoring the surprise of the witnesses and the "unnatural" way in which Christ enters the scene: for instance, by coming through closed doors or through walls. Although the scriptures explicitly underscore all this, they do not allow for the duality of illusion versus empirical reality with respect to the reality of the resurrected Christ. Occasionally, however, they note this problem, for instance, when the text says that Jesus' followers were frightened because they thought they saw a ghost (Luke 24:37). On the whole, the resurrection witnesses very calmly acknowledge that this presence is not a simple empirical reality, although it bears several characteristics of such a reality.

On the one hand, the experiences of the resurrected Christ and of his reality are as various and unique as our own individual experiences of love, joy, trust, and sorrow are various, highly unique, never fully communicable, and certainly not experimentally reproducible. On the other hand, according to the witnesses of the scriptures, the experiences of the resurrected Christ are quite the opposite of any existential experiences that either are beyond words or can only be narrated individually. All the witnesses to the resurrected Christ refer to the new presence, the presence in a different mode, of the pre-Easter Jesus Christ. Despite their witness-character they are communal experiences and they generate communal experiences. In intelligible ways they are directed toward a new reality. And this is the reality we have to understand.

Cultural and Canonic Memory and the Living Christ

In his book *Das kulturelle Gedächtnis*[6] the Heidelberg Egyptologist Jan Assmann gives a brilliant examination of the cultural shaping power of cultural memory. He takes up ideas from Maurice Halbwachs,[7] Claude Lévi-Strauss,[8] and other theorists of the culture of memory and shows that memory is not only an individual

---

6. Jan Assmann, *Das kulturelle Gedächtnis. Schrift, Erinnerung und politische Identität in frühen Hochkulturen*, 2d ed. (Munich: Beck, 1992), 1997.
7. Maurice Halbwachs, *Das Gedächtnis und seine sozialen Bedingungen* (Paris, 1925; Frankfurt, 1985); also *Das kollektive Gedächtnis* (Paris, 1950; Frankfurt, 1985).
8. Claude Lévi-Strauss, *Das wilde Denken* (Frankfurt, 1973) (Paris, 1962).

or a common mental phenomenon. It is also the power to construct a common world. Cultural memory shapes not only a common past, but also a shared presence and, to a high degree, an expected future. It shapes cultural and moral spaces[9] that condition human life and communal life no less than natural spaces. The power of cultural memory becomes obvious as soon as we observe in what ways it transcends the fluid communicative memory. The "communicative memory" of a community is a memory that is constantly reconstructed. It is constantly enriched, and constantly parts of it fade away. The communal memory shifts, rearranges, and regroups itself all the time. But beside this communal memory human beings develop a cultural memory that as a rule lasts much longer. Cultural memory imposes meaning, control, and forms on memories, actual experiences, and expectations in ways that are difficult to change.[10]

Cultural memory can help to stabilize communities and societies against change, for instance, against change by the flux of the communicative memory. Lévi-Strauss used the term "cold societies" for societies that resist the change of those structures that normally history would shape and reshape.[11] Assmann speaks of "cold options" of the memory. However, cultural memory can also turn into a "hot memory" that enables societies to make the historical dynamics a motor of their own development. This happens when historical events or clusters of historical events are lifted up to the level of myth. Thereby cultural memory starts a process that Assmann calls *Mythomotorik.*[12]

"Hot" dynamizing and "cold" stabilizing memories are not abstract alternatives. Highly developed human societies, it seems, strive to attain a cultural memory that allows them to stabilize their identity and, at the same time, provides a dynamic development. Assmann shows that the *canon,* for instance, the canon of the biblical traditions, is such an achievement that allows cultural memory to operate in dynamizing and stabilizing modes simultaneously.[13] The canon stabilizes the common identity and at the same time requires a living development in a multitude of individual and communal perspectives and interpretations. The canon conditions the interplay of hot and cold memory and thus stimulates a cultural memory that I would like to term "living cultural memory" or "canonic memory."[14]

Living cultural memory, the canonic memory, is an amazing power. On the one hand, the living cultural memory is bound by a certain stock of texts (e.g., the biblical traditions that grew for about 1,500 years). As a fixed stock of texts, the

---

9. Cf. William Schweiker's "Time as a Moral Space: Moral Cosmologies, Creation, and Last Judgment," chap. 9 in this volume.

10. Cf. Assmann, *Das kulturelle Gedächtnis,* 48ff.; Siegfried J. Schmidt, "Gedächtnis — Erzhlen — Identität," in *Mnemosyne. Formen und Funktionen der kulturellen Erinnerung,* ed. Aleida Assmann and Dietrich Harth (Frankfurt a.M.: Fischer, 1991), 378ff.

11. Lévi-Strauss, *Das wilde Denken,* 270.

12. Assmann, *Das kulturelle Gedächtnis,* 75.

13. Ibid., 103ff., esp. 126ff.; J. Assmann, *Fünf Stufen auf dem Wege zum Kanon. Tradition und Schriftkultur im frühen Judentum und in seiner Umwelt,* MTV 1 (Münster: Lit, 1999).

14. M. Welker, *What Happens in Holy Communion?* (Grand Rapids, Mich.: Eerdmans, 2000), chap. 8.

possibilities for change are limited. On the other hand, a pluralistic multitude of perspectives in the canonic traditions stimulates a liveliness, a liveliness of permanent exegesis and interpretation that functions like hot cultural memory but does not swallow up the historical basic stock of texts and does not devour the common identity. A canon and a canonic memory cannot be planned, launched, or constructed. They arise out of complex historical and cultural lives and patterns. It is historical and cultural reality that gives shape to the canonic remembrance.

The memory of Christ, the memory that is established and instituted by the resurrection and is renewed in proclamation and in the celebration of the sacraments, is a key example of such a living cultural and canonic memory. It is conditioned by the synoptic gospels, with their (in part highly similar, in part subtly divergent) ways of presenting Jesus' life, proclamation, death, and resurrection. It is stimulated by the perspectives of the Gospel of John and the different perspectives of the New Testament letters, by the images of Christ in Acts, and by the complex Christology of the Apocalypse. It is stimulated by the different roles of the earthly Jesus and the different christological titles (Son of God, Kyrios, Our Lord, Son of man, the Messiah, and so on) with their different realms of memory and expectation. These perspectives, roles, and titles are modes of an approach to the reality of the resurrected Christ in its liveliness and fullness. They are — substantially — generated by the life of Christ, his proclamation, his death, and his resurrection.

The living cultural or canonic memory connects together a multitude of perspectives on the presence of Christ which are all interdependently related in a continual interplay. In this canonic memory, which is only one dimension of faith and of the working of the Spirit — although a most important one — the resurrected Christ, in the fullness of his person and in the fullness of his pre-Easter history, brings his presence to bear. From a multitude of witnesses to the presence of the resurrected Christ, the unfolding of the full life of the pre-Easter Christ, his sayings and his deeds and intentions, arises and in all this a rich and living memory and doxology with respect to his person and his continuous effectiveness.

Narratives about the encounter with the resurrected Christ are wonderful examples of the ignition and the inflammability of the canonic memory. The breaking of the bread, the perception of his wounds, the modes of address, his opening up of the scriptures, all these canonic elements bring the presence of Christ to bear and release the knowledge of the presence of the resurrected Christ. From his turning to the children, to the sick, the suffering, and the obsessed, to his acceptance of outcast people and collaborators in the table-fellowship, a multitude of events can ignite the canonic remembrance with respect to Christ's life.[15] Furthermore, the symbol-political arguments with the cult of the temple and with the Roman empire,[16] and analogous arguments in historically analogous

---

15. Cf. John Dominic Crossan, *The Historical Jesus: The Life of a Mediterranean Jewish Peasant* (San Francisco: HarperSanFrancisco, 1992); also *Jesus: A Revolutionary Biography* (San Francisco: HarperSanFrancisco, 1995).

16. Cf. the excellent article of Gerd Theissen, "Jesus und die symbolpolitischen Konflikte seiner Zeit. Sozialgeschichtliche Aspekte der Jesusforschung," *EvT* 57, no. 5 (1997): 378ff.

constellations, can provide such stimulation of the canonic memory. Complex normative fields become operative through Jesus' new interpretation of the law and by his proclamation of the coming reign of God. This, and Jesus' claim to the intimate relation with the Creator, as well as his laying claim to the power to forgive sins, explicitly bring religious dimensions into the canonic memory, which in itself has a religious quality. In these and other references to the historical Jesus canonic memory can become active and can become a witness to the presence of the resurrected in the interplay of highly stabile and highly fluid forms.

The memory that Jesus established in the celebration of the Lord's Supper allows the canonic memory — on the basis of the biblical traditions — to become highly concentrated, concrete, and existential. It involves those who celebrate Holy Communion in the memory of Christ in a much more basic and elementary mode than proclamation or exegesis could do. In the action of the breaking of the bread, the Emmaus disciples recognize the resurrected, and only then do they see that "their hearts burned within them while he opened to them the scriptures." The living cultural memory in which the crucified and resurrected Christ again and again brings his influence to bear is a result of the resurrection and the working of the Holy Spirit. The Holy Spirit is the power that again and again brings human beings together to strengthen, to renew, to enliven, and to enrich the memory of Christ. The Holy Spirit is on the one hand the spirit of Jesus Christ by which the resurrected Christ makes himself present among his witnesses. The Holy Spirit is on the other hand the power by which the human beings become witnesses to the presence of Christ and gain participation in Christ's life and in the creative life of God. It is through the working of the Spirit and through the working of God's creativity that the memory of Christ does not sink to a merely historical remembrance, or even to a multitude of remembrances.

This cannot be grasped at all if we think only along the lines of a remembered individual or of an objectified and attuned communal memory. For living memory, it is crucial that there is a connection between the multifariousness of the witnesses, the establishment of a common medium, *and* the reference to the historico-empirical past person or event. All these factors have to come together. In the case of the resurrected Christ they do all come together in an exemplary way, through the establishment of what the Bible calls faith, namely the objective faith that has come with Christ (Gal. 3:25).

The Life of the Resurrected and Eternal Life

In the canonic memory, and in faith, the incarnated life of Christ is present in a way that allows the witnesses to gain a share in this life. The presence of the resurrected is — as Luther and Barth in his late writings would put it — *"nicht ohne die Seinen."* He is not without his witnesses. They shape the realms of common remembrance, common expectations, and common experiences in proclamation, in the celebration of the sacraments "in remembrance of Christ," and in a life lived in accordance with his guidance. In that they live in the remembrance of Christ, their lives are shaped to diverse degrees, and they shape other people's lives to diverse degrees by living as witnesses. But this process of bearing witness is finite. It is limited by individual lives, and it is limited by the finitude of the existence of the human species on this planet.[17] Impressive and important as the chain of cultural remembrance and the loving activity of faith are, they do not fully explain the power of eternal life. Amazing as the vitality and power of common remembrance are, amazing as the cultural and ethical consequences of this remembrance may seem, the resonance to Christ's life and proclamation alone is at best a mirror that permits only a dim view of the power of eternal life.[18]

The power of eternal life becomes visible as soon as we make it clear that it is not the activity of the memory which is the power of the resurrection, but the substance and the glory of the life of Christ incarnate. It is the fullness of the life of Christ that can rightly be called "eternal life." This life in its worth and in its glory does not depend on memory. It is no less fulfilled under the cross than in Christ's parousia. In this life the witnesses gain a share and give a share. By this life they are ennobled and made holy. Participation in this life is the ground of Christian hope.[19]

Participation in this eternal life is not a question of the quantity of that re-membrance and of the spreading of that remembrance through the activities of faith. It is its quality that brings the fulfillment. But it is also its quality that directs us to intensify the remembrance of Christ and to give our fellow human beings a share in it. And it is its quality that challenges us to shape and reshape our lives to become more similar to Christ and to make the Gestalt of this life already on this earth as clear as possible.

This gaining of Gestalt, of participation in Christ's life, is not simply a source of comfort, but a very dramatic event. It gives us participation in a reality that elevates us along with our finite lives into a life that is indestructible. At the same time, this process works in our lives in judging and redeeming ways. The biblical traditions speak of the judging and redeeming workings of God in the "coming of God's kingdom,"[20] in the dynamic presence of the resurrected, in faith, and in other spiritual forms and symbols. The divine judgment is grasped as the opening up of truth and righteousness and as their preservation. Eschatological judgment is presented through metaphors of purification, or surrender to the negative consequences of one's life-behavior,[21] and thus it is happening already during one's earthly life.

---

17. Cf. William Stoeger, "Scientific Accounts of Ultimate Catastrophes in Our Life-Bearing Universe," and John Polkinghorne, "Eschatology: Some Questions and Some Insights from Science," chaps. 2 and 3 in this volume.

18. Cf. Hans Küng, *Eternal Life? Life after Death as a Medical, Philosophical, and Theological Problem*, trans. E. Quinn (Garden City, N.Y.: Doubleday, 1984).

19. Cf. Kathryn Tanner, "Eschatology without a Future?" and Gerhard Sauter, "Our Reasons for Hope," in this volume.

20. Cf. Michael Welker, "The 'Reign' of God," *TToday* 49 (1992): 500–515; Michael Welker and Michael Wolter, "Die Unscheinbarkeit des Reiches Gottes," *Marburger Jahrbuch Theologie XI*, hg. W. Hrle u. R. Preul (Marburg: Elwert Verlag, 1999), 103–16.

21. Cf. Jürgen Moltmann, "Is There Life after Death?" and Miroslav Volf, "Enter into Joy! Sin, Death, and the Life of the World to Come," chaps. 16 and 17 in this volume.

The fulfillment of the law — that is, the exercise of righteousness, mercy, and the striving for the knowledge of God and for truth — is the Old Testament criterion for measuring in judgment. The christological *Aufhebung* of this orientation in the New Testament goes along with an altogether utterly heightened sensitivity to the fact that even the good law can be perverted and its normative dynamics distorted. Concentration on God's justice and God's truth again and again is made concrete in acts of mercy. "As you did it to one of the least of these my brethren, you did it to me" (Matt. 25:40) — thus runs one of the most important formulae for the orientation of life, whose observation grants acceptance at the eschatological judgment.

In this perspective — relative to individuals, times, and epochs — on the judgment of the world in its historical process, we encounter the purifying and preserving, judging and redeeming, workings of God, the search for righteousness and truth which in our lives grasps, elevates, and preserves eternal life. Yet also we find another idea of judgment and another mode of transition into eternal life in the New Testament. This idea of judgment appears in a perspective on the judgment of the world in its totality, eschatologically transcending all definite conditions of the world and all particular processes of history. The coming of the Son of man with his angels, the fleeing of heaven and earth before God's face — these are images that the New Testament traditions use to describe this state of affairs.

The image of the Son of man who comes with the angels does not simply want to portray a final epoch or episode of human life on this earth in a manner rich in fantasy. The images of the New Testament are intended as provocations that make it necessary to problematize all the conceptions of world, reality, and future, which are only generalizations of certain well-practiced ideas of world, reality, and temporalities.[22] The eschatological texts say that the Son of man comes with the elect and with the angels and that they come together not only from *one* certain time and place, but from all the times and places of the world. Mark 13 puts it thus, that the Son of man will gather *all* the elect — not only from one end of the earth to the other, but "from the ends of the earth to the ends of heaven" (Mark 13:27).

The more or less dramatic descriptions of the perishing or the fleeing of heaven and earth correspond to this, since the eschatological gathering of the fullness of times and the fullness of realities must dissolve and transform the present creaturely and historical texture of the world. This form of the judgment does not speak of purification and the merciful transformation of the world in Christ. It pointedly aims at decision, separation, the abstract preservation for eternal life, and the similarly abstract condemnation. Judgment is reduced to sentence and decision, to abstract condemnation or redemption.

One could talk of an "eschatological complementarity," which on the one hand makes it necessary for us to grasp and to think the transformation of earthly life into eternal life, and on the other the difference between earthly and eternal

---

22. Cf. Klaus Berger, *Wie kommt das Ende der Welt?* (Stuttgart: Quell, 1999), esp. 148ff.

life.[23] Contrary to the idea of judgment we meet with a reality in the life of the resurrected, and in faith in him, that in a thoroughly "evangelical" way includes and leads us into the eternal life.

Eternal life that finds its form in Christ's life presses for its anticipation already here on this earth. It presses for the new creation to become present already under the conditions of the old, vanishing creation. It wakes a delight and joy in this life which although it wants to be carried on to others also rests in itself. The existential dimension, the dimension of historical memory, and the dimension of practical and ethical formation are entwined into each other. Existential access to and the participation in eternal life have a clear and rich form.[24] Their content is accessible to us. The perception of eternal life in the life of the resurrected is the foundation of a meaningful and genuine hope that understands and ennobles this world in the light of the incarnated and the coming Christ.

---

23. This religious eschatology of Jewish-Christian origin combines two achievements. (a) It can offer a connection of norms which concentrates individual and cultural processes of development and education on the interdependencies of a striving for righteousness, the inculturation of the protection of the weak, and the search for truth, and which at the same time cultivates sensitivity for the corruptibility of even highly developed morals and the corresponding readiness for self-criticism. (b) It withdraws this connection of norms from any attempt by peoples, cultures, and powerful interest groups to fix it for their respective ethos, no matter how tentative and searching these attempts may be.

24. The experiences of the resurrected Christ are individual and unique and cannot be reproduced in experiments. This certainly does not mean that they are all "existential" experiences in the sense of Neo-Protestantism, in which the standardized modern individual comes to his or her abstract encounter with an "ultimate point of reference" or a "ground of being." Nor does this mean that they are all "existential" experiences in the sense in which the unique postmodern individual simultaneously encounters God and her or his radical *Eigentlichkeit* à la Bultmann. Or rather, since Bultmann oscillates between modern individuality and the search for radical uniqueness, it would be more appropriate to say that the biblically attested experiences of the resurrected Christ are not "existential" experiences that strive for what is sensationally erratic and bizarre, in the hope of reaching the realm of religion.

Appendix

METAPHOR AND REALITY

Hans Weder

The dialogue between theology and natural science can only make sense if they share a common subject. My suggestion is to define *reality* as this subject. This implies, however, a certain epistemological disposition in both: theology and natural science both produce a construction of reality that can and must be distinguished from reality itself. The scientific character of an approach is established by defining the rules and axioms according to which the construction of reality is to be achieved. The term *construction* must not, of course, be understood in a merely constructivistic sense. On the contrary, every single construction of reality must be judged by the criterion of adequacy to reality itself. There is an inescapable degree of circularity here. Different sciences can be taken as multidimensional approaches to the same reality, and dialogue aims to broaden the notion of the real by taking into account as many dimensions as possible.[1] There are, of course, considerable differences in the account of constructing accounts of reality, first of all among the different natural and social sciences, and then between theology and all other sciences.

I

Natural science (as in all secular sciences) constructs its reality presupposing a uniform secularity: the reality of the world is to be understood without any extraworldly factor, a closed system with continuous chain of cause and effect (this is not to postulate a certain system of causality).[2] Theology, on the other hand, has to respect the religious approach to the same reality, an approach that discovers God in the midst of secular experiences and that therefore describes reality by using words evoking transcendence. Dialogue would be impossible if either (1) natural science were to claim a secular character for reality itself instead of sticking to the secularity of its construction, or (2) if theology were to claim that transcendent factors are *indispensable* for describing reality, so that any secular approach would be excluded as false and inadequate.

---

1. See J. C. Polkinghorne, *The Faith of a Physicist: Reflections of a Bottom-Up Thinker*, Gifford Lectures for 1993/94 (Princeton, N.J.: Princeton University Press, 1994), 9: "We all need to form a world-view going beyond the particularities of our individual disciplines."

2. Cf. Troeltsch's principle of correlation: E. Troeltsch, "Ber historische und dogmatische Methode in der Theologie," in *Gesammelte Schriften*, vol. 2, *Zur religisen Lage, Religionsphilosophie und Ethik* (Tübingen, 1913), 729–53.

Two conditions are necessary for dialogue to avoid these pitfalls: (1) natural science has to keep in mind the limitations of its construction of reality and has to acknowledge the basic openness of reality to a deeper (and eventually religious) dimension; and (2) theology has to use the word God in such a way that transcendence is not an *indispensable factor in explaining* reality, but rather a dimension enriching the perception of reality (e.g., describing the weight or dignity of reality, or discovering the true shape of moral space).[3] Theology therefore must not use religious concepts in such a way that secular explanations are excluded. Its religious interpretation of reality must fully respect the *possibility* of secular explanation (e.g., the conversion of Paul can be seen as a work of the Spirit with full respect for psychological descriptions or even explanations of the same fact). Moreover it can be imagined that the interpretations of theology are actually improved if they do not exclude secular explanations. Theology, to sum up, has to use the word God not as the counterpart of secular perception, but as the opportunity for deeper insight: to discover the secret of reality in the midst of riddles, solved as well as unsolved.

II

In the philosophy of language (and in New Testament exegesis) an important form of speech (*Sprachform*) has gained attention in recent decades: metaphor. Metaphor is predominant in religious language, for it is a very appropriate way of speaking of transcendence. A typical metaphor consists of a subject that is related by a copula to a predicative noun. Let us take an example: Nature is a temple.[4] This metaphor (by Baudelaire) combines two phenomena that cannot be combined literally or in conceptual language. Nature is not really a temple, and *temple* is not really a predicate of *nature*. Yet the semantic value of the metaphor consists in the fact that two things are brought together which are literally incommensurate. A metaphor is able to express truth that cannot be expressed in any other way. This means, among many other things, that in metaphorical predication the qualitative difference between subject and predicate is not a disadvantage hermeneutically, but rather it has hermeneutical potential. This potential looks very promising if applied to the dialogue between theology and natural science.

A religious metaphor (differing from a common metaphor that combines two literally incommensurate phenomena of the world) can be defined as combining a transcendent subject with an immanent predicate. Many parables of Jesus, for instance, have the following structure: the kingdom of God is like ..., followed by a secular story, the parable story itself. The semantic value of the parables consists in the fact that everybody is aware of the difference between the kingdom of God and the secular story.[5] Thus the secularity of the world is an advantageous presup-

---

3. See William Schweiker, "Time as a Moral Space: Moral Cosmologies, Creation, and Last Judgment," chap. 9 in this volume.
4. Cf. H. Weder, *Neutestamentliche Hermeneutik* (Zurich, 1989) (ZGB), 155–66.
5. Cf. H. Weder, *Die Gleichnisse Jesu als Metaphern: Traditions- und redaktionsgeschichtliche Analysen und Interpretationen*, FRLANT 120 (Göttingen, 1990), 75–80.

position for this way of using the word *God*. A religious metaphor has therefore a positive relationship to the secularity of the world which is the result of a scientific approach. The metaphor does not aim to replace the secular description of experience but, rather, discloses or discovers a deeper dimension within secular reality. It is able to fully respect secularity and yet to evoke transcendence in a deep sense of the word.

My suggestion is to model the dialogue between theology and natural science according to metaphorical process: Theology and natural science are related to each other in analogy to the subject and the predicate in a metaphor (for the present purpose, it does not actually matter which is the subject and which is the predicate). I shall try to apply this model to particular subjects later.

III

Religious interpretation of reality is always based on the perception of a single phenomenon, a person's very special experience of the world. In the New Testament we encounter a set of ideas that is based upon the perception of the particular. This concentration on the particular marks one decisive difference between the religious approach to reality and a scientific or empirical approach. Perceiving the particular leads into the realm of the contingent. What is called experience in the New Testament must not be confused with empirical statements. This is true in two ways. First, empirical knowledge is based on experiment.[6] The experience thus derived can, in principle, be repeated at any time. Religious experience, on the other hand, is shaped by contingency. The key contrast here is between the experimental (contrived) and the historical (contingently given). Nevertheless both categories are of experience. In common with all personal experience religious experience cannot be reproduced on demand (it is indebted to epiphany and revelation). Experimental experience produces and controls its phenomena; religious experience, on the other hand, must wait for them to appear. Experimental experience prescribes questions that the phenomena must answer; religious experience, on the other hand, tries to grasp what is shown by a phenomenon.

To give an extreme example in Christian theology: the epiphany of Christ. It is detached from any experimental access. As a historical event it is essentially not reproducible, though it may have caused more reflection than the biggest experiments of humanity. Regardless of the role creative imagination may have played in the accounts that have come down to us, in the person of Christ a truth has been manifested that is not within the range of any experiment. This difference cannot, of course, simply be equated with the difference between theology and natural science. In theology, too, regularity is of some interest, and in

---

6. There are, of course, exceptions, e.g., in microphysics and physical cosmology: cf. P. Janich, *Art, Experiment, Enzyklopdie, Philosophie und Wissenschaftstheorie*, vol. 1, ed. J. Mittelstrass (Mannheim, Vienna, Zurich, 1980), 622; J. Audretsch, "Physikalische Kosmologie II: Das Inflationre Universum oder der kosmologische Münchhausen-Effekt," in *Vom Anfang der Welt: Wissenschaft, Philosophie, Religion, Mythos*, ed. Audretsch and K. Mainzer (Munich, 1990), 111.

natural science, too, we encounter processes of perception that are concentrated on the particular (a very interesting example is cosmology).

Second, experimental experience approaches the particular in a way that is fundamentally different from the experience of life or religious experience. In experimental perception particular phenomena are viewed as examples, whose summation constitutes basic facts for a scientific theory.[7] Scientific knowledge is not directed to the particular, but rather to achieving a general theory, for which particular phenomena are examples. Religious experience, on the contrary, is exclusively directed to the particular. Christ could never serve as an example for a theory of God; in the New Testament he is perceived rather as the embodiment of the highest God. In this particular person, the faith of the New Testament bears witness to what holds the world and God together as its innermost center.[8] While experimental knowledge aims to formulate theories, religious knowledge is primarily concerned with the perception of the particular. When theology speaks of cosmology, it is not by abstraction from a plurality of particular phenomena. Cosmological statements become necessary, because Christ is seen (e.g., by the prologue of the Gospel according to John) not only as a human exemplar but as the cosmological principle, the fount of the universe embodied in a particular human being. This makes a fundamental difference between theological statements on the cosmos and the cosmology of natural science.

IV

Some religious systems have their starting point in the transcendent realm of spirit, for example, in the purity of a world of ideas. For such systems, statements about the world are situated in a very specific context. They speak about the world in the context of the question of what has led from the purity of the spirit to the impurity of matter, from the clarity of ideas to the mixture of the world (as in the writings of the Hellenistic-Jewish philosopher Philo). It is characteristic of such a cosmology that the real world fundamentally has an ontological deficit, it is basically imperfect.

The New Testament, in this respect representative of the Jewish-Christian approach to reality, differs considerably from such religious systems. It is not concerned with the explanation of how it happened that the imperfect material world came out of the perfect divine realm. It is concerned with the question of how a human being can rise to the demands of the dignity of the given reality, how a human being can appreciate the true weight of the world. According to Rom. 1:20 the things of the world are creatures, in which the everlasting power and

---

7. To this and the specific problems in the field of physical cosmology cf. Audretsch, "Physikalische Kosmologie II," 111–13.

8. Cf. E. Jüngel, "Metaphorische Wahrheit. Erwgungen zur theologischen Relevanz der Metapher als Beitrag zur Hermeneutik einer narrativen Theologie," in P. Ricoeur and E. Jüngel, *Metapher: Zur Hermeneutik religiser Sprache* (Munich, 1974), 71–122.

deity of God can be perceived, if they are considered thoughtfully.[9] Paul reminds us of the creative dimension of things in order to ensure their particular dignity. The reason why he speaks of the Creator is not to get beyond the material world. Theological cosmology, then, does not function as a means of overcoming and leaving the world in order to rise into the high spheres of the Creator, but rather it serves to draw the attention of human beings to the dignity and inviolability of the things that exist, that all can see. Theological cosmology is concerned with the foreground of the world, not with the background of heaven, and here is the point where theology and natural science meet. The latter describes the function of the universe; the former tries to explain its dignity and weight. The latter explores a world that seems to be inexhaustibly rich in its nature; the former makes more or less reliable maps of that world. The former must stay away from all definitions and images of God that turn out to be idols, ultimately to be broken in the face of an Infinite Reality.

V

The New Testament texts, in this respect again in accordance with the Old Testament, make a fundamental distinction between the world and God, between immanence and transcendence. Thus the things of the world, however high their dignity, are perceived strictly as secular phenomena. Cosmology always remains cosmology; it does not become a hidden or declared theology. The divine does not appear in secular shape or form (the one and only exception is the embodiment of the divine Word, the incarnation). Thus the divine is not accessible to a human eye; as far as that eye can see, it always perceives secularity.

Yet the New Testament speaks of the perspicuity of God's power and deity. This perspicuity, however, is not taken in by the eyes (nor by any other of the human senses). It is generated if the things seen by human eyes are contemplated by reason. According to Paul, the invisible things of heaven have been understood and seen ever since the creation of the world through the things God has made (Rom. 1:20). The invisible God becomes apparent to reason, when it turns thoughtfully to the things of the world. The divine is perceptible in the form of a deep dimension that is accessible only to thoughtful reason. The things of the universe lie before everybody's eyes. Their secret, however, is invisible, to be perceived only by reason that turns to their deeper dimensions.

Unlike the knowledge of the world, which can be compulsory, the knowledge of God is unconstrained in principle. It is the very nature of this truth that it cannot be forced on a man. For it would die straightway if it were to be enforced on someone. It is absolutely essential to the divine secret that it meets the free consent of reason. Religious cosmology and, consequently, eschatology are, therefore, unconstrained on principle, in contrast to the power of the factual. A systematic theory of everything, or a scientific prediction of the future, if it is

---

9. Cf. H. Schlier, *Der Römerbrief* (Freiburg, Basel, Vienna, 1977), 52–54; U. Wilckens, *Der Brief an die Römer. 1.* Teilband: Rm 1–5 (Zurich, 1978), 105–6.

based on the laws of nature, can enforce its acceptance eventually, even against resistance. On the contrary, religious cosmology and eschatology have the nature of address. They do not just speak about the world, but speak to somebody to suggest a certain perception of the world and its future. Their truth, therefore, differs on principle from that of science. It would not be wise to restrain the concept of the reasonable to enforceable truths, while one assigns all other insights to the field of opinion or of subjective taste. There is a status of truth that is not governed by the necessity of proof nor by deliberate taste, but that speaks to people of distinctly perceived experience and its meaning for life. In the face of such a truth, a free space is generated for the human "yes." In this respect, the insights of religion are much like works of art.

VI

It is characteristic of Christian theology that it makes a distinction between creation and the world. This entails a difference between cosmology and the doctrine of creation. This distinction is again an important difference from natural science. In natural science the world is a unity, and if science would use the word *creation*, it would apply it to the whole universe. The religious texts of the Jewish-Christian tradition contain the notion of a distinctive present in the universe. Creation is the world as it was originally created by God; with regard to the creation of the firmament in Genesis 1, we read: God saw that it was good. Creation is the name of the world, insofar as it is a home for humanity, a space for life as intended by God. It was always a world of finitude, but it was not always a world of destruction and sin.

There is a certain distance between the world, as it actually exists, and that creation. That is why Paul speaks of the suffering of creation (Romans 8), and of the great longing for deliverance from the futility that dominates the whole world until now. In many texts this gap is related to the rise of the human species. In mythological language, Adam's fall is told as that which has torn down the whole creation. This mythical idea contains the interesting insight that a human being is free to leave the conditions of nature, possessed by the idea to be like God or even to replace God. In the mythological idea of Adam's fall, the insight is preserved that a human being can live in opposition to himself and to the bare necessities of life.

Whatever one thinks about that idea, in a theological perspective the world is not identical with creation.[10] Neither is there a radical dualism between creation and world; the world continues to bear the traits of creation. Nevertheless one may choose not to call the world creation. The world is, to express it metaphorically, a garden run wild.[11] This distinction between creation and world has to be

---

10. Cf. I. U. Dalferth, "Schöpfung–Stil der Welt" (unpublished manuscript), 18: To name the world a good creation ascribes more to the world than our experience can prove (translation by H. W.).

11. E. Fuchs, *Hermeneutik* (Tübingen, 1970), 67–68; see also Chr. Link, "Die Transparenz der Natur für das Geheimnis der Schöpfung," in *Kologische Theologie: Perspektiven zur Orientierung*, ed. G. Altner (Stuttgart, 1989), 166–95.

kept in mind in any interdisciplinary dialogue; if not, the resulting equivocations would lead to almost insoluble problems. The world of experience, then, is to be seen as a garden run wild. One can still perceive the traces of creation, but in a faint and vulnerable way. In the approach of natural science, this world is made unequivocally secular, and the success of the dialogue depends on how open the participants are to a multidimensional approach and to the enrichment of their mutual perspectives.

CONTRIBUTORS

Larry D. Bouchard is Associate Professor of Religious Studies at the University of Virginia. He received his Ph.D. in Religion and Literature from the University of Chicago Divinity School. He is the author of *Tragic Method and Tragic Theology: Evil in Contemporary Drama and Religious Thought* (1989).

Walter Brueggemann (Ph.D., Yale) is the William Marcellus McPheeters Professor of Old Testament at Columbia Theological Seminary in Decatur, Georgia. He is interested in interpretive issues that lie behind the development of Old Testament theology. He is the author of numerous publications, including *Theology of the Old Testament: Testimony, Dispute, Advocacy* (1997).

Donald H. Juel (Ph.D., Yale) is the Richard J. Dearborn Professor of New Testament Theology at Princeton Theological Seminary. His primary research interests are the Gospels, especially Mark and Luke-Acts, Christology, and Jewish-Christian relations. Among his many publications are *Messianic Exegesis: Christological Interpretation of the Old Testament in Early Christianity* (1992) and *The Gospel of Mark* (1997).

Detlef B. Linke, Dr. med. (Bonn), is Professor of Clinical Neurophysiology and Neurosurgical Rehabilitation at the University of Bonn. He won the Alfred Hauptmann Prize for Epilepsy Research in 1990. He is Co-Founder of the journal *Ethica: Wissenschaft und Verantwortung.*

Patrick D. Miller is Professor of Old Testament Theology at Princeton Theological Seminary. He is editor of *Theology Today* and of the *Westminster Bible Companion* and Old Testament editor of the *Interpretation* commentary series. Among his books are *Interpreting the Psalms* (1986), *Deuteronomy* (1991), and *They Cried to the Lord: The Form and Theology of Biblical Prayer* (1994). In 1998, he was President of the Society of Biblical Literature.

Jürgen Moltmann began the study of theology and philosophy as a prisoner of war in England in 1946 and continued after his repatriation in 1948 at Göttingen University. He taught at Wuppertal, Bonn, and Tüubingen. Today he is regarded as one of the foremost living theologians. Among the American editions of his works are the following: *The Theology of Hope: On the Ground and the Implications of a Christian Eschatology* (1967), *The Crucified God: The Cross of Christ as the Foundation and Criticism of Christian Theology* (1975), *God in Creation: A New Theology of Creation and the Spirit of God* (1985), and *The Coming of God: Christian Eschatology* (1996).

John Polkinghorne, K.B.E., F.R.S., is a Fellow and former President of Queens College, Cambridge. He is an Anglican priest and former Professor of Mathematical Physics at the University of Cambridge. Among his many books on this subject are his Gifford Lectures, *The Faith of a Physicist* (1994), *Scientists as Theologians* (1996), *Belief in God in an Age of Science* (1998), and *Science and Theology* (1998). He was knighted in 1997.

Gerhard Sauter is Professor of Systematic Theology and Director of the Ecumenical Institute at the University of Bonn. He is the author of *What Dare We Hope?: Reconsidering Eschatology* (1999), the inaugural volume in the "Theology for the 21st Century" series, and *Eschatological Rationality: Theological Issues in Focus* (1997).

William Schweiker is Associate Professor of Theological Ethics at the University of Chicago. Holding degrees from Simpson College (B.A.), Duke University Divinity School (M.Div.) and the University of Chicago (Ph.D.), he has taught at the University of Iowa and the University of Chicago. He is author of three books: *Mimetic Reflections: A Study in Hermeneutics, Theology, and Ethics* (1990); *Responsibility and Christian Ethics* (1995); and *Power, Value and Conviction: Theological Ethics in the Postmodern Age* (1998).

Christoph Schwöbel, Dr. theol. (Marburg), is Professor of Systematic Theology and director of the Ecumenical Institute at the University of Heidelberg. His publications include *Persons, Divine and Human* (1991), *God: Action and Revelation* (1992), and (ed.) *Trinitarian Theology Today* (1995).

Janet Martin Soskice is University Lecturer in Modern Theology at the University of Cambridge and Fellow and Director of Studies at Jesus College. Her research interests include the interrelation of body, self, and society, and Christianity and gender. She is the author of *Metaphor and Religious Language* (1987) and the co-editor of *Medicine and Moral Reasoning* (1994).

William R. Stoeger, S.J. is a staff scientist for the Vatican Observatory Research Group, specializing in theoretical cosmology, high-energy astrophysics, and interdisciplinary studies relating to science, philosophy, and theology. He entered the Society of Jesus in 1961 and was ordained to the priesthood in 1972. He pursued doctoral studies in astrophysics at Cambridge University, England, and completed his Ph.D. in 1979. Stoeger's research has dealt with various problems connected with the physics of accretion onto black holes, and mathematical and physical issues connected with torsion and bi-metric theories of gravity, as well as the harmonic map structures contained in gravitational theories, including general relativity. In recent years, Stoeger has also been actively involved in interdisciplinary dialogue between science and philosophy, science and theology, and science and culture.

Kathryn Tanner teaches theology at the University of Chicago Divinity School. She is the author of *God and Creation in Christian Theology* (1988), *The Politics of God* (1992), and *Theories of Culture: A New Agenda for Theology* (1997). She is currently preparing for publication a series of lectures entitled *A Systematics in Brief.*

Miroslav Volf is Henry B. Wright Professor of Theology at Yale University Divinity School and a Visiting Professor of Theology at the Evangelical Theological Faculty, Osijek, Croatia. He has published widely on dogmatic issues as well as on the themes at the intersection between social sciences and humanities and theology. His most recent books include *Embrace* (1996) and *After Our Likeness: The Church as the Image of the Trinity* (1998).

Fraser Watts is Starbridge Lecturer in Theology and the Natural Sciences at the University of Cambridge, Fellow of Queens College, and Vicar-Chaplain of St. Edward, King and Martyr. He was formerly at the MRC Applied Psychology Unit, working on cognitive aspects of emotional disorders, and has been President of the British Psychological Society.

Hans Weder has been Professor of New Testament at the Universität Zurich since 1980. He will become the President of the University in 2000. He is the editor of many journals and academic series and the author of *Die "Rede der Reden": Eine Auslegung der Bergpredigt heute* (1985, 1994).

Michael Welker, Dr. theol. (Tübingen), Dr. phil. (Heidelberg), is Professor for Systematic Theology and director of the Internationales Wissenschaftsforum of the University of Heidelberg. His recent publications include *God the Spirit* (1994), *Creation and Reality: Theological and Biblical Perspectives*, Warfield Lectures 1991, 1999, and *What Happens in Holy Communion?* (2000).

INDEX